Western Political Thought

========= Second Edition =========

Western Political Thought

From Socrates to the Age of Ideology

BRIAN R. NELSON
Florida International University

Prentice Hall, Upper Saddle River, New Jersey 07458

Library of Congress Cataloging-in-Publication Data

Nelson, Brian R.
  Western political thought : from Socrates to the age of ideology / Brian R. Nelson
    p.   cm.
  Includes bibliographical references (p.   ) and index.
  ISBN 0-13-191172-4
    1.   Political science—History.   I.   Title.
  JA81.N44   1996
  320—dc20
                                                    94-48427
                                                    CIP

Acquisitions editor: Michael Bickerstaff
Editorial assistant: Nicole Signoretti
Editorial/production supervision
    and interior design: Linda B. Pawelchak
Cover design: Jane Conte
Manufacturing buyer: Robert Anderson

©1996, 1982 by Prentice-Hall, Inc.

Printed in the United States of America
10   9   8   7

ISBN 0-13-191172-4

90000

9 780131 911727

To the Memory of
CARL O. NELSON
My father
and
MARY F. NELSON
My mother

Contents

2   Plato   23

Plato: the unity of philosophy and politics; the Academy and the trip to Syracuse; the question of Justice; the ideal and the best possible state; Justice as the interest of the stronger party; the case for injustice; the Just state and the Just man; the unity of ethics and politics; Justice and the division of labor; the paradox of philosophic rulership; communism and education; the Good; the theory of form; Plato's dualism; politics and the cave; public opinion as sophistry; the decline of the ideal state and the unjust man; the myth of metals and the injustice of politics; individual versus political ethics; the tyranny of reason.

3   Aristotle   51

Plato's influence; the Lyceum; political science as a practical science; the theory of immanent form; matter and form; actuality and potentiality; teleology; the unity of ethics and politics; virtue as reasoned action; virtue as a mean; virtue and opinion; the state and subordinate communities; the state and the good life; the private and public domains; form and constitution; the classification of constitutions; constitutional types and social class; polity and the mixed constitution; Justice as the rule of law; Justice as proportional equality; the aristocratic ideal; the critique of Plato; the radical versus the conservative temperament.

4   Cicero   69

Cicero and the classical tradition; Alexander the Great and the age of empire; the Hellenistic age and the new schools; Skepticism and the New Academy; Cicero's eclecticism; individualism, subjectivism, and cosmopolitanism; universal equality and apolitical virtue; Cynicism, Epicureanism, and the theory of contract; Stoicism: natural law and the two cities; fate and the rational will; politics as duty; the statesman-philosopher; the res-publica; *Cicero, Caesar, and Augustus; the* concordia ordinum *and the senatorial ideal; the Scipionic Circle and humanitas; the commonwealth and natural law; commonwealth and civitas; Polybius and the composite state; the theory of the ideal republic; natural law, civil law, and justice; Cicero as conservative; law as political philosophy; the unity of law and magistracy; consuls and tribunes; the Senate and the rule of wisdom; the people's assemblies and republican liberty; the failure of the classical city-state model; the Principate and the end of the Republic; the rise of Christianity.*

5   St. Augustine   103

The evolution of Roman law; Justinian's codification; the collapse of the Roman Empire; the decline of political philosophy; political withdrawal and the Stoicism of Seneca and Marcus Aurelius; Plotinus and neo-Platonism; philosophy, religion, and salvation; the rise of Christianity; St. Augustine and the origins of Christian political philosophy; St. Augustine's Manichaen dualism; sin and the Christian concept of evil; the psychology of evil; the two cities; the value of peace; the state as convention; the displacement of the classical vision; the separation of ethics and politics; the decline of political theory; the theocratic theory of the state; sin as a political solution; Augustinian political analysis and the theory of realpolitik.

6 St. Thomas Aquinas 123

The Church and the nation-state; the rediscovery of Aristotle and the synthesis of classical and Christian thought; John of Salisbury and the organic metaphor; St. Thomas's Aristotelianism; the monarchical ideal; teleological naturalism and Christian spiritualism; the natural and the supernatural; the hierarchy of law; human reason and natural law; natural law as participation in eternal law; the compatibility of political and spiritual life; human nature: the predominance of reason; the supremacy of the sacred and the legitimacy of the secular; theology, philosophy, faith, and reason; liberation from the metaphor of the two cities; the disintegration of the Thomistic synthesis; the disjunction of ethics and politics.

PART II MODERN POLITICAL THEORY

7 Machiavelli 137

Machiavelli and the Renaissance; realism and empiricism; the decline of feudalism and the emergence of the modern nation-state; Machiavelli and nationalism; the modern conception of human nature; the rules of power politics; the anti-Machiavellian tradition; the logic of violence and the art of manipulation; popular rule and political stability; Machiavelli's republicanism; civic virtue, pluralism, and equality; a political religion, a theology of action; power versus authority; the Platonic order inverted; modern sophistry; virtue as power; authority as illusion; the divorce of ethics and politics; ethical naturalism; the state as an end in itself; the illusion of nationalism; virtue and fortune.

8 Hobbes 161

The Reformation and the nation-state; the Puritan revolution and the scientific revolution; the revolt against Aristotle; materialism and the new empiricism; body and motion; mathematical truth and nominalism; the physics of psychology; knowing and willing; appetite and aversion, pleasure and pain; the will to power; the rejection of the Socratic conception of freedom; the modern theory of contract; consent versus divine right; the state as rationally constructed machine; human behavior and the state of nature; the compositive and resolutive methods; the state of war; the paradox of power; the modern theory of natural law; the theory of absolutism; the theory of sovereignty; the paradox of consent; law as command; the nominalist theory of justice; the language of power; modern Hobbesianism; the theory of the negative state; power and self-interest; Hobbes's sovereign and the weakness of power; Hobbes and the summum bonum; *modern science and the theory of authority.*

9 Locke 193

Locke and liberal democracy; the Glorious Revolution; radical individualism and the negative state; Locke and Hobbes: materialism, empiricism, and nominalism; the tabula rasa *and the theory of toleration; Locke versus Hobbes and Filmer; paternal versus political power; the theory of contract reconsidered; the state of nature and natural law; the two-stage contract; popular sovereignty; the right of revolution; the state of nature reconsidered; the right of property;*

and Locke united; the economic theory of classical liberalism; the physiocrats, Adam Smith, and laissez faire capitalism; the unseen hand and enlightened self-interest; Herbert Spencer and Social Darwinism; classical liberalism and the condition of the working class; the political failure of the middle class.

13   Modern Liberalism   298

De Tocqueville: the sociology of democracy; the tyranny of the majority; equality and liberty; public opinion and bureaucratic despotism; pluralism, mass society, and the theory of association; the social structure of democracy; John Stuart Mill: utilitarianism revised; the quality of pleasure and the superior individual; simple expediency versus higher values; the revised theory of liberty; moral progress and the quest for truth; proportional representation and mass education; T.H. Green and the Oxford Idealists; German idealism and modern liberalism; the classical view and the rejection of utilitarianism; the unity of will and reason; the theory of positive freedom; the social basis of rights; the right of property and the positive state; modern versus classical liberalism; modern liberalism in theory and practice: ambiguities and paradoxes; self-development as social engineering; democracy: moral progress versus moral anarchy; liberal ideals and the civilized state.

14   Marxism   326

Marx: scientific versus utopian socialism; the materialist conception of history and the critique of idealism; the historical acts and the relations of production; property and the division of mental and material labor; history as class conflict; life and consciousness; substructure and superstructure; ideology as false consciousness; idealism as ideology; the inevitability of communism; capital, profit, and surplus value; the labor theory of value; the theory of alienation; the law of the falling rate of profit and the anarchy of production; the dialectic; Marx versus Hegel; the historical significance of the working class; the unity of theory and practice; revolution as an epistemology; communism and the end of alienation; liberalism as alienated theory; Marx as antipolitical theorist; Eduard Bernstein and revisionism; Lenin's theory of imperialism; the party; spontaneity versus consciousness; Marxism and nationalism; Marxism and the end of communism and the rebirth of Marxism; Marxism as ideology.

15   The Age of Ideology   359

Western political thought and the critique of ideologies; ideologies and the unity of ethics and politics; the higher principles: classical and ideological; ideologies versus moral autonomy; Mazzini: nationalism and the subversion of ideology; state centralization and the loss of moral autonomy; the sociology of ideology: industrialism and secularism; the nation state and the higher principles; ideology and the problem of authority; authority as science; ideology, the state of war, and the weakness of power.

Preface

The second edition of this book includes, among other changes, a new chapter on Cicero. In fact, that chapter is more than its title indicates because it includes a substantial introduction to the major Hellenistic political philosophies as well as a historical overview of the events surrounding the rise of the Roman Empire. Because of this expanded coverage of the larger Greco-Roman tradition of political discourse, I have changed the title of Part I from "Ancient-Medieval" to the more inclusive "Classical and Medieval" Political Theory.

I included the new chapter because of requests from instructors who have used the text as well as my own increasing sense that the brief discussion of Hellenistic political philosophy in the first edition, and the even briefer references to Roman political thought, was inadequate given the basic intent of the book. The intent was to present the introductory student with a basic comprehension of Western political thought from the perspective of a limited number of key thinkers viewed in historical context and understood in terms of the changing relationship of ethics and politics in political philosophy from Socrates to the contemporary period. The addition of Hellenistic political thought and its great transmitter Cicero, the most important and influential of the Roman political thinkers, enhances the book's objective. Not only is a considerable historical period in the evolution of Western political thought now covered in some detail, but important perspectives in the classical conception of ethics and politics are elaborated in the process.

It is from this broadest historical and thematic perspective that the chapter on Cicero becomes a necessary addition to the book. Cicero is important not because he is a great political thinker in the sense of a Plato or an Aristotle. Clearly he is not. But as a transmitter of Hellenistic thought and as a thinker who, more than any other, integrated it with Roman political ideas, most notably with the Roman emphasis upon law as the foundation of political community and as the source of the classical unity of ethics and politics, he is crucial.

But there is another, in some ways more fundamental, reason for adding a chapter on Cicero. This book was written with a pedagogical intent. As I noted in the preface to the first edition, the thinkers and themes chosen are those that seem most useful in encouraging the student to think critically about the subject of political philosophy, and about his or her own theoretical assumptions about the nature of politics. In this regard, Cicero is of particular importance, for he illustrates something that in my experience few students ever consider—that political ideas from one era are passed on and modified to meet the exigencies of another, and in this way become part of the political consciousness of later generations. To understand our own political assumptions is to have some understanding of the evolution and modifications of these earlier ideas that have implicitly, unconsciously, become our own. More than any other thinker, with the exception of Aristotle, Cicero modifies and passes on classical ideas about the nature of law, the political community, and republican ideals that form the unconscious substructure of those political ideas and ideals most Western students value. For this reason alone, Cicero is important.

There are, in addition, several other revisions and modifications of the first edition. The introductory part of the St. Augustine chapter now includes a discussion of some of the key political ideas of the Roman Empire as well as a more detailed analysis of St. Augustine's theocratic theory of the state. John of Salisbury, important as a late medieval pre-Aristotelian thinker, is briefly discussed in the St. Thomas chapter. In the Locke chapter I have added a section on patriarchy and the political exclusion of women in Locke's theory of contract. The obvious inconsistencies and paradoxes inherent in Locke's and later liberals' treatment of women, their actual defense of patriarchy, are hardly dead issues and should not only arouse the interest of students but provide the instructor with a useful vehicle for explaining the theory of contract and for probing some of the issues raised by feminist critics of Locke and "patriarchal liberalism." Finally, the conclusion to the Marx chapter has been updated to reflect the demise of Soviet and East European communism and the current "death of communism" debate.

Given its pedagogical intent, the general format and style of the book continue to be designed with the student in mind. It is assumed that the student has no background in the history of political thought. Hence, all specialized terms are clearly defined in the text and used in a variety of contexts to better enable the student to grasp their meaning. In addition, an expanded glossary of terms is provided at the end of the book. And insofar as possible, given the inevitable limitations imposed on any introductory textbook, each thinker is dealt with in detail; basic concepts are explained in depth; and the implications of various political theories are drawn out and analyzed. The object has been to render the material understandable by writing at an appropriate level, not by overly simplifying difficult concepts and issues.

As for the specific thinkers discussed, although they do represent most of the genuinely important theorists in the Western tradition, at least those that the introductory student should be expected to have some comprehension of, there are some exceptions. Montesquieu is only briefly mentioned in passing. Hegel is discussed in conjunction with his influence upon modern liberal and Marxist thought; he is not given separate treatment. And in the contemporary period only those thinkers within the major ideological systems of thought who are intellectually important are analyzed in any real depth.

Where appropriate, I have cited sources that are recognized as classics in their respective fields. The most current literature is not always cited, but some of the most enduring is. The object has again been pedagogical: to introduce the beginning student to the mainstream of scholarship in political philosophy, not to the most current debates in the field. The bibliography includes some of the most important, or most useful, of the works cited.

The last section of the book, contemporary political theory, covers the age of ideology from Burke through Marx and the rise of modern nationalism. Although the term *contemporary* is usually employed to describe a more recent period of time, I have chosen to use it in this broadest context because the major ideological systems of thought that emerge following the French Revolution still constitute the major focus of political debate. Burke or Marx or Green are not contemporary political thinkers, but their respective philosophies have remained the touchstones of contemporary political thought. This remains so even in this "post-modern" era when the boundaries of political thought have been stretched at times to the point of obliteration.

Finally, I have made some changes in style and format that, I hope, will make the book more attractive and useful to both instructor and student. I have eliminated gender specific language wherever possible. I use the male pronoun only when it is necessary to keep the sense of the thinker being discussed, to maintain historical facticity, or when for other reasons substantive or stylistic it seems appropriate to do so. I have also reduced and simplified the index, which I believe was too long and complex in the first edition to be as useful to the student as it ought to be.

It is traditional and appropriate to end the preface with a note of thanks to all those who have helped bring the book to fruition. Those thanked in the first edition for critically reading the original manuscript are thanked again: Joyce and Stuart Lilie, Lynn Berk, and Joel Gottlieb. I should also like to thank those who critically reviewed the new Cicero chapter and the entire manuscript of the second edition; their criticisms and suggested revisions were most helpful. The reviewers of the second edition were Richard Franklin, University of Akron; Mark N. Hagopian, American International College; and W. Wesley McDonald, Elizabethtown College. In addition, I must now add to this list those who have used the text and have been kind enough to offer their criticisms and suggestions. Where possible, I have tried to follow their suggestions in this edition. Special thanks are due to Linda Pawelchak for her fine editorial supervision; the book reads much better because of her work. Finally, thanks to Linda Whitman for her much appreciated help in typing and manuscript preparation. I alone, of course, am responsible for the inevitable shortcomings of this work.

Brian R. Nelson

Western Political Thought

Introduction

Western political thought, from its inception to the present time, is the subject of this book. Not all of the political thinkers who have contributed to the historical evolution of that tradition of discourses are dealt with, but many of the most important are. Those who are discussed have been chosen for two reasons. First, they raise the perennial issues of politics and, as such, are most useful to the student who is just beginning to study political theory seriously. Second, they seem to best illustrate, or embody, the changing relationship of ethics and politics in Western political thought, the basic theme of this work.

The precise meaning and implications of that theme will be developed in the following chapters, not here; but the reader should know in broad outline what to anticipate. In its simplest terms, the book will argue that all political theories establish, explicitly or implicitly, some thesis about the relationship of ethics and politics. At a deeper level, it will be argued that the relationship of ethics and politics is a theme that defines key historical junctures in Western political thought and, more importantly, that explains certain crucial dilemmas within that tradition of discourse.

The organization of the book follows that theme: It analyzes, from the perspective of specific thinkers, the shifting relationship of ethics and politics from the beginning of Western political thought to the present time. Part I, the Classical and Medieval period, is seen as a time in which political theorists conceived politics as an activity rooted in ethical considerations, and political theory, above all, as a moral science. Part II examines the breakdown of this presumed unity in the thought of key modern political thinkers and the corresponding development of those categories of political analysis that define the modern political perspective. Part III analyzes the major ideological systems as one response to the dilemmas arising out of the modern divorce of ethics and politics. The final chapter will attempt to explain the assumptions behind that response and some of the political dangers inherent in it.

This brief synopsis, however, raises an issue, the first of many we will face in the following chapters, but clearly an issue prior to all others. To organize a book such as this around a theme is by definition to adopt a particular perspective, a certain "point of view," that will differ from the perspective of others within the field of political thought. This is inevitable, for there simply is no scholarly agreement that any perspective best characterizes the Western tradition of political discourse. Indeed, there is not even universal agreement that there is a tradition of discourse from which themes and perspectives can be derived.

The issue is resolved in recognizing that it is precisely in disagreement, not consensus, that our understanding of political matters has evolved. What ultimately is significant is not whether or not a perspective is valid in some absolute sense, but whether or not that perspective enlarges our understanding. This applies not only to questions of perspective and to scholarly interpretations of political thinkers, but to those thinkers themselves. Political theorists are important not because what they say is necessarily "True" with a capital "T," but because what they say enlarges our understanding of politics. This is not always understood by the student beginning the study of political thought. Frequently, the initiate will make the mistake of attempting to determine whether or not a theorist's philosophy is "True" or "False" and upon that basis to accept or reject the thinker's arguments.

Apart from the fact that the "Truth" cannot be so easily ascertained (just as there exists little scholarly agreement on matters of perspective and interpretation, there will be even less on the question of "Truth") sophisticated students of political thought will not raise the question of "Truth" at all. At least they will not do so in the manner of the initiate, for they will understand that some of the greatest political thinkers have arrived at conclusions and have employed methods of analysis that are profoundly important whether "True" or not. Indeed, it is often in pursuing a line of reasoning that may be erroneous, or that many consider to be so, that some of the most important insights into the nature of politics have been discovered and elaborated.

The following chapters, it is hoped, will offer numerous examples of thinkers with whom students will disagree, but from whom they will also find new insights despite, indeed often because of, that disagreement. In the same way, it is hoped that the student's understanding of political theory will be enlarged and deepened whether there is agreement with the premises of this work or not. Certainly the theme of this book, and the interpretations and arguments that follow, are presented in this spirit.

Part I

Classical and Medieval Political Theory

Unless . . . political power and philosopy meet together . . . there can be no rest from troubles . . . for states, nor . . . for all mankind . . .

—Plato, *The Republic*

1

Socrates

Western philosophy began in the sixth century B.C. in Greece. The sixth century philosophers—the pre-Socratics—were physicists who directed their speculation to determining what the universe is made of. The first of them, a man named Thales, claimed that the universe is made of water. He meant that water is the most basic substance out of which other elements are constituted. Those who followed Thales argued that the universe is made of earth, or fire, or air, or some combination of these basic "elements." In the fifth century a thinker named Democritus finally solved the riddle; he claimed that all things are composed of atoms.

But as time went on it became apparent to many thinkers that the most important questions were not being addressed. Even if everything is composed of water, how does the water change into something else, they asked. How does anything change from one thing to another? And, even more important, what is the ultimate nature of the universe? Is everything in a state of change, or is there a more basic reality that is permanent and unchangeable?

Thinkers gave widely varied answers to these questions. Some, such as Heraclitus, argued that the basic nature of reality is change itself. Others, such as Parmenides, insisted that change is a deception of the senses, that reality is ultimately unchangeable. Still others took positions between the extremes of Heraclitus and Parmenides. A thinker named Pythagoras, for example, claimed that beneath the changeable universe that we see around us is a substructure of unchangeable mathematical principles. If you want to understand the cosmos, Pythagoras argued, you must understand it mathematically.

Yet, as varied as these different doctrines were, we can see, in retrospect, two general and opposing tendencies.[1] Those who continued to ask the kinds of questions that interested Thales and the early physicists (What is the universe made of?) tended to take the position that the cosmos must be understood strictly in terms of materialist principles. They claimed that reality is nothing more than material—nothing more, that is, than what we can see or sense. As such, they argued that we must assume that change is real, and we must assume, further, that there is no divine or spiritual principle behind it. Democritus, for example, argued that everything is made of material atoms that move and combine in different ways purely by accident. What exists, therefore, exists as the result of an unplanned combination of atoms, nothing more.

Thinkers such as Parmenides and Pythagoras, on the other hand, insisted that beneath the reality we sense is a more basic reality. Without this more basic reality, they argued, the universe makes no sense. Despite change and impermanence there must be an unchanging pattern and purpose to things. What exists must be the reflection of some underlying structure.

The Greeks called these two tendencies in pre-Socratic thought philosophies of *being* and of *becoming*. The *materialists,* the philosophers of becoming, believed that all things change (become) without any inherent purpose or direction. Their opposites, the philosophers of being, believed that at the most basic level of reality things "be"—they exist perfectly and unchangeably. Pythagoras would argue, for example, that mathematical principles are perfect and unchangeable and that these principles constitute reality, not the imperfect world of our senses.

For our purposes, what is important about this debate is that the doctrines of being and becoming are applicable to human beings' social and political life. Pythagoras was the first to grasp this. He argued that by intellectually comprehending mathematical principles, we instill within the soul that same mathematical harmony found around us and thereby change ourselves and our communities for the better. In this way, Pythagoras showed the link that exists between metaphysics and ethics, between our basic notions about reality and our conception of how we should live as individuals and as members of society.[2] Those who found themselves in the materialist camp, however, drew radically different conclusions. And as we shall see throughout this book, the history of Western political philosophy can be seen as a debate between the theorists of being and the theorists of becoming, although these particular terms eventually disappear in common philosophical usage.

That debate begins with Socrates (470?–399 B.C.), one of history's great personalities. Indeed, in the history of Greek philosophy Socrates plays a role almost equivalent to that of Jesus in the history of the Christian religion. Both men were great teachers. Both were brought to trial on false charges (Socrates was accused of corrupting youth and religious impiety by the authorities of democratic Athens.) Both died for their beliefs; Jesus on the cross, Socrates by taking hemlock.

Aside from this, we do not know a great deal about Socrates; like Jesus, he wrote down nothing of his philosophy. What we do know about him comes primarily from Plato, his greatest student, just as we know about Jesus from his followers who wrote the New Testament. The new testament of Greek philosophy is the Platonic dialogues, a series of dramatic confrontations that pit Socrates against a variety of protagonists, the most important of whom were a group of teachers known as the *Sophists*.

The Sophists were roving teachers who began to appear around the early fifth century B.C. They went from city to city offering their services for a fee, and some of them, such as Gorgias and Protagoras (whose names became the titles of two important Platonic dialogues), were famous and eminent men. The Sophists taught young men from wealthy families who wanted to learn how to get ahead in life, and particularly those who wanted to learn how to get ahead in politics. Thus, the Sophists were the first political educators in Greece, and their teachings represented the first attempt to "philosophize" about politics, although it is not until Plato that we can speak in any real sense of a political philosophy.

Despite the fact that Socrates opposed the Sophists, they did have one thing in common. Both believed that the sixth-century philosophers' investigation of nature was leading nowhere and, more importantly, was not dealing with the significant questions. Even if it could be shown that the universe is composed of water, or of atoms, or of some other substance, what difference would that make to human beings, they asked. For both the Sophists and Socrates the significant questions were questions of ethics: How should we live? What is really important in life? What is the good life?

Of course, Socrates and the Sophists were aware of the earlier debate between being and becoming. The Sophists almost surely were influenced by Heraclitus. The link between Socrates and the pre-Socratics is more tenuous, but his greatest student, Plato, drew upon the work of such philosophers of being as Parmenides and Pythagoras. The point, however, is that it was the concern with physical questions as such that Socrates and the Sophists rejected. They wanted to raise the ethical question of how human beings ought to live their lives.

Here we must briefly discuss what we mean by ethics. *Ethics* has to do with values, that is, with whether or not an action or, more broadly, a way of life is good or evil, right or wrong. As such, ethical statements are immediately recognizable because they are always *ought* or *should* statements: "We *ought* not to commit murder" or "We *should* love our fellow human beings" are examples of such statements. When we make such assertions, we implicitly claim to have knowledge of what is right and what is wrong, what we ought or ought not to do.

There is another kind of statement we can make about reality based upon empirical observation (*empirical* means knowledge attained by the

senses). Such statements are *is* or *are* statements: "The earth is round," "Th
flower is red," or "The material world is composed of atoms" are all empir
cal statements because they all assert knowledge attained either directly
indirectly through the senses. (We cannot directly see atoms, but we can ind
rectly "see them" or "infer them" through special methods of observation
Modern science is an empirical discipline because it claims to deal with th
world as perceived by the senses alone, with objects of knowledge that c
be directly or indirectly observed. It is concerned with what *is*, not with wh
ought to be.

These distinctions between is and ought, empirical knowledge and eth
cal or normative knowledge as it is sometimes termed, are more clea
drawn in our own day than they were in Socrates' time. Our knowledge
these matters has expanded considerably since then. But we must bear i
mind, and this will become clearer as our analysis of Socrates' philosophy
proceeds, that Socrates did much to lay the basic framework of thought that
eventually allowed these distinctions to be made.

It is important at this juncture to emphasize again that Socrates and the
Sophists were interested in ethical or normative questions, not with the empirical questions that concerned the pre-Socratic physicists. And they realized, although again not as surely and consciously as we do today, that answering such questions required a way of thinking different from that needed
to answer empirical questions of the *is* variety. For in the case of ethical matters, whether we ought or ought not to do something depends upon the ends
we wish to achieve. (To employ an obvious example, we ought not to commit
murder if our goal is to preserve life.) And in order to say that an end is good,
we must first posit some ethical standard that establishes the validity of our
end, goal, or objective. It is for this reason that ethical questions always deal
with ends and, therefore, raise the issue of standards. Empirical questions do
not do this since they are concerned only with what in fact exists.

In the broadest terms, all ethical questions deal with how we ought to
live our lives. As we have seen, the answer to this question depends upon
what end, or goal, human beings ought to strive for, and this in turn depends
upon what the standard of life ought to be. All the ancient Greek thinkers, including Socrates and the Sophists, agreed that the ultimate end of human action should be happiness. Their disagreement was over the larger question:
What is the human standard of happiness?

Even then, there was a superficial agreement. Both Socrates and the
Sophists maintained that virtue, which they both claimed to teach, ought to
be the standard of happiness. They even agreed on the meaning of *virtue* in a
general sense because it was a commonly used term. Virtue meant *arete* or
excellence. (*Arete* is related to the word *aristocracy*, which originally meant
rule by the excellent.) The Greeks employed this idea of virtue very broadly
and comprehensively to describe a variety of human activities. They would
say, for example, that the virtue of a shoemaker is his ability to know and use

his materials to produce a fine product; the virtue of an athlete is his ability to use his body to its fullest potential. Thus virtue presupposed some end (the final product of a craftsman, the winning of an athletic event, and so on) and a standard of excellence. In other words, virtue, or arete, was the measure of a person's ability to perform well a specific function in life. And, of course, the Greeks believed the ultimate end of virtue to be happiness. A shoemaker who cannot make good shoes or an athlete who cannot perform well will not be fulfilled, they would argue, and therefore will not be happy.

While the Greek idea of virtue is a standard of excellence, it does not appear from these examples to be strictly an ethical standard. "Should I make good shoes?" may or may not be an ethical question, but to the extent that it is, it certainly does not raise the larger moral issues that people face. But virtue does become an ethical standard when it is used to judge how human beings should live, not simply in narrow occupational terms, but in terms of the goodness or evilness of their entire lives. This is why Socrates came to insist that there is such a thing as moral excellence that will produce not simply the limited happiness of performing well a simple task, but the complete happiness of living life well.

More than anyone else, Socrates transformed *virtue* from a morally neutral term to one with moral connotations, because he discovered that being a good craftsman and being a good human being hold something in common.[3] Unfortunately, Socrates maintained, people fail to recognize this shared quality. Thus, while they can easily agree about what constitutes virtue or excellence when it comes to making good shoes, they cannot agree at all when it comes to the much more important matter of living a good life. In the first case, failure to know what virtue is simply means sore feet. In the second, it means an unhappy and unfulfilled life. That people should know how to make shoes and not know how to make their lives fulfilled is absurd and tragic Socrates argued.

How, then, does Socrates define virtue, and how does his definition differ from that of the Sophists? Both definitions are, at first sight, quite simple and quite understandable. This simplicity is deceptive, however, because behind the differing conceptions of virtue lie two profoundly contrary visions of humankind, of society, and of politics. And here we must add yet another dimension to our discussion of ethics: Ethical and political questions are intimately connected. Before Robinson Crusoe met his man Friday, he had a number of problems, but not ethical or political ones. People do not live as individuals on deserted islands, however, they live among other human beings in political communities in which political decisions must be made. And political decisions involve questions of the ought variety: Ought we to make laws against abortion? or Ought we to go to war? are typical political questions that directly affect people for good or evil.

The point, given this ethical dimension to politics, is that how one defines virtue will depend in large part upon one's understanding of the nature of society and polity (*polity* is the generic term for political community whatever form it may take, be it a clan, a tribe, or as in ancient Greece, the *polis* or small city state). Let us look first at the Sophists' definition of virtue, specifically their definition of political virtue. Given the link between ethics and politics, we should be able to deduce their social and political theory from their definition.

The Sophists argued that virtue in general is the ability to acquire those things that people agree give pleasure—wealth, honor, status, and so on—and that political virtue in particular is the ability to acquire these things by the successful use of power. If this seems a shocking definition of virtue, remember that virtue originally meant nothing more than the ability to attain a given end. If the end of politics is the acquisition of power as the Sophists believed, then the virtue of a politician is simply his ability to master the techniques of attaining it. Interestingly, the Sophists were the first teachers of rhetoric, that is, of the art of speaking well. They saw it as a most important technique for gaining power because it gave the politician the means to sway public opinion to his side. For this reason, the political education of the young men who came to the Sophists included lessons in rhetoric, and rhetoric was considered a prime component of political virtue.

The Sophist's definition of virtue clearly implies a particular conception of society and politics and a corresponding view of human nature. The Sophist view holds that society and the state are conventional, that they are nothing more than artificial arrangements (conventions) created to serve limited purposes such as providing security and maintaining order. There is nothing natural about society and polity, the Sophists argued, because human beings are not innately social creatures. They are, rather, individual egotists who are more concerned about themselves than about some larger social good. Behind the Sophists' philosophy of society and politics lay an individualistic and egotistical psychology or theory of human nature.

The conventionalist view of society and the state explains why the Sophists defined virtue as they did. If the social and political order and its traditions, customs, and laws are simply pragmatic arrangements between individual egotists, then there is nothing intrinsically good or right about them. Hence, the Sophists taught their students to use the social order to their own benefit. Why be constrained by laws that are ethically meaningless?

Not all the Sophists went so far as to say that anything goes, but the more extreme ones did. And in order to justify their teaching they engaged in a radical critique of state and society, which they saw as an unnatural constraint upon the individual. In nature the strongest rules, they argued, but the conventions of society stand in the way of this natural order of things. The laws of society create a false equality among human beings, while in nature the powerful are superior to the weak. Their argument is best summed up in a famous Platonic dialogue entitled the *Gorgias* in which a young man named Callicles argues the Sophist case:

. . . we take the best and strongest of our fellows from their youth upwards, and tame them like young lions, enslaving them with spells and incantations, and saying to them that with equality they must be content, and that the equal is the honourable and the just. But if there were a man born with enough ability, he would shake off and trample under foot all our formulas and spells and charms, and all our laws which are against nature; the slave would rise in rebellion and be lord over us, and the light of natural justice would shine forth.[4]

It is evident that Sophists such as Callicles were preaching a doctrine of radical individualism at the expense of the larger society. Their political theory glorified the individual and encouraged him to do what he wanted in spite of law and custom. They addressed themselves to the potentially "great man." Foreshadowed by the Sophists' position, as the great classical scholar Sir Ernest Barker has argued, was Nietzsche's doctrine of the "overman" or "superman" who tramples underfoot all social constraints.[5]

It is easy to see why the Sophists became so popular with young men who were, so to speak, on the political make. Here were teachers who taught every adolescent what he wanted to hear; that he is a "superior man" who should let nothing stand in his way. And what young person does not suppose he or she really is superior and does not have an almost natural contempt for traditional authority? The adolescent is a ready-made Sophist in almost any society, and the Greek youth were no exception.

It is equally easy to see why the Sophists were unpopular with the average citizen. Most people believe their traditions and laws to be socially necessary, sacred, and above criticism. The Sophists attacked these deeply held beliefs and, so it seemed, thereby threatened the stability of the social order.[6]

How did Socrates respond to the Sophists? He argued that their definition of virtue is wrong, and that the whole conception of man and society upon which it is based is erroneous. According to Socrates, virtue is knowledge, not merely instrumental knowledge of how to attain power, but a larger ethical knowledge of how we ought to live our lives. Just as we recognize that knowledge is required to exercise a craft, says Socrates, so too must we recognize that knowledge is required to learn the art—the arete—of living a good, that is, an ethical, life. This is why we find Socrates constantly making analogies between the good craftsman and the good man in his dispute with the Sophists. We all recognize, Socrates argues, that what makes a good shoemaker is his knowledge of how to make shoes. Why can we not recognize, therefore, that that which makes a good or virtuous human being must be knowledge of how to live a good life?

The Sophists say that political virtue is power, but power for what, asks Socrates. The Sophists claim that power gives men the ability to appropriate the goods of this world, and that the pleasures derived from these goods will make them happy. But in point of fact, Socrates argues, the ceaseless search for pleasure will produce just the opposite because all pleasures, rooted as they are in our basic biological urges, are intimately connected to pain. Eating produces pleasure, for example, only if first we experience the pain of hunger. And this is true of all pleasures, says Socrates. This is why the desire for pleasure, which is as ceaseless as our biological drives, can only lead to constant pain and unhappiness. Thus, when you give power to a man and tell him that political virtue is the exercise of that power to satiate his passions, you are really contributing to his unhappiness. The more successful he is as a politician, the more unhappy he will become. Moreover, Socrates concludes, because he is concerned only with his own self-interest, he will fail to rule society properly and therefore will produce unhappiness in the citizenry as a whole.

In rejecting power and pleasure as the basis of human happiness and putting knowledge in their place, Socrates proposes a theory of society and politics radically different from that of the Sophists. He argues that if people can know ethical truths, then these truths should be embodied within their social organizations. This means that society, government, and law are much more than conventions. They are, Socrates would say, natural to the extent that they embody ethical truths. They are not simply artificial constructs; they are intimately connected to people's moral well-being.

This view that society and its political institutions are natural carries with it, of course, a radically different psychological theory than that of the Sophists. Socrates insists that society is natural because he believes human beings are social animals, not egotistical individualists. No one is self-sufficient says Socrates; people need others in order to survive. And since humans are by nature social beings, there must be social and political arrangements that are naturally good, that contribute to the harmonious functioning of the social organism. Clearly, given this view, the doctrine of the Sophists could only disrupt society and thereby the lives of all of its members.

This distinction between nature and convention is perhaps the single most important philosophical dichotomy in the history of Western political thought. As a general, but almost invariable rule, those thinkers who hold to a conventional theory of society, as do most modern theorists, view ethical standards as purely relative. Those, on the other hand, who take the position that society is natural, as do most classical and medieval theorists, believe that there are certain knowable ethical truths that ought to be recognized socially. We shall see this distinction between nature and convention raised repeatedly as an issue in the works of subsequent political thinkers.

For now, it is sufficient to recognize that in showing that there are knowable ethical truths that will produce happiness if they are embodied within people's social and political relationships, Socrates was able to demonstrate what he believed to be the utter wrong-headedness of the Sophists. How, he asks, can the Sophists possibly teach virtue if they admit there is no ethical standard that can be known? What is there to teach? Nothing, beyond certain political techniques, says Socrates. It is as if the Sophists had the technical know-how to make shoes, but no notion of what constitutes a good shoe. They had the technical know-how to acquire power, but no knowledge of the appropriate end or purpose of power. Their assumption that the end is pleasure merely demonstrates their ignorance.

Moreover, Socrates asks, how can the Sophists claim to teach virtue, and political virtue in particular, when their theory of state and society denies any real validity to the social and political order? In fact, they teach the individual how to triumph over society's rules and thereby ignore the needs of all the members of that society. They forget the necessary unity of ethics and politics; they forget that political questions are always ethical ones that involve moral relationships among people. The issue is not How shall the individual live life simply as an individual?, but How shall he or she live it in community with other human beings? To teach political virtue is, by definition for Socrates, to teach people how to live together for a common good that transcends the individual. This is why Socrates responds to Callicles' earlier paean to the "superior-individual" with a defense of social order.

> Philosophers tell us, Callicles, that communion and friendship and orderliness and temperance and justice bind together heaven and earth and gods and men, and that this universe is therefore called cosmos or order, not disorder or misrule, my friend.[7]

Socrates, then, defends the social order; the Sophists attack it. This is the explicit and obvious political difference that follows from their differing ethical, social, and psychological assumptions. But this political difference is more complex than Socrates' response to Callicles would suggest, for Socrates does not support the social order uncritically. Quite the contrary— he is a greater social critic than the Sophists, but in a different way. What Socrates argues is that while law is natural, any given law may, and frequently does, violate basic ethical precepts. For example, if the laws are made by men such as Callicles, they will fail to create that order and harmony that is essential to the well-being and happiness of the whole community. Such laws are merely conventional. What Socrates proposes to do, therefore, is to reform the state and politics in accordance with correct ethical standards. In a sense, he wishes to mediate between nature and convention; to make the social and political order compatible with that which is natural (ethical).

The problem was that in order to unite the social and ethical, Socrates was compelled to both defend and attack society at one and the same time. His contemporaries missed the subtlety. They thought he was simply another radical Sophist engaged in tearing down those values that hold society together.[8] This is the real reason why Socrates was brought to trial and put to death. The specific charges leveled against him—"religious impiety" and "corrupting young people"—were simply the form in which the court gave legal expression to this, the real issue. The trial was in fact a political trial aimed at preventing Socrates from continuing to teach his philosophy. When, in the name of a higher duty to follow his philosophic conscience, Socrates refused to abide by the court's demand that he cease his teaching, he was condemned to death.

That Socrates chose to die rather than cease his teaching illuminates the real political meaning of his philosophical system. For Socrates' death was a political act aimed at demonstrating that philosophy is not simply a set of ideas, but a way of life superior to that of politics, at least politics as conceived by the Sophists. The story of Socrates' incarceration and death, and the events leading up to it, are told in several dialogues. One of these, the *Crito,* best illustrates Socrates' position.

In this dialogue Socrates' friend Crito comes to his jail cell with a plan for escape. (It was a common practice to allow prominent citizens to escape rather than suffer the penalty of death.) Socrates refused to flee, however, even though he knew that his sentence was utterly unjust. He based his refusal on the argument that the state had raised him and nurtured him like a parent, and that he could not now turn his back upon it. He owed obedience to it, but only to a point. The state demanded that he stop teaching, and he could not do that without violating his conscience. He could, however, affirm the right of the state to make laws and impose penalties by suffering the consequences of following his conscience.

We would today classify Socrates' decision as an act of civil disobedience. Civil disobedience is a political act that attempts to affirm the individual's conscience as the highest law, yet at the same time recognizes the social necessity of civil law and order. This is accomplished by violating the law where it contradicts the urgings of conscience, yet affirming the necessity of law by suffering willingly the consequences of one's acts. This was precisely Socrates' intent. In civil disobedience Socrates had discovered a way, the only way in fact, to carry his philosophy into real life. By refusing to stop teaching, he affirmed the superiority of conscience and the philosophical life upon which it is based. By refusing to escape, he affirmed that the state is a natural and a necessary good, even though specific laws and institutions may be only conventional.

Moreover, in choosing to die as he did, Socrates demonstrated the appropriate relationship between philosophy and politics. His teaching had been that the political sphere, the state, should be founded upon philosophical truths, but in his own case the relationship seemed to Socrates to be breaking down. The men of thought and the men of action seemed to be of different minds. What to do? Given his situation, Socrates' only solution was to die. To live would be to concede that the commands of the state are superior to philosophical truth. His greatest student, Plato, would propose another, and ultimately more radical, solution; but this is a subject for the next chapter.

There will be those who take exception to Socrates' reasoning, of course. It might be argued, for example, that if Socrates is correct in what he teaches, he is correct whether he lives or not, and that had he chosen to live he could have had a continuing influence upon people. Crito made precisely these kinds of arguments, and others like them (What about your family, Socrates?—Your friends?) but to no avail. Socrates refused to do the prudent thing, because prudence is not philosophical. To be prudent means to act upon one's political judgment of the relative merits of a course of action. To be philosophical means to act strictly on the basis of truth, regardless of the consequences. This, at least, is what Socrates meant by philosophy. The philosopher must behave strictly according to knowledge of what is right and what is wrong.

These abstract principles are linked with real life through Socrates' definition of virtue. If virtue is knowledge, then to act upon any other basis than that of knowledge would be unvirtuous or evil. And to lack virtue is to be unhappy and unfulfilled. So Socrates' decision to remain philosophical and die was no mere posturing; it was the only action he could take that would be consistent with his completeness as a human being.

Any difficulty one may find in comprehending Socrates' decision to die is most likely due to failure to consider seriously Socrates' definition of virtue. When Socrates says that virtue is knowledge, he means just that. This definition expresses the very essence of Socratic ethics, and it means exactly what it says. According to Socrates, if one knows, really knows, what is ethically correct, one cannot help but act accordingly, for no one would knowingly do something that produces unhappiness.

The obvious objection to this line of reasoning, an objection that was raised against Socrates in his own day, is that our desire to do something may be stronger than the force of our knowledge that we ought not do it. We may know that it is wrong to steal, for example, but given the opportunity we might do it in any case. Socrates insists that this cannot happen. The fact that people steal is proof that they do not really know that it is wrong, although they may have thought they knew. It is ignorance of the real human consequences of unethical behavior that compels us to misbehave, not the weakness of reason in the face of great passion.[9]

Can Socrates really mean, then, that because he knows dying is the ethical thing to do, his death is the necessary condition for his happiness? This is precisely what he means. Had he chosen to follow Crito's advice and live, he would have admitted thereby that virtue is not identical to knowledge, that the philosophical life is a sham, and that his life of teaching was for naught. His life would have been thereby rendered meaningless and miserable by not choosing to die. And Socrates would have immediately rejected the conventional argument that an unhappy life is better than no life at all, for implicit in this objection is the idea that mere biological pleasure is the greatest good. This Socrates would never concede. Mere existence can only produce pleasure in its narrowest sense. We may continue to eat, sleep, and procreate, but this is not the condition of genuine human happiness as Socrates defines it. To his mind, to merely live is not to live at all. This is why he denies that virtue is pleasure as the Sophists maintained.

Moreover, he would argue that conventional wisdom is based upon an unphilosophical fear of death. To fear something means to know that there is something to fear. But since we cannot know for certain what death will bring, we have no basis to fear it. In fact, for Socrates the fear of death is a form of intellectual arrogance that he finds typical of men such as Callicles. Like Callicles, who thinks he knows what the purpose of life is without really knowing, the necrophobe thinks he knows death is to be feared without in fact really knowing.

So confident was Socrates that knowledge is the real basis of a fulfilled life, so certain that, as he says, "the unexamined life is not worth living," that he was able to die as he lived—philosophizing. In the *Phaedo,* the last of the dialogues that deal with his final days, Socrates is shown discussing the meaning of death with his friends while waiting for the deadly hemlock to be brought to him.

But was Socrates' confidence misplaced? This is the real issue. If knowledge is the source of truth about how we ought to live our lives, and if Socrates possesses such knowledge, his decision to die makes perfect sense. The question is, "Does such knowledge really exist as Socrates claims, and if it does exist, does Socrates possess it?" In short, "How does Socrates know that he knows, and how does he know what he claims to know?"

These are what we call *epistemological* questions. An *epistemology* is a theory of knowledge; it is a theory about what and how we can know. Every political theory, as with every other kind of theory, is based upon some kind of epistemology, if only implicitly. For it is impossible to assert knowledge about anything without first demonstrating that we know our knowledge to be a valid source of truth. This certainly is the case with Socrates whose epistemology is explicit and absolutely crucial to his whole philosophy of life. This is why the real dispute between Socrates and the Sophists is not simply over the purpose of life, but over how we know that we know that purpose. And this is why the really fundamental question here is epistemological: How does Socrates know that he has knowledge with such certainty that he is willing to die for it?

Socrates' answer is given in a number of dialogues, but it is best to begin with the *Apology,* the dialogue that deals with his trial and conviction. In this work, Socrates explains by way of a story the basis of his claim to possess knowledge or wisdom. A friend, he says, was told by the Oracle of Delphi that he, Socrates, is the wisest man in Greece. Now, Socrates did not believe that this was so and determined that if he could find someone wiser than himself he could refute the Oracle. "Accordingly," says Socrates "I went to one who had the reputation of wisdom and observed him—his name I need not mention, he was a politician."[10] And I found, continues Socrates, that I was wiser than the politician, because "he knows nothing, and thinks that he knows; I neither know nor think that I know. In this one little point . . . I seem to have the advantage of him."[11] This same procedure, says Socrates, he followed with others, and the results were always the same. He found that he was wiser than others because he alone seemed to know that he was ignorant.

Socrates' assertion that he is wiser than others "in this one little point" is not to be taken to mean that he believes knowledge is unattainable. It is simply that one must first admit ignorance in order to acquire knowledge. If, like the Sophists and politicians, one begins with the assumption that one is already knowledgeable, it will be impossible to engage in the quest for truth. The ignorant who think they are wise are unteachable; those who know they are ignorant are willing to learn and, in this Socratic sense, are already "wise."

It is of more than passing interest that Socrates initiates his experiment in wisdom with a politician. To his mind the politicians, like the Sophists, were not only the most arrogant in their ignorance, but the most dangerous. They were the teachers and leaders of society. Their ignorance, therefore, was a public concern. From the beginning, Socrates' theory of knowledge was employed by himself and by his students in critiques of existing political practices. In such critiques the ignorance of the Sophists and the leading politicians in Athens was demonstrated. But the criticisms did not always have the desired effect. As Socrates wryly observes in the *Apology,* they frequently caused him to be hated, a matter not wholly unconnected with his trial and death.

But even had the leaders of Athens become aware of their ignorance, how could they have gotten beyond it? As we have noted, the admission of ignorance is only the starting point for Socrates. The next steps are to define knowledge and determine how it can be attained. Socrates does this in one manner or another in all of the dialogues because knowledge is the key to the whole Socratic system. But for our purposes the dialogue entitled the *Meno* is most useful.[12]

In this dialogue, Meno engages Socrates in a discussion about whether or not virtue can be taught. Socrates' response is at first perplexing, for he argues that it can neither be taught nor, in the usual sense of the term, learned. It can, however, be drawn out, for knowledge of such matters is already within us. We need simply learn to know what we already know—a paradox that Socrates explains by way of a demonstration. He borrows one of Meno's slaves, a young boy who has had no formal education, and by a process of questioning gets him to discover for himself the Pythagorean theorem that the square of the hypotenuse of a right triangle is equal to the sum of the squares of the other two sides. Now, Socrates asks, how could the boy have discovered the theorem without in some sense already knowing it? He had had no mathematical training; there was nothing in his experience that could explain his knowledge. How, then, did he come by it except that he already knew it? And, Socrates continues, what is true of mathematical knowledge is true of other branches of knowledge, including ethics. Just as the slave boy discovered for himself a principle of mathematics, in the same way we can discover for ourselves the principles of leading a good life. We need only look within ourselves.

Concealed in this simple analogy between mathematics and ethics is an epistemological discovery of momentous import in the development of Western thought. Socrates had discovered the *concept,* which is a generalized, abstract idea by which we classify and organize particular ideas about the world around us.[13] For example, the slave boy in the *Meno* is able to recognize all three-sided polygons as triangles when he sees them, Socrates would argue, because he already has within him the concept—the generalized idea or ideal—of "triangleness." In the same way, according to Socrates, people recognize courage, or temperance, or justice, or any other virtue because they have prior conceptual knowledge of what constitutes virtue. Philosophers would call this a priori knowledge.

It is this conceptual knowledge, then, that is already within us (not, of course, empirical knowledge). And because this knowledge is general and "ideal" it must be universal and unchanging. That is, it must always be true, and it must be the same truth for all. There is only one Pythagorean theorem, and it will be as true an infinite number of tomorrows from now as it is today. In the same way, Socrates asserts, since ethical knowledge is also conceptual, it must be universally true and unchanging. It cannot be merely conventional as the Sophists claim.

It is clear that conceptual knowledge must be arrived at in a particular way. Since this knowledge is within us, it needs to be drawn out; it cannot be imposed. It does no good, Socrates would argue, to lecture to students about virtue. People already know what virtue is but must be helped to know that they know. This requires a form of questioning the Greeks called the *dialectic.* Through dialectic the student's initial definition about what constitutes virtue (or some equivalent conceptual issue) is countered on the part of the "teacher" by critical questioning that demands a more inclusive definition. Seeing the inadequacy of a first opinion, the student will attempt to modify it in light of the teacher's questioning. The process continues until a definition is reached that is complete, inclusive, and genuinely conceptual. But it is the student who ultimately recognizes the inadequacy of the initial opinion and who, by the very logical structure of the mind, is forced to learn the truth. The Socratic or dialectical method of questioning is designed to tap this logical structure, not to impose the truth upon it.

The dialectic, then, is a method that begins with opinion and ends with knowledge. And herein lies a crucial distinction in Socrates' debate with the Sophists. For Socrates, opinion is the precise opposite of knowledge because it is not conceptual. Everyone has opinions, but the philosopher alone has knowledge, that is, a conceptual grasp of the underlying order of things. He alone has an understanding of the nature of being, as opposed to that of becoming, which is in the realm of opinion.

Now it is Socrates' claim that the Sophists teach opinion, not knowledge. This is so, he argues, because they do not understand that opinion is simply ignorance masquerading as knowledge. And the reason they do not understand, Socrates insists, is that they have no concept of the concept. Hence, they never teach more than commonsense opinion about virtue. Their theory that virtue is pleasure is, in reality, an idea that has been accepted by every Philistine throughout the ages. And the Sophists never go beyond this general and mistaken theory of virtue.

For example, they never adequately define the essence (the concept) of virtue as such, says Socrates, but have as many different opinions of what virtue is as there are virtues. When they define courage, or justice, or any of the other virtues, their definitions have nothing in common. It is as if, to return to the analogy in the *Meno,* they have one definition for an isosceles triangle, another for a right triangle, and others for the whole variety of triangles, without ever having a concept of triangleness as such.

It is now clear why the Sophists taught rhetoric instead of dialectic. Rhetoric has to do with swaying public *opinion,* not with the acquisition of genuine conceptual knowledge. The Sophists taught their students how to change people's opinions; Socrates taught his students how to rise above opinion. Clearly the Sophists had the easier job of it. They only had to tell people that which they wanted to hear. Socrates taught what they should but would rather not hear. People do not willingly give up their opinions, as Socrates discovered. The dialectic works only if the student first commits to the quest for truth. Then, and only then, will the logical structure of the mind come into play and the conceptual knowledge within emerge into full consciousness.

This leads us to the culminating point of Socrates' theory of knowledge, and to his ultimate criticism of the Sophists. It was apparent to Socrates, and it became even more apparent to Plato, that the logic of the mind must be part of a larger cosmic order. It seemed inconceivable to them that truth exists in the mind only. It must be, they thought, that the concepts in our mind reflect some real order and purpose in the universe as a whole. This idea, in fact, was discovered before Socrates by some of the pre-Socratic thinkers, most notably Pythagoras. He claimed, you will recall, that mathematical principles undergird the empirical world. Hence, Pythagoras came to believe that the whole universe works upon logico-mathematical principles that are reflected in the mind.

Socrates did not adopt the Pythagorean view; the kinds of ethical questions he was interested in led him in other directions. But Socrates did believe, as did Pythagoras that the universe is orderly and purposeful, and that our ideas are reflections of this fact. And, most important for Socrates, this purposefulness went beyond the physical dimension. It included the ethical as well. Since human beings can attain ethical knowledge, Socrates believed the universe as a whole must have an ethical purpose.

It is easy to see why classical thought, which begins with Socrates, was so easily absorbed by medieval Christianity. Clearly Socrates' moral universe could be construed as the mind of God, and his idea of inner knowledge could be seen as the illumination of God's divinity within the soul. In fact, Socrates believed something very much like this. His epistemology indicated to him the existence of God, of a soul, and of life after death (although of this he was not certain).[14] And his belief in the immortality of the soul was linked to a theory of reincarnation. It seemed to Socrates that since knowledge is within us, we must have learned it somewhere in another life. Hence, he came to view learning as a recollection of that which we have forgotten in the process of being reborn.

But Socrates' theology is no longer of real importance to us. We now understand that his religious theories were a reflection of the fact that the rules of logical thought were not yet fully developed. We no longer need to rely on such notions to explain conceptual knowledge. On the other hand, the question of whether or not human reason is a reflection of some larger order and purpose is by no means a dead issue. And in retrospect we can see that it is precisely this larger order that Socrates wished to structure into people's social and political relationships.

Is this not ultimately Socrates' criticism of the Sophists? They recognize no order or purpose to anything, whether it be the universe, the state, or the individual. Hence their idea of virtue: Where no ethical purpose or order exists, "virtue" reduces itself to a struggle for power and nothing more. But the other side of this inability to see order and purpose, Socrates maintained, is the Sophists' inability to understand the nature of knowledge. They have no concept of the concept. As a result, they have no conception of an inner order that would clue them to the existence of an outer order. And their political theories simply reflect this inability to conceptualize order. This is why they justify a politics of chaos and disorder.

Socrates' insight into the nature of knowledge transformed Western consciousness. The central role accorded to reason in Western philosophy, and the idea that human institutions ought to reflect a larger rational order—ideas that have become almost the sine qua non of Western thought—we owe to Socrates. But in political philosophy, Socrates only laid the foundation. He was not a political philosopher as such because his concern was primarily with the individual (although he did emphasize that the individual could not be conceived apart from politics). And while he was, from all we can surmise, a ceaseless critic of Athenian democracy, he never created a thoroughgoing political philosophy as an alternative to existing political practices.

Plato did. He picked up where his teacher left off. He united Socrates' insights with those of pre-Socratic thinkers of being such as Pythagoras, who claimed that beneath everything we see is a perfect and unchangeable order.

The result was not only great political philosophy, but the beginning of a tradition of political thought that extends to the present day.

Notes

1. See W.K.C. Guthrie, *The Greek Philosophers From Thales to Aristotle* (New York: Harper & Row, 1960), for a brief but excellent discussion of these two tendencies in early Greek philosophy.
2. Sir Ernest Barker, *The Political Thought of Plato and Aristotle* (New York: Dover Publications, 1959), pp. 19–21.
3. See Laszlo Versenyi, *Socratic Humanism* (New Haven: Yale University Press, 1963), pp. 83–86, for an excellent discussion of Socrates' transformation of virtue from a morally neutral to an ethical term.
4. B. Jowett, trans., "Gorgias," in *The Dialogues of Plato*, 4th ed. (Oxford: Oxford University Press, 1968), II:577.
5. Barker, *Political Thought*, p. 96.
6. Francis MacDonald Cornford, *Before and After Socrates* (Cambridge: Cambridge University Press, 1968), p. 43. Cornford frames the issue in its simplest and most human terms: "In this philosophy of individual self-assertion parents . . . [recognized] something analogous to the spirit of adolescent reaction against the authority of the home. . . . To the boys, on the other hand, it . . . [came] as [a] . . . welcome expression of the rebellion against those stupid rules."
7. Jowett, "Gorgias," p. 606.
8. Cornford, *Before and After Socrates*, p. 43.
9. There is more to Socrates' insistence that evil is ignorance than the failure of evildoers to grasp the real human consequences of their actions. Ultimately, for Socrates, to know the truth is to be so moved by it that the personality itself is altered such that the desire to do wrong no longer exists. [See Arthur Kenyon Rogers, *The Socratic Problem* (New York: Russell & Russell, 1971), pp. 135–36.] This idea that philosophical knowledge leads to a radical psychological reorientation will become more understandable in the chapter on Plato. For now, it is sufficient to note that Socrates' ethical system involved a whole new vision of humanity, one of great power and beauty, and that his almost saintly reputation is based on the fact that others could see in him that psychological transformation, that actual embodiment of virtue, that he claimed inherently followed from the possession of philosophical knowledge.
10. B. Jowett, trans., "Apology," in *The Dialogues of Plato*, 4th ed. (Oxford: Oxford University Press, 1969), I:345.
11. Ibid.

12. See Jowett, *The Dialogues of Plato,* vol. I, pp. 252–63, for an analysis of the connection between the *Meno* and the development of Plato's thought, particularly of his doctrine of Form, which will be discussed in the next chapter. See also Norman Gulley, *Plato's Theory of Knowledge* (London: Methuen & Co., Ltd., 1962), pp. 4–23.

13. See, for example, Barker, *Political Thought,* p. 47; and B. Jowett, trans., "Parmenides," *in The Dialogues of Plato,* 4th ed. (Oxford: Oxford University Press, 1969), II: 640–41. See also Max Weber, "Science as a Vocation," in H.H. Gerth and C. Wright Mills, trans./eds., *From Max Weber: Essays in Sociology* (New York: Oxford University Press, 1946), p. 141. In this classic essay on the scientific life, Weber points out the enormous importance of Socrates' discovery of the concept to the whole development of Western science and to those rational modes of inquiry that define the Western world view.

14. There has long existed a dispute regarding Socrates' position on the question of life after death. No definitive answer to this issue can be given. See W.K.C. Guthrie, *Socrates* (Cambridge: Cambridge University Press, 1971), pp. 153–64, for a discussion of the issue, and for an interesting analysis of Socrates' religious beliefs in general.

2

Plato

Plato (427–347 B.C.) was born into an aristocratic Athenian family. His life spanned the period of the Peloponnesian War, which began in 431 B.C. and did not end until 404 B.C. The war involved the whole Hellenic (Greek) world, with Sparta and Athens the chief antagonists, and it resulted in the common ruin of all concerned. It marked the beginning of the end of that glorious period in Greek history when in art, literature, philosophy, and politics the Western world was given its enduring form.

The disintegration of the Hellenic world was paralleled at home by ceaseless political discord. Different classes with irreconcilable disagreements engaged in bitter struggles for power. Some members of Plato's own family seized power and created an oligarchy in 404 B.C. only to be deposed shortly thereafter in 403 B.C. by the democrats. It was this democratic regime that tried and executed Socrates.

Common to all these political struggles, as both Thucydides (the great historian of the Peloponnesian War) and Plato observed, was people's unwillingness to look beyond their immediate self-interest. They seemed incapable of conceiving of any kind of larger good beyond themselves. The result was common ruin and common misery. Surely, Plato thought, there must be a better way. And, for Plato, there was: He became Socrates' student.

Socrates transformed Plato's life. As an aristocrat, Plato was expected to go into politics, which was then considered an honorable and noble profession for members of the upper classes. But the politics of that time appalled Plato, and Socrates showed him that the philosophical life is superior to the life of a politician. With Socrates' death, however, Plato came to recognize, more intensely than had his teacher, that philosophy and politics cannot be kept apart. This recognition compelled Plato to think philosophically about politics in a deeper and more radical sense than had his teacher. Thus Plato became the first real political philosopher in the Western world.

Now Plato's political theory is but a part of a much larger philosophical system based upon Socrates' initial insights. As such, Plato's political theory, like his larger system, resembles a huge building in which each part has its place, and in which neither the parts nor the whole can be understood apart from each other. His political theory, therefore, includes a theory of ethics, as well as of psychology, economics, and sociology.[1] The current separation of modern social science into discrete subfields would have struck Plato as absurd—like a building made of parts that did not fit into an integrated whole.

Plato's political theory is based upon Socrates' teaching in another way also. It was intended to change existing conditions, not to be merely an exercise in abstract thinking. Unlike his teacher, however, Plato was not content simply to wander the streets of Athens discoursing upon his philosophy. Plato founded the first university, which he called the Academy, the function of which was not only to teach young men philosophy but to reform Greek politics. Teachers were sent out to train political leaders in the philosophical truths learned at the Academy. The results, however, were rarely what Plato would have desired, for the same irrational politics prevailed no matter what the philosopher taught. This was a cause of great dismay to Plato and the source of much of his hostility toward the political domain.

Plato himself went on some legendary teaching expeditions, all of which turned out disastrously. The story of these trips is worth recounting because it will help us understand Plato's basic hostility toward politics.[2] In 387 B.C., when Plato was in his early forties, he visited Sicily. There he met Dion, the brother-in-law of Dionysius I, the tyrant of Syracuse. Dion was impressed by Plato's philosophy and, according to legend, persuaded Plato to teach Dionysius I. Unfortunately, Dionysius was not enchanted by what Plato had to say and reportedly sold him into slavery. Plato escaped with the aid of friends and returned to Athens.

Upon his return he founded the Academy, where he remained for twenty years, glad to be rid of politics. But when Dionysius I died, Dion summoned Plato back to Syracuse to attempt with young Dionysius II what he had failed to do with his father. Initially Dionysius II was quite enthusiastic and spoke of reforming Syracuse's politics in light of Plato's teachings. But he soon wearied of philosophy and became distrustful of Plato's relationship with Dion. Dion was banished and Plato was put under virtual house arrest. Eventually he managed to secure his release and once again returned to Athens.

Several years later he returned at the request of Dionysius II with the hope of reconciling the young tyrant with Dion. The reconciliation failed, and the trip turned out as disastrously as the first two. Worse, events went in a direction designed to utterly disgust Plato with politics and to ensure his final withdrawal from public activity. Dionysius II became increasingly tyrannical, and Dion eventually overthrew him. Then Dion himself was assassinated by one of Plato's own students who, in turn, established himself as a tyrant. Later he too was assassinated. What had begun many years earlier in philosophical enthusiasm ended in cabals and intrigues and, for Plato, utter despair.

Here was the paradox and agony of Plato's life. His attempt to teach philosophy to tyrants indicates his unflagging belief that politics could be rationalized by truth. Yet the attempt failed utterly; Plato barely avoided the fate of Socrates. No matter how loudly and insistently the truth was proclaimed, the same irrational element in politics prevailed.

Even though over the years the reality of politics slowly chipped away at Plato's bedrock belief in the power of philosophy to transform the human condition, the belief was never destroyed. It was modified in Plato's more mature works such as his last great political dialogue, the *Laws,* but it was never destroyed. Plato never lost hope that at some propitious time philosophy might enter people's lives and transform them. He, at least, could prepare the way philosophically. His most famous dialogue, the *Republic,* is just such a preparation.

The *Republic,* let it be said from the beginning, is by all accounts a great work of political philosophy. It failed to rationalize politics every bit as much as did Plato's attempt at practical reform, but that failure is no longer important. The *Republic* is quite simply a remarkable work of the human mind. One cannot read it and be untouched by its spirit and by the profundity of its insights. And this was precisely Plato's intent: If the *Republic* could not alter people's politics, it could at least alter the lives of those who read it. For the *Republic* is not just about politics; it is about the individual and how he or she should live his or her life.

The *Republic* is about justice—what it is, and whether or not it is a desirable virtue for people and for states. We are, of course, to deal with justice as a universal ideal, as *justiceness,* just as in the *Meno* we dealt with a universal triangle or *triangleness.* Because it deals with an ideal, the *Republic* has often been described as a utopian work of political philosophy. But Plato's utopianism cannot be equated with modern utopian thinking. The *Republic* is not an early form of science fiction or an ancient version of contemporary futurist writing. Rather, it is a work that attempts to establish an ideal standard, a normative measuring rod, by which to judge existing political practices. As such, the *Republic* is about the ideal state of perfect justice. Plato's later works discuss the best possible states of less than perfect justice. The ancients were realists who understood that the ideal cannot as a general rule be attained in the "real world." But they also understood that without an ideal standard they could say nothing about the real. How, they would ask, can we say that an existing political system or political practice is unjust if we do not know the ideal of justice? It would be as if we were to attempt to measure something without a ruler.

The opening pages of the *Republic* set the philosophical framework of what is to follow, for they give us hints that point to the conclusion that justice is the greatest good that people can attain as individuals and as members of a larger political community. These hints are contained in a dialogue that begins at the house of an old and respected man named Cephalus whom Socrates and others are at the time visiting. In innocent enough fashion a question arises as to what is right conduct or justice. Cephalus answers that justice is simply telling the truth and paying back one's debts. But Socrates argues that the definition is not inclusive enough and therefore does not always apply. For example, Socrates points out, if "a friend who had lent us a weapon were to go mad and then ask for it back, surely . . . we ought not to return it."[3]

Cephalus's son, Polemarchus, then suggests that justice is giving every man his due, which he takes to mean harming your enemies as well as helping your friends. This definition is more inclusive than Cephalus's, but Socrates responds by pointing out that hurting a person makes that person worse, or "less excellent," as the Greeks would put it. And, he continues, "justice is a peculiarly human excellence. . . . To harm a man, then, must mean making him less just."[4] But clearly, says Socrates, justice cannot be the cause of injustice. To bolster his point, Socrates employs a familiar analogy. A craft requires a special skill, he says, and it would be absurd to argue that "a musician or a riding master [can] be exercising his special skill if he makes his pupils unmusical or bad riders."[5] In brief, the teacher of virtue, whether we use that term in its narrowest meaning of mastering a specific craft or in its broader ethical connotation, cannot logically make his pupils less skillful or less ethical.

Now enters a new character, Thrasymachus, a Sophist and a renowned teacher of rhetoric. He vociferously objects to Socrates' method of asking questions rather than giving answers. He tells the assemblage that "Socrates [is] at his old trick of shamming ignorance."[6] But Socrates is not shamming. His "ignorance" is a starting point, and his questions are a dialectical method of attaining conceptual knowledge. Thrasymachus understands nothing of this because he understands nothing of the underlying philosophy that Socrates teaches. He is an extreme Sophist who, without fully realizing it, denies the possibility of attaining conceptual knowledge of ethical principles. Hence, he misunderstands the purpose of Socrates' questioning; he assumes it is merely a rhetorical trick and that Socrates is simply another clever Sophist. And because of Thrasymachus's lack of philosophical sophistication, Socrates quickly traps him with what he initially assumes to be an unassailable definition of justice.

According to Thrasymachus—and here the discussion becomes political—what is "'just' or 'right' means nothing but what is to the interest of the stronger party."[7] In other words, might makes right. We can immediately recognize that this definition is identical to Callicles' in the *Gorgias*. And the reader will recall that Socrates had responded to Callicles by saying that if justice or right reduces itself to power, then all will be disorder and disharmony. So we already know, in broad outline, how Socrates will define justice. Justice, like any other virtue, will be an expression of harmonious relationships within the individual and within society as a whole.

But Socrates does not yet respond to Thrasymachus with his own definition of justice. Once again he returns to his questioning and exposes a serious flaw in Thrasymachus's notion of justice. Is it not true, asks Socrates, that those in power make mistakes? And if the powerful mistakenly make laws that are harmful to themselves, will they not in the process violate the principle that the exercise of their power is to their own self-interest? To all of this Thrasymachus must agree. But in agreeing Socrates has gotten him unwittingly to admit to the basic Socratic premise that virtue, in this case the virtue of statesmanship, is knowledge, not power, for clearly knowledge is required if mistakes are to be avoided. Of course, by "knowledge" Thrasymachus means simply knowledge of the leader's self-interest. Socrates must show that knowledge refers to something much broader than this. But the fact that he has forced Thrasymachus to introduce knowledge into his definition of justice gives him an opening wedge that, eventually, will expose the fallacy of Thrasymachus's position.

What is this broader aspect of knowledge? Socrates' answer again takes the form of a question. Tell me, says Socrates, is it a physician's "business to earn money or to treat his patients?"[8] Thrasymachus admits that the physician's proper objective, insofar as he is acting as a physician, is to treat his patients. Socrates continues: "can it equally be said of any craft that it has an interest, other than its own greatest perfection?"[9] In other words, is it not the interest of a physician as physician to efficiently and properly treat his patients just as, say, it is the interest of a shoemaker as shoemaker to make fine shoes? Thrasymachus again agrees because it would be absurd to argue that it is a physician's interest to produce sick patients or a craftsman's interest to produce shoddy products. But Thrasymachus's admission is reluctant because he now senses that his definition of justice no longer suffices. By admitting that the interest of a physician lies in treating his patients, it must follow that the real interest of the statesman lies in his subjects. In other words, it follows that the public interest is the proper concern of the political leader, not his self-interest. Thus, Socrates concludes:

> With government of any kind: no ruler, so far as he is acting as ruler, will study or enjoin what is for his own interest. All that he says and does will be said and done with a view to what is good and proper for the subjects for whom he practices his art.[10]

First, Socrates had gotten Thrasymachus to admit that statecraft, as with any craft, requires knowledge. Now he demonstrates that political knowledge has to do with the public interest, not with the interest of the politician. Thrasymachus is not willing to concede defeat, however, and makes a dramatic shift in his argument. He now decides to argue the case for injustice!

> Why, you imagine that a herdsman studies the interests of his flocks or cattle, tending and fattening them up with some other end in view than his master's profit or his own; and so you don't see that, in politics, the genuine ruler regards his subjects exactly like sheep, and thinks of nothing else, night and day, but the good he can get out of them for himself. . . . Innocent as you are yourself, Socrates, you must see that a just man always has the worst of it. . . . It is to one's own interest not to be just.[11]

It is important to understand the new position that Thrasymachus has adopted, and to be critical of it. Thrasymachus has "appealed to the facts" and that is not a valid argument. It does not follow that because human beings in fact act unjustly that they ought to so act. For example, simply because some of them commit murder (an indisputable fact) does not mean that they ought to commit murder. Thrasymachus commits the logical fallacy of deriving an *ought* (a normative or value proposition) from an *is* (a factual proposition).

That Thrasymachus's argument is based upon this fallacy cannot be stressed too strongly because the political "realist" so often defends his ethical position by employing it. For this reason Plato is frequently and unthinkingly criticized for being unrealistic by those who pride themselves on their hardheadedness. But they fall into Thrasymachus's logical trap. Plato is not unrealistic. The *Republic* is about the ideal just state; it is, remember, an ethical measuring rod. Neither Socrates nor Plato ever claimed that existing political practices were anything but corrupt and unjust. They do not dispute the facts; they simply want to change them.

But Socrates does not object to Thrasymachus's illogic. He knew all along that his definition of justice really meant injustice. The purpose of Socrates' questions was to make Thrasymachus face that fact and thereby define the real issue: Is injustice better than justice? And while Socrates rejects Thrasymachus's defense of injustice, he agrees with him that the end that people should seek is happiness. The question is, will the just person be happier than the unjust?

At this critical juncture another character, Adeimantus, enters the fray on the side of Thrasymachus. Adeimantus actually sides with Socrates, but in order to get Socrates now to explain what he thinks justice is, he puts Thrasymachus's argument in a more sophisticated guise. Suppose, says Adeimantus, that one behaves unjustly but conceals his "ill-doing under a veneer of decent behavior?"[12] Then, as everyone agrees, he would have the best of both worlds. He would have all the advantages of being free from ethical constraints, and all the rewards of appearing to others to be a good person.[13] There is only one way that Socrates can respond, and Adeimantus throws out the challenge:

> You must not be content merely to prove that justice is superior to injustice, but explain how one is good, the other evil, in virtue of the intrinsic effect each has on its possessor, whether gods or men see it or not.[14]

Now Plato proposes to proceed with his argument in the following way (from this point on we shall speak of Plato rather than Socrates): The question before us is whether or not justice is intrinsically superior to injustice and, therefore, whether or not human beings ought to be just. Plato suggests that it would be easier to look first at justice in the state, then at justice in the individual. The state, says Plato, is simply the man writ large, and it will be easier to look first at this larger picture and then apply what we have learned to the smaller picture of the individual. This procedure is agreed to, but its full implications are not to be revealed until much later. It is sufficient to recognize that in getting agreement to pursue his analogy, Plato has once again gotten the discussants, without realizing it, to adopt a major element of Socrates' theory of knowledge. For the analogy of the state to the individual can work only if justice is something that transcends both and is more universal than either. From acceptance of this idea it follows that a genuine philosophy of justice is possible, for if justice is a universal there can be conceptual knowledge of it, contrary to the argument of Thrasymachus and the Sophists.

Moreover, Plato has gotten unwitting agreement on another critically important point by way of his analogy. If the just political organization of the state can serve as a model of the just man then, conversely, ethical principles applied at the individual level must be substantially the same as political principles applied at the societal level. In other words, politics and ethics must be made of the same cloth, and political science must be a branch of ethics. And, again contrary to Thrasymachus and the Sophists, this means that political questions such as What is the just state? cannot be treated apart from ethical considerations.

Plato begins his discussion of justice in the state by arguing that the state is natural because no one is self-sufficient. Human beings need each other. The question is, What makes for social self-sufficiency? Plato argues that it entails maintaining an appropriate division of labor. Every state, he argues, will require artisans first of all. Plato includes in this group all those who produce goods and perform socially necessary services—craftsmen, farmers, traders, and the like. Theirs is an economic function. Second, every state will require a class of warriors whom Plato calls the *guardians*. Theirs, of course, is a military function. Finally, every state will require rulers whose function is rulership—making decisions, formulating policy, and so on. Plato proposes that this third class of rulers be drawn from the guardians. Thus, the guardians really should form two classes according to Plato: those who are selected to rule, and those who are charged merely with the execution of the rulers' decisions. The latter element of the guardian class Plato calls the *auxiliaries* to distinguish it from the higher guardians who will be trained specifically to rule.

To this point, there is not really that much to dispute in Plato's argument. We might argue that Plato's threefold division of labor is too simple, that a truly self-sufficient state would require a much more complex and extensive division of labor. It must be remembered, however, that the polis was a small and relatively self-contained community; it did not require the complex division of labor characteristic of modern industrial societies. What is important, in any case, is the underlying principle involved in Plato's scheme, not its technical viability.

Now, Plato continues, it is apparent that each class within the division of labor must manifest specific kinds of virtues. That is, each class must have a certain end or purpose in view and must have the requisite skills to attain its end. This argument should be thoroughly familiar by now; its implications, however, are yet to be seen. Let us simply note again that Plato has not yet said anything with which his antagonists can reasonably disagree. Obviously a division of labor is essential to the state, and just as obviously each class must possess virtue, that is, the necessary skills to perform its tasks. The meaning of *virtue* is to this point still ethically neutral, and any Greek of the time would have understood and accepted Plato's meaning.

What, then, are the specific virtues required for each class? The upper-level guardians—the rulers—must possess the virtue of wisdom. They must have the requisite knowledge to know how to appropriately order the state as a whole. The lower-level guardians, or auxiliaries, must obviously embody the virtue of courage; otherwise they would make poor warriors indeed. The artisans must have the virtue of temperance, that is, the ability to restrain their passions. They must understand that theirs is an economic function and not allow cravings for wealth or status to lead them to take over those functions, such as rulership, that they are not equipped to handle.

What has just been said about the artisans in fact applies to all of the classes. The virtue of temperance is the virtue of self-restraint, and self-restraint in this context means keeping one's place in the division of labor. Clearly, then, each class in society must be temperate. The auxiliaries, no less than the artisans, must restrain any desire to perform a function for which they are ill equipped. The point, however, is that the artisans need only to be temperate, while the auxiliaries must be both courageous and temperate. The rulers must be wise in addition to possessing these other virtues. The division of labor, in short, is a division of virtues, and those who have a superior role in the division of labor are, in Plato's ideal society, those who have a superior degree of virtue. The rulers possess complete virtue because they have wisdom or knowledge, which you will recall is identical to virtue in Socratic philosophy. Other classes have incomplete virtue because their knowledge is limited and, in the case of the artisans, almost nonexistent.

What then is a just state according to Plato? He has just described it. It is one ruled by philosophers, and that means a state in which the appropriate division of classes, and therefore of virtues, is maintained. Thus, justice is the virtue of virtues—it is the virtue of maintaining the proper relationship among wisdom, courage, and temperance. Injustice is rule by non-philosophers, which means the appropriate ordering of classes and virtues has broken down. In political terms this breakdown is identical to class war in which those not equipped to rule struggle among each other to acquire power. This was occurring during Plato's lifetime. The poor wanted to overthrow the rule of the rich; the rich wanted to suppress the poor. Neither was in the least concerned about justice; they wanted simply to promote their own class interests. They were practicing Sophists as far as Plato was concerned.

Given this analysis, the supposed advantages of philosophic rulership are clear, but what precisely makes such rulership the defining characteristic of the just state? Plato's answer brings us back to our starting point. Justice is a virtue, and in the Socratic system virtue is identical to knowledge. Hence, a "just" state must by definition be one ruled by philosophers, by those with knowledge. And the kind of political knowledge they must have is knowledge of how to maintain the division of labor, for this is the necessary condition for philosophical rulership and thus for the appropriate ordering of virtues within the state. In its most general sense, then, political justice is simply the virtue of harmony within the state and the absence of conflict. It is a condition in which each performs his or her task well for the benefit of the whole. This conception of justice accords perfectly with its traditional usage. The Greeks had always conceived of justice as the principle of order and harmony, whether they used it in reference to a person, a state, or the universe (the pre-Socratics frequently described the cosmos, which means *order,* as just). Even our contemporary usage of *justice* as equal to *fairness* still retains this idea of order and harmony.

But herein lay, in Plato's own words, the central paradox of the *Republic.* Philosophers must rule, yet it is precisely philosophers who have no desire to rule. Unlike Thrasymachus and his kind, they are lovers of knowledge, not of power. Yet rule they must, says Plato, for

> unless either philosophers become kings in their countries or those who are now called kings and rulers come to be sufficiently inspired with a genuine desire for wisdom; unless, that is to say, political power and philosophy meet together, there can be no rest from troubles . . . for states, nor yet, as I believe, for all mankind.[15]

At this point in the *Republic,* Plato must begin to deal with some very practical issues. Assuming we can make philosophers rulers, how can we assure that they will continue to rule? The danger is not only that those unfit to rule may attempt a *coup d'état;* the philosophers themselves may come to promote their self-interest rather than the public interest. They may become so tainted by desire that the just state will not continue to exist. This, at least, is Plato's fear. Plato proposes to resolve this problem in a variety of ways, almost all of which involve the rulers. To begin with, he proposes an elaborate system of ruler selection. We need not discuss that system in any detail here except to note that any child, regardless of sex or class position, may become a ruler if he or she indicates a capacity to learn philosophical truths. The selection process, in other words, is not to be based upon artificial class or sex biases. Plato is not advocating an hereditary male-dominated ruling class. Such a proposal would utterly contradict the whole premise of the *Republic* that knowledge is the only criterion for rulership. Clearly, Plato argues, the class into which one is born or one's sex is an irrelevant consideration.

Selecting the best candidates for rulership, however, is not sufficient. In addition, says Plato, the objects of desire must be removed from the society of rulers. To this end he proposes that society be based upon communist principles. The auxiliaries and rulers will not be allowed to own property, nor will they have families of their own. Mating will be carefully regulated to ensure a pool of future rulers, but it will take place outside of any family structure. Children will be held in common, and they will not know who their real fathers or mothers are. They will come to identify the state as their family. In this way, Plato believes, not only will the familial objects of desire be removed from the ruling class, but those children who will later be selected for training as rulers will come to identify their interests with those of the larger community.

Plato's communism shocked his contemporaries, as it may shock the modern reader; private property and the family are still sacrosanct. Yet, if, as Plato claims, the just state is one ruled by philosophers, that state clearly cannot exist unless desire is eliminated in the ruling stratum. It must be remembered, however, that Plato's communism applies only to the ruling elite, not to the vast majority of the population. The artisans will be allowed to own private property and to have families. Moreover, there is no relationship between Plato's communism and its contemporary meaning. Plato was not an ancient Karl Marx. Plato proposes an ascetic communism, the purpose of which is to remove objects of desire, not to distribute them more equitably.

It is Plato's educational system, however, that is most important in maintaining the rule of philosophers. It is through education, Plato claims, that the future rulers will come to recognize that the desire for power and pleasure is not the basis of political or individual happiness and fulfillment. Since Plato's educational philosophy illuminates the whole of his political theory, we must analyze it in some depth.

Plato argues that education should begin at a young age with the learning of basic skills such as reading, writing, recitation, and so on. His proposed program of studies is not markedly different from what actually existed at the time. Plato does advocate one major reform, however: censorship of poetry, and particularly that of the great epic poet Homer. His reason is that people took from the poets what they thought to be sound ethical knowledge when, in fact, says Plato, the poets are no different from the Sophists—they teach people opinions of what is true, not genuine knowledge. Besides, he complains, they present unacceptable models of human behavior. Both heroes and gods frequently act unjustly, if not downright bestially, in the epic poems. It would be inappropriate, Plato argues, for potential rulers to be influenced by such models at a young and impressionable age. How, he asks, are they to become just rulers if their literature exposes them to acts of injustice?

In addition, Plato points out that poetry appeals to the emotions, and unless it is carefully censored it will lead the young guardians astray. Instead of learning to control their lives rationally, they will become subject to their passions. Plato is a classicist; he believes that art should reflect order and harmony so that the same order and harmony will begin to be reflected in the lives of those exposed to it. He is opposed to romanticism, to art that simply appeals to feeling and emotion and that he believes thereby disorders the soul. For this reason, Plato concludes that

> we must not only compel our poets, on pain of expulsion, to make their poetry the express image of noble character; we must also supervise craftsmen of every kind and forbid them to leave the stamp of baseness, license, meanness, unseemliness, on painting and sculpture, or building, or any other work of their hands; and anyone who cannot obey shall not practice his art in our commonwealth.[16]

It may seem to the modern reader that Plato's proposed reform of the arts, and poetry in particular, is excessive. But the great epic poets, such as Homer, and the great dramatists, such as Sophocles and Aeschylus, had enormous influence in Greek society. All Greek boys learned Homer, whose works were the bible of the Hellenic peoples, and the great dramatic tragedies were played before the whole community and had a real moral and religious significance for the onlookers. People were influenced by these art forms as intensely as Americans are influenced by television. Seen in this light, artistic censorship makes eminent sense, for without it the underlying ideas and values that make the just state possible could not exist no matter how refined the formal educational system was made to be. Education does not occur in a vacuum; Plato is quite correct about this. It is of little use to teach children one set of values in the classroom if the whole society outside the school is organized around different values.

Now the key values that Plato wishes to inculcate in the personalities of the young guardians are those of order and harmony because these, as we have seen, constitute the very essence of justice. This is the purpose behind his proposed censorship of the arts, and this is why he argues that even primary education should aim at instilling harmony in the young guardians' personalities. But advanced education must complete the process much more directly. It must go beyond the simplicities of grammar school to the complexities of theoretical knowledge. The future rulers must come to know justice philosophically, says Plato, that is, as a rational principle of order, not simply intuitively as do youngsters in their primary education. In other words, advanced education must teach not particular kinds of justice but justice itself, that is, the ideal concept of justice.

This is to be accomplished, says Plato, by introducing the students to increasingly abstract and generalized truths. They must be made to look beyond the empirical world to those principles that underlie it. The first step in this process, he argues, should be to teach the young guardians basic mathematical and geometrical truths. Mathematics not only teaches how to think logically, but introduces the students to the ideal of conceptual truth. They will come to understand, for example, that—as in the *Meno*—a triangle is a concept that has certain logical properties, and that the way to understand the triangle in the sensory world is to first grasp the logic of the concept of triangleness.

But learning mathematics is not sufficient, says Plato. It leads the young guardians only part of the way to perfect knowledge. One problem with mathematics is that one must use numbers or diagrams as an aid in thinking and, therefore, remain partly bound to the senses. The goal is to get beyond the senses to pure conceptual knowledge. So after ten years of mathematical training that begins at age twenty and is preceded by three years of military training (remember that the lower-level guardians or auxiliaries are to be soldiers), a select few will be chosen for training in the dialectic.

The dialectic, you will recall, is simply a method of disputation leading to knowledge of universal principles. Unlike mathematics, however, dialectics does not rely upon visual images of geometrical forms or numbers but aims directly at truth itself. Moreover, Plato argues, it does not begin with unproven axioms or assumptions as does geometry, but moves directly to a comprehension of the eternal and unchanging structure of the entire cosmos. As such, dialectical knowledge is furthest removed from the empirical world and is closest to those universal principles that underlie the world of sensation. But most importantly for Plato, dialectics leads to knowledge, not only of physical principles, but of ethical principles as well. Hence, the student of dialectics will come to know the true meaning of justice, not justice in its various forms, but justice itself—as a perfect and unalterable concept.

But Plato now tells us that there is an even higher truth than that of justice that only a few—a very few—will come to know. This higher truth Plato calls the *Good,* which is the cosmic principle of order that unites both physical and ethical principles in a grand synthesis.[17] It is that which gives the whole universe, and everything in it, a meaning and a purpose. It is really impossible to explain beyond this what the Good means. In part this is because it is something that cannot be grasped simply in logical terms. Knowing the Good, for Plato, is to have a suprarational insight into the rational structure of the whole universe. There is, therefore, an element of mysticism in Plato's theory of the Good, but this in no way contradicts his emphasis upon rational knowledge. The dialectical acquisition of knowledge is the necessary condition for grasping the Good, but its illumination in the human mind comes, after years of training, as a flash of insight that transcends mere logic.

Only those who attain this final vision will be allowed to become philosophical rulers, and Plato expects only a few to attain it, and these only when well into middle age. They will all have had practical political experience following their training in the dialectic, so we need not worry about their being too abstract and philosophical. Those who are unable to attain this highest truth will be auxiliaries. The artisans, of course, will have no role in rulership since they will not have been educated for it.

At this point we must say something of Plato's theory of form because the education of the guardians is, in fact, an education into the reality of forms. Although many students find this the most difficult part of Plato to understand, approached correctly it is not really difficult at all. Plato's theory of form is simply an extension of Socrates' idea of the *concept*.[18] In Plato the concept becomes not merely a logical structure within one's head but an objective—transcendent—reality. Forms, Plato argues, transcend the empirical world of sensation, and they include both the physical and ethical dimensions. This means that everything we see has a corresponding form, as does every virtue. There is a form of a tree, and of a human being, and of a flower, just as there is a form of temperance, courage, and justice.

Now, just as concepts are perfect ("ideal") universal ideas, so too are forms, except that forms exist as transcendental realities. This means that the things we see, for example "real" trees, are imperfect representations of their perfect transcendent form, as with the perfect form of *treeness*. And in the same way, what most people define as justice is really an imperfect representation of the perfect transcendent form of *justiceness*. Plato would say that just as the trees we see participate in the ideal form of *treeness,* so too do good people participate in the ideal form of *justiceness*. "Real" trees and "real" people are imperfect, of course, but they are understandable because they reflect a transcendent reality of pure, unchanging form. And all of the forms, Plato argues, themselves participate in an ultimate form. It is this that Plato calls the Good: the form of all forms.

Many students have difficulty grasping Plato's theory of form because they try to visualize what a form looks like. They imagine *treeness,* for example, as an ethereal tree floating somewhere in space. And when they try to visualize the form of justice, they simply give up. But to try to visualize a form is to miss the whole point. Forms cannot be visualized because they are not objects of sensation any more than simple concepts are. They are, however, objects of understanding, and that is something entirely different from objects of sensation. We understand the Pythagorean theorem, we do not see it, although we can use diagrams to illustrate it. (Recall here that Plato views mathematics as an imperfect science precisely because it can be translated into visual terms.)

How then are the forms to be understood? The reader will no doubt be disappointed by the answer, but no other can be given. They are to be understood only through years of training in mathematics and dialectics. And the ultimate form of the Good will be grasped, even then, by only a very few. For those of us who cannot take this long and arduous intellectual journey, we must be content to grasp the basic idea of form, and that really is not difficult if we avoid the error of trying to picture forms in our heads.

There are many logical problems with Plato's theory of form, which, however, we shall not pursue here. In the next chapter, Plato's greatest student, Aristotle, will discuss some of them. It is important to keep in mind that despite these problems the general idea of form—that the universe is structured upon principles that cannot be seen but that surely exist—may be quite valid. In this sense, as the classical scholar A.E. Taylor has noted, Plato's forms are not unlike the modern scientist's "laws of nature."[19] Of course, modern scientists would not subscribe to the idea that these laws transcendentally exist, nor would they accept the idea of ethical forms. But the general idea of form cannot be easily dismissed, and it has cropped up in various guises throughout the history of Western philosophy.

But there is one problem with Plato's theory of form that should be mentioned at the outset because it will help us to understand his educational philosophy and to grasp a basic contradiction in his political theory. Note that the theory creates a dualism between the empirical world of sensation and the nonempirical, nonsensory world of form. Plato calls the former the world of appearances. This constitutes the world of becoming, the realm of endless change and of ceaseless flux. The latter he calls the intelligible world of pure being. This, of course, is the world of perfect stability. We can now see that the whole purpose of education for Plato is to train the future rulers to understand the intelligible world of forms. This requires, as we have seen, a focus away from the realm of appearances. Mathematical objects belong to the intelligible world, which is why Plato insists that early training in mathematics is essential to turning the young guardians away from the objects of sensation and toward the unchanging, intelligible objects of pure being. Dialectical training completes this process.

The problem is that politics is part of the world of becoming, and a political theory that focuses upon the intelligible world of being faces enormous difficulties in translating itself into human terms. It is not that Plato is unrealistic. As we have seen, he is well aware of the reality of politics. Rather, the problem is that his dualism makes the application of his theory to human realities uniquely difficult and, as we shall see, potentially destructive of some important human values. But this is not yet the time to criticize. First, let us see what implications Plato's theory of form and educational philosophy have for his theory of politics.

In the *Republic,* Plato employs a famous allegory to explain these implications and to help his listeners better grasp his philosophy of form. Imagine, says Plato, that people live in a cave and are chained so that they can only see the back wall of the cave. Behind them is a parapet in back of which men walk back and forth while holding up objects that resemble people and animals and other things we commonly see in the everyday world. Finally, behind the parapet is a fire that casts shadows of these objects onto the back wall of the cave. People who had spent their whole lives facing the back of the cave and who were prevented from turning around would naturally assume that those shadows represented reality. They would be unable to comprehend that the shadows are nothing more than ethereal projections—Plato calls them *images*—of a more basic reality. These images are the lowest objects of contemplation, according to Plato, because they are the furthest removed from reality. The state of cognition that corresponds to these objects he calls *imagining.*

Suppose, however, that one of the cavemen were freed from the chains and forced to turn around. At first the light of the fire would blind him, says Plato, but eventually, as his eyes became accustomed to the light, he would see the objects that were the source of the shadows. This state of cognition Plato calls *belief,* and while it is a higher state than imagining, it is still not knowledge of reality. The objects of belief, after all, are themselves mere images of the real things.

Suppose, now, that our caveman were dragged out of the cave into the world above. He would once again be blinded by light, this time emanating from the sun. Eventually, however, his eyes would become accustomed to the light, and he would see real living things rather than their crude representations. This state of cognition Plato calls *knowledge.* Finally, as his eyes adjusted completely, he would be able to look at the sun directly. At this point the caveman would grasp the true nature of reality. He would see that the sun is the cause, or source, of all things and that the life around him in the upper world owes its origin and sustenance to the sun. He would now understand that the objects and shadows in the cave were only imperfect representations of this ultimate reality.

The meaning of the cave allegory is clear. The cave represents the world of appearances, the world in which most people live. Outside the cave is the intelligible world of forms. The sun represents the ultimate form of the Good. It is the source of all other forms in the upper world and the cause of their mutual order and harmony. The search for philosophical truth is represented allegorically as leaving the cave of false, or imperfect, images of reality and entering the upper world of pure unchanging forms that alone are the true objects of knowledge.

Clearly, we cannot have "knowledge" of shadows because they are not real; they are ceaselessly shifting images of something much more basic. And precisely because these images change and alter their shapes and positions, there is no way that people can agree among themselves on their meaning. The shadows and images in the cave belong to the world of becoming and, therefore, cannot be the proper objects of knowledge. The upper world outside the cave, the intelligible world of pure being, is alone the proper object of knowledge because it represents the unchanging reality that transcends mere appearances.

Broadly speaking, the cave is the realm of opinion. Most people have opinions about many things, only the philosopher has knowledge of the one underlying reality. The problem is that people come to believe that their opinions constitute knowledge; having spent their whole lives in a cave contemplating shadows, they naturally come to believe in the reality of those shadows. The problem is compounded by the fact that people become so attached to their opinions and so fervent in the belief in the reality of those opinions that they are unwilling to give them up. This is why Plato describes the unchaining of the caveman and his emergence into the upper world as a painful experience. When he first turns around and confronts the "truth" of the cave, his eyes ache from the light. Plato emphasizes here that truth, or knowledge, does not come easily to people since they prefer to hold on to their illusions. No wonder Plato speaks of the caveman being forcibly dragged from the cave; he certainly is not going to leave on his own initiative. And it is clear in this analysis that it is to be the philosopher who does the dragging.

What does Plato's philosophy of form and his allegory of the cave have to do with political theory? The answer is deceptively simple. Justice is a form, as is courage or temperance or any other virtue or ethical concept. To know the form of justice, to have real knowledge of it, we must leave the underworld of appearances where are found only shadows (opinions) of justice and, therefore, as many different definitions of it as there are people in the cave. The whole intent of Plato's educational theory is to drag the young guardians out of this cave and into the real world by introducing progressively, as objects of contemplation, increasingly abstract universal concepts until the forms, and ultimately the Good itself, are revealed and comprehended.

It is fundamentally important to understand that Plato's definition of the "real world" is precisely the opposite of the popular definition. When we hear people say, in a very emphatic and hardheaded way, "I am speaking about the real world," we understand them to mean that they are speaking of the way society really works as opposed to our ideals about how it should work. But this is not the real world at all, according to Plato; it is the illusory world of the cave. As far as Plato is concerned, the Sophists, the politicians, and all the so-called men of the world who pride themselves on their hardheaded realism live in an unreal world of shadows and illusions that they mistake for reality. But it is not just worldly people who refuse to learn the truth, says Plato. "The public itself [is] the greatest of all Sophists"[20] he argues. It is the public, and public opinion, that constitutes the chief source of those illusory values in which people mistakenly come to believe.

Given this analysis, Thrasymachus's defense of a life of injustice is simply a false opinion so far as Plato is concerned. Thrasymachus is a man of the cave, and he is defending the politics of the cave. Hardheaded people, Thrasymachus notes approvingly, say that wealth and pleasure are to be valued, and that power is the means by which to attain them. But wealth and power, says Plato, are mere shadows on the wall of a cave. People think that these forms of pleasure will make them happy, but their notion of happiness is an illusion. The truth would set them free but, like Thrasymachus, they prefer not to leave the cave.

What is worse, says Plato, is that people like Thrasymachus are arrogant in their ignorance. They laugh at the philosopher as muddleheaded and naive. They are so ensnared in their illusions that they cannot, like Socrates, admit to their ignorance and leave the cave of appearances. And because they refuse to leave, the philosopher who does so appears odd and his ideal outrageous; he becomes an object of scorn. Worse yet, the philosopher lives a precarious existence because the truth is inevitably a threat to the established order of things; to those illusions that bind societies together. This, as we have seen, is the real reason for Socrates' death, and the cave allegory helps us to understand why Socrates could not clear himself before the Athenian tribunal. In an obvious reference to Socrates, Plato notes that it is not

> at all strange that one who comes from the contemplation of divine things to the miseries of human life should appear awkward and ridiculous when, with eyes still dazed and not yet accustomed to the darkness, he is compelled, in a law court or elsewhere, to dispute about the shadows of justice or the images that cast those shadows, and to wrangle over the notions of what is right in the minds of men who have never beheld justice itself.[21]

Philosophers must rule, then, if genuine justice as opposed to what people "think" is just is to be made a reality. The first problem is to train a class of philosophic rulers who know what justice is. The second problem is to compel them to rule once they have left the cave of appearances. If it is painful for people to leave the cave, it is doubly painful to return. The pleasure that political power brings to someone like Thrasymachus is an illusory happiness that can have no attraction for the philosopher; having once seen the ultimate reality, the shadows of power, wealth, and status are no longer worthy of consideration. Thus, Plato concludes

> It is for us, then, as founders of a commonwealth, to bring compulsion to bear on the noblest natures. They must be made to climb the ascent to the

vision of Goodness, which we called the highest object of knowledge; and when they have looked upon it long enough, they must not be allowed, as they now are, to remain on the heights, refusing to come down again to the prisoners or to take any part in their labours and rewards, however much or little these may be worth.[22]

Such, then, is Plato's vision of the ideal state. The question is, What relationship does Plato's political theory bear to the question of what is the just human being? We know that Plato had argued that the state is simply the man writ large, and that the ideal of the just state should provide us with a model of the just person. If one thinks for a moment about the characteristics of Plato's ideal state, the model should be apparent. Justice in the state exists when each class maintains its appropriate position within society and thereby ensures a harmony of the virtues of wisdom, courage, and temperance. This is possible, as we have seen, only when wisdom rules the state or, in other words, when philosophers are made political rulers. It follows, then, that the just person is one in whom the philosophic element (that is, reason) "rules the soul." The three virtues of the state are as necessary to the individual as to the collective, and it is essential to both that wisdom maintain its superior position relative to the other virtues and to the baser instincts.

Conversely, the unjust person is one in whom the division of labor in the soul or psyche has broken down and the passions and desires begin to rule rather than reason. The unjust person, in other words, is irrational, driven this way and that by uncontrolled desires, ceaselessly chasing illusions of happiness because of a lack of knowledge of what constitutes real happiness and real fulfillment.

At this point Plato is ready to answer Adeimantus's challenge and show the intrinsic value of justice. But clearly an answer is no longer required. The unjust person obviously is a slave to the desires, in short neurotic: unfulfilled, lacking in purpose and direction, and chasing illusions of happiness. The just life is intrinsically the best because it is the happiest.

The contrast between the happiness of a just life and the misery of an unjust life is dramatically illustrated by Plato near the end of the *Republic*, where he discusses the decline of his perfect state. Plato understands that the ideal state must inevitably disintegrate because it is a human institution and, therefore, not beyond the laws of the world of becoming. For a short time people may create institutions that are patterned on the ideal and transcendent forms of pure being, but these institutions nevertheless remain patterns—imperfect representations of an ultimate reality. Change is in the nature of this sensory world and influences everything in that world including the ideal state of Plato's *Republic*. Plato had no choice but to end his political treatise on a note of pathos.

What is for our purposes important about Plato's theory of political decline is his assertion that it will lead to a corresponding decline at the level of the individual. If the state is simply the man writ large, Plato argues, then we must expect that as justice and the other subordinate virtues begin to deteriorate at the collective level, they will deteriorate within the souls or personalities of the citizenry as well. This means that the decline of the ideal state, from perfect justice to perfect injustice, will be matched by an equivalent decline of the inner life of the citizenry, from genuine happiness to utter misery.

The decline of the just regime begins, Plato argues, within the ruling class. At some point an error will be made in the selection of the children who are to be trained as future guardians. Some will begin to deviate from philosophical principles of governing when they become full members of the ruling class. They will reinstitute private property, and desire will begin to rule reason. The new ruling class will eventually enslave the citizenry in order to free itself for pursuits other than philosophy, primarily warfare. The virtue of the new ruling class will be courage, and its members will hold honor above knowledge. Plato calls this new type of regime or constitution *Timocracy:* a garrison state ruled by the auxiliaries, or a warrior class, rather than by philosophic guardians.

But this new ruling class will itself become increasingly disordered, Plato argues. Where the auxiliaries had acquired wealth and possessions in order to have leisure for warfare, their children will come to desire wealth and property for their own sake. They will possess neither wisdom nor courage, but they will have the virtue of temperance, although their version of this virtue will be imperfect. It will be imperfect because their temperance will be a reflection, not of philosophical principles, but of greed. Their desire for wealth, Plato argues, will be matched by their fear of losing it. Hence, they will have the "temperance" of a miser who manages to keep his desire for illicit pleasures under control in order to concentrate on amassing more wealth. People of this new class will maintain an outward respectability; they will believe in the ethic of working hard and saving money, but inwardly their souls will be corrupted by the lust for gold. This new class Plato calls *oligarchs,* and the corresponding type of constitution *oligarchical,* which means rule by the few rich.

The children of the oligarchs will have become accustomed to having money, but not to saving it. Their souls will be totally devoid of temperance, Plato argues, not to speak of courage and wisdom. They will be characterized by their desire for the whole variety of petty pleasures available to people. Above all else they will want liberty: freedom to pursue their every passion without restraint. Moreover, Plato tells us, equality will prevail among them because the hierarchy of virtues and classes in the ideal regime has now been utterly destroyed. This new type of humanity Plato calls *democratic,* and the corresponding constitution he calls *democracy,* meaning rule by the many.

It is worth pausing for a moment to reexamine Plato's underlying assumptions, and to see where he is leading us. His argument, remember, is that as the constitution of the state begins to disintegrate, we may expect to see an equivalent disintegration within the souls or personalities of the citizenry. Like the modern social scientist, Plato emphasizes that human beings are largely a product of their social environment. This is why he believes that people will be corrupted if their social order is corrupted. And while it is true that, unlike the social scientist, Plato's analysis focuses on the constitution rather than the society, the term *constitution* means for Plato, as it did for his contemporaries, the whole complex of social and political relationships we call society, not simply a legal document. So Plato's method of analysis is not so far removed from our own social understanding as we might at first think. The question is, how accurate is that analysis?

The answer, of course, is debatable. It depends in part upon one's political perspective. But if other thinkers confirm the analysis, there is good reason to take it seriously. Such is the case with Plato's description of the democratic type, for it is amazingly similar to Alexis de Tocqueville's description of early nineteenth-century Americans. DeTocqueville was a brilliant political analyst who, recognizing that democracy was the wave of the future, determined to study it firsthand in the United States. As a result of his studies, he wrote *Democracy in America,* which has now become a classic. De Tocqueville noted, as had Plato over two thousand years earlier, that democratic citizens have an insatiable demand for liberty and equality. And he also noted, as had Plato, that they use their liberty, not for great and noble purposes, but to glut their lives with petty and paltry pleasures. Because they believe they have an absolute right to pursue their interests, but no real knowledge of what to pursue or for what ends, their life lacks nobility and direction. It is not surprising, then, that Plato's analysis of democratic man in the following quotation closely parallels de Tocqueville's description in *Democracy in America:*

> [When democratic man] . . . is told that some pleasures should be sought and valued as arising from desires of a higher order, others chastised and enslaved because the desires are base, he will shut the gates of the citadel against the messengers of truth, shaking his head and declaring that one appetite is as good as another and all must have their equal rights. So he spends his days indulging in the pleasure of the moment, now intoxicated with wine and music, and then taking to spare diet and drinking nothing but water; one day in hard training, the next doing nothing at all, the third apparently immersed in study. Every now and then he takes a part in politics, leaping to his feet to say or do whatever comes into his head. Or he will set out to rival someone he admires, a soldier it may be, or, if the fancy takes him, a man of business. His life is subject to no order or restraint, and he has no wish to change an existence which he calls pleasant, free, and happy.[23]

This is a disturbing picture of democratic man, and to the extent that it is an accurate picture, we are compelled to take seriously the philosophic insights upon which it is based. The fact that Plato's analysis so closely corresponds to that of de Tocqueville, and to many critics of democracy since, even though many centuries separate Plato from these thinkers and the types of democratic regimes they studied are so different, leads us to conclude that Plato's philosophy is not to be taken lightly.

With these thoughts in mind, let us continue our discussion of Plato's description of the decline of the ideal state. We can now see that democratic types are full-fledged citizens of the cave. They are chained so that they can see only the shadows that move back and forth on the wall of the cave. This explains why they ceaselessly move from one object of desire to another. The shadows represent the whole variety of opinions about what is pleasurable and "good." One shadow says pleasure is possessing material things, another that it is being a businessman, another that diet and exercise are the basis of happiness. Occasionally a shadow crosses the wall saying that people should be involved in politics, and the democratic citizen leaps to the defense of a favorite politician or a pet social concern, remaining committed to an endeavor only till another shadow, another opinion of what ought to be done is brought to the democrat's attention. Then the democrat begins a new project, ceaselessly chasing the illusion of happiness without ever achieving its reality.

Yet, for all of this, democratic types are almost comical in their humanness. They are Walter Mitty characters who dream of doing great things without the knowledge or discipline to do anything well. They are certainly not just people, but they mean no harm. Their actions have evil consequences, for both themselves and others, but they are not intentionally evil.

Such is not the case with the *despot,* who represents the final and absolute decline of the ideal state. The despot or tyrant and the corresponding despotic constitution are the inevitable outgrowth of democracy, says Plato. What happens, he argues, is that the mass of the poor people come to believe that the wealthy classes in society are oppressing them. As a result, the poor put forward one man to champion their cause. When their leader comes to power, he begins to oppress the rich. It becomes necessary, therefore, to hire bodyguards to guard the new leader against the constant danger of assassination by the men of property. Initially the people support the use of bodyguards in their anxiety to protect their leader. But eventually the bodyguards are turned against the people themselves and the whole society becomes enslaved to an absolute dictator.

Now we can see the full implications of Thrasymachus's definition of justice as "might makes right." If politics is reduced to a struggle for power, the inevitable result will be despotism. It is obvious that the despotic constitution enslaves everyone and cannot, therefore, claim to make people happy. But what about the despotic leader? It was Thrasymachus's argument that those who could gain absolute power would be absolutely happy. Let us recall Plato's reasoning. If the oligarchical constitution organized on the principle of property produces rulers whose souls are corrupted by the desire for wealth, if the democratic constitution organized on the principle of "liberty" produces rulers whose souls are corrupted by the desire to satiate their every whim, what kind of ruler will be produced given a constitution organized on the principle of slavery? The answer, says Plato, is obvious:

> If the individual . . . is analogous to the state, we shall find the same order of things in [the despot]: a soul laboring under the meanest servitude, the best elements in it being enslaved, while a small part, which is also the most frenzied and corrupt, plays the master.[24]

Note that the despot's soul has a peculiar structure to it; it is organized upon a principle of action that subordinates the many desires of the democratic personality to one supreme, or master, passion. In this sense the despotic ruler is analogous to the philosophical ruler—but in reverse. The philosophical ruler subordinates the lower elements of the soul to the principle of wisdom. The despotic ruler eliminates wisdom from the soul entirely and subordinates everything to the satiation of a master passion. Thus, the master passion is the opposite of wisdom. It is the principle of evil for its own sake, just as wisdom is the principle of virtue for its own sake. Here is Plato's description of the despotic type under the control of the master passion:

> When those terrible wizards who would conjure up an absolute ruler in the young man's soul begin to doubt the power of their spells, in the last resort they contrive to engender in him a master passion, to champion the mob of idle appetites which are for dividing among themselves all available plunder.[25]

Note, further, how closely Plato follows the analogy of state to individual. The despot comes to power as the champion of "the people" who desire to plunder the wealthy, just as the despot in the ruler's soul (the master passion) comes to power as the champion of the many idle appetites that aim at plundering the soul. And just as any reasonable ordering of society ceases once the despot has seized power, in the same way all rational control ceases once the master passion has gained control over the despot's soul. Then, at last, says Plato:

> This passion, as leader of the soul, takes madness for captain of its guard and breaks out in frenzy; if it can lay hold upon any thoughts or desires that are of good report and still be capable of shame, it kills them or drives them forth, until it has purged the soul of all sobriety and called in the partisans of madness to fill the vacant place. . . . Is not this the reason why lust has long since been called a tyrant? A drunken man, too, has something of this tyrannical spirit; and so has the lunatic who dreams that he can lord it over all mankind and heaven besides. Thus, when nature or habit or both have combined the traits of drunkenness, lust, and lunacy, then you have the perfect specimen of the despotic man.[26]

Is it even necessary at this point to refute Thrasymachus's thesis that the absolutely unjust ruler is the happiest of men? Can any man whose character combines drunkeness, lust, and lunacy be happy? Clearly not, says Plato, and just as clearly the more power he acquires to satiate his lust the more enslaved he becomes to his master passion and the more miserable his life.

We might say that the despot is a citizen of the very depths of the cave. His life is a total illusion; he is driven by the master passion to seek a forever unattainable happiness. In this sense, the master passion is the very opposite of the sun in Plato's cave allegory. The sun, representing the ultimate good, is the light of truth. The master passion, representing evilness itself, is a blackness that blots out the light, allowing only shadows and illusions to be seen.

How accurate is Plato's description of the despotic ruler? We have no de Tocqueville to corroborate Plato's analysis, as we did with the democratic type. Yet, a variety of scholars who have studied modern despotisms tell us that Plato is correct, and folk wisdom about the abuse of political power, summed up in Lord Acton's famous aphorism that "power corrupts; absolute power corrupts absolutely" is in agreement with Plato. One need only look at the examples of the great tyrants in history, such as Nero, to recognize that power without knowledge corrupts personality to the point of madness. We know that the two major totalitarian leaders of this century, Josef Stalin and Adolph Hitler, were quite as mad as the political regimes over which they ruled.

What, then, are we to say about Plato's grand political vision? If we are to judge a political theory on its ability to help us comprehend people's political and social reality, we must credit the *Republic* as a huge success. Plato's analysis of the relationship between self and polity has illuminated our understanding of politics through the centuries. It has stood the test of time.

But if we are to judge the *Republic* on its ability to change people's politics, what then are we to say? Certainly we cannot claim that politics has changed for the better since Plato's time. Nonetheless, we can grant a certain practical success to the *Republic*. While it has not altered people's collective political lives, for over two thousand years it has continued to inspire some people to transform their own lives. And this was precisely Plato's intent in his famous analogy of justice in the state and in the individual. If justice is unattainable at the political level, it may still be acquired by the individual who desires to possess it. Since ethics and politics are one, the mastery of the political principles Plato teaches in the *Republic* will enable the individual to master the principles of leading a just life. Referring to this fact near the end of the *Republic*, Plato gives us one of his most beautiful passages. The dialogue includes Glaucon, another member of the discussion circle:

> (Socrates:) . . . In accepting power and honors he [the just man] will . . . [be] . . . ready to enjoy any position in public or private life which he thinks will make him a better man, and [avoid] any that would break down the established order within him.

(Glaucon:) . . . Then, if that is his chief concern, he will have no wish to take part in politics.

(Socrates:) . . . Indeed he will, in the politics of his own commonwealth, though not perhaps in those of his country, unless some miraculous change should come about.

(Glaucon:) . . . I understand . . . : you mean this commonwealth we have been founding in the realm of discourse; for I think it nowhere exists on earth.

(Socrates:) . . . No . . . ; but perhaps there is a pattern set up in the heavens for one who desires to see it and, seeing it, to found one in himself. But whether it exists anywhere or ever will exist is no matter; for this is the only commonwealth in whose politics he can ever take part.[27]

The *Republic* is a noble work, and Plato's vision profound and moving. Nevertheless, the *Republic* is not above criticism. There are serious contradictions and inconsistencies in it. Even these inconsistencies help, however, to illuminate our understanding of politics. When theorists are merely inconsistent, we dismiss them as being unworthy of serious study. When their inconsistencies lead us to the heart of their philosophy and raise fundamental theoretical questions, then we must take them seriously. Plato is unquestionably the kind of theorist we must take seriously.

The major inconsistency in the *Republic* has to do with Plato's proposals for maintaining the division of labor within the state. The key is to ensure the continued rule of the wise. Ideally, other classes within the state will accept this arrangement to the extent that they understand its purpose. They need not be philosophers themselves, but they must at least grasp the rational necessity of philosophical rulership. It turns out, however, that Plato doubts even the rulers' ability to understand fully the need for philosophical rule. Thus, despite the elaborate procedures for selection of class types and the extensive education of guardians and auxiliaries, he is concerned that the rulers may become corrupted and rule unphilosophically. This is why Plato proposes communism for the rulers; he wants to remove those things that lead to corruption. But here is the problem: If virtue is knowledge, how can the rulers be tempted to act unjustly? Remember, Socrates had insisted that this cannot happen. It seems that Plato doubts the very Socratic premise he wishes to prove.

That Plato does indeed have doubts is confirmed by another of his proposals for ensuring that the wise continue to rule. The proposal, which we have not discussed until now because it illustrates so well the problems inherent in his political theory, is that the whole community including the rulers be induced to accept a *noble lie,* a myth, about the reason for their class position within society. People are to be told that they were fashioned from a common stock down inside the earth; and the rulers are to be told that their years of education and training were really a dream. The god who fashioned them, they will be taught, mixed different proportions of metals in their souls. Those who are fit to rule he mixed with gold, the auxiliaries with silver, and the artisans with brass and iron. Occasionally golden parents will have silver or brass children, or brass or silver parents a golden child. This explains why the child of an auxiliary or an artisan may become a ruler. It is never permissible, however, that a person of brass or silver become a ruler; otherwise, according to the myth, ruin will come upon the state.

The problem, of course, is that this myth, or noble lie, is contrary to Plato's assertion that justice or any virtue is identical to knowledge or truth. A myth is a shadow, an illusion, part of the world of becoming. This remains true regardless of the good intent behind the myth. And the fact that Plato feels compelled to hold his ideal state together with a lie—that is, with an act of "injustice!"—indicates that even he recognized the limited capacity of truth to reform politics.

It would have been easy for Plato not to have included the myth of metals in the *Republic*. But he was too great a theorist to achieve consistency at the expense of honesty. In the final analysis, Plato may have doubted his own theory. Perhaps at the very heart of politics is a fundamental irrationality. Perhaps the human condition is too ambiguous ever to conform to strict dictates of truth. Perhaps philosophy and politics can never be united as wholly and completely as Plato had hoped.

There is another related flaw in Plato's political theory. The myth of metals is one that Plato hopes will be accepted by all classes in society, but it must absolutely be accepted by those who do not rule, that is, by those whose ability to reason is most limited. Thus, while Plato doubts the power of reason to transform people ethically, he particularly doubts it in regard to those who are not philosophers. For this reason, Plato excludes most from engaging in the philosophical quest for knowledge. But since knowledge is the necessary condition for justice, Plato assigns the greatest part of humankind to lives of injustice. Of course, Plato would argue that most people can approximate justice in their lives by accepting the authority of philosophers. But this is a far cry from the ideal of justice that Plato wishes to found upon this earth.

Moreover, the division between philosophers and nonphilosophers exposes a basic incompatibility between justice in the state and justice in the individual. It is Plato's argument that justice in the state and justice in the individual are identical, and that the one is the condition for the other. But in fact Plato's just state cannot exist unless large numbers of individuals are relegated to subordinate class positions and thereby denied the possibility of attaining justice in its fullest sense. Plato's analogy between self and polity, then, does not fully hold, and this means that political ethics are not entirely identical to personal ethics. Perhaps "perfect justice," if it is at all possible, is attainable only within the individual, and any attempt to apply it collectively is destructive of both it and other important human values.

There is one final criticism we might make of Plato's political theory. Plato took from Socrates an abiding faith in the power of reason to liberate. Just people do not repress their passions; they are liberated from them because they understand their limited importance. This, at least, was Socrates' teaching. But in Plato we get an uncomfortable feeling that reason is more monastic than Socratic, that it tyrannizes rather than liberates.[28] The state is controlled by the wise, just as the soul is controlled by reason, but the control is so absolute that it approaches tyranny. Plato, of course, would argue that the rule of reason is the very opposite of tyranny, but rule is not the same as absolute control. Plato seems to cross the narrow line between liberation and repression.

In giving philosophical form to Socrates' theory of knowledge, Plato may have taken his teacher's insights too far. Socrates did believe that reason liberates—all people. In this sense, Socrates was a democrat. He was critical of Athenian democracy because those who ruled lacked wisdom, but he did not, so far as we know, claim that only the few could attain wisdom.[29] In putting philosophy beyond the reach of most, Plato not only made justice impossible for the many, he perhaps made reason more a repressive than a liberating element within the state and within the individual.

Our criticisms of Plato all have to do with his conception of the role of knowledge in human affairs. In showing that knowledge points to ethical truths that people ought to incorporate into their lives and political institutions, Plato perhaps goes too far. But the contrary position of Thrasymachus and the Sophists errs in the opposite extreme. Is there some way in which Plato's vision could be modified to reflect better the realities of the human condition? Plato himself had begun this modification in his later works. His greatest student, Aristotle, completed it.

Notes

1. See G.M.A. Grube, *Plato's Thought* (London: Methuen & Co., Ltd., 1935), p. viii: "Plato's mind was synthetic rather than analytic. He never treats subjects separately. . . . Metaphysics, Ethics and Psychology would have seemed to Plato a meaningless classification. . . . Each of these terms he would have thought to include all others."

2. The account that follows is but one of many versions of Plato's journeys. There is little agreement on the story of his travels, and much of what has been written about it is fanciful. Despite this problem, the story is worth recounting because it does provide some interesting insights into Plato's view of politics. The version given is based upon accounts given in Alfred E. Taylor, *Plato* (New York: Books for Libraries Press, 1911) and David Grene, *Greek Political Theory: The Image of Man in Thucydides and Plato* (Chicago: University of Chicago Press, 1950).

3. From *The Republic of Plato,* translated by Francis MacDonald Cornford (New York: Oxford University Press, 1941), p. 11.

4. Ibid., p. 13.

5. Ibid., p. 14.

6. Ibid., p. 16.

7. Ibid., p. 18.

8. Ibid., p. 22.

9. Ibid.

10. Ibid., p. 24.

11. Ibid., p. 25.

12. Ibid., p. 51.

13. The foregoing account of the opening arguments in the dialogue does not include all the relevant protagonists, but only those who, for our purposes, best illustrate those ideas about justice that lay the groundwork for Plato's own view on the subject. At this juncture it is worth noting that all the discussants, including those not mentioned, view justice as something external to the individual (for example, traditional rules, a form of power, a cloak of morality, and so on). As will become evident, Plato, in the Socratic tradition, will define justice as an internal attribute (an "order of the soul"). See Sir Ernest Barker, *Greek Political Theory: Plato and His Predecessors* (London: Methuen & Co., Ltd., 1918), p. 186.

14. Cornford, *The Republic of Plato,* p. 53.

15. Ibid., pp. 178–79.

16. Ibid., p. 90.

17. Ibid., pp. 211–12. The classical scholar, R.L. Nettleship, in his *Lectures on the Republic of Plato* (London: MacMillan and Co., Ltd., 1901) explains Plato's concept of "The Good" as follows: "The good is at once: first, the end of life, that is, the supreme object of all desire and aspiration; secondly, the condition of knowledge, or that which makes the world intelligible and the human mind intelligent; thirdly, the creative and sustaining cause of the world." (p. 218).

18. Although the theory of form is generally attributed to Plato, some scholars argue that the theory belongs to Socrates. See, for example, A.E. Taylor, *Socrates: The Man and His Thought* (Garden City: Doubleday and Co., 1953).

19. Taylor, *Plato,* p. 72.

20. Cornford, *Republic of Plato,* p. 199.

21. Ibid., pp. 231–32.

22. Ibid., p. 233.

23. Ibid., p. 286.

24. Ibid., pp. 303–04.

25. Ibid., p. 298.

26. Ibid.

27. Ibid., pp. 319–20.

28. See Sir Ernest Barker, *The Political Thought of Plato and Aristotle* (New York: Dover Publications, 1959), pp. 161–63, for an excellent discussion of Plato's tyranny of reason—in Barker's words, his "tyranny of principle"— as contrasted with the more moderate system of Aristotle.

29. Whether or not Socrates was agreeable to democracy as a constitutional form has become in recent years a matter of scholarly dispute, although the clear consensus seems to be that he was not. See W.K.C. Guthrie, *Socrates* (Cambridge: Cambridge University Press, 1971), pp. 89–96, for a discussion of this debate.

3

Aristotle

Where Plato's emphasis is upon the ideal state, Aristotle is interested primarily in the best possible form of government. For this reason, Aristotle's vision is more practical and more worldly than Plato's. This is no doubt due in part to his social background, which was broader than his teacher's. Plato was a native Athenian; Aristotle was born in 384 B.C. in the town of Stagira near the Macedonian border. His father was court physician to King Amyntas II of Macedonia, and Aristotle later became tutor to a young Macedonian prince—Alexander the Great. There is no small irony in this, because Alexander's conquest of the Hellenic world destroyed the polis that was Aristotle's model for his theory of politics. But we will discuss the implications of the age of empire in the next chapter.

We know little of Aristotle's life before he came to Plato. At the Academy, Aristotle distinguished himself as Plato's most brilliant student. In his later years, however, Aristotle began to break from his intellectual master. Some scholars speculate that this was the reason Aristotle eventually left the Academy after Plato died in 347 B.C. It is also possible, again on speculation, that Aristotle left because he was rejected by Plato's most devoted disciples who wished to deify the master.[1] Certainly Aristotle would have resisted any attempt at deification of Plato. He believed too strongly in the intellectual life to consider any thinker beyond criticism, and in his mature works he freely criticizes both Plato and Socrates.

Whatever the reason for his departure, Aristotle embarked upon a period of travel after leaving the Academy and also tutored Alexander the Great. He returned to Athens in 335 B.C. and established his own school, the Lyceum. There he remained until he was forced to flee for political reasons, and in 322 B.C., shortly after fleeing, he died.

The story of Aristotle's flight from Athens is worth recounting because it gives us an insight into the man's philosophical temperament. Following Alexander's conquests, the Greek city-states were put under the "protectorate" of the Macedonian empire. Athens, no longer an independent power, was ruled by Antipater, a Macedonian dictator and a friend of Aristotle. Needless to say, Antipater was unpopular—he was not only a dictator, he was a Macedonian dictator. Thus, when Alexander the Great died, the Athenians revolted against Antipater and Aristotle found himself compromised by his friendship with the tyrant. As a consequence, Aristotle fled, justifying himself, it is reported, by claiming that he "did not wish to see the city commit another crime against philosophy." Aristotle was clearly the kind of man who would rather take leave than take hemlock.

Aristotle's statement provides us with a clue to the nature of his political philosophy. He could not agree with Socrates that one's life should be sacrificed to philosophical principle because he did not believe that life could be frozen into a set of philosophical abstractions. According to Aristotle, political philosophy should provide people with general guides and rules of action, but more than this it should not attempt. Political science is not, he argues, a precise theoretical science as Plato had assumed. It is a practical science that deals with practical people who do not—and should not—reduce their lives to pure logic.

Given this attitude towards life and politics, it is not surprising that we find Aristotle's political analysis much more practical than Plato's. Aristotle was a worldly philosopher who loved politics, the most worldly of occupations, as much as Plato despised it. Thus, rather than railing against the injustices of politics, Aristotle looked continuously for ways to improve it without expecting perfection. But Aristotle's attitude toward political theory is not to be explained on the basis of his temperament alone. He was too profound a thinker to express an attitude without having a sound philosophical basis for it. That basis is his theory of form, which constitutes an important modification of Plato's theory.

Aristotle objected to Plato's separation of form (the intelligible world of being) from matter (the sensory world of appearances or becoming). Form, Aristotle argues, is immanent in matter, not transcendentally separated from it. (*Immanent* means to "be within.") We need not, therefore, speak of a perfect form of a tree or of any other object of sensation existing apart from "real trees" or "real objects," says Aristotle. Every tree manifests form, that is, an ideal pattern of *treeness* that is inherent within it, just as every human being inherently manifests the form of *humanness*.

One of the clear advantages of Aristotle's theory of form is that it avoids the difficulty Plato had in demonstrating how matter "participates" in form. More important, it overcomes the problem of change that so troubled Greek thinkers from the pre-Socratics to Plato. Plato insists that form is transcendent because matter changes. Since form is perfect and unchangeable it cannot, in Plato's mind, be united with matter. But it can, says Aristotle, if we understand the real relationship of form to matter. This is a relationship of potentiality to actuality, he says. Matter is potentiality (becoming) but it develops toward form or actuality (being). For example, if we look at an acorn we understand that immanent within it is the form of an oak tree. The acorn is potential and, given the necessary conditions, it will produce a tree; it will actualize itself. In the same way, a fertilized human ovum is pure potentiality that, again given the necessary conditions, will actualize itself as an adult human being. In Aristotle's biological works, species is the form or actuality that shapes the development of living things. This is why the fertilized egg of any living creature will produce only that given species or form that is immanent within it.[2]

It is apparent that the key to Aristotle's theory of form is the idea of development. Things develop to their own perfection and completeness, Aristotle would say, and the function of theory is to explain this process and the purpose that it serves. This is why he insists that a science of any subject matter (physical, biological, or political) must be teleological. *Teleology* means the study of ends or purposes *(telos)*. To return to an earlier example, a biologist in the Aristotelian tradition would study an acorn from the perspective of the fully mature oak tree. The acorn has a purpose to fulfill, an end toward which it moves; and its structure, growth, and transformation must be analyzed in light of that end. This same reasoning holds true for the study or science of humankind or of anything else.

What does all this have to do with Aristotle's political science? A great deal, because Aristotle's theory of form fundamentally shaped his science of politics, as much so as Plato's theory shaped his. This shaping influence can be seen in the *Politics,* his greatest and most comprehensive political work, and in the *Nicomachean Ethics.* Aristotle intended the *Politics* and *Ethics* to be read together because he believed the study of ethics and politics has the same purpose. Ethics is the study of the meaning, purpose, or end—the telos—of human life. But these same questions are the subject matter of political science according to Aristotle because the "end in politics as well as in ethics can only be the good for man."[3] In fact, ethics is really just a branch of political science for Aristotle. In ethics we study the Good from the perspective of the individual, in political science from the perspective of the whole community.

Aristotle's argument for the unity of ethics and politics is identical to Plato's. But Aristotle's method for studying ethics, and subsequently for studying politics, radically differs from that of his teacher, and the reason is his theory of immanent form. Where Plato had looked for ethical values such as justice in the realm of pure transcendence, Aristotle looks for them in the very facts of the human condition. Ethics, after all, refers to real people and to their real behavior, Aristotle argues. The fact that humans behave according to certain moral principles is, he believes, the most important part of their development to their unique end. So, just as we would study human beings as biological organisms by analyzing their real biological makeup and the end that it serves, in the same way we should study them as ethical beings by analyzing their real ethical behavior in light of the end or purpose it serves. Just as we should expect to find the form of biological humanness in human beings themselves, we should expect to find the form of justice, or any other ethical value, in people's actual behavior says Aristotle.

The *Ethics,* then, treats of real people and their actual behavior, but within the context of Aristotle's teleological system. The employment of this system requires Aristotle to begin with basic theoretical questions. First he asks, What is the Good? It is, he says, "that at which all things aim."[4] What do people aim at above all else? Happiness, says Aristotle. The end or telos of humans as ethical beings is happiness, and here, of course, he is in perfect agreement with Socrates and Plato. But what makes for happiness in human terms? It must be something that is unique to humans. This something, Aristotle argues, is people's capacity to reason and to carry what they reason into practice. This being the case, happiness must be related to people's capacity to act appropriately upon a rational basis, and to shape their behavior according to the dictates of reason.[5] Happiness, in a word, is virtue—which means, you will recall, the ability to perform a specific function well. And for people to perform well, their actions must have a rational basis.

The *Ethics* is a treatise on the whole variety of virtues (liberality, courage, temperance, justice, and so on) that people praise as good and necessary for a genuinely human and happy life. But, as we have noted, Aristotle's method of analyzing these virtues, owing to his modified theory of form, is radically different from Plato's. To begin with, Aristotle develops his catalogue of virtues from what people actually say about courage, or temperance, and so on. Unlike Plato, he does not reject as mere opinion commonsense beliefs about these matters. People practice virtue because they recognize that it contributes to happiness (for example, they recognize that a courageous person is happy; a coward, miserable), and they "philosophize" about virtue because they understand the enormous importance of it to their development as adult human beings. In other words, virtue is not something that exists in the sky attainable only by the few. For Aristotle, virtue is precisely the proper end of the human being, and it exists as an integral part of the development of each of us. How we actually behave and what we say about that behavior are part of our end or telos and, therefore, virtue must be understood as part of this human context.

Moreover, Aristotle cannot accept Plato's assertion that moral virtue is strictly identical to knowledge. Again, if we look at real people and how they actually develop to their end as ethical beings, we note, says Aristotle, that habit and training play a profoundly important role. By and large, we learn to be virtuous by practicing virtue. Aristotle argues this point with an analogy that should be familiar by now:

> The moral virtues we do acquire by first exercising them. The same is true of the arts and crafts in general. The craftsman has to learn how to make things, but he learns in the process of making them. So men become builders by building, harp players by playing the harp. By a similar process we become just by performing just actions, temperate by performing temperate actions, brave by performing brave actions.[6]

This emphasis on practice as opposed to pure reason in the development of a virtuous life is uniquely Aristotelian. Human happiness for Aristotle is the result of reason plus action, not reason alone. People act to shape their lives and institutions to a given end; it is through action that they actualize the form of virtue. Moreover, Aristotle's conclusion about virtue in general is also uniquely his own, and quite different from that of Plato. Virtue, says Aristotle, is a mean. Again, if one looks at the real human meaning of any given virtue, we find that it is equidistant between extremes. For example, courage is a mean between cowardice on the one hand and foolhardiness on the other. Courage involves *knowing* what is and is not to be feared and *acting* upon that knowledge (courage, in short, is reasoned action). Cowards fear everything because they do not know what is not to be feared; the foolhardy fear nothing for the opposite reason, and therefore neither develop in their behavior the proper habit of courage. We may surmise that Aristotle thought he struck the mean when he fled Athens.

When Aristotle's theory of ethics is taken as a whole, we note the profound influence of his notion of immanent form. His idea that practice and habit are essential in the development of virtue is in accord with the idea that the form of virtue is immanent within people's lives and can be actualized only through real, concrete action. It is for this reason that Aristotle believes that the function of social and political philosophy is to modify and perfect commonsense notions of what constitutes a virtuous life, not automatically to reject people's opinions.[7]

These ideas lead directly to Aristotle's theory of politics because politics is a collective form of reasoned action. Like Plato, Aristotle believes the primary function of the state to be the inculcation of virtue in its citizenry in order to achieve those purposes specified in the *Ethics*—human happiness and fulfillment. But given Aristotle's philosophy of form, we find that his theory of the state differs from Plato's in a number of important respects. His starting point in the opening pages of the *Politics,* nevertheless, is perfectly compatible with Plato's views:

> Every state is a community of some kind, and every community is estab-
> lished with a view to some good; for mankind always acts in order to ob-
> tain that which they think good. But, if all communities aim at some good,
> the state or political community, which is the highest of all, and which em-
> braces all the rest, aims at a good in a greater degree than any other, and at
> the highest good.[8]

Note Aristotle's claim that the state, like every other human community, aims at some good. This logically follows from his premise in the *Ethics* that all things aim at the good. The good for human beings, the end to which they direct themselves, is happiness. The good at which the state aims is the virtue and happiness of the whole community. But why is the state's end the highest good? Partly, of course, because it is concerned with the whole community, which is more important than the individual. But the reasons go deeper than this, for the state, Aristotle insists, allows people to acquire virtue to a higher degree than in any subordinate community.

We can best understand Aristotle's argument if we put it in the context of his larger theory of community. According to Aristotle, the human com-munity is a complex interrelationship of three different kinds of communi-ties, the simplest of them evolving teleologically into the more complex. The primary social unit is the household or family. Over time, various families unite to form the village that, in turn, unites with other villages to form the state or polis. In historical terms, of course, the household and village are prior to the state. In teleological terms the opposite is the case. Teleologi-cally, the state is the end toward which people's social life ultimately aims. Since the state is our final end, or telos, other kinds of communities are sub-ordinate to it and are simply stages leading to this most complete form of community. This is why, despite the historical reality, Aristotle insists that the state is prior to the household and village.

It is apparent from this analysis that Aristotle considers the state as well as the subordinate communities to be natural. Like Socrates and Plato, Aris-totle rejects the Sophist argument that people are naturally self-interested in-dividuals, and that the state is a mere convention designed to frustrate the de-sires of the "superior man." Human beings are above all social animals for Aristotle; they are naturally political animals as well. Politics is simply the highest expression of humanity's sociability.

Because politics is the highest expression of human sociability the polis or city-state is able to inculcate virtue in its citizenry to a greater degree than the household or village. This is so because it allows for the expression of reasoned action to a greater degree. This is why Aristotle argues that slaves and animals cannot form a state. They lack free choice and, therefore, cannot engage in reasoned action. As a consequence, they cannot attain virtue. And since a virtuous life is the basis for a happy life, slaves or animals can have no share in genuine human happiness. Says Aristotle:

> A state exists for the sake of a good life, and not for the sake of life only: if life only were the object, slaves and brute animals might form a state, but they cannot, for they have no share in happiness or in a life of free choice.[9]

But why does Aristotle assume that reasoned action can occur only within the state? Why not within the household or village? The reason is that in subordinate communities, particularly the household, free choice is severely limited. The function of the household is to maintain biological existence and there are no "free biological choices." Survival dictates that people eat, sleep, and procreate, and it dictates the means by which to do these things as well. To live, people must make a living somehow; they must labor, acquire property, and manage the household. All these activities are economic and all are rooted in biological necessity. (For Aristotle, biological existence and economic activity are two sides of the same coin.) And these activities, Aristotle argues, require strict hierarchical relationships. The husband must rule like a monarch and the children must obey their parents. (We would no longer agree that the husband should "rule," but the idea of hierarchy and discipline in raising children is still influential.)

The state, however, is above mere biology argues Aristotle. Unlike the private domain of the household, the state is a public arena in which people come together to make decisions affecting the whole community for good or evil. This requires debate, hence free speech. This is why speech is the preeminent political virtue for Aristotle. Politics could not exist without it, although a primitive form of social organization could. Aristotle distinguishes between animals and human beings precisely on this crucial point. Bees, he notes, have an elaborate social organization, but no politics. Their sociability is purely instinctual; they have no free choice about how they shall live because they have no capacity to speak (reason) to the issue. This is why animals cannot attain virtue. Virtue comes from reasoned action, and speech is simply reason made active.

The necessity of free speech, further, means that the state must be organized differently from the household. The public sphere can function only where there is equality, says Aristotle. (Aristotle's conception of equality, however, is quite different from our own, as we shall see.) The words of one person must count as much as those of another, otherwise there would be no equality of speech and no genuine debate. Thus, Aristotle insists that rulership of the state is distinctly different from management of the household. The state must be ruled constitutionally, which means that the whole citizenry must in some way participate in an equality of rulership, whereas the inequality of the household demands the rule of one person. This is why Aristotle believes that only in the state, only in the public arena of political action, can people acquire virtue and thereby attain genuine human happiness and fulfillment. And this is why he believes that, among all the kinds of communities, the state alone aims at the highest good.

Aristotle's analysis, once again, is thoroughly teleological. The historical development of household, village, and state is teleologically conceived, a movement from necessity to freedom, freedom being the distinguishing telos of human beings because it is the condition necessary for their happiness. Grasping the teleological nature of this development, people should understand, says Aristotle, that their true home lies in the public arena. Unless people devote themselves to political activity they will not be genuinely free. They will be incapable, therefore, of the highest form of human happiness. In fact, they will be no better than slaves, because slaves are distinguished precisely by their inability to enter the political arena, the only arena in which they can be treated as equal and free members of the community. The slave is tied to the household, like women and children, and subject to the rule of the household manager. This is why Aristotle insists that the whole purpose of household (economic) activity is to provide the necessities so that people will have leisure for political activity. (For Aristotle, leisure is the sine qua non for all "higher" activities such as philosophy, art, politics, and so on.) Those who spend their lives acquiring wealth and property as an end in itself, therefore, are really no different from slaves. Their idea of freedom, Aristotle argues, is not genuine human freedom at all.

Unfortunately, Aristotle believed that slavery and male supremacy are natural. This is why he justified the exclusion of slaves and women from the political arena. And since this arena alone allowed for reasoned action, it was a logical step to conclude that slaves and women, like children, are not fully rational. The legacy of this kind of reasoning is still with us. But it is a legacy that has no necessary connection to Aristotle's political theory. We now know that slavery and male supremacy are purely conventional, and we can eliminate Aristotle's defense of them without rejecting the whole of his political thought. Indeed, to the extent that Aristotle's theory is valid, to that same extent we should encourage women and others traditionally excluded from the public arena to engage in politics. In this way alone, if Aristotle is correct, will their full humanity be recognized.

Having established the importance of political life, Aristotle turns to classifying and then analyzing forms of the state. (Aristotle believed that classification was the first step in any science, and he is known for his elaborate systems of classification in physics, biology, and political science.) His classification is premised upon his theory of form. The structure of the state is determined by its constitution, and the constitution of a state, says Aristotle, is nothing other than its form.

We can best explain Aristotle's reasoning by way of an analogy. Recall that the form of anything for Aristotle is its final end, its actualization, which occurs after a period of development. Thus, as we have seen, *species* refers to the form immanent within a given biological category. A constitution is a kind of "political species," and it emerges or becomes actualized only at the end of a period of social development that begins in the household and culminates in the state.

We must be very careful with this analogy, however, because there is a fundamental difference between a biological species and a political constitution. Biologically there is no choice. A dog, for example, cannot choose to be other than a dog. But human beings are not merely biological creatures. They live among other human beings in elaborate social arrangements and, ideally, they choose freely the kinds of social and political organizations they wish to have. Here we come full circle back to Aristotle's starting point: Humans are ultimately ethical beings who may choose (or choose not) to become virtuous through reasoned action. It is people's telos to make moral choices, and the choice of a constitution is the most important choice they make because a constitution determines to what extent they can collectively attain a life of virtue and happiness.

But what, precisely, is a constitution? According to Aristotle, it is an arrangement of political offices that effectively determines who shall be allowed to participate in ruling the state. Obviously, as you expand or circumscribe the number of those engaged in rulership you alter the character of the state. But Aristotle's classification of states, or constitutions, involves more than mere numbers. We may have two different states, each ruled by one person, but the quality of rule in one state may be quite different from that in the other. One person may rule to his own advantage, the other to the public's advantage. Thus, Aristotle argues that the simplest and most basic classification of states must involve two considerations—the number of rulers and the quality of rulership.

Given these considerations, Aristotle proposes a sixfold classification of constitutions, three good and three bad. The three good constitutions are *monarchy* (rule by one), *aristocracy* (rule by the few), and *polity* (rule by the many). The corresponding types of perverted constitutions are *tyranny, oligarchy,* and *democracy.* In this scheme, the absolute best kind of constitution is monarchy, the absolute worst is tyranny. Here, Aristotle agrees almost exactly with Plato's classification of constitutions developed in the *Republic.*[10] Note that his six basic constitutional types closely parallel those discussed by Plato in his theory of the decline of the ideal state.

Aristotle and Plato, then, arrive at very similar conclusions about what are the best and worst constitutions despite their differing theories of form. The reason for this agreement is clear and explains why political theorists often speak of Plato and Aristotle as "one" despite their differences. Any theory of form, transcendent or immanent, asserts the existence of an objective, knowable ethical standard. Given such a standard, we have a basis for classifying constitutions as good or evil. And Plato and Aristotle agree on what that standard is. When Aristotle divides his three good constitutions from the three evil, his standard is justice. The good constitutions are characterized by rulers, whether one, few, or many, who rule justly for the public good, perverted constitutions by those who rule unjustly in their own private interest. Plato's theory of political justice is rooted precisely in this question of public versus private interests. The *Republic* begins, you will recall, with a debate between Plato, who argues that the just statesman should rule for the public good, and Thrasymachus, who argues he should rule for his own private good.

But in the *Politics* Aristotle focuses on the best possible constitution under the variety of circumstances that confront people most of the time. Thus, when Aristotle agrees with Plato that monarchy is the ideal constitution, he does not thereby dismiss all other constitutions as inferior or relegate them to the shadow world of the cave. Justice is the key to Aristotle's classification of constitutions, and constitutions are more or less good to the extent that they embody the ideal of justice. The tendency of Plato to see an irreconcilable gap between the ideal and the real is thereby overcome by Aristotle. This is why the theory of immanent form is so much more practically useful in political science than the theory of transcendent form. If justice is immanent within people's political arrangements, then they always have the possibility of further actualizing justice in their political communities. Life is movement, not stasis, Aristotle insists. We must look at the variety of constitutions on a continuum of worst to best, therefore, not simply at the ideal or final point.[11]

If actual states lie on a continuum from perfect injustice through perfect justice, the possible types of constitutions are infinite. This is why Aristotle's initial classification soon gives way to a much more complex system. In reality there are various types of monarchies, democracies, oligarchies, tyrannies, and so on. Moreover, it follows that if justice is a continuum, then some oligarchies or tyrannies are better than others. Even the perverted constitutions can be made better or more just according to Aristotle, and it is the task of political leaders, no matter what kind of state they live in, to move toward the ideal within the limits of possibility.

It is this question of the limits of possibility that really concerns Aristotle in the *Politics*. It does no good to advocate Plato's philosophical monarchy if it is impossible to achieve. And, as we have seen, lesser constitutions are not to be considered merely as perversions of this ideal. Certainly Aristotle would not say, as Plato does in the *Republic*, that we should refuse to participate in any state other than the ideal. Most people are not philosophers who can retreat from real politics and establish the ideal commonwealth within their souls.

For Aristotle, then, rule by a philosopher king is a purely theoretical possibility that is, for all practical purposes, impossible to realize. But other types of states face real practical limitations as well. Aristocracy is close to the ideal, but it is not always possible to attain. In ordering the constitutional structure of the state, the limitations that leaders face are, in fact, many: the size of the population, the temperament of the people, their geographical location, and so on. But above all else, Aristotle focuses on social class as the most important factor in determining what is constitutionally possible.

Aristotle was exceedingly sensitive to the economic basis of politics, so much so that some have seen in him the prefiguration of Karl Marx. This goes a bit too far, but it emphasizes the enormous importance Aristotle attached to the economic class system in his analysis of various states. He argues that the fundamental conflict in all societies is the conflict between rich and poor. It is thus the distribution of wealth and property that really determines the character of perverted constitutions.[12] Oligarchy really means rule by the few rich in their own class interest; democracy means the equivalent rule by the many poor; and tyranny means the self-interested rule by one who comes to power when either the poor or the rich cannot maintain control.

Aristotle's economic analysis constitutes a clear admission that people will tend to seek their own class advantage at the expense of the public good. How, then, can he speak of any form of just constitution as a real possibility? It was precisely this pessimistic assessment that drove Plato to his extreme political solution: Institute a philosophical ruling class that is propertyless and that will have, therefore, neither the desire nor the opportunity to rule unjustly in its own class interest.

Aristotle's solution is radically different from Plato's. To begin with, he regards property as natural and as a means to people's ethical betterment if used appropriately. Plato's communist ideal is not, therefore, acceptable to Aristotle. At the same time he takes it as given that people tend to seek their own economic advantage and that, therefore, class conflict undergirds any political system. But there is no contradiction here. We find in human institutions both the bad and the good, argues Aristotle. Property is both an ethical good and a potential evil. The function of leadership is to draw out the good and to direct people's institutions toward the just and the virtuous. We do not deny the "real world" because of its ethical ambiguity, as Plato comes very close to doing; rather, we use its contradictions and irrationalities to arrive at an ethical end. This is the political logic inherent in Aristotle's theory of form.

Thus, Aristotle advocates not the elimination of economic classes but rather a balancing of one against the other. This idea is particularly applicable to polity, the "lowest" form of just constitution. Polity is Aristotle's best average constitution under most circumstances.[13] It is a form of democracy in which the many participate in ruling but, unlike "pure" democracy, under the constraints of law and for the public good. Polity is created by combining the principles of democracy and oligarchy— that is, by constitutionally balancing the rich and the poor such that neither group is able to grasp control of the state to further its own ends at the expense of the other. Such balancing can occur only when there is a large and stable middle class that acts as a buffer between the poorest and wealthiest classes in society. In this sense, polity is rule by the middle-class majority.

Aristotle was one of the first to stress the importance of the middle class in creating a stable and lawful political system. His insight is as valid today as it was in the fourth century B.C. Modern political scientists, for example, would argue that the chronic political instability of underdeveloped countries is caused by the lack of a large middle class. In these areas we typically find a small and wealthy oligarchy ruling to its advantage over a multitude of poor. Class conflict and political instability are the inevitable consequence. For this reason, political scientists have argued that the solution to these problems lies in industrialization that leads to a dispersion of wealth and the emergence of a middle class. Like Aristotle, they look for a political solution to class conflict, not directly in politics itself, but in the social and economic arena.

Aristotle's emphasis on the political importance of the middle class must be credited as a mark of his insight into the real, the practical, dimension of politics. But particularly important is his idea that different political principles can be combined to produce a desired political effect. We owe to Aristotle the theory of the *mixed constitution,* which is really what polity is. The mutual balancing and checking of different social classes is to be accomplished by giving each class a different role within the power structure of the state. Remember that a constitution for Aristotle is a particular arrangement of political offices that effectively determines who will rule. By combining or "mixing" the principles of oligarchy and democracy, we create a constitution that allows substantial numbers of citizens to participate in ruling but that at the same time limits access to certain offices of state. The ways in which this may be done are myriad as Aristotle shows (for this reason there are many forms of polity), but the principle of the mixed constitution is all we are concerned with here.

The importance of Aristotle's theory of the mixed constitutions is twofold. First, it sensitizes us to the fact that we ought not become fanatical in defense of our preferred form of government. We may, for example, argue that what we would today call representative democracy is the "best," but we need not go to the extreme of arguing that the majority should have total power. In fact, we have found that the majority can be utterly tyrannical. The task of those who would found a democracy, Aristotle argues, is to temper its excesses by "mixing" other political forms with it. If one looks carefully at the American Constitution, it will be noted that our founders did just that. Congress is directly elected by the people, in accord with the democratic principle, but the Supreme Court is appointed for life. In effect, the Court is a kind of "aristocratic" element that checks the potential excesses of democratic rule.

Second, the theory of the mixed constitution further illustrates Aristotle's insight that it is an oversimplification to view politics simply in terms of good or evil. Evil may be turned into good in the hands of a wise leader. Polity, a just state, is a mixture of two unjust constitutions! In Aristotle's teleological scheme two "wrongs" may indeed make a "right." Once again, the theory of immanent form leads not to a rejection of this world because of its ambiguities and contradictions, but to a realistic and creative response to it. Thus, political justice for Aristotle is a complex thing requiring sophisticated analysis of the various available types of constitutions, not simply of the rational ideal.

Because of this complexity, we must look more deeply at Aristotle's theory of justice in light of his classification of constitutions. We note again a basic difference between Aristotle and Plato. Plato had argued that justice in the state is identical to the rule of philosophers because philosophers have no desire to rule selfishly. While Aristotle concedes that there is the possibility that a ruler may be found who will be so superior in virtue that he will rule only for the public good, he denies that this is probable. Polity, however, and occasionally aristocracy are within the realm of probability. And, Aristotle argues, justice in the less-than-perfect states is still possible because *law* may take the place of the philosophic ruler. Law, in Aristotle's view, is "reason unaffected by desire" and, hence, precisely analogous to Plato's philosophical ruler. Rule of law is thus identical to justice. Says Aristotle:

> He who bids the law rule may be deemed to bid God and Reason alone rule, but he who bids man rule adds an element of the beast; for desire is a wild beast, and passion perverts the minds of rulers, even when they are the best of men. The law is reason unaffected by desire.[14]

Plato and Aristotle agree, then, that justice and reason "unaffected by desire" are synonymous. They differ only in respect to the means they recommend for embodying such reason in the structure of the state. Plato rejects law in his *Republic* because it constrains the wise ruler who knows at any given time what is the best decision to make. Law is imperfect because it covers only general matters. But Plato is concerned with the ideal state while Aristotle is concerned with the best possible, and rule according to law is the closest we can come to just rulership in the "real world" Aristotle argues. Even Plato in his later years came to accept law as the best approximation of just rule that human beings could attain in this life.

Aristotle gives another meaning to political justice, a meaning that is closely related to rule of law. For Aristotle, equality and justice are also synonymous, but his conception of equality is radically different from our own; in fact, it is the opposite. Aristotle always speaks of justice as proportional and the just state as one in which rulership is allotted to individuals proportionate to their political virtue or ability. Since, as we have seen, politics requires freedom of speech, and since such freedom requires equality (that is, all must have an equal chance to speak), it follows that those who speak and reason best ought to hold higher political office than those with lesser abilities. An equality of talent is Aristotle's political ideal.

How, then, do we know who has the greatest political virtue? Quite simply by observing how people speak and act in their public lives. Politics for Aristotle is not only a means to solve pressing social problems, it is a testing ground—a process—in which we select as rulers those who demonstrate the greatest political abilities. And, Aristotle argues, this principle of proportional equality is intimately connected to the rule of law, for:

> It is . . . just that among equals everyone be ruled as well as rule, and therefore that all should have their turn. We thus arrive at law, for an order of succession implies law. And the rule of law . . . is preferable to that of any individual.[15]

A state in which equals rule and are ruled in turn is by definition a state organized around the principle of rule of law. Law regulates who will rule and in what manner they will rule. In this way, those such as Thrasymachus who want power for its own sake will be kept in check. The principle of proportional equality, regulated by the rule of law, will ensure that public spirited people attain the important offices of state. Unless they demonstrate public spiritedness and political virtue, they will not be chosen to rule. And once chosen, the rule of law will constrain the rulers to rule legally and rightfully, if not philosophically.

Aristotle's emphasis upon rule of law and the corresponding ideal of an (proportional) equality of political participation points to an interesting conclusion about his political ideal. Clearly these ideas fit precisely his notion that the necessary condition for a virtuous life is reasoned action within a public arena. Yet, as we have seen, in his classification of constitutions Aristotle put monarchy forward as theoretically best. Here there is an apparent contradiction because rule by one excludes others from political activity. We must keep in mind, however, that for Aristotle monarchy, although "ideal," is not a practical possibility in most circumstances; and he therefore feels free to advocate aristocracy and polity, which do allow for wider political participation. And it is apparent from a close reading of the *Politics* that Aristotle in fact prefers aristocracy rather than an "ideal" monarchy because it does provide people with a genuine life of political action; and he considers that polity best that comes closest to aristocracy. Conversely, since polity gives the greatest scope to political action, Aristotle prefers those aristocratic constitutions that embody some of the democratic principles of polity.

Such, then, is the basic outline of Aristotle's political philosophy, a philosophy that has become an enduring part of the Western tradition of political thought. The ideals of political participation, rule of law, the mixed constitution, and so on have become such an unconsciously accepted part of our

Western tradition of political discourse that we sometimes forget their initial originality.

We can best understand the depth and originality of Aristotle's political thought through contrast with Plato. We have already seen how, on specific issues, Aristotle disagrees with his mentor. But the disagreement extends to the whole conception of the state and of politics generally. This is why in the *Politics* Aristotle directly attacks Plato's theory of the state that was developed in the *Republic,* and in the process illuminates the originality of his own political theory.

Aristotle's argument against his teacher's theory of the state may be summed up in one fundamental criticism: There is too much unity in Plato's ideal republic. The real nature of the good state, argues Aristotle, is not unity, but plurality. Plato wants to make the state equivalent to the family, but the state is not at all similar to the family, says Aristotle, or at least it ought not to be. The family is totally unified and hierarchically organized. It must be in order to survive. But the state exists so that people may engage in public speech and action. Such speech and action require many different kinds of people possessing different beliefs and organized on a basis of equality rather than of hierarchy. It is in part for this reason that Aristotle rejects Plato's communism, which aims at destroying any basis for individualism or any kind of political equality.

In essence, Aristotle's criticism is that Plato failed to see the necessary distinction between private and public activities. Plato's ideal state is like a gigantic household in which all distinctions between individuals are destroyed for the "common good." But in destroying these distinctions Plato destroys public life, which, for Aristotle, is the very basis of virtue and happiness and the real source of the common good.

We concluded our discussion of Plato with the criticism that his ideal republic comes close to being a tyranny of reason. The excessive unity that Aristotle criticizes is the ultimate consequence of this tyranny. "Pure reason" admits no plurality; syllogistic logic posits only one truth. But life cannot be forced into a logical mold; it is too complex for that, says Aristotle. His theory of immanent form allowed him to escape the tyranny of reason and excessive unity that characterizes Plato's political and ethical doctrines. For Aristotle, there are many roads leading to the just state; it is not the task of political philosophy to point one way only. Political philosophy must begin with the social world as it is, in all its complexity and ambiguity, and on that basis evolve a theory of the just state that will aid people in actualizing virtue in their lives.

Aristotle's originality lay in his recognition that the complexity of life required plurality in politics, and that plurality is not something that contradicts the theory of form. Thus, in uniting matter and form, being and becoming, Aristotle was able to bring together the reality of politics with a genuine ethical standard. This is something Plato could never quite do. Even in his later works, such as the *Statesman* and the *Laws,* where he more directly confronts the complexities of the human condition than he does in the *Republic,* the spell of the ideal of justice still holds sway over the "real world" of politics.

Yet, it must not be thought that Aristotle's "realism" is irreconcilable with Plato's "idealism." His originality lay in uniting Plato's "ideal" with an appreciation for the "real." Without Plato, Aristotle's work would not have been possible. Aristotle made his teacher's philosophy of form and his theory of justice more compatible with the everyday world. He did not reject Plato's philosophy so much as modify it.[16]

Does this modification make Aristotle's political theory superior to Plato's? Here we enter the realm of judgment. Certainly we can say that Aristotle's theory is more practically useful. A leader facing concrete problems would do better to have a copy of the *Politics* to consult than a copy of the *Republic.* But for the political theorist, practical usefulness is not the only criterion of value. The theorist wants to understand politics, and to this end the *Republic* may be "superior" to the *Politics.* Some of the greatest works in political philosophy are utterly useless from a practical point of view.

Whether or not one finds one thinker preferable to another is really a matter of intellectual temperament. Those with a pragmatic bent will likely appreciate Aristotle's grasp of the complexity and plurality of politics. Those who are inveterate rationalists, who love the abstractions of pure theory, will probably prefer Plato. In political philosophy these two tendencies are usually described generically as *conservatism* and *radicalism.* Seen in this light, the real political difference between Plato and Aristotle becomes apparent. Almost invariably rationalists are radicals. Like Plato, they want politics to correspond to an ideal, and they are impatient with anything less than the ideal. For this reason, radicals of all stripes, whether of the right or of the left, typically dislike real politics because it seldom, if ever, corresponds to the ideal.

Pragmatists are conservative. They have their ideals, of course, but they have perhaps a greater appreciation of the limits of the ideal, and they tend to be more comfortable with—and have a greater appreciation for—the imperfect world around them. Moreover, conservatives are even a little distrustful of the ideal. If the ideal were really good or really workable, they argue, then people would ascribe to it. That they do not should be a cue to us that, in real human terms, the ideal is not always the best. This is why Aristotle, the conservative, argues, in what has become the rallying cry of conservatives throughout the centuries, "that we should not disregard the experience of the ages."[17]

Clearly then, whether or not Plato is "superior" to Aristotle depends upon one's most fundamental intellectual and political convictions. But from a theoretical point of view the question of which thinker is superior does not really apply. As we have seen, at the most basic level Plato and Aristotle work from the same assumptions. Both are convinced that ethics and politics are one, and that politics is a human affair that ought to contribute to a human good. The difference between them is a difference of emphasis only, and the serious thinker ought to read, appreciate, and criticize both rather than reject one for the other.

In the case of Aristotle, our criticism of his political philosophy is connected precisely to his conservative point of view. We know from our analysis of Plato that one of the dangers of radicalism is that in striving for the ideal the radical thinker may fail to take into account the realities of the human condition and, therefore, propose reforms that may be destructive of important human values. But conservatism has the opposite fault. In accepting the concrete and the real, the conservative thinker frequently accepts without questioning things that perhaps ought to be changed. The ideal may not always be right or proper for human beings, but the same can be said about the real. Sometimes the ideal would be better and more workable than the real.

This criticism of conservatism applies directly to Aristotle because in accepting the good around him, he also accepted the bad. Recall that, unlike Plato, he defended male supremacy and slavery as natural, and he did so precisely because he did accept "the experience of the ages." He fell into the conservative fallacy of assuming that because a particular social practice or institution has existed over time it therefore ought to exist. Radicals escape this fallacy because the logic of the rational ideal is, in their mind, superior to the irrationalities of the real.

The lesson we learn from reading Plato and Aristotle, then, is that both have their virtues and their defects, and that we ought therefore to temper our own political attitudes with a healthy dose of the point of view opposite to our own. If we are temperamentally radical, we ought to listen carefully to the conservatives who warn us of the dangers of the ideal. And if conservative, we ought to take seriously the opposite advice from the radicals.

Notes

1. There is general agreement that Aristotle left the academy, at least in part, because he disagreed with Plato's successor.
2. See Marjorie Grene, *A Portrait of Aristotle* (Chicago: University of Chicago Press, 1963), pp. 211–26, for a brief but admirable discussion of the doctrine of "potency and actuality" as applied to biological analysis, as well as to the whole range of phenomena to which Aristotle intended it to be applied.
3. J.A.K. Thomson, *The Ethics of Aristotle* (Harmondsworth: Penguin Books, Ltd., 1955), p. 27.
4. Ibid., p. 25.

5. Henry B. Veatch, *Aristotle: A Contemporary Appreciation* (Bloomington: Indiana University Press, 1974), p. 106. Veatch explains Aristotle's concept of rational-action as follows: For Aristotle "man's proper function or activity is not simply one of having intelligence in the sense of a certain I.Q., which one can then show off upon occasion, but rather in the sense of actually being intelligent in the living of one's life and of actually using one's intelligence in making the day-to-day decisions of one's life."

6. Thomson, *The Ethics of Aristotle*, pp. 55–56.

7. Richard Robinson, in *Essays In Greek Philosophy* (Oxford: Clarendon Press, 1969), p. 147, notes that Aristotle "thinks of his works as justifying rather than as superceding common sense He ventures only to raise certain 'unpleasantnesses' . . . and to make a few alterations in order to remove them."

8. Benjamin Jowett, trans., *Aristotle's Politics* (New York: Random House, Inc., 1953), p. 51.

9. Ibid., p. 142.

10. Aristotle's classification of constitutions even more closely parallels that of Plato's in the *Statesman*.

11. See Werner Jaeger (Richard Robinson, trans.), *Aristotle: Fundamentals of the History of His Development* (Oxford: Clarendon Press, 1934), p. 292: "The great, the new and comprehensive feature in Aristotle's work is his combination of normative thought . . . with a sense of form capable of mastering and organizing the multiplicity of actual political facts. This sense of form kept his striving for the absolute standard from leading to stiffness, and revealed to him a thousand kinds of political existence and methods of improvement."

12. See Sir Ernest Barker, *The Political Thought of Plato and Aristotle* (New York: Dover Publications, 1959), p. 312: "This teaching is not . . . extended beyond democracy and oligarchy: the previous use of number is not systematically replaced by the new criterion of class."

13. Ibid., p. 472. It is interesting to note that as the "best average" constitution, polity fulfills Aristotle's criterion of virtue (virtue is a mean) developed in the *Ethics*, p. 474.

14. Ibid., p. 163.

15. Ibid.

16. See, for example, A.H. Armstrong, *An Introduction to Ancient Philosophy* (Boston: Beacon Press, 1965), p. 66: "However drastic his later disagreements with Platonism he always remains as it were within the same country of thought."

17. Jowett, *Aristotle's Politics*, p. 90.

4

Cicero

We now turn to the period shortly before the beginning of the Roman Empire and Rome's most eminent political thinker, Marcus Tullius Cicero (106–43 B.C.). That our focus should now be Rome is clear, for next to ancient Greece and the Greek world following Aristotle's death, the Roman experience is most important in the subsequent development of Western political thought. Indeed, we speak of the whole Greco-Roman contribution in art, literature, and philosophy, including political philosophy, as belonging to a common tradition we now call *classical*. Cicero's importance as a political thinker lies precisely in the fact that he, more than any other thinker, passed on to the Roman world not only Greek political philosophy but Greek philosophy in general. He was, therefore, a key figure in the development of the classical tradition. And, just as important, it was largely through Cicero that this tradition was transmitted to the Western world after Rome had ceased to exist as a viable political entity.[1]

In order to grasp what Cicero passes on as a political philosopher, as well as to come to terms with the specifics of his political thought, it is necessary first to return to Aristotle. Recall that Aristotle's *Politics* was written with the Greek polis in mind. The polis as he understood it, however, was disappearing in his own day. In its place the Macedonian Empire arose under Alexander the Great (356–323 B.C.). That empire came to encompass most of the known civilized world, and the Greek city-states lost their autonomy and self-sufficiency. They were absorbed by a new political entity that Aristotle had never even considered. The comparatively intimate governments of the city-states were replaced by a distant emperor ruling over a seemingly limitless expanse of peoples who had nothing in common except their new government.

The form of government during this period was monarchy, but not the ideal type of monarchy envisioned by Plato or Aristotle. The new monarchs were, on the whole, Oriental potentates asserting absolute power and claiming to rule by divine right, that is, by the will of God. In some cases they actually claimed God-like status—Alexander was eventually deified, a pattern that was repeated for later Roman emperors. And this extreme centralization and bureaucratization of monarchical power and the ideals of divine right characteristic of this period did indeed derive from Oriental sources, for one of the fateful consequences of Alexander's conquests was the incorporation of parts of Asia into the empire with the resultant fusion of Greek and Oriental cultures.

These new political realities required a transformation of political theory as well. It was useless to speak any longer of the state, justice, or citizenship in the traditional Aristotelian manner. Aristotle's theories of public life and the importance of political activity, of reasoned action, and of virtue and happiness all presumed the existence of a city-state small enough to be a genuine community, something Alexander's empire clearly was not even after it was broken into smaller units shortly after his death—nor was the later Roman Empire that began to emerge in Cicero's time.

The new theories, all Greek in origin, began to develop early on, well before Aristotle's death, and spread beyond the Hellenic world during what we now call the Hellenistic period. The term *Hellenic* is derived from *Hellenes,* which is what the Greeks called themselves (it was the Romans who gave them the name *Greek*). The Hellenic period refers to the time before Alexander the Great's conquests had ended Greek autonomy and intermixed Greek and Oriental cultures. The Hellenistic period refers to the time subsequent, beginning it is agreed from Alexander's death in 323 B.C. to, with less agreement, about the middle of the second century B.C. (some scholars would argue that the Hellenistic age extends well into the era of the Roman Empire). In terms of political philosophy, we could say with rough accuracy that the Hellenistic period stretches from the death of Aristotle in 322 B.C. to the death of Cicero in 43 B.C.

In one form or another the major Hellenistic theories persisted throughout the age of empire to the final disintegration of the Roman Empire in the fifth century A.D. and, primarily through Cicero, to the medieval and even modern worlds. And while they were not on the whole entirely novel nor in themselves terribly original, for they drew upon the whole range of earlier Greek philosophies from the pre-Socratics and Socrates in particular to Plato and Aristotle, they did modify the ideas of these thinkers to fit the new political realities of empire.

Of the various new schools of the Hellenistic period, the three most important were Cynicism, Epicureanism, and most notably Stoicism. In addition, the older schools of Plato and Aristotle continued to exist alongside these new schools as did even some of the pre-Socratic schools and doctrines. The Academic school of Plato lasted into the early medieval period, and largely through the writings of Cicero, so too did Stoicism, the most important of the new schools for the subsequent development of Western political thought.

The new schools as well as the old preached a variety of doctrines. This led eventually to the development of Skepticism as a distinct school of thought as well. Since each of these schools, the new ones in particular, asserted its doctrines dogmatically to the exclusion of others, the Skeptics concluded that none of them was true and, finally, that ultimate truth about anything is impossible. The only truth is that there is no knowable truth, a position that ultimately becomes self-contradictory. As one later Skeptic stated, "he was certain of nothing—not even of the fact that he was certain of nothing."[2]

Paradoxically, it was the Platonic Academy that from about the middle of the third century B.C. most seriously expounded the skeptic position. Under the leadership of Carneades (214–129 B.C.), the New Academy, as it came to be known, most fully and powerfully developed Skepticism as a serious intellectual position. While Carneades drew upon the Platonic dialogues of the earlier "skeptical" Socrates who claimed only to know that he did not know,[3] it is nonetheless striking that Plato's claim to universal truths should culminate in Skepticism. It was one mark of how intellectually transforming were the new political realities of empire.

If Skepticism was one logical outcome of the diversity of Hellenistic schools, Eclecticism was another. Rather than reject all schools, borrow from each what seems to be true or useful. This was Cicero's method. While considering himself a follower of the Academy, he was in fact the greatest of the Roman Eclectics for he could never accept the extreme skepticism of a Carneades. Cicero took the more moderate position of his teacher Philo (head of what is sometimes called the "Fourth Academy," a later, less skeptical, development of the Academic school) that if we cannot claim to know absolute truths we have good reason to assert knowledge of probable truths, and these are not to be found in one school of thought only.[4]

It was the new schools, however, Stoicism particularly, that most clearly illuminate the new political consciousness of the Hellenistic period and that will have the most bearing on our analysis of Cicero's political thought. And what is important to recognize at the outset is the great similarity that existed among these schools despite their philosophical differences.[5] In this, they were all reflecting the vastness, psychic rootlessness, and ethical dislocations characteristic of empire.

They all, for example, emphasized the importance of the individual rather than the community.[6] Since the community as Aristotle had understood it was moribund, it seemed that the individual alone must create the conditions of fulfillment and happiness. And closely linked to this concern with the individual was an emphasis on the subjective dimension of life. The new thinkers stressed the inner life at the expense of the outer. Like the ancient Greek theorists, and Socrates in particular, they argued that power, status, and wealth are not the basis of happiness but that virtue, which alone produces inner peace and serenity, is the real condition of a fulfilled life.

The new schools were also decidedly cosmopolitan in outlook. While individuals must acquire their own virtue and create their own subjective well-being, each was in this regard like every other individual. At this level, all human beings are equal whether Greek or Roman, slave or noble. As a consequence, the individual was seen in the first instance as a citizen of the world, indeed of the whole cosmos, not merely of this or that particular polis. Every human being is, as both the Cynics and Stoics would say, a citizen of the *cosmopolis.*

In one sense, this expanded conception of citizenship was a great advance in Western political consciousness for it eliminated the parochial elements of ancient Greek thought. No longer could one say, as does Aristotle, that some forms of slavery are natural, or divide the world into Greek and barbarian in which political and civic rights accrue to the dominant group only. Indeed, from this point on the "modern" concept of universal equality emerges, not merely Aristotle's proportional equality, which divides human beings on the basis of intellectual or political ability, but the radical equality of all human beings.

Another important similarity among the new schools was that they were largely apolitical and sometime downright antipolitical. The politics of empire seemed to them to be the precise opposite of that inner virtue and harmony that they all claimed to teach. Consequently, with the partial exception of Stoicism (but, as we shall see, a very important exception), they advocated withdrawal from civic life as a necessary precondition for the acquisition of virtue.

All of these characteristics can be seen in Cynicism, the first of the Hellenistic schools. Founded by Antisthenes (445–365 B.C.), a follower of Socrates, and developed by Diogenes of Sinope (died c. 324 B.C.), a student of Antisthenes, the Cynics not only advocated a radical individualism and withdrawal from civic life, they carried their advocacy to its most logically extreme conclusion. Claiming that virtue alone, which they defined as inner peace and acceptance of the vicissitudes of fortune, is the only thing necessary to a happy and fulfilled life, they rejected all traditional values. To make their point, many of them dressed in rags and wandered the streets flaunting social and political authority, which they saw as purely conventional and contrary to the dictates of virtue. It is not without reason that *cynic* means dog in Greek; the Cynics could be quite outrageously "uncivilized" in making their point, and none was more outrageous in behavior than Diogenes, who lived in a tub to demonstrate his contempt for civilized comforts and, with rapier wit and sarcasm, demonstrated his contempt for "civilized opinions." Plato is reputed to have said of Diogenes that he "is a Socrates gone mad."

The Cynics were, as well, thoroughly cosmopolitan in outlook. Human beings are by nature citizens of the world they argued and, as such, are all equal. They saw no difference between the slave and the master; that distinction was purely conventional they insisted, and, in their wanderings, they mocked this and other deeply rooted traditional values. Indeed, much of their impact occurred through these kinds of actions rather than through any deep philosophical speculation. Cynicism's real intellectual impact, in fact, was its influence on the early development of Stoicism, which ultimately came to supplant it as a more attractive and workable philosophical system.[7]

Epicureanism possessed these same general characteristics: individualism and subjectivism, cosmopolitanism, and a profound rejection of politics. Beyond this, its basic premises were quite simple and, in its psychology, probably too simple. Founded by Epicurus (341–270 B.C.), it propounded a hedonistic ethics, that is, one that asserts that the virtuous is the pleasurable, a concept of virtue premised upon the fact that human beings are psychologically predisposed to maximize pleasure and minimize pain. Given this predisposition, the Epicureans reasoned, virtue must be the acquisition of pleasure since any other principle would be contrary to nature and, conversely, pain must be evil.[8] (Note the individualism and cosmopolitanism—all are equal in their desire for pleasure—inherent in the Epicurean ethics.)

The problem, a much more difficult one than might first be assumed, is determining what constitutes pleasure and pain in the overall scheme of life. As we have seen in Socrates' critique of "Sophistic hedonism," if one gives oneself completely over to the more basic pleasures, chronic pain will result. Epicurus and his followers agreed and, as a consequence, advocated not a life of wild abandon but rather one of balance and harmony. Indeed, the object for Epicurus was not so much to acquire pleasure as avoid pain, and thus a virtuous life was to his mind the one least likely to produce pain.[9]

For this reason, Epicurus and members of his school were proponents of the simple life and the gentle pleasures. The ideal was moderation in all things, the inculcation of friendship and human affection, and the primacy of philosophy and the intellectual life.[10] And what clearly contradicted this ideal for Epicurus was politics, a most immoderate activity, certainly so in the age of empire and, as such, one likely to produce more pain than pleasure. The acquisition of power, therefore, was not for Epicurus and his school a valid goal since it produces conflict and anxiety rather than inner peace and serenity. Says Epicurus, "we must release ourselves from the prison of affairs and politics."[11]

Clearly, such views had to make for an impoverished political theory, but the Epicureans did develop at least the outlines of one. Like the Sophists before them, and in line with the Cynic and Skeptic positions as well, the Epicureans insisted that the state and the political community are strictly conventional. They advanced a contract theory of the state not unlike that propounded by Glaucon early in Plato's *Republic.* The state is seen as nothing more than an agreement to band together for mutual protection. It is not, as Plato asserted, founded upon some universal of justice. Says Epicurus, "Justice never is anything in itself but . . . is a kind of compact not to harm or be harmed."[12] And the reason human beings obey the law, he insists, is not as Plato claimed because "injustice is . . . an evil in itself, but only in consequence of the fear which attaches to the apprehension of being unable to escape those appointed to punish such actions."[13]

Clearly, were it only for Cynicism and Epicureanism, Hellenistic political thought would have contributed little to the subsequent evolution of Roman political theory and, ultimately, to the Western tradition of political discourse. True, their cosmopolitanism was a great advantage in the age of empire. This was particularly so in the Roman Empire, which, with this more universalistic perspective, granted citizenship to many of its conquered peoples, something not typical of ancient empires. But these schools were far too meager in content and negative in their view of the political domain to lay the basis for a thoroughgoing political philosophy. The emergence of Stoicism, however, did provide the necessary link to Rome and, largely through the eclectic Cicero, to the medieval world.

Stoicism was founded by Zeno (335–263 B.C.). Early Stoicism had its roots in Cynicism and espoused ideas and attitudes not unlike Cynicism, indeed in some ways not unlike Epicureanism despite its clear rejection of that school's ethical philosophy.[14] Unlike these other schools, however, Stoicism was able to create a political theory that reflected the actual conditions of empire and to develop it beyond the meager outlines of the earlier schools.

The key terms in Stoic ethical and political thought are *reason* and *nature.* For the Stoics, human beings are rational creatures because nature, of which they are a part, is rational. Reason permeates the universe as a whole. Hence, when human beings behave on the basis of rational principles, they are simply giving expression to the "divine" *logos* (the Greek term for reason) that permeates all things including human consciousness. We are not, therefore, merely individuals among other individuals but are connected to each other as part of a larger rational order. As such, we are most certainly equal citizens of the cosmopolis as the Cynics and Epicureans maintained, but we are also social and political creatures in the narrower and more concrete sense, for our rational capacities compel us to recognize our sociability and therefore the necessity of living with each other on the basis of common ethical principles. This means, contrary to the Epicureans in particular, that the state is natural. Says Marcus Aurelius, emperor of Rome (A.D. 161–180) and one of the greatest of the later Roman Stoics, "the rational animal is consequently also a political (social) animal."[15] Human beings, therefore, can acquire virtue only as citizens of the state and members of society, not in withdrawal from their public duties and obligations to their fellow citizens.

These obligations, the Stoics argued, are known by all human beings on the basis of reason alone. They are, therefore, what the Stoics called *natural laws,* that is, ethical obligations we have to one another that exist by nature, not by convention, and are therefore universally valid. They are known and apply in all societies the world over. We all know, for example, that it is wrong to harm another or to kill without just cause whether or not any existing law or tradition prohibits murder. These natural laws of moral reason, embedded in human consciousness itself and reflecting the larger rational ethical order of nature ought, then, to govern our behavior in all circumstances regardless of the status of our conventional legal rules or ethical values.

This concept of natural law was the Stoic's great and enduring contribution to Western political thought. Its influence upon Cicero was profound, as we shall see. Yet this all sounds very similar to the theory of form developed by Plato and Aristotle, for there is the same assertion of universal ethical principles that are known by reason alone. The theory of natural law, however, does not assert the existence of forms as such. It simply states that reason is a natural capacity of human beings and that reason points to certain broad ethical principles. Nor does the theory of natural law presume, as does the theory of form (Plato's theory in particular), that ethical truths can be known only by the educated few. All human beings who have not lost the capacity to reason can know right from wrong, not just the philosophic elite.

The similarity, nevertheless, is very real. Thus, the theory of natural law proclaims the same unity of ethics and politics that characterizes the theory of form and the whole of what we call the classical tradition of political thought. This means for the Stoic thinker that the state must be erected upon ethical principles derived from natural law, and that the state has an ethical purpose to play. Consequently, the state must be more than a mere agreement or contract between people not to harm each other as the Epicureans had asserted.

Clearly, the theory of natural law meant that state or civil law, what we now call *positive law,* must be in conformity with the principles of natural law. This was a basic element of Stoic political philosophy and was expressed in its concept of the *two cities.* All human beings, the Stoics argued, are in the first instance citizens of the world-state or cosmopolis and only secondarily citizens of their own particular city or polis. The cosmopolis represented the universal moral principles of natural law. To be a citizen of the cosmopolis meant, simply, to know these principles and to obey them. The polis, or state, was thus legitimate to the extent that its laws did not violate the principles of natural law. Since these were quite broad and general, positive law could vary considerably from state to state, but not to the point of transgressing natural law. A state organized to kill its own citizens, unfortunately not an unknown phenomenon, could never be legitimate in terms of natural law.

As for the individual, the sole object of life must be to live in accord with these universal ethical principles. This was the way to virtue that the Stoics defined as "living according to nature." Since nature embodies those rational principles that are the source of ethical knowledge, to live according to nature is to live as an ethical being. And since by nature humans are social animals, it follows that virtue requires, among other things, treating others as you would wish to be treated. Stoic ethics is replete with exhortations to follow what we call the "golden rule," a rule that has traditionally been seen as the essence of all natural law principles.

Apart from this, the individual should seek only inner peace and harmony, for this too is in accord with nature, that is, reason. Here the Stoics sound very much like the Cynics and Epicureans, but they, and subsequently Cicero, rejected the Epicureans' argument that pleasure is virtue or, conversely, that pain is evil. For the Stoics (in fact, for the Epicureans as well despite their hedonistic ethics), pleasure or pain, success or failure, even life or death are "indifferent things," that is, things that should have no impact upon our inner peace, our virtue. Death, for example, is a part of nature, and since nature is based upon rational principles, to live according to nature (reason) means not to fear death. The same reasoning holds for all of life's supposed tragedies and disappointments, for these too are a part of life and are accepted with equanimity by the wise person.

In the final analysis, the ideal of Stoic virtue reduced itself to accepting one's fate, for the Stoics recognized that we are masters only of our own rational will, not of our outer circumstances.[16] We cannot choose not to die, but we can rationally choose to accept death as an indifferent thing, in which case it no longer affects us. We cannot choose whether or not we shall be a Caesar or a slave, wealthy or poor, honored or humiliated, healthy or sick, but we can understand that these are indifferent things and choose not to resist them or to wish that they would be otherwise. Certainly pleasure and pain, contrary to the hedonistic philosophy of the Epicureans, are indifferent things and ought not to affect our will. Indeed, if we see the rational order of nature correctly, we shall actively will that which exists and thereby put our will in conformity with our particular circumstances. We shall then be free and at peace, for as the great Stoic philosopher Epictetus (A.D. 50–138) states, "if . . . nothing beyond our will's control is either good or evil, and everything within our will's control depends entirely on ourselves . . . what room is left for anxiety?"[17]

There is in this, quite noticeably, an emphasis upon the inner person that seems so characteristic of that subjective individualism that had led the other Hellenistic schools to advocate withdrawal from public life. The difference, as we have seen, was that the Stoics recognized that the state is natural, a part of the rational order of things, and that human beings are therefore obligated to live in political union with others. The political leader, in particular, had a duty to rule justly for the public good, an idea that had a profound influence on Cicero and subsequently on the Roman Empire's ruling classes. Nevertheless, it remained a duty, not something in itself ennobling or the source of ethical well-being as it had been for Aristotle. While it is therefore true that the Stoics originally never advocated that radical withdrawal from political life characteristic of Cynicism and Epicureanism, a certain tension always existed between the Stoic concept of political duty and its emphasis on the morally independent individual. During the later period of the Roman Empire, for reasons we will examine in the next chapter, the tendency toward political withdrawal was reemphasized by the Stoics.

This is the broad philosophic context to Cicero's political thought, but there is a more immediate political context. Cicero lived during the period of the late Roman Republic and the beginnings of the Roman Empire. We must, therefore, say something about this fateful time and Cicero's role in it, for it is the cojoining of Hellenistic thought and the actual facts of Roman politics at this crucial juncture between republic and empire that defines Cicero's political philosophy.

It is easiest to discuss this political context from the perspective of Cicero's own biography. Born in 106 B.C. into the equestrian class, a lower-level aristocracy comprising Rome's landed and financial elites, Cicero was educated in Rome and abroad in Athens and Rhodes, two of the most important intellectual centers in the ancient world. Greece had retained its reputation as the home of philosophy since Socrates, and Athens in particular had become a "university town" that drew students and scholars from the whole of the ancient world. Here Cicero absorbed Greek philosophy, including the philosophy of the various Hellenistic schools, the Peripatetic (Aristotelian) school, and the teachings of the Platonic Academy, which, with modifications, he adopted as his own. Recall, however, that Cicero was an eclectic who drew upon a variety of Greek schools in developing his political philosophy.

The object of Cicero's studies was not to become a scholar or a political philosopher, but rather a statesman-philosopher. This is not the same as Plato's philosopher-statesman who rules upon the basis of absolute truths. As a follower of the modified Skepticism of the Academy, Cicero was well aware of the limited capacities of human beings to know such truths or, at any rate, to try to make the political order strictly conform to them. His ideal was to take the actual facts of a political situation and by political skill direct them toward an end that most reasonable human beings would agree is ethically appropriate—for example, toward broad natural law principles. For this reason, Cicero held the statesman in higher regard than the philosopher, and in this too he differed with his master Plato.

Tragically, however, statesmanship failed him. He was unable to save his beloved Republic despite his own considerable political skills. He had risen over the years from the practice of law in Rome through various executive positions to that of consul, the most powerful executive office in the state. And he had done so by dint of sheer political ability and the highest ethical standards as befitted his ideal of a statesman, for Cicero was not a member of the nobility who controlled access to the key political positions. Yet by his death in 43 B.C., and in retrospect long before then, the Republic was gone, to be replaced by an empire premised upon radically different political principles than those advocated by Cicero. Sometimes, during periods of massive political transformation such as those Cicero confronted, statesmanship is not enough. This, as we shall see, was one lesson Cicero never learned and, in some ways, his political philosophy suffers for it.

What was this thing called *republic (res publica)* that Cicero wished to save? It is difficult to give a precise definition to the term; it is an ancient idea going back to the Romans that, over time, has undergone a variety of modifications. In general, however, a *republic* is a form of government that is based upon some kind of popular rule and correspondingly a certain degree of liberty and personal freedom. As such, a republic, in its ideal sense, is premised upon the inclusion of all citizens in a common enterprise of searching for the public good. The corresponding English term is *commonwealth,* as Cicero's greatest work of political philosophy, the *Republic,* is sometimes translated. Clearly the substance of Cicero's *Republic* is not to be confused with that of Plato's work of the same name, which rejects absolutely the idea of popular rule, although the title is intended to honor Plato's great work.

In this sense, the United States is a republic and was so termed by the founding fathers. It would be a mistake, however, to read into the Roman Republic a modern democracy with its panoply of civil rights and liberties. This was neither the fact nor what Cicero desired. An "aristocratic republic" was his ideal, as it was of the American founders incidentally, for like Cicero they believed neither popular government nor republican liberty could exist apart from a wise and experienced political class of statesmen.

That Cicero did fail to save the Republic is hardly surprising from our historical perspective. The Roman Republic was a city-state, initially not unlike the Greek polis, and its relative smallness and homogeneity was what made possible its being a commonwealth of relatively free and equal citizens. But by Cicero's day Rome had become a huge empire encompassing all of Italy and beyond. It was simply not possible to rule an empire on the basis of ideal republican principles. How in such an extended and diverse polity without modern mass communications could a commonwealth, or popular government, exist in any meaningful sense? Clearly, as the earlier Hellenistic empires had demonstrated, monarchy was the way to govern an empire, not a republic.

This is precisely what happened in one of the most storied periods of Roman history, and this is precisely what Cicero attempted to prevent.

Everyone knows the major players but one in this drama: Pompey, Caesar, Mark Antony, and Octavian, the future Augustus and first emperor of Rome. Few know the other: Marcus Tullius Cicero. With the partial exception of Pompey whom Cicero hoped, wrongly, would support his policies, the other protagonists destroyed the Republic. They were all military men with armies at their command, and Caesar, Cicero's greatest nemesis, was the mightiest of them. Cicero was simply a statesman steeped in Greek philosophy and Roman republican ideals, increasingly isolated and alone, who resisted the inevitable until, in revenge for a series of speeches known as the *Philippics,* which attacked Mark Antony's character following Caesar's assassination, was himself brutally assassinated. Cicero's death perfectly symbolized the death of the Republic, for Cicero was its greatest defender.

Cicero's failed plan was to restore the Republic by creating a *concordia ordinum* (harmony between classes) based upon a coalition of the Senate, the propertied middle classes, and those throughout the Italian peninsula who supported moderate and stable republican rule.[18] The middle classes were crucial for stability, for reasons that Aristotle made clear in his *Politics,* and, in this and other ways, Cicero's Republic resembles Aristotle's polity or "mixed constitution."

What is new here, however, and the crucial political element in Cicero's scheme, is the Senate, the most important political institution of the Republic. The Senate was composed of life-tenured ex-magistrates. The magistrates were the governing officers of the state. Drawn largely from the nobility, their powers were extensive. While in office they ruled as executive leaders; they exercised important controls over various legislative assemblies; and they possessed some judicial authority as well. Most importantly, when they left office their influence in shaping policy continued for a lifetime in the Senate. In this way the magistrates continued to shape and direct the Roman state long after their tenure as official executive agents.

While the Senate did not technically initiate legislation (it passed binding decrees only at the request of an acting magistrate), its actual authority and influence were enormous. It quite literally comprised the whole of the Republic's political class, the most powerful, influential, and experienced leaders in Rome. It is no wonder that Cicero, himself a member of the Senate as an ex-magistrate (consul), saw it as the key to his reforms. Here was to be found not only the requisite source of power but the skill, experience, and education, in short the statesmanship, that Cicero believed necessary to save the Republic.

Unfortunately, the Senate failed to play the role Cicero had so valiantly encouraged it to play. The reasons for this are complex, but in essence the narrow class interests of the senators predominated over the interests of preserving the Republic. While class conflict had been a feature of Roman politics from the beginning, the expansion of territory had exacerbated it. As a consequence, necessary reform was subordinated to maintaining the nobility's prerogatives. They resisted, for example, the growing power of the new middle classes, which supported moderate government. New men *(novo homo)* of this class such as Cicero attained leadership positions with difficulty.

In this deadlock of the Senate and the political class, power increasingly began to devolve upon the military and to those such as Caesar who were able to build their political base upon the army. In the end, military leaders would destroy the Republic and lay the basis for imperial rule that would culminate in the Principate of Augustus, a monarchical form of government disguised by the outer forms of the Republic, a system better suited to ruling the vast empire that Rome had become.[19] Thus began the long reign of Roman emperors. And while Augustus maintained some of the outer appearances of the Republic, such as its prestige, the reality became over time the absolute power of the emperors based upon the loyalty of the army. The Senate met but Augustus ruled, and Cicero's writings became proscribed reading.

This is the political background to Cicero's political philosophy, and it must be understood in this context. As statesman-philosopher, when Cicero thought about politics philosophically he did so always with his beloved Republic in mind and with the actual realities of Roman politics always before him. But it is equally true, and this is what was ultimately important for the subsequent development of Western political philosophy, that Cicero employed the whole of Greek thought since Plato as the framework for his thinking about Roman politics. This, not any impact he had in his own day, constitutes Cicero's importance as a political thinker.

Most of Cicero's major political works were written during enforced lulls in his public activities caused by the increasingly deteriorating political conditions. As a statesman first and foremost, Cicero would have preferred action but, fortunately for posterity, his temporary retirement from political involvement allowed time to philosophize about politics. And while he produced a great number of writings, many of which touch upon political issues, his major works on political philosophy are two: *De Republica* (the *Republic* or the *Commonwealth*), and *De Legibus* (the *Laws*), both of which, unfortunately, are fragmentary. A third work, *De Officiis (On Duties),* a treatise on practical ethics might be added here, but it is only of secondary interest to us although it was a primary source in the middle ages.[20]

The *Republic* or *Commonwealth* is considered Cicero's primary work on political philosophy for in it he develops his concept of the ideal state, that is, of the ideally just and ethically best form of political organization. His *Laws* establishes the type of legal system and laws best suited to this ideal state. In this sense the *Laws* is subordinate to the concept of the ideal developed in the *Commonwealth,* but in fact the two works, while not entirely consistent with each other, constitute a complete statement of Cicero's political philosophy.

The classical thrust of Cicero's thinking is clear. He proposes to analyze the state from the perspective of the ethical ideal, precisely the starting point of Plato and subsequent Greek thinkers in that tradition. Indeed, Cicero clearly is modeling his approach on his beloved Plato. Even the titles and format of his works betray this link, for they are both dialogues obviously patterned on Plato's *Republic* and *Laws.* There are differences, however. Whereas Plato's *Laws* constitutes a second-best state, or best possible compromise to the ideal established in his *Republic,* Cicero's *Laws* indicates the actual laws necessary for the functioning of his ideal state. Indeed, the difference here is even more dramatic, for Plato's ideal state was ruled by philosophers unconstrained by law, something few Romans, certainly not Cicero the lawyer, could have seriously entertained. Given the legal cast of the Roman mind and the importance of law in the evolution of the Roman state, a state without law was inconceivable.

Since the *Commonwealth* lays out the basic framework of Cicero's ideal state, we shall begin our analysis with that work. It is, as noted, a dialogue. The discussants are important public men who manifest Cicero's ideal of the statesman, the political leader who philosophizes about politics from the perspective of practical political experience. Cicero, recall, ranks the statesman higher than the philosopher, for, among other reasons, through his laws he "obliges all men to adopt that course which only a mere handful can be persuaded to adopt by the arguments of philosophers."[21]

Moreover, the key discussants are all members of a now famous philosophical discussion group known as the *Scipionic Circle,* named after its leader Scipio Aemilianus (185–129 B.C.), the chief protagonist of the dialogue. The Scipionic Circle, which was greatly influenced by Stoic ideas, had a profound impact on subsequent Roman and ultimately Western social and political thought by integrating Roman ideals with earlier Greek and Hellenistic philosophy. One of the enduring contributions of the Scipionic Circle was its concept of *humanitas,* an ideal of the gentle-man whose goodness and decency are derived from an appreciation of the "higher" activities of philosophy, literature, and art, that is, of the humanities.[22]

The dialogue opens with Gaius Laelius, next to Scipio Aemilianus the most important member of the dialogue, requesting Scipio to expound upon his concept of the ideal state, in short, on "the best form of constitution for the state."[23] Scipio's response, which constitutes the core of the dialogue and reflects Cicero's own views, begins with a definition of the commonwealth, that is, of the political community. The definition has become one of the most enduring in the history of Western political thought. Says Scipio:

> The commonwealth . . . is the people's affair; and the people is not every group of men, associated in any manner, but is the coming together of a considerable number of men who are united by a common agreement about law and rights and by the desire to participate in mutual advantages.[24]

The "people's affair" is a simple but by now famous definition of the commonwealth. However commonwealths may vary, they are, according to Cicero, truly commonwealths only so long as they remain the "people's affair." They are not the affair of the king only, or of the aristocracy, or for that matter of a democratic leadership, but of the whole community of citizens. When this ceases to be the reality, as increasingly was the case in the Roman Republic of Cicero's day, the commonwealth no longer exists. The Third Reich, therefore, was not a commonwealth, nor Stalin's Russia, nor any regime that terrorizes its citizenry, for in these cases community disappears. The mere existence of some form of government, or law, or administration does not constitute a political community and, without this, there can be neither ideal state nor even a best possible approximation to it.

Of course, we would no longer accept that only a "considerable number of men" constitute a genuine political community. Women too must be included, for a "men's affair" is not the same as the whole "people's affair." Given Scipio's definition, a patriarchy, no matter how democratically organized, cannot be a commonwealth. Clearly Cicero, like Aristotle, is the victim of the traditional conventions of his society. Were he writing his *Commonwealth* today, he would include women, as would Aristotle. Indeed, if we strip away the ancient prejudice against women's political participation, both thinkers provide powerful arguments for the full inclusion of women into the political community and the political process. And, at bottom, has not the women's movement implicitly legitimized its position precisely along lines first articulated by Cicero? To say "It's our country too" is simply to assert that it's "our affair" also, and that without this recognition no genuine political community can exist.

So, let us remove the archaic patriarchal element in Cicero's definition and say that a commonwealth involves a substantial number of human beings, but not just any number "associated in any manner." People associate for all kinds of reasons, but a real community implies agreement on some basic values and a political community or commonwealth on key political values. These values exist, says Cicero, when there is "common agreement about law and rights and by the desire to participate in mutual advantages." A commonwealth, in other words, requires for its continued existence a common legal system, a recognized body of rights that determine the legitimate powers of government and the liberties of people, and perhaps above all a recognition of the value of the existing social and political order.

Now it would follow that if the political community rests upon commonly accepted values regarding law and rights, then human beings must be by nature political and ethical creatures. Indeed, Cicero is quite explicit on this point and stresses it again and again. The previous quotation defining the commonwealth, for example, goes on to note that "the original cause of this coming together is not so much weakness as a kind of social instinct natural to man."[25] This reasoning, of course, is perfectly consistent with Aristotle's insistence that human beings are by nature "political animals."

Cicero stresses the social and ethical basis of the commonwealth, that is, the classical unity of ethics and politics, in contradistinction to the Epicureans and various other Hellenistic thinkers who, you will recall, took a quite different position. Later in the dialogue Cicero has Philus, the third most prominent character in the *Commonwealth,* take the position of Carneades, the extreme Skeptic of the New Academy. Attacking Plato's, Aristotle's, and the Stoics' assertion that justice is a universal, Philus argues that since laws vary from one commonwealth to another, it follows that there is no commonly accepted ethical standard of justice. Moreover, he asserts, in line with both the Epicurean and the Skeptic tradition, laws are obeyed not because of any sense of justice but because of the fear of punishment. He therefore concludes that "the law has no sanction in nature. It follows, then, that men are not just by nature."[26] Justice, and the laws that supposedly institutionalize it, are purely conventional.

Consequently, and again in line with the Epicureans and Skeptics, Philus proposes a contractual theory of the state. People, he says, contract to form a political society not because of any innate social instinct or ethical capacity as Scipio asserts, but because it is in their self-interest to do so. It is the fear of our own antisocial tendencies and our love of injustice that compels us to unite politically for mutual protection from one another and, in particular, of the weak from the strong. In an argument reminiscent of both Epicurus and the Sophist Thrasymachus in Plato's *Republic,* Philus claims that "neither nature nor deliberate choice but weakness is the mother of justice."[27] And he concludes that Scipio's supposed ideal state reflects nothing more than this kind of conventional justice created by a purely utilitarian contract.

It is important to recognize, therefore, that when Cicero has Scipio state that the commonwealth is based upon an agreement regarding law and rights, he does not mean agreement in this contractual sense. It is, rather, an implicit understanding inherent in the very social and ethical nature of humankind. It is there from the beginning as an a priori category of human existence. The political community and its ethical underpinnings, the commonwealth, are for Cicero natural, not conventional as Philus claims.

It is in fact the Stoic concept of natural law that ultimately lies behind Scipio's claim that justice is a universal and that law, society, and the state are natural. It is Laelius, however, who in responding to Philus first articulates the natural law position. Says Laelius: "There is in fact a true law—namely right reason—which is in accordance with nature, applies to all men, and is unchangeable and eternal."[28] And since it is unchangeable and eternal, he continues, "it will not lay down one rule at Rome and another at Athens, nor will it be one rule today and another tomorrow."[29] It follows, therefore, and this is terribly important to Cicero's legal theory developed in his *Laws,* that "to invalidate this law by human legislation is never morally right."[30] In short, civil law must never contradict the precepts of natural law, an argument first developed by the Stoics.

Who is correct: Laelius or Philus? The reader must decide for him- or herself. Is Socrates correct, or the Sophists? Plato or Thrasymachus? It is the same ancient nature–convention debate renewed by Philus and Laelius. All that we can say is that in adopting the natural law position Cicero roots himself squarely in the classical tradition: The state and law, reflecting a universal of justice, are natural and manifest the ultimate unity of ethics and politics.

What, then, is Cicero's ideal state? The answer depends in the first instance on what we mean by state. We have used the term in our discussion of the ancient Greek thinkers, but it is time to give it a more precise meaning. Actually, the term was not even used until the modern era, Machiavelli being the first to employ it in anything like its present meaning. We often translate the Greek word *polis* as state, but the two are not entirely identical. The Roman term *civitas,* however, which we also translate as state, comes much closer to what we mean by the term in its modern sense.

The state or *civitas,* says Scipio, "is an organization of the people . . . which . . . needs to be ruled by some deliberating authority . . . [government] . . . in order that it may endure."[31] At first glance this may appear confusing, but in fact Cicero is making some crucial distinctions. The commonwealth is a political community of commonly held ethical values regarding law and rights, but the state is the organization of that community into a real political and legal structure without which it could not survive. Indeed, it is only in theory that we are able to separate the state from the commonwealth. A political community without a state, that is, without a legal constitutional structure, could not long endure.

In theoretical terms, however, this separation is crucial. It involves distinctions that certainly go beyond the ancient Greek thinkers who were much less clear in distinguishing state from political community, distinctions that were to be crucial in the subsequent evolution of Western thinking on the state. Ultimately, the West came to recognize the state as a legal organization that for conceptual purposes must be understood as something not identical to the political community that it is created to preserve, although in real terms it always exists along with the political community.

Given this, it is logically apparent that the ideal state is that state or *civitas* that maintains the commonwealth as "the people's affair," that is, as a political community based upon law and justice. The question is, What type of state, what constitutional structure in other words, is most likely to do this? Scipio rejects the simple forms of government or constitution as incompatible with his definition of a commonwealth. Monarchy, aristocracy, and democracy have their specific virtues, but they all tend in the long run toward their perversions of tyranny, oligarchy, and ochlocracy (mob rule). They become states premised on the class interest of the rulers rather than the public interest of the whole citizenry.

In order to overcome these destructive tendencies, Scipio advocates what he terms the *composite state,* one that combines the simple forms in such a way that they mutually check their potential excesses. The scheme proposed is to combine those existing institutions of the Roman state that manifest the basic principles of the simple forms: The people's assemblies manifest the democratic principle; the magistrates and Senate the aristocratic; and a rector, a kind of philosopher-statesman, the monarchical principle. The rector is actually Cicero's invention and is not mentioned in the *Laws,* in which the consuls, the two most important magistrates, constitute the monarchical principle. What precisely constitutes the monarchical element in Cicero's composite state, therefore, is never made entirely clear, but it is probable that the consuls are his ultimate choice.[32]

Such an arrangement, Scipio argues, will ensure both governmental stability and liberty, the essence of a republican constitution. Liberty will be maintained by the democratic processes of the people's assemblies, but the potential of anarchy and mob rule will be mitigated by the wise and prudent leadership of the consuls and other magistrates representing the monarchical and aristocratic principles. And, as Cicero intended, inherent in these political structures would be distinct class interests since the magistrates would be comprised of the economically dominant and better educated social groups.

There is, of course, nothing terribly original in Cicero's conception of the composite state. This idea of balancing political principles and class interests in the constitution of the state is reminiscent of Aristotle's mixed constitution. It was not Aristotle directly, however, but another Greek and member of the Scipionic Circle, Polybius, who influenced Cicero's theory of the composite state. A noted historian of Rome, Polybius (c. 200–118 B.C.) drew upon Greek political thought and applied it to the actual evolution of Roman political institutions. His basic thesis, adopted with modifications by Cicero, was that the greatness of Rome is due to its mixed constitution.[33]

Herein lies what is in fact original in Cicero's theory of the composite state. Cicero very much follows the Greek tradition of distinguishing between the ideal and the real in his theory of the state. But, following the lead of Polybius, Cicero proposes to locate his ideal state in the actual evolution of the Roman constitution. The ideal is to be found in the real.

But how in fact do we know that the republican constitution of Rome really is the ideal? The answer lies in Cicero's analysis of its evolution from the simpler forms of state that characterized the earlier development of the Roman polity to its "final" republican form. The Roman state, like the earlier Greek polis, had evolved from monarchy to the inclusion of aristocratic and democratic elements creating ultimately a republican system composed of a mixture, if not a genuine balance, of the three simpler types. By looking at the history of the simpler forms, their respective strengths and weaknesses as demonstrated in how they actually worked over time, and by comparing them to their culmination in the composite republican form, the ideal character of the republican system can be established. Thus, says Scipio, "[I shall] picture our commonwealth at the moment of its birth, in the course of its development, and then in the strength and vigor of its maturity, instead of arbitrarily creating an imaginary state, as Socrates does in Plato's *Republic.*"[34]

We need not go into Scipio's subsequent historical analysis of the Roman polity. Suffice it to say that he finds the earlier and simpler forms of the state inadequate for the reasons we have already discussed, and that the composite republican form, "in the strength and vigor of its maturity," to enhance the positive features of the simpler forms of which it is composed while eliminating their excesses. As such, the Roman Republic constitutes the ideally just state, that is, that form of state most capable of preserving the commonwealth as the "people's affair."

But herein lay the obvious problem with Cicero's method of analysis, a problem of which Cicero is himself well aware: The existing Roman Republic quite clearly was not an ideally just state. It had ceased to be in any meaningful sense a "people's affair," a genuine commonwealth, but had increasingly become an arena of class conflict that would culminate in the tyranny of Caesar and ultimately the end of the Republic and the rise of empire, the precise opposite of Cicero's definition of a just state. How, then, could the ideal be located in the real, given that by Cicero's time the actual evolution of the Roman polity was anything but ideal?

Clearly, either Cicero's method is flawed or something needs to be added to his analysis that could explain the apparent inconsistency. This is precisely what Cicero, through the mouth of Scipio, does. Recall that Scipio had located the ideal republic "in the strength and vigor of its maturity," probably around the middle of the second century B.C. before class conflict had begun to erode what Cicero believed to be a harmonious balance of monarchical, aristocratic, and democratic elements in the constitution of the state.[35] In other words, Cicero's method was valid until the recent time of troubles, and this he has Scipio attribute to a decline in the quality of leadership, particularly in the Senate, the collective body of ex-magistrates that constitutes the aristocratic element in Cicero's ideal republic. It is not that Rome had failed to produce the ideal, but that the ancient virtues that an earlier generation of leaders had employed in maintaining it had become corrupted. In Cicero's words, "It is by our defects of character, and not by accident, that we have long since lost the substance of the commonwealth though we still retain its name."[36]

This emphasis on leadership is typical of classical political thought. Recall that the decline of Plato's ideal state began as a decline in the quality of the philosophic rulers, so it is natural for Cicero to view the decline of his ideal republic in the same terms. The difference, of course, is that Cicero's ruling elite are not philosophers but practical Roman statesmen. The issue for Cicero, then, is what kind of knowledge must these practical politicians possess in order to return the Republic to its "pristine condition." It is not pure theoretical knowledge of Plato's ideal form of justice, since that is neither Cicero's method of determining the ideal nor is it the capacity of practical politicians to acquire. On the other hand, it must be something more than that mere political expediency that had characterized the ruling elite's behavior for some time and that, according to Cicero, had been the primary reason for the decline of the Republic.

In the most general sense, Cicero emphasizes that the statesman must understand that politics is a dynamic affair. As Scipio notes, there is a "cycle of changes in the life of states."[37] The composite state that he praises had evolved out of just such a cycle of changes. Again, Cicero's ideal is not derived from pure philosophical speculation, as in Plato, but from an analysis of the actual evolution of the Roman state. Consequently, says Scipio, while it is the task of the philosopher "to understand the order in which these changes occur; . . . to foresee impending modifications, and at the same time to pilot the state, to direct its course, and to keep it under control, is the part of a great statesman."[38]

There is much in this reminiscent of Aristotle and his reliance on "the wisdom of the ages," as there is of Edmund Burke, the founder of modern philosophical conservatism (see Chapter 11). Like these thinkers, Cicero is a conservative who wishes to preserve what is best in existing political institutions, to reform them where necessary, and not to impose some philosophical abstraction no matter how logically coherent it may be. Note that even his concept of the philosopher is of one who understands political change, not Plato's philosophical ruler who turns his back upon this world of change and appearances.

Clearly this change is not random for Cicero. Politics is not just storm and strife signifying nothing. If it were, mere politicians, party hacks, would do. The genuine statesman grasps the ideal that is implicit in the real and uses his political skills to steer the state toward the ideal. And, in the broadest sense, that ideal is the very same that shaped the whole of classical thought from Socrates on: justice.

So, we might then say, again in perfect conformity with the classical tradition, that what the statesman needs to know above all else is the nature of justice. But how precisely is he to know this? In part, by observing it as it manifests itself in existing political institutions. This, however, rather begs the question, for how can we know this without first knowing the principle of justice itself? This was Socrates' and Plato's whole point, and for that matter, Aristotle's. Their ideal states were premised upon some knowable principle of justice.

The answer is twofold. In the first place, while Cicero relies primarily on a concept of the ideally just state drawn from the actual evolution of the Roman Republic, he never entirely jettisons Plato's philosophically derived ideal state. He continues to employ it as a kind of benchmark or ultimate reference point in his analysis of the Roman polity. As Scipio states, "I shall strive to follow the same principles which Plato perceived, and to illustrate them, not in an unreal and shadowy state, but in our own glorious commonwealth."[39] The statesman, then, is not devoid of an ideal of justice, but he employs it within an existing political context that shapes and modifies as well as illuminates it.

In the second place, and more important, the statesman knows the first principles of justice because he knows, or ought to know, natural law. Here Cicero returns to the Stoic's natural law as a rule of moral reason that establishes the unchangeable principles of justice to which civil law must conform. Thus, says Scipio, in the law of nature the statesman must

> be perfectly versed, for without this no man can be just. In the Civil law he must not be unversed, but in the latter field his knowledge should resemble the pilot's knowledge of astronomy or the doctor's of natural philosophy, which these men adapt to their own uses but never allow to be an obstacle in their profession.[40]

Thus, in the final analysis the knowledge the statesman must possess is knowledge of the law. Natural law he must know absolutely, for without this knowledge he cannot direct the commonwealth to its proper end of justice. Civil law he must understand in a different way. Civil law is changed over time by the wise statesman to move the commonwealth in the direction of justice. It was in fact precisely in this way that the Roman polity evolved into its ideal republican form according to Cicero. Hence, the statesman must know civil law as a ship's pilot must know astronomy, as a means to an end: the port for the pilot, justice for the statesman.

Note how this view of law encompasses the whole of Cicero's notion of the wise statesman. Natural law produces those first principles of justice that make the dynamic of politics something more than mere chaos. Civil law is the practical means by which the statesman confronts those dynamics and guides them in the direction of justice. Bear in mind that civil law will vary from state to state for it reflects different cultures and traditions, and broad natural law principles allow for wide variations in civil law. Thus, to know civil law means to know intimately one's own history and political culture.

This brings us to Cicero's second major work, the *Laws,* for here he proposes to specify those laws that will govern the ideal commonwealth. Recall that Cicero's *Laws,* unlike Plato's, is not merely an exposition of the second-best possible state: It is an analysis of the laws necessary to maintain the ideal composite state developed in the *Commonwealth.* Moreover, it must be kept in mind that for Cicero the law is the expression of a whole political philosophy, not merely a set of legal proscriptions. As Atticus, a discussant in the *Laws* emphasizes, Cicero does not believe "that the science of law is to be derived from the praetors edict . . . , but from the deepest mysteries of philosophy."[41] Hence, to analyze the law is to engage in political theorizing. In this sense, Cicero went beyond the Greeks to whom law was important but not nearly as primary and formative as it was for the Romans.

Even a cursory reading of the *Laws* makes clear this crucial point. Like the *Commonwealth*, the *Laws* is a dialogue, in this case between Cicero; Quintus, his brother; and his lifelong friend Atticus. From the beginning, Cicero emphasizes the necessity of knowing natural law as the necessary basis for determining the character of his ideal civil laws. His complaint is that his contemporaries had tended to ignore this "universal law" and thus treat civil law from a purely pragmatic point of view.[42] Lawyers want to win cases, not contemplate the first principles of law, that is, of justice.

Indeed, without the Stoic concept of natural law, Roman law would have remained largely a pragmatic set of rules devoid of philosophical content. Unlike the Greeks, the Romans were a practical people not easily given to theoretical speculation. They would have remained so without Greek philosophy, and by employing Greek theory and the Stoic concept of natural law in particular, Cicero intends to make the study of law a philosophical rather than simply a pragmatic activity.

Thus, in conformity with the Stoic view, Cicero defines law not simply in terms of what the magistrates or courts say it is in any particular case but "as the highest reason implanted in Nature, which commands what ought to be done and forbids the opposite."[43] Law is first and foremost reason, that is, moral reason, and it is natural not merely conventional. But it is a particular kind of moral reason. In Cicero's words it is "right reason applied to command and prohibition."[44] Law commands and prohibits us, the commands and prohibitions of conscience in the case of natural law, the commands and prohibitions of the state in civil law. And what distinguishes the civil law is that commands and prohibitions are backed up by actual coercion or the threat of it. Cicero sums this all up as follows:

> Law is the distinction between things just and unjust, made in agreement with that primal and most ancient of all things, Nature; and in conformity to Nature's standard are framed those human laws which inflict punishment upon the wicked but defend and protect the good.[45]

This all may seem clear enough, but in fact Cicero devotes a substantial portion of his treatise to restating and reformulating these basic propositions, and not only because he desires to instruct his pragmatic countrymen in the deeper philosophy of law. The reality is that a radically different concept of law and consequently of politics could be derived from the fact that civil law commands and prohibits by the threat of coercion. It could be argued that the whole basis of law is not moral reason, that is, justice, but coercion alone.

Precisely this kind of argument was being made by members of various Hellenistic schools including the extreme Skeptics of Cicero's own Academy. And once this argument is accepted, the whole philosophy of politics that Cicero extracts from his concept of law is abolished. If, for example, law is nothing more than an instrument of state coercion, then it and the state must be purely conventional. Natural law would be a meaningless concept as would justice, which Cicero equates with natural law principles. Justice itself would be a mere convention, nothing more than a human construct created, as the Epicureans asserted, to serve certain interests. Cicero could not sustain his claim that "we are so constituted by Nature as to share the sense of Justice with one another and to pass it on to all men."[46] The classical unity of ethics and politics that defines his political philosophy would, as a consequence, be hopelessly undermined.

Cicero's affirmation of the rational and moral basis of law, then, contains within it a much deeper philosophy of politics. This is what makes Cicero so typically Roman, and what differentiates him from the ancient Greek thinkers. He philosophizes about politics from the perspective of law. We have already seen this in his initial definition of a commonwealth as a "people's affair" in which the citizens "are united by a common agreement about law and right." In the *Laws* Cicero further elaborates this view when he states that "those who share law must also share Justice; and those who share these are to be regarded as members of the same commonwealth."[47]

In the final analysis a commonwealth for Cicero is a political community with a shared system of law for, given his philosophy of law, a shared system of law will inherently be a "people's affair." It must be shared, however. A mere set of legal rules existing for the benefit of a particular group or class would not be just or constitute a commonwealth. Indeed, contrary to the Epicureans, it would not be law, for an unjust law is in Cicero's view a contradiction in terms.[48]

As to the specific laws Cicero recommends for his ideal republic, most would have little relevance for us today. Like Plato, Cicero proposes to regulate many things we would now relegate to the private domain, but the classical city-state was premised upon the inculcation of virtue in its citizens, and this required much greater social control than is characteristic of the modern state. Of particular importance to Cicero but of little to us, for example, are laws concerning religion. Religion in the Roman Republic, as in the Greek polis, was a state religion and as such assumed enormous political importance. In the modern Western state this is no longer true. We have separated church and state or at a minimum allowed for full religious freedom even where, as in England, there is an established religion. Religion is now constitutionally a private affair, although certain religious issues, such as prayer in public schools, may still be politically relevant, particularly in this country.

The laws that will most interest us, and that were most important to Cicero, are those that directly shape the structure of the state, that is, constitutional laws. We know from the *Commonwealth* that the composite state, a mixed constitution composing a balance of monarchical, aristocratic, and democratic elements is Cicero's ideal. This is the form of state or *civitas* most likely to maintain the commonwealth as a "people's affair." The constitutional laws Cicero recommends in the *Laws,* then, are those that will best maintain the composite state.

Of these, the most important are the laws of the magistrates, which, Cicero emphasizes, are "next to the establishment of religion . . . surely the most important in the formation of a commonwealth."[49] As the governing agents of the Republic and in their various capacities as the monarchical and aristocratic parts of the ideal constitution, the magistrates' authority is to be extensive. Recall that they possessed legislative and judicial authority as well as executive powers. Most important, they constituted that group of statesmen that Cicero insisted was the key to reforming the Republic. It is hardly surprising, then, that in his view "the whole character of a republic is determined by its arrangements in regard to magistrates."[50] Indeed, for Cicero "different types of States are recognized by their constitution of these magistracies."[51] Recall here that Aristotle's classification of constitutions was also based upon its arrangement of the ruling groups within the offices of state.

We have seen that for Cicero the law constitutes a whole political philosophy and that the knowledge his ideal statesman must possess is knowledge of the law. This view is maintained in his treatment of the magistrate's role for, according to Cicero, "the function of a magistrate is to govern, and to give commands which are just and beneficial and in conformity with the law."[52] In his ideal state the magistrate's commands are in accord with the civil laws of the state, which themselves are in conformity with the principles of justice inherent in natural law. In this way the magistrate is subject to the very law he is expected to enforce; in Cicero's words "as the laws govern the magistrate, so the magistrate governs the people."[53]

In the final analysis, then, we may say that Cicero's ideal state is one premised upon a unity of law and magistracy for, as he concludes, "it can truly be said that the magistrate is a speaking law, and the law a silent magistrate."[54] In the ideal state it is ultimately the law that governs, for to say that the magistrate governs as a "speaking law" is to assert the rulership of law. This constitutes the ideal of the rule of law, hence justice. This all presumes, of course, that the magistracy understands it is "speaking law," that it is subordinate to law while speaking it, and that the function of law is to preserve the commonwealth. In Cicero's day this increasingly was forgotten by the political elite.

This brings us back to Cicero's constitutional theory, for it is the arrangement of magistrates in the constitution of the composite state that, ideally at least, is to ensure that the magistrates rule only in the name of law. Clearly, if only one magistrate or one small group held power exclusively that would not constitute a composite state. Such concentration of power would create a simple form of constitution that, as with all simple forms according to Cicero, has the tendency to degenerate into tyranny and the destruction of the commonwealth as a shared system of law. A balance between types of magistrates should have the opposite effect, and this, not unlike Aristotle's mixed constitution, is the whole point of Cicero's composite state.

We need not review all the various magistrates that Cicero discusses. Suffice it to say that the Republican constitution was a complex combination of different types of magistrates who possessed those executive, judicial, and indirect legislative powers necessary to the functioning of any state. It was complex because it was not designed logically and deductively by a philosopher but evolved historically out of the struggle of different classes to acquire a share of power in the state. But, at one time at least, it worked, according to Cicero: It produced the ideal state. This is why Scipio states that "since the wisest and most evenly balanced system has been devised by our own ancestors, I had no innovations, or at least only a few, which I thought ought to be introduced into the constitution."[55]

There were, however, two key types of magistrates who were of particular importance to Cicero: the consuls and the tribunes. The two consuls were the supreme executive power in the state. Elected in one of the popular assemblies for a two-year period, they possessed, as we have noted, more than just executive powers and, when waging war, were the supreme military power. They had authority over all other magistrates except the tribunes. In Roman terminology, they possessed *imperium,* which meant that their rule reflected the full power of the state, not simply the circumscribed power or *potestas* of a minor official.[56] As such, in the *Laws* the consuls replace the rector of the *Commonwealth* as the monarchical element in Cicero's composite state.

The tribunes, all ten of whom were elected by the common people or *plebeians* for a period of ten years, were created to check the power of the consuls, who tended to reflect the interests of the nobility. Over time, the power of the tribunes increased, and Cicero emphasizes that in his ideal republic "their prohibitions and resolutions passed by the plebeians under their presidency shall be binding."[57] As such, the tribunes have a certain connection to the democratic element of Cicero's composite state for they are elected by the common people and preside over their assemblies. As members of the Senate, of course, they formed a crucial part of the aristocratic component of the constitution.

The consuls and tribunes, in effect, were the constitutional reflection of distinct and potentially violent class differences between the nobility and the common people. Like Aristotle, Cicero proposes a political solution to class conflict that ideally would abolish violence and produce rule of law. The problem was that the tribuneship increasingly had been the vehicle by which ambitious men increased their power at the expense of those republican ideals Cicero wished to preserve. Given this, the question is, Why does Cicero not advocate its abolition? This question is put forcibly to Cicero by Quintus, who views the creation of the tribuneship as "a great misfortune, for it . . . brought about the decline in the influence of the aristocracy and the growth of the power of the multitude."[58]

Cicero's response should by now be easily surmised: "Consider the wisdom of our ancestors in this matter."[59] They created the tribuneship for a reason, and it is our task to understand their reason, not simply to reject it because we now see difficulties with the institution. If that were our method, says Cicero, we would have to abolish the consulate as well, which also had been corrupted.[60] Indeed, given the overweening power of the nobility and the rebellion it produced, the creation of the tribuneship, says Cicero, "was the only salvation of the State."[61]

For Cicero, it is the preservation of liberty that constitutes the real importance of the tribuneship. Without it, the liberty of the people would be nonexistent, for the power of the consuls and the noble classes whose interests they reflected would destroy the people's freedom. It was, in fact, precisely their desire for liberty that had caused the people to create the tribuneship in the first place. And without liberty there could be no republic, for a republic is characterized by the existence of liberty. For this reason, Cicero concludes, "it is clear that either the monarchy ought never to have been abolished, or else that real liberty, not a pretence of it, had to be given to the common people."[62] (Recall that monarchy had been the form of government that the ancient Roman city-state initially possessed.)

The Senate constitutes the aristocratic element of Cicero's composite state. As such, it acts as a check not only upon the magistrates currently holding office but upon the people as a whole. It thus ensures that both the monarchical and democratic parts of the constitution do not degenerate into their respective perversions of either one-man despotism or mob rule. It is, in this sense, the fulcrum of the whole republican system. More than this, as a body of life-tenured ex-magistrates, the Senate constitutes the political class of Republican Rome, those with real political knowledge and experience. It was that assembly of statesmen upon which Cicero placed all his hopes for a *concordia ordinum* and upon which his theory of the ideal state rested.

Those specific legal powers that Cicero recommends for his ideal senate conform more or less to existing practice, but its real power resides in its moral authority, which ideally becomes actual political authority. Thus, Cicero proposes a law that states that the Senate's "decrees shall be binding."[63] This means, ideally, that "all the other orders defend its decrees."[64] And this they will do, Cicero argues, because the Senate will be recognized as the rule of wisdom. The acting magistrates and most importantly the people, therefore, will willingly obey it.[65] The people in particular will be led to obey since their magistrates, the tribunes, are also members of the Senate. In this way, says Cicero, "Supreme power is granted to the people and actual authority to the Senate."[66] Putting actual authority in the Senate is, in the final analysis, the real basis of Cicero's ideal composite state, for as he concludes, it makes "possible the maintenance of that balanced and harmonious constitution which I have described."[67] It makes possible, in short, the composite state.

The problem, of course, was that the existing Senate's decrees were increasingly ignored, for the Senate was not perceived as a source of political wisdom but as a center of self-interested cabals and class-oriented politics. Atticus pointedly notes its misdeeds, but Cicero again stresses that he is speaking of an ideal future senate. Clearly the Senate would have to be reformed, and to this end Cicero proposes another law that, he believes, will ensure the survival of his ideal state. That law states that the Senate "shall be free from dishonour, and shall be a model for the rest of the citizens."[68] All other laws are subordinate to this, for without an uncorrupted Senate they will be meaningless. It is not without reason, therefore, that Cicero concludes:

> If we secure this, we shall have secured everything. For just as the whole State is habitually corrupted by the evil desires and vices of its prominent men, so is it improved and reformed by self-restraint on their part.[69]

Here Cicero's analysis follows the classical Platonic model of the just state, which is premised upon the character of the ruling class. Basing his analysis on the actual evolution of the Roman polity, Cicero notes that "whatever change took place in the lives of the prominent men has also taken place in the whole people."[70] Thus, the corruption of the Senate like the corruption of Plato's philosophic rulers is the source of a much more general corruption of society as a whole. Fix that and "everything is secured"; on this Cicero and Plato are one.[71]

They differ, of course, on what constitutes the ideal ruling elite. For Plato it is philosophic rulers who derive their authority from pure philosophical principles. For Cicero it is practical statesmen who derive their authority from the people. Supreme power is to reside in the people while actual authority remains in the Senate. Cicero, after all, is a republican. But both Cicero and Plato agree that their respective ideal states cannot exist apart from the rule of wisdom and that requires, above all, an uncorrupted ruling elite.

The democratic part of Cicero's composite state is constituted by the people's assemblies. While their specific jurisdictions varied, their primary role was legislation. Accordingly, Cicero proposes various laws to regulate their meetings, for the most part mundane rules of order and decorum. Clearly he does not consider the assemblies to be as important as the Senate and the magistrates. This subordination of the assemblies is most clearly seen in a related law on voting.

The law proposed is that in voting for magistrates, in trials of criminals, or in assemblies on legislation, the vote "shall not be concealed from citizens of high rank, and shall be free to the common people."[72] In granting the vote to the common people Cicero certainly includes a democratic component in his composite state. But how truly democratic is it if the vote "shall not be concealed from citizens of high rank"? And what about the people's liberty, a crucial element in a republican system of government? Won't the people be reluctant to express their real wishes if even in their own assemblies their vote can be revealed to important nobles such as magistrates and senators? Cicero, however, concludes that the people's liberty is actually secured by the open ballot for he asserts that "the people may enjoy liberty . . . in this very privilege of honourably winning the favour of the aristocracy."[73]

None of this is likely to be very convincing to those of us who are citizens of a modern democratic society. We cannot conceive of democratic government apart from the secret ballot, nor of liberty that is not at a minimum defined as freedom from outside influences and pressures. In fairness to Cicero, however, open declaration had existed in the past and was, in fact, not uncommon in classical democracies. Moreover, Cicero is not advocating a pure democracy where the "people rule," but a republic or composite state in which checks are to be placed upon the democratic part of the constitution as much as (in fact more than) on the aristocratic and monarchical parts. Even with the secret ballot, all modern constitutional democracies limit the power of the people. The founders of the American polity, for example, rejected pure democracy for a republican system that set very definite limits on popular rule, and this they did precisely to preserve liberty.

Yet, having said all this, there remains something troublesome about Cicero's law. Even within the context of his own time and place, it is difficult not to conclude that the law goes too far, that the open ballot gives the senatorial class too much power, that the people's liberty will not be secure.[74] Cicero himself seems to recognize this when he has Scipio conclude that the law in fact only "grants the appearance of liberty."[75] But the appearance of it is not the same as the reality, and Scipio had been adamant in his debate with Quintas on the tribuneship that a genuine republic requires real liberty, not merely the pretence of it.

Such, then, is Cicero's political philosophy. There is certainly more that we could discuss: other types of laws regarding magistrates and officials important to the ideal republic and the courts. This would not notably enhance our understanding of his political thought, however, and unfortunately the sections in the *Laws* on the courts and the specific legal powers of the various magistrates are lost. It is worth noting, however, that the concluding part of the *Laws* available to us once again affirms the importance of natural law. The whole of Cicero's theory of the ideal republic, both in the *Commonwealth* and the *Laws,* is derived ultimately from this great Stoic concept.

What criticisms might we make of Cicero's political thought? We have already suggested that his law on voting calls into question the viability of the democratic and libertarian elements of his ideal state. Moreover, the powers of the magistrates, and through them the noble classes, are even more extensive than we have indicated. We might conclude, then, that Cicero does not provide a valid theory of the ideal state since his republic is not a real commonwealth or "people's affair" inclusive of all classes, not a true composite state or *civitas* based upon a genuine balance of political principles. Most scholars have adopted this view. We should temper this criticism, however, for surely Cicero's law on voting could be modified without jeopardizing the whole of his theory of the ideal state, and there are more real checks upon the admitted power of the nobility in his ideal state than is sometimes conceded. Recall again his defense of the tribuneship as a protector of the people's liberty. Cicero's intent certainly is not to deprive the people of their liberty even if he is ambiguous about the extent and exercise of it.[76]

Cicero's not always satisfactory treatment of liberty and popular rule is, at any rate, derived from a more fundamental problem inherent in his whole theory of political reform. He advocates returning to the principles of the earlier Republic, which means, above all, a reconstituted Senate comprised of able and uncorrupted statesmen most of whom would be from either the noble classes or, like Cicero, aristocratic in their sentiments. If Cicero is at times ambiguous on the actual extent of the people's power and of their liberty, it is in large part because of his anxiety to preserve the autonomy of the Senate and shield it from popular pressures.

The problem is that his solution to the decline of the Republic is little more than a statement of the problem. Cicero tells us that if he can reconstitute the Senate he "shall have secured everything." Who can doubt it? A Senate composed of politically experienced statesmen imbued with the principles of natural law would of course preserve the Republic in its ideal form. But how is this to be accomplished? Cicero says little in his *Laws* or the *Commonwealth* beyond recommending special training and education for the senatorial class, and even this begs the issue for it presumes a class willing to be educated.[77] Mere assertion of the goal desired is not a solution to the problem; it is simply a recognition of it.

The objection might be raised, of course, that Cicero is in the classical tradition of constructing a theoretically ideal state whose value is not determined by its concrete political usefulness. There is something to this, and if our critique were of Plato it would be entirely accurate. Plato, recall, had derived his political theory from philosophical concepts beyond "the world of appearances." For this reason, the Platonic ideal state remains unsullied regardless of existing political conditions, so much so that people of justice could always withdraw and found the ideal commonwealth within themselves when real politics became too messy.

But Cicero is not Plato. To be sure, he is influenced by Plato's analysis of the ideal state and he does in part employ Plato's pure philosophical method where appropriate. But his primary method, derived from Polybius and more in line with the Aristotelian tradition, sees the ideal of justice emerging out of what Plato had devalued as the shadowy cave world of appearances. Cicero cannot, therefore, simply dismiss the existing Republic because of its corruptness since the evolution of the Roman polity to its republican form constitutes his ideal. Nor can he withdraw in the name of some higher ideal as would Plato or his own contemporary Cynics and Epicureans. Cicero is as much committed to an active public life by his method as he is to a political philosophy whose ideals must be validated in actual political practice.

In the final analysis, the root problem with Cicero's political theory, the one from which all others derive, is that it never comes to terms with the real cause of the decline of the Republic. As we have seen, Rome had already become a huge empire that could no longer govern itself on purely republican principles any more than the Alexandrian Empire could model itself on the Greek polis. As with the earlier Hellenistic empires, Rome would become in effect a monarchy ruled by emperors with increasingly centralized and absolute powers. This was inevitable, for without modern mass communication so large an empire with such a diversity of peoples and cultures could not hope to create even that relative intimacy and those minimum of shared political values necessary to a republic.

Despite these facts, so obvious today, Cicero remains in thrall to the early Republic, more broadly to that model of the small classical city state that goes back to the early Greeks and that he believes remains valid for the Roman polity of his day.[78] It was not. Cicero fails to face what his method of determining the ideal should have made him face. If the ideal is in the real, then the actual evolution of Rome to an empire should have caused Cicero at least to modify his republican ideal to fit the new political realities. Perhaps this would have been futile, but at least his political philosophy would have posited an ideal more in accord with reality and less with nostalgia for a dead past.

As is, Cicero's failure to confront the facts of empire lies behind most of the other criticisms directed at his political philosophy. The corruption of the Senate that so dominated his thinking, for example, was not so much the cause of the Republic's decline as the result of it. Yet Cicero believes that he can reconstitute the Republic by somehow reforming the Senate as a body of wise and public-spirited statesmen. This may have been a valid approach in a small city-state, but it was woefully inadequate when applied to a large empire under conditions of radical change. In this sense, his political philosophy fails in the same way, and for the same reason, as his practical attempt to create a *concordia ordinum*. Both were premised upon a republican city-state model no longer applicable to the reality of empire.

Only in this sense, however, can we say it fails. Like Aristotle, Cicero sums up the experience of the small city state at the very point it had ceased to exist as a viable form of polity. And, like Aristotle, Cicero's political philosophy proved inadequate to the new reality. For the later development of Western political thought, however, none of this was important, for his political philosophy had a great impact upon subsequent republican and democratic theories of government from the Renaissance on.[79] Had Cicero been more imperial in his thinking, less of this republican tradition would have been available to posterity.

More than this, as an eclectic thinker Cicero transmits much of the entire classical tradition of ethical and political thought from Socrates on, including that of the major Hellenistic philosophies. The impact on the West of such concepts as natural law, the commonwealth, and republicanism is due in no small measure to Cicero. There is, it must be admitted, a negative side to his eclecticism. While it makes him an excellent transmitter of many classical ideas and ideals, it does not enhance him as an original thinker. Eclectic thinkers are rarely original. Certainly Cicero is not equivalent to a Plato or an Aristotle, as he would be the first to admit. He employs them but he does not transcend them.

Yet, having said this, it cannot be claimed that Cicero is simply mindless in his eclecticism. He relies on others: Plato, Aristotle, Polybius, the Stoics; but he integrates their philosophies in often imaginative ways. His view that the ideal state is to be located in the actual evolution of the Roman constitution is based upon the ideas of others such as Polybius, but it constitutes a not entirely unoriginal application of those ideas.[80]

Whatever our final assessment of Cicero as a political thinker, there is no gainsaying his subsequent influence as a transmitter of classical ethical and political thought. There is equally no question that events soon rendered his political philosophy irrelevant in immediate terms. When Augustus established the Principate, the already dead Republic was formally laid to rest although the forms of the Republic and Cicero's beloved Senate were retained for appearance's sake.

With Augustus began a long line of emperors and imperial rule. New forms of political thought, or rather modified forms, would emerge that would be more compatible with the reality of empire than the republicanism of Cicero. But these new ways of political thinking would themselves be challenged and ultimately supplanted by a revolutionary religious faith unlike anything that Cicero or other classical thinkers could have imagined. Christ was born in the reign of Augustus; his followers would revolutionize the politics of the later Empire, shape the political structure of medieval Europe, and alter radically the way we think about politics down to our own times. This is the subject of the next chapter.

Notes

1. Giovanni Reale, *The Systems of the Hellenistic Age,* 3rd ed., John R. Catan, ed./trans. (Albany: State University of New York Press, 1985), p. 357.

2. Frederick Copleston, S.J., *A History of Philosophy: Greece and Rome* (Garden City, N.Y.: Doubleday and Co., 1962), I, pt. 2:158.

3. Eduard Zeller, *Outlines of the History of Greek Philosophy,* 13th rev. ed., Wilhelm Nestle, ed., L.R. Palmer, trans. (New York: Dover Publications, 1980), pp. 242–45.

4. Reale, *Systems of the Hellenistic Age,* pp. 358–59.

5. This was true even of Stoicism and Epicureanism, which were engaged in constant controversy with one another. See Zeller, *History of Greek Philosophy,* p. 230.

6. The following general characteristics of Hellenistic thought are common knowledge. For a brief analysis of these and other such general features, see Reale, *Systems of the Hellenistic Age,* pp. 5–15.

7. More than this, Cynicism influenced as well the development of Epicureanism and Skepticism and, indeed, the whole of the Hellenistic emphasis upon the autonomous individual as the only real source of virtue and happiness. See Reale, *Systems of the Hellenistic Age,* pp. 37–38.

8. See Phillip Mitsis, *Epicurus' Ethical Theory: The Pleasures of Invulnerability* (Ithaca, N.Y.: Cornell University Press, 1988), for a detailed analysis of the difficulties in connecting an overly simplified psychology to a rational ethical theory.

9. Zeller, *History of Greek Philosophy,* p. 238.

10. See Robert Drew Hicks, *Stoic and Epicurean* (New York: Russell and Russell, 1962), pp. 184–89, for a brief summary of these Epicurean ideals.

11. Bailey, trans., "The Extant Writings of Epicurus," in Whitney J. Oates, ed., *The Stoic and Epicurean Philosophers* (New York: Random House, 1940), p. 43.

12. Ibid., p. 38.

13. Ibid.

14. Stoicism went through various periods of development, the most important being the so-called Middle Stoa under the leadership of Panaetius, who began eclecticizing the Stoic doctrine (as a member of the Scipionic Circle, Panaetius both influenced and was influenced by Roman ideals). As a result, Stoicism was not only influenced initially by Cynicism but subsequently by the Skeptic, Platonic, and Peripatetic (Aristotelian) schools. See Reale, *Systems of the Hellenistic Age,* pp. 291–92.

15. G. Long, trans., "The Meditations of Marcus Aurelius," in Oates, *Stoic and Epicurean Philosophers,* p. 562.

16. Robert Mark Wenley, *Stoicism and Its Influence* (New York: Cooper Square Publishers, 1963), pp. 97–98. According to Wenley, for the Stoics "the 'whole duty of man' may be summed in two brief precepts: submission to

the Providence or Fate governing the world, and realization of the 'divine spark within.'"

17. P.E. Matheson, trans., "The Discourses of Epictetus," in Oates, *Stoic and Epicurean Philosophers,* p. 306.

18. See Mason Hammond, *City-State and World State in Greek and Roman Political Theory Until Augustus* (Cambridge, Mass.: Harvard University Press, 1951), pp. 107–10, for a more detailed analysis of Cicero's political program, which was actually more complex than indicated, as were the class relationships he hoped to establish. It was a congruence between the senatorial class of nobles and the landed equestrian class of which Cicero was a member that constituted the real basis of his *concordia ordinum.*

19. Ibid, p. 140. Hammond notes that "the Augustan compromise combined the inheritance of Caesar, concealed monarchy, with that of Cicero, the restored Republic guided by the authority of its chief citizen."

20. Antony Black, *Political Thought in Europe 1250–1450,* Cambridge Medieval Textbooks Series (Cambridge: Cambridge University Press, 1992), p. 9. While *De Officiis* was widely read in the medieval and Renaissance periods, Cicero's political works were not as available. Parts of *De Republica* were extant in the medieval period but not recovered in more complete form until the early nineteenth century. However, Cicero's political philosophy was known through other secondary sources such as St. Augustine.

21. Reprinted with the permission of Simon & Schuster from the Macmillan college text *On the Commonwealth* by Cicero, translated by George Holland Sabine and Stanley Barney Smith. Copyright 1976 by Macmillan.

22. See Sabine and Smith's "Introduction," in *On the Commonwealth,* pp. 34–38, for a brief but excellent discussion of the many contributions of the Scipionic Circle to the Western tradition of thought and, in particular, on its role in the subsequent development of Roman law.

23. Cicero, *On the Commonwealth,* p. 126.

24. Ibid., p. 129.

25. Ibid.

26. Ibid., p. 206.

27. Ibid., p. 210.

28. Ibid., p. 215.

29. Ibid., p. 216.

30. Ibid., pp. 215–16.

31. Ibid., p. 131.

32. See Sabine and Smith's "Introduction," in *On the Commonwealth,* pp. 92–98, for a brief but thorough discussion of this issue.

33. See Polybius, *The Rise of the Roman Empire,* Frank W. Wallbank, ed., Ian Scott-Kilvert, trans. (New York: Penguin Books, 1979), Book VI, pp. 302–18.

34. Cicero, *On the Commonwealth*, p. 155.

35. See Hammond, *City-State and World State*, p. 110: "Cicero's program for practical politics was in fact to restore the Roman constitution of the second century B.C., which Greek political theorists had identified as a close approximation to the ideal mixed constitution."

36. Cicero, *On the Commonwealth*, p. 243. This quotation is in Cicero's own words rather than through the mouth of Scipio.

37. Ibid., p. 134.

38. Ibid.

39. Ibid., p. 181.

40. Ibid., pp. 245–46.

41. Marcus Tullius Cicero, "The Laws," in G.P. Gould, ed., Clinton Walker Keyes, trans., *The Loeb Classical Library, Volume XVI: De Re Publica–De Legibus* (Cambridge, Mass.: Harvard University Press, 1928), p. 315.

42. Ibid., p. 313.

43. Ibid., p. 317.

44. Ibid., p. 333.

45. Ibid., pp. 385–87.

46. Ibid., p. 333.

47. Ibid., p. 323.

48. Ibid., p. 385.

49. Ibid., p. 457.

50. Ibid., p. 461.

51. Ibid., p. 473.

52. Ibid., p. 459.

53. Ibid., p. 460.

54. Ibid., p. 461.

55. Ibid., p. 473.

56. Ibid., p. 467.

57. Ibid., p. 469.

58. Ibid., p. 477.

59. Ibid., p. 487.

60. Ibid., p. 485.

61. Ibid., p. 487.

62. Ibid.

63. Ibid., p. 491.

64. Ibid.

65. Ibid., p. 493.

66. Ibid.

67. Ibid.

68. Ibid.

69. Ibid., p. 495.

70. Ibid.

71. Cicero goes on to note that unlike Plato who thought that by changing the character of a nation's music he could reform the state, he believes this is effected by reforming the aristocracy. Cicero fails to note, however, that for Plato a reformed state is ultimately premised upon a reformed ruling class.

72. Cicero, "The Laws," p. 497.

73. Ibid., p. 505.

74. See Sabine and Smith's "Introduction," in *On the Commonwealth*, p. 88. This is the editors' view of Cicero's law on voting.

75. Cicero, "The Laws," p. 505.

76. See Sabine and Smith's "Introduction," in *On the Commonwealth*, pp. 83–93. The editor's views are more negative than our own. They see the preponderance of power in the senatorial class overwhelming the power of the people, and the tribuneship to be a repressive rather than a liberating agent of the commons. The reader must decide ultimately for him- or herself just how "imbalanced" Cicero's composite state really is. That the popular element of his ideal constitution is subordinated to the Senate and noble classes (the "optimates") is incontrovertible. How subordinate, and with what ultimate effect upon the people's liberties, is debatable.

77. Cicero, "The Laws," p. 493. Cicero says somewhat more about the education and training of the ideal statesman in Books IV and V of the *Commonwealth*, but much of this discussion has been lost.

78. See Hammond, *City-State and World State*, pp. 159–65. Hammond's thesis, which is our own, is that Cicero and the whole corpus of Greco-Roman political thought failed to transcend what he terms the "orthodox theory of the city-state" (i.e., the theory of the "mixed constitution") when confronting the reality of empire.

79. Black, *Political Thought in Europe 1250–1450*, p. 19.

80. A.A. Long, *Hellenistic Philosophy: Stoics, Epicureans, Sceptics*, 2nd. ed. (Berkeley: University of California Press, 1986), p. 230. While medieval scholars rated Cicero highly, modern scholars have been less enthusiastic, but as Long notes "we should judge Cicero by what he achieved and not what we should like him to have achieved."

5

St. Augustine

If the Greeks are known for philosophy, the Romans are known for law; and in the centuries following Cicero's death, Roman law went through its greatest period of development. It became a great civilizing agent, not only in Rome, but subsequently in the whole of the Western world. Fortunately in the sixth century A.D. Justinian, emperor of the Eastern Empire (the Roman Empire had long before been split into eastern and western branches), codified this law into what became known as the "Justinian code" (the *Corpus Iuris Civilis*), which was recovered in the West in the twelfth century. There it continued to be developed as a civilizing force and the source of medieval political thinking.

Justinian's codification was fortunate because in the fifth century A.D. the Western Empire, whose capital was Rome, collapsed under barbarian invasions. The greatness that was Rome ceased to be, forever, except in the imagination of later generations. In Western Europe the "dark ages" would last for centuries. The Eastern Empire, however, whose capital was Constantinople, continued to flourish and become the repository of classical learning. Much later in Western Europe this learning, including not only Roman law but, in the thirteenth century, classical Greek philosophy including political philosophy, would be recovered from the East.

If Roman law continued to flourish in the early centuries of empire, the same could not be said for political philosophy. As the Empire expanded and the emperors became increasingly autocratic, the tendency toward political withdrawal, so characteristic of the early Hellenistic philosophies of the Alexandrian period, reasserted itself. The Empire was simply too vast and the state too remote and arbitrary to allow for the development of creative political thinking. Law could develop slowly, piecemeal, and in the end leave a repository of embedded political philosophy such as the Stoic theory of natural law. Political philosophy, such as Plato's or Aristotle's or even Cicero's, must be produced whole, and this requires an entirely different political situation, one of at least minimal openness to political ideas.

We find in the political thought of the Roman Empire, therefore, little that was truly political. While the ancient Socratic search for virtue continued on the part of the surviving Hellenistic schools, it was a virtue largely devoid of political content. The domain of politics had become radically devalued, even for the Stoics who had made at least some attempt to create a political philosophy. And in this there was a real paradox, for Stoicism had become the dominant philosophy of the Roman ruling classes. The political class, such as it was, increasingly rejected politics as a source of moral virtue and human fulfillment.

This paradox can be seen perhaps most consistently in the Stoic philosopher Seneca (4 B.C.–A.D. 65), who had the misfortune to be advisor to the emperor and madman Nero until Nero had him executed. In Seneca we find this psychic withdrawal from politics in its most dramatic form. He is extremely pessimistic about politics and advocates a life of contemplation and inner virtue that seems at times almost otherworldly. Such views were not unique to Seneca, however. The *Meditations* of Marcus Aurelius, a noble Stoic and emperor of Rome from A.D. 161–180, is suffused with a melancholy world-weariness. Imagine the most powerful man in the world writing these lines:

> Leaves . . . are thy children, and leaves, too, are they who cry out as if they were worthy of credit; . . . and leaves, in like manner, are those who shall receive and transmit a man's fame to aftertimes. For all such things as these "are produced in the season of spring"; . . . then the wind casts them down; then the forest produces other leaves in their places. But a brief existence is common to all things, and yet thou avoidest and pursuest all things as if they would be eternal. A little time, and thou shalt close thy eyes; and him who has attended thee to thy grave another soon will lament.[1]

The self-same withdrawal to the point of otherworldliness can be noted in other key philosophies of the Roman Empire, most notably neo-Platonism. Founded by Plotinus (A.D. 205–270), neo-Platonism extended the Platonic dualism between the intelligible world of form and the sensory world of appearance. Plotinus's assertion that "as there are two worlds, the intelligible and the sense world, it is better for the soul to live in the intelligible world,"[2] is taken to the point of religious mysticism. Thus, the "sense world" of politics pales to insignificance. Plato had at least urged the philosopher to reenter the cave world of the senses and reform the state; Plotinus is concerned only with uniting the soul with the ultimate reality, what he called the "One," not with reforming this world, and certainly not politics.

Indeed, in Plotinus we find as much a religion as a philosophy. Seneca, too, often sounds as much religious as philosophical in his sentiments. And there was good reason for this. The political realities of empire had not only exhausted the optimism of classical thought in the efficacy of politics, it had produced a kind of hopelessness that philosophy alone could not assuage. People no longer wanted Socratic, Platonic, or Stoic virtue as an end in itself; they wanted salvation. Philosophy could give them this only to the extent that it became religious, but as it became religious it lost its connection to the classical ideal of philosophy as a purely rational and anthropocentric enterprise.

In fact, for the vast majority of people at least, it was religion, not philosophy, that came to offer the salvation craved. To be sure, people had always had religion, but the ancient pagan religions of Greece and Rome had been state religions, part of the political order that was now incapable of providing meaning, much less salvation. The traditional pagan gods were dying. The new religions, imported from the Hellenized East (yet another fateful consequence of Alexander's conquests), were outside the political order. There were any number of such religious sects, all promising salvation of one sort or another, but the one that came to dominate and, ultimately, to transform the whole of the Western world and Western consciousness was Christianity.

Christianity was not simply a new element in the ancient world that, like earlier philosophical schools of thought, could easily be absorbed into the classical tradition because, most obviously to the Roman elite at the time, it was not a state religion. Indeed, it was positively hostile to the state. It demanded from its adherents that their primary obligation be to God and the teachings of the Church, not the state. Such a conflict of church and state would have been unthinkable in the classical world because the two were never separate.

At a deeper level, however, the Christian doctrine itself, at least in its pure primitive form, was incompatible with classical thought and ideals. The belief that God had entered history and dwelt among human beings marked a radical rupture with all that had gone before. It required a complete rethinking of the meaning and purpose of existence. Certainly political philosophy ceased to be important any longer, much less so than it had been for the later Roman Stoics and even the neo-Platonists. The belief in the imminent second coming of Christ made philosophizing about this world senseless. This, coupled with the persecution of the Church by the state, made Christianity hostile to the whole political order and thus unsuitable for the development of theories about such a worldly activity as politics.

All this changed in A.D. 381, however, when, through an extraordinary series of events, emperor Theodosius I made Christianity the officially recognized religion of the Roman Empire, an event that would forever alter the course of Western history. By this time the second coming appeared much less imminent, and the state's adoption of Christianity made politics once again important. It appeared that the Church would be around for a long time and that the appropriate relationship between church and state would have to be established. Christians would have to become political philosophers.

We shall see in this and the next chapter how Christianity slowly developed its own unique political philosophy. Given its inherent otherworldly perspective, this was no easy task. Suffice it to say for now that classical thought, which was initially rejected, was finally grafted on to the body of Christian doctrine. Beginning with Platonic, Stoic, and neo-Platonic ideas, all of which with modification could be given a Christian content, and culminating in the thirteenth century with the recovery of Aristotle's works, Christianity evolved a distinct theory of politics. St. Augustine, while at best ambivalent about politics, and largely rejecting the ability of classical philosophy to understand and shape it, begins this process.

This is not to suggest that St. Augustine was the first Christian to write about politics, but he was the first genuinely important Christian political theorist. Even then, he was an unwilling theorist. He was too close to the otherworldly attitudes of early Christianity to take politics completely seriously. The need to define the appropriate roles of church and state, and to defend the Church from its pagan detractors, compelled St. Augustine to think and write about politics.[3] But he did not become a political philosopher because of any inherent interest in the subject matter.

St. Augustine's life (A.D. 354–430) spanned the period of Rome's decline. In his own lifetime he saw Rome sacked by the barbarians and in the process the whole of Western civilization threatened. Clearly, the old pagan political order was crumbling; but the new Christian order had yet to emerge. People who live in such chaotic and uncertain times as these are profoundly affected by them. Certainly this was the case for St. Augustine. His personality was dramatically shaped by the contradiction between the old pagan order and the emerging Christian order. He personally confronted this contradiction at every stage of his life. His mother (St. Monica) was a Christian, his father a pagan. When, as a young man, he was sent to Carthage for an education, he was trained in the pagan classics. When he later journeyed to Rome, he met and was counseled by some of the great Christian saints. And before his conversion to Christianity at the age of thirty-two, after which he renounced the pleasures of this world, he spent much of his life in "pagan excess."

Not surprisingly, St. Augustine came to embody the contradictions of the times. For some years before his conversion, moreover, St. Augustine belonged to a religious sect called the Manichaeans that further shaped his personality around these contradictions. The Manichaeans taught that the universe is divided into the contradictory yet autonomous and coequal principles of good and evil. Christianity itself emphasized the irreconcilability of good and evil, of course, but Christian thinkers could not accept that the forces of evil are coequal with those of goodness. While St. Augustine later came to accept the Christian view theologically, temperamentally he remained very much a Manichaean dualist. This was all the more the case given that his early training in the classics brought St. Augustine into contact with Platonic and neo-Platonic ideas. These helped give philosophical shape to his Christian faith. But neo-Platonism could only push St. Augustine further toward a kind of philosophical Manichaeism. Its distinction between the intelligible world of forms and the sensory world of appearances involved a dualism not unlike the Manichaean distinction between the forces of good and the forces of evil.[4]

This is the key to understanding St. Augustine: He is a dualistic thinker. For St. Augustine things are either black or white, good or evil; there is no in-between. The historical circumstances of his life, coupled with the early religious and philosophical influences that came to bear upon him, inexorably impelled him to think in these either-or terms. It is not surprising, then, that his political thought manifests a profound dualism, a fact that, as we shall see, explains both the weaknesses and strengths of his political philosophy.

That philosophy is most consistently developed in *The City of God,* St. Augustine's major political work. *The City of God* was written over a period of thirteen years while St. Augustine was Bishop of Hippo, a city in North Africa. (Following his conversion, St. Augustine joined the priesthood and rose to the office of bishop, which he held until his death.) It was begun following the sack of Rome by the Goths in 410 and was written in response to pagan apologists who claimed that the adoption of Christianity as the official state religion was the cause of Rome's downfall and advocated a return to paganism. Since the pagan critique of Christianity was in essence a political critique, St. Augustine was compelled to engage in a political analysis of what he believed to be the real nature of Roman institutions and the real cause of Rome's decline. His intent was not to write political philosophy for its own sake, but to defend Christianity. In the process, nevertheless, he evolved a distinctive political philosophy.

The basic structure of that philosophy is premised upon the doctrine of sin and salvation. Originally, says St. Augustine, God created human beings to live together in peace and harmony, but by Adam and Eve ". . . so great a sin was committed, that by it human nature was altered for the worse, and was transmitted also to their posterity."[5] This, of course, is the Christian doctrine of original sin, which teaches that humans are tainted by evil from the moment of birth. Christian doctrine also holds, however, that Christ died for humans' sins and offered them the possibility of salvation. In Augustine's view, this is interpreted to mean that salvation is the result of God's gift of grace, a gift not given to everyone. For this reason, St. Augustine insists that human beings are predestined to heaven or to hell. This is a harsh doctrine no longer accepted by the Catholic Church, but it did not seem harsh to St. Augustine. He believed sin to be so horrible that all deserve the torments of hell simply by being born. That some get to heaven seemed to St. Augustine proof of God's goodness and mercy.

Now this idea of sin deserves special note because it was a radically new departure in Western thought. The ancients were concerned with the problem of evil, but evil carried quite different connotations for them than it did for Christian thinkers such as St. Augustine. When the Greek philosophers spoke of evil (or virtue), they spoke in essentially secular terms. They accepted the great Sophist Protagoras's dictum that "man is the measure of all things." Evil and virtue were to be understood within a human context; they were to be measured against man himself. Virtue was praised, therefore, because it contributed to human happiness; evil disparaged because it contributed to unhappiness. But *sin* is not a secular term. It has a religious meaning, and it is rooted in the Judeo-Christian worldview in which God, not human beings, are the measure of all things. Thus, to sin is to violate God's laws; it is to revolt against the very order of the cosmos, not simply to manifest a human failing.[6] For this reason, the Christian notion of evil carries with it the connotation of depravity.

The Christian idea of evil contrasts with the ancient view in another way as well. The general consensus among ancient thinkers was that evil resulted from ignorance (Socrates and Plato) or a combination of ignorance, temperament, and upbringing (Aristotle). The point is that these thinkers understood evil to be a human problem resulting from human error. People would not behave evilly if they really understood, or had been trained to understand, the advantages of behaving virtuously. This reasoning lay behind Socrates' insistence that virtue is knowledge. But St. Augustine argues that the problem of evil is not simply the absence of knowledge or correct upbringing. It is, rather, a positive inclination to violate God's law. Human beings desire evil for evil's sake, he claims. Sin is thus doubly depraved for St. Augustine: It is not only a violation of God's law—it is an intentional violation.

To understand the intensity of his belief in the depravity of sin, it is helpful to turn to his *Confessions,* one of the most remarkable works of self-analysis in Western literature. In this great spiritual odyssey St. Augustine is intent on showing that he too is a sinner, that the indictment he throws at humanity applies equally to himself. He wants us to understand that only by the grace of God can we overcome our depravity, and he uses himself as the prime example of how degraded an evil life without God can be.

Poor St. Augustine, good man that he was, lacerates himself for the most trivial of faults. But they were not to his mind trivial because they were all violations of God's law. Certainly the most famous example in the *Confessions* of this tendency to see the darkest evil in what most would take to be mere peccadilloes is St. Augustine's agonized admission that as a small boy he stole some pears from a neighbor's tree. This he did, he informs us, not because he wanted the pears, but because "I loved my own perdition and my own faults, not the things for which I committed wrong, but wrong itself. . . . The evil in me was foul, but I loved it."[7] St. Augustine concludes this confession by noting that "even Catiline did not love crime for crime's sake."[8] (Catiline was an infamous Roman governor of Cicero's time.)

If most would find it difficult in this day and age to view such childhood pranks as a manifestation of evil, they would find it impossible to believe in the moral depravity of the newborn. Not St. Augustine:

> Who can recall to me the sins I committed as a baby: For in your [God's] sight no man is free from sin, not even a child who had lived only one day on earth. . . . What sins, then, did I commit when I was a baby? Was it a sin to cry when I wanted to feed at the breast? I am too old now to feed on mother's milk, but if I were to cry for the kind of food suited to my age, others would rightly laugh me to scorn and remonstrate with me. So then too I deserved a scolding for what I did.[9]

St. Augustine concludes this analysis by noting that "if babies are innocent, it is not for lack of will to do harm, but for lack of strength."[10]

One cannot imagine a more radical view of human evil than this. And while the reader may think that St. Augustine was a narrow puritanical sort who refused to see the good side of humanity, he was from all we know a kind and gentle person, and in his *Confessions* he writes a good deal about God's goodness and the power of love. But we stress his concept of sin because "sinful man" constitutes his psychological model or theory of human nature, a theory that has a direct bearing upon his political philosophy. Clearly, if humans are by nature evil, they will need to be controlled by coercive political institutions. If they were good then, conceivably, government might not be necessary at all. St. Augustine's psychology leaves him no choice but to advocate some form of coercive governmental control.

It is apparent that St. Augustine's political theory will make sense to the extent that his psychology is an accurate reflection of the way people really are. Unfortunately, it is not an easy matter to determine the validity of basic psychological assumptions. Thinkers disagree about human nature, which largely explains the variety of political theories. One has simply to judge for her- or himself whether or not St. Augustine's psychology is correct. Before making any judgment, however, we should put his psychology in its most acceptable light.

St. Augustine's psychology is much more plausible to the modern reader if it is translated into secular terms. We can eliminate its religious element (for instance, we can drop his concept of evil, his notion of original sin, and so on) and still retain his basic psychological insight. What we have then is simply a psychology that asserts an innate biological predisposition in human beings to maximize their own self-interest regardless of the interests or needs of others. This predisposition St. Augustine calls *lust,* again a term with religious connotations with which we can dispense. But we must give the idea behind the term serious consideration. That idea is that humans are innately egotistical and self-regarding; they think that the world centers upon them, existing for their pleasure alone.

This psychological theory has been predominant since the seventeenth century. (This is one reason why some scholars call St. Augustine the first "modern" political thinker.) Thomas Hobbes, one of the giants of modern political thought who will be discussed in the next section, adopts this theory. We might also mention Sigmund Freud with whom the reader will be more familiar. Freud claims that every individual is born with an instinctual sexual or pleasure drive he calls the *libido,* which is simply a secular version of St. Augustine's lust. For this reason, Freud agrees with St. Augustine that humans are born egotists, that they are self-centered, self-interested pleasure seekers. And this is why, like St. Augustine, Freud insists that not even infants are "innocent" and that it is only by society's imposition of rules of behavior on them that civilization becomes possible. Left to themselves, both St. Augustine and Freud agree, infants would all grow up as beasts of the jungle. In his *Civilization and Its Discontents,* therefore, Freud argues, as does St. Augustine in *The City of God,* that some form of social and political order is essential.

Seen in this light, what St. Augustine says in the *Confessions* is not as farfetched as it may have at first seemed. Stealing pears, for example, is not psychologically trivial. In terms of the motivational structure of the personality, it is no different from, say, robbing a bank. And this really is all St. Augustine is attempting to show—that people's motivations are innately lustful. The specific manner in which they express their lust, whether stealing pears or robbing banks does, of course, make a practical difference to society. But for the psychologist the differences of expression are secondary to the primacy of the motivation.

We must, then, take St. Augustine's psychology or theory of human nature seriously. We may disagree with it, but we cannot simply dismiss it because it is framed in a religious language not easily accepted by the modern mind. And if we do disagree, we must be sure that we are not being dishonest with ourselves. If it is unpleasant to think of one's fellows as selfish and egotistical, it is intolerable to think of oneself in these terms. For this reason, we have a tendency to mask our all-too-often selfish behavior in high-flown altruistic terms rather than face the hard facts about ourselves. St. Augustine, like Hobbes and Freud, refuses to hide the truth about himself or others; he is brutally honest.

Yet, given his religious system, St. Augustine's psychology clearly does differ from modern theories such as we find in Hobbes and Freud in one crucial respect. While he believes all human beings are born innately lustful or self-regarding, he also believes that some few are saved by the grace of God. These, says St. Augustine, are able to "overcome" the ravages of original sin and thus organize their lives around the principle of love rather than that of lust. Love, which is manifested first of all as love of God and then as love of one's fellow human beings, is the opposite of lust, says St. Augustine, because love is by definition "other-regarding."

Modern thinkers in the Augustinian tradition would not concede that human nature can be transformed by the mediation of God. They are all secular rather than religious theorists. Yet, even here, St. Augustine is not so far removed from modern assumptions, for he never suggests that some people are other than inherently self-interested and self-seeking. Even those who have been saved, and they are few indeed, may at any time fall from grace. In the final analysis, human beings never completely escape the ravages of their all-too-human nature according to St. Augustine. Man, the sinner, remains his psychological model.

Now it is this pessimistic view of humanity, coupled with his notion that some are saved, that makes the development of a political theory so perplexingly difficult. This difficulty is immediately apparent when St. Augustine shifts from psychological to political and sociological analysis. The following quotation from *The City of God* illustrates the problem:

> Two cities have been formed, . . . by two loves: the earthly by love of self, even to contempt of God; the heavenly by love of God, even to contempt of self. . . . In the one, the princes and the nations it subdues are ruled by the love of ruling; in the other, the princes and the subjects serve one another in love, the latter obeying, while the former take thought for all.[11]

This statement describes St. Augustine's "political sociology," which is simply the logical extension of his psychology. The two cities (not to be confused with the "two cities" of Stoicism although St. Augustine may have been influenced by that concept) is St. Augustine's metaphor for his two human types viewed at the social and political level. They are not real cities; they are sociopolitical concepts. The earthly city comprises all those whose souls are organized upon the principle of lust. The heavenly city, or the City of God, is "inhabited" by those few who have been saved by God's grace and whose souls, therefore, revolve around the love of God rather than around the love of self.[12]

The political problem for St. Augustine is twofold. The more serious problem is that the citizens of the earthly city are antisocial individualists. How then is any kind of social and political organization possible? How can the state exist? St. Augustine's brutally honest assessment of human beings seems to leave little for the political theorist to work with. The subsidiary problem is that the citizens of the heavenly city who, by the grace of God, have been made social beings (love is by definition social) must find some way to coexist with the citizens of the earthly city. But how? Let us first see how St. Augustine proposes to solve the problem of the saints, since his solution also resolves the larger problem of socializing the sinners.

The most obvious "solution" St. Augustine rejects outright. He tells us that God alone knows who belongs to which city. It is impossible, therefore, to physically separate the two types of humanity. The good people cannot go off by themselves to found the ideal republic envisioned by Plato. Saints and sinners will have to live together somehow. St. Augustine thus eschews any kind of utopianism. He believes the human condition is such that people of all types must find mechanisms for living together.

This antiutopianism is one mark of St. Augustine's realistic assessment of the nature of politics, and of his importance as a political theorist. It is an easy matter to argue that the solution to political problems lies in separating the "good" people from the "bad." Religious thinkers and political utopians have thus argued from time immemorial. They have advocated separating Christians from Moslems, political ideologues of one kind from those of another, true believers from the multitude of erring humanity. Behind many of the communitarian movements of the nineteenth and twentieth centuries has been this belief that separation is the answer to getting at least some people to live together in harmony and community.

But separatism is not a solution, as sophisticated political analysts such as St. Augustine recognize. Communitarian settlements historically have failed because they have been organized around political principles most people cannot accept. Eventually the saints die off, or leave, and few if any come to replace them. Besides, these saintly settlements can exist only within a larger political system that will protect them. Unless the state or its equivalent were there to control the sinners, they would destroy the cities of the saints in their drive to acquire more worldly goods.

Had St. Augustine advocated separatism, therefore, we would dismiss him as unworthy of serious study. He is, in part, an important political thinker because he refuses such easy "solutions." But what, then, is his solution? How is he to unite the saints and sinners, to reconcile the earthly with the heavenly city? It is apparent that he must find some commonly held value that all people can unite around regardless of the state of their souls or of their ideologies and political beliefs.

St. Augustine claims that peace is just such a value. Without peace, neither the lover of God nor the lover of self can organize his or her life appropriately to the ends sought. The saint requires peace to worship God, the sinner to enjoy worldly pleasures. Social disorder and chaos are desired by no one. The desire for peace, therefore, is a relative good, for it is the basis for a political reconciliation between the two cities. As such, it is the necessary precondition for civilized life and the existence of the state, according to St. Augustine.

Note that this analysis also solves the deeper problem of getting the mass of the sinful to live harmoniously with each other. The egotists, the self-centered, and the self-interested require peace among themselves in order to pursue their drive for worldly goods. If each and every person pursued his or her own individual interest without any political constraints, society would break down into chaos and civil war and the state would disintegrate, a condition in which no one could enjoy the goods of this world. This, St. Augustine argues, is why even the members of the earthly city desire peace among themselves and why, therefore, they will support the state.

St. Augustine's theory of the state ingeniously overcomes the dilemma inherent in his psychology and sociology. He turns the problem into the solution, for if self-interest is the source of social disorder, it is also the source of that desire for peace that makes the state possible.[13] But it is a theory that contrasts sharply with those of Plato and Aristotle. In St. Augustine's political theory people, most people at any rate, band together to form the state because it is in their self-interest, not because of any mutual respect and affection. His theory, in short, conceives the state as an artificial institution created to serve certain limited, and ultimately selfish, purposes. Although he is not always consistent in this matter, St. Augustine does not believe, as did the classical thinkers, that the state is a natural institution that is an organic part of people's lives.[14] Indeed, if all people were citizens of the heavenly city, the state would not be necessary.

The contrast here with classical theories of the state is dramatic. We know, for example, that Socrates, and later Plato and Aristotle, argued against the view held by Augustine in their dispute with the Sophists. So too did Cicero. The classical thinkers could not conceive of people existing apart from society and polity. Social and political institutions were seen as natural, as an organic part of human existence. Moreover, the classical thinkers, again contrary to the Sophists, assumed the state to be above all else a moral community organized to promote moral goodness.

Clearly, St. Augustine has a radically different perspective. If, as he maintains, the state is conventional, it is a community in name only since *community* refers to a natural form of human organization. A community is not merely an artificial set of arrangements between people. And it certainly cannot be a moral community. To say, as St. Augustine does, that humans create the state out of their own self-interest means that the state can exist only so long as it appeals to people's "sinful needs" rather than to any capacity for virtue that he denies most possess in any case.

The other key elements of St. Augustine's political philosophy also contradict classical views, for they are simply logical extensions of his theory of the state. For example, St. Augustine believes law also to be conventional, to be nothing more than artificial rules people create to serve the limited purpose of maintaining social order. Moreover, he argues, people obey law because it is in their self-interest to do so, not because they believe it is the morally correct thing to do. If people did not fear the possible consequences of breaking the law, says St. Augustine, they would break it with impunity. This is why he believes that the primary function of law is to engender fear since fear alone can appeal to people's self-interest. Given his psychological theory, it is inconceivable to St. Augustine that human beings, or at least the vast majority of them, would obey the law for altruistic reasons.

Here the contrast with classical thought and most clearly with Aristotle and Cicero is stark indeed. They had argued that because people cannot be fully human outside the state, by the same token they cannot live without law. To them, making and obeying law are part of people's telos. By legislating, they are compelled to think and speak about what is good for themselves and their community. And they do not obey law simply out of fear and self-interest but because they believe in the moral rightness of obeying and because they believe obedience will benefit the whole community.

But the contrast, with Aristotle in particular, is even more apparent in St. Augustine's view of political action, for St. Augustine does not consider political activity to be natural to people, nor does he believe that people, at least most people, engage in politics for any reason except promoting their own self-interest. They enter politics because of their lust for power, not, as Aristotle claimed because they wish to improve themselves morally.[15] Those who "are ruled by the love of ruling," as St. Augustine puts it, are sinners plain and simple. Politics makes them morally worse, not better. Moreover, he will have none of Aristotle's talk about politics as an arena of excellence. To his mind, the desire to excel is a form of pride, the deadliest of Christian sins.

How might we criticize such a dark and pessimistic theory of political life? It is clear from the foregoing discussion that our criticisms of St. Augustine are best made within the context of his rejection of classical thought. But it must be kept very clear precisely what it is that St. Augustine rejects. He does not deny the classical notion that virtue and happiness are our proper telos; what he denies is that this telos can be realized in this world. He believes that it can be attained only in heaven, and that the rewards of nobility and immortality that Aristotle claims attach to a virtuous life come from God, not human beings. St. Augustine makes heaven rather than the polis the source of human values and the real end to which people ought to direct their lives. In other words, St. Augustine displaces the classical vision more than he rejects it.[16] He wishes to direct people's ethical strivings away from this world and toward the next.

But the problem with St. Augustine's political theory lies precisely in this displacement because it separates ethics and politics into two distinct and irreconcilable categories. Ethics now has to do with otherworldly values, politics with the values of this world. There is no way in which the two can be reconciled; they contradict each other. The inevitable result is that the importance of political theory is radically denigrated. (Why waste time on a subject that does not, as the classical thinkers had thought, contribute to people's fulfillment and moral well-being?) For this reason, St. Augustine's political theory lacks that comprehensiveness that was part of the greatness of classical thought.

We note, for example, that in radically divorcing the ethical domain from the political, St. Augustine is left with little to say about the specifics of political organization. If the state is nothing more than a necessary evil, it does not really matter what form it takes. Tyranny, oligarchy, democracy—they are all the "same" in the sense that they are all variations on a worldly institution based upon worldly values. Given that the ethical realm is detached from the political, that worldly and otherworldly values are utterly incompatible, it is impossible to improve humans individually or collectively by altering the form of the constitution.[17]

We do not find in St. Augustine, therefore, a detailed discussion of the best forms of the state. There is no attempt to reconcile the best constitution with the best possible because there is no "best" or final good in this world for St. Augustine. This is why in *The City of God* he says (and this would have astounded classical thinkers such as Aristotle and Cicero) "as far as this life of mortals is concerned, which is spent and ended in a few days, what does it matter under whose government a dying man lives."[18]

This same lack of comprehensiveness affects the rest of St. Augustine's political theory, and for the same reason. For example, while he recognizes the necessity of lawmaking and of political activity, he denies any real ethical content to them. He thereby diminishes the status that once accrued to citizenship: to making and obeying laws. By portraying political participation as lust for power and glory, St. Augustine debases an activity that had the greatest significance for the major classical thinkers. He does not deny that the Christian has civic duties, of course, but he does not glorify citizenship as Aristotle had done. Beyond insisting that people must obey political authorities regardless of the quality of their rule, he says little. Indeed, St. Augustine's view of authority is thoroughly paternalistic and authoritarian. He does agree that the subject must not obey if commanded to commit a sinful act; but if as a matter of conscience disobedience is required, it must be a purely passive disobedience says St. Augustine.

Ultimately, St. Augustine possesses this view of authority because he believes that all authority, including that of the state, is derived from God, not, as in modern political thinking, from the people. Such a view constitutes what is called the *theocratic* theory of the state. Since the authority of the state, and of those who rule it, is derived from God, it is an absolute authority limited only by God-given ethical rules such as natural law or divine revelation. It is the ruler alone, however, who determines whether or not these precepts will be honored. As a consequence, the theocratic ruler's powers are quite absolute, the "citizen's" nonexistent. Indeed, in theocratic theory the "citizen" is properly speaking not really a citizen at all, either in the modern sense of being the repository of certain rights or in the classical sense of being an active participant in the political community, but is merely a passive subject.

It is important to emphasize that St. Augustine's theocratic theory applies to all states regardless of whether the rulers are Christian or atheist, good or evil, benevolent or tyrannical. St. Augustine is not suggesting that the theory is valid only for "Christian" states ruled by true defenders of the faith, likely a rare occurrence in any case given his pessimistic view of politics. To be sure, this was his ideal, partly realized in the Roman state of his day and very incompletely realized in the Holy Roman Empire of the later medieval period, but it was not a requirement. Even tyrants derived their authority from God, and it was therefore as absolute and legitimate as the authority of the ideal Christian ruler. The good Christian, therefore, must submit even to the yoke of a tyrant, refusing to obey only immoral commands and suffering the consequences of that disobedience, never attacking the state or the right of the ruler to rule.

St. Augustine's theocratic theory does not contradict his view that the state is the consequence of human sinfulness and a convention created for pragmatic political reasons to preserve peace. It simply asserts that once created the state's authority ultimately is legitimate because it is sanctioned by God. As a consequence, whatever the actual political reasons for the state's formation or the quality of its rulership, however sordid these typically may be, its authority remains God given.

St. Augustine's theocratic views became accepted Christian doctrine throughout most of the medieval period. In the later middle ages modifications began to occur as conflict between Church, Empire, and various secular authorities over respective roles of church and state increased. Toward the end of the medieval period St. Thomas Aquinas softened St. Augustine's extreme theocratic perspective, as we shall see in the next chapter. But St. Augustine remained adamant in his theocratic views and, consequently, in his authoritarian and paternalistic concept of authority that reduces the classical citizen to the status of a mere subject.

Clearly, St. Augustine's theocratic views will not appeal to the civil libertarian or to anyone who thinks that people ought to change the government if it does not rule properly, or overthrow the state if it is dictatorial. But those who think along these lines take politics quite differently than St. Augustine. They assume that politics is directly connected to people's moral well-being and that this world is really important. But St. Augustine does not, and that is the point. He wants people to direct their attention to God and away from the life of the city. The form of government, and how the leaders rule, is utterly irrelevant to those who seek salvation. They must be obedient but beyond this they must not go. In fact, St. Augustine even suggests that passively submitting to an evil regime may be beneficial to the saint in that the suffering experienced will help to prepare the soul for eternal life.

The ultimate problem with St. Augustine's political philosophy may be traced back to that dualism of good and evil that is so characteristic of his thought. It is reflected throughout *The City of God* at the psychological, sociological, and political levels. Lust versus love, earthly city versus heavenly city, politics versus ethics—all are versions of the same extreme distinction between good and evil. And just as good and evil can never be reconciled for St. Augustine, neither can ethics and politics. He does not try to reconcile them. His general lack of concern about politics and the poverty of detail in his political theory inevitably follow.

It should not be thought, because of its position on the irreconcilability of good and evil, that the Christian church imposes upon its political philosophers the extreme dualism we find in St. Augustine. It must be remembered that St. Augustine was heavily influenced by the Manichaeans, and that he lived at a time when Christianity's ecstatic otherworldly attitudes were still intense. Most important, he lived amid the ruins of the old order, and he was compelled to answer those who blamed Christianity for the demise of the Roman Empire. As we shall see in a moment, his political theory with its sharp dualisms served to defend Christianity from its detractors. The defensive position that St. Augustine found himself in contributed, therefore, to the theoretical inadequacies we have just discussed. Later, when these circumstances no longer existed, Christian thinkers would attempt to reconcile St. Augustine's two cities.

But here is the great paradox of St. Augustine's political theory—its weaknesses are at the same time its strengths. To begin with, note that while St. Augustine's dualism deprecates the importance of politics and political theory, it is a dualism predicated upon a psychological theory that cannot be entirely dismissed. If people really are as St. Augustine describes them, then clearly politics cannot aid them in realizing a moral end. Politics and ethics are indeed irreconcilable if humans are innately self-interested and antisocial. Hence, if St. Augustine's political theory is in some senses impoverished, it is so because the human condition itself is impoverished. His weaknesses as a political theorist, then, are a mark of his realistic assessment of the limitations of politics.

It is also a mark of his realism, moreover, that he does not take these limitations to mean that human beings can do nothing to improve their collective lives. He avoids both cynicism and utopianism. Rather, he takes what is worst in humanity (where the ancients took what is best) and shows how it can be used for a political good. Recall that St. Augustine turns the problem of human nature into a political solution. He realizes that the values of the earthly city can be turned against it for socially useful purposes. Sin can be used to control the consequences of sin. (This idea stripped of its religious connotations, like his psychology, prefigures much modern thought.) Where the state and indeed civilization itself would appear a hopeless ideal given people's antisocial tendencies, St. Augustine shows that these very tendencies can be employed to create social and political order. This is precisely the logic behind his theory of law.[19] St. Augustine shows that where law inculcates fear, people's natural self-interest will impel them to obey despite their inclinations to disobey. By the same token, St. Augustine shows how the love of power can be turned to socially beneficial purposes. If people did not desire power the state could not exist nor, therefore, could law. The lust for power ensures that the offices of state will be filled and that laws will be legislated.

St. Augustine's dualism contributes to his political theory in another important way. In drawing a sharp distinction between ethics and politics, he is able to strip away the front of respectability that hides the often brutal and vicious facts of political life. As such, his political philosophy contributes to a consistently honest and realistic assessment of politics. We can best see this dimension of his political thought in his response to the pagan critics of Christianity. Remember that *The City of God* was written with the specific purpose of defending the faith from its pagan detractors.

St. Augustine's argument, in its essentials, is that the pagan critics wrongly blame Christianity for Rome's decline. They fail to understand that decline has befallen every other earthly kingdom in the past, as it will befall those in the future. This world has a principle of decay structured into it. All that exists will eventually perish, whether it be an individual or a state. Death is the price paid for Adam's original sin. Only in the heavenly city can we find eternal life.

And, Augustine continues, as pagan thinkers fail to grasp the inherent instability of history, so do they fail to read their past history accurately. They see in Rome's decline the loss of a civilization that they believe had embodied the noblest aspirations of humanity. Rome had been great, they think, because its laws and institutions were the greatest ever created by humankind. In short, they believe Rome to have been the very embodiment of justice. But was Rome ever just? Not if we look at the facts, says St. Augustine. "Away with deceitful masks, with deluding whitewashes," he says, "look at the naked deeds: Weigh them naked, judge them naked!"[20]

St. Augustine strips away all the pretentious claims of Rome's defenders. He shows, in case after case, how Rome has abused its power; how it has fought unjust wars, subdued its provinces by force, and employed violence against innocent people. He notes the war of one class against the other that has marked Rome's history and shows how the power of the state was consistently used by one group to suppress another. He takes us back to the so-called golden age of the Republic, before Rome had become an empire, and shows, contrary to Cicero, that even then Rome was unjust. The great and noble leaders of the Republic, he argues, were in reality men who lusted after fame and glory. Their concern for the public good was a cover for their pride and vanity.

St. Augustine's exposé of Rome applies to all states, which he says, are without justice because justice, except in the most imperfect sense, cannot exist on this earth, and as he notes "without justice, what are kingdoms but great robberies?"[21] To emphasize his point he recounts the story in Cicero's *Commonwealth* of a pirate who was captured by Alexander the Great. When Alexander asked the man to justify his piracy, he responded "what thou meanest by seizing the whole earth; but because I do it with a petty ship, I am called a robber, whilst thou who dost it with a great fleet are styled emperor."[22]

And how would our own political institutions stand up to an Augustinian analysis? Is the United States just? Has it ever been just? Let us recall St. Augustine's admonition to Rome's pagan patriots: "Look at the naked deeds: Weigh them naked, judge them naked!"

How shall we judge the settling of this country? Under the policy of manifest destiny our forefathers, with the aid and succor of their government, almost exterminated a whole people. Ask Native Americans about American justice. What shall we say about slavery, a practice once protected by the Constitution and condoned by the most respectable and "God-fearing" pillars of American society? And how should we view our domestic politics today? Is the public weal the first consideration of our political leaders, or do they represent special interests contrary to the public good? Do our politicians enter the public realm because, as they always insist during campaigns, they care deeply about America and its future? Or do they enter to increase their status, extend their power, and frequently to make personal financial gain at the expense of the public treasury? Do our politicians use their public trust ethically, or do they engage in unethical behavior more frequently than we might care to admit?

You can see how devastating an Augustinian analysis of politics can be. And its effectiveness is due to St. Augustine's dualism, to his theory of the two cities. By displacing the classical vision, by making virtue an other-worldly value, St. Augustine is free, so to speak, to look for the worst in this world. His theory of politics tells him that political justice is impossible, that politics is an arena of corruption, that self-interest is the driving force behind political activity. It is therefore to injustice, corruption, and self-interest that he looks.

St. Augustine's method of analysis has come to be known as the theory of *realpolitik*. It is a theory that eschews all sentimentality. It comprehends politics as nothing more than a struggle for power, domestically and internationally. It denies the unity of ethics and politics and the idea that the state is a moral community.

St. Augustine does not suggest that politics should be this way, of course; he simply says that it *is* this way. Realpolitik is a fact, not a goal. And terrible as this fact may be, St. Augustine at least holds out the promise of moral fulfillment and human happiness in a world to come for members of the heavenly city—for those who refuse citizenship in the kingdoms of this world.

It would be a serious mistake to think that St. Augustine's political theory has become outmoded. Great ideas transcend historical time and become part of the wisdom of the ages. We no longer care about the specific historical circumstances that impelled St. Augustine to write *The City of God.* Paganism, the decline of Rome, the politics of the church in the fifth century, these are all issues that no longer concern us. But what does remain important for us is the general theory of politics that St. Augustine developed in response to these issues. In focusing on the hidden underside of humanity and its politics, St. Augustine bequeathed to us a dark and timeless vision. Those who have read *The City of God* can never again look at their own political institutions, their own leaders, or themselves without "judging naked" that which they would rather not see.

Notes

1. Marcus Aurelius, "Meditations," in Whitney J. Oates, ed., *The Stoic and Epicurean Philosophers* (New York: The Modern Library, 1940), p. 569.

2. Plotinus, *Enneads* IV, viii, in Joseph Katz, ed., *The Philosophy of Plotinus* (New York: Appleton Century Crofts, 1950) p. 111.

3. St. Augustine had no interest in elaborating a consistent theory of church-state relations however [see John Neville Figgis, *The Political Aspects of St. Augustine's 'City of God'* (Gloucester: Peter Smith, 1963), p. 54]. Later in the medieval period, the relationship of church to state would become the dominant theoretical issue.

4. See R.L. Ottley, *Studies in the Confessions of St. Augustine* (London: Robert Scott, 1919), pp. 44–64 (chapter 33) for a discussion of the impact of Manichaean dualism and neo-Platonism on Augustine's thought.

5. St. Augustine, *City of God,* Marcus Dods, D.D., trans. (New York: Random House, 1950), p. 441.

6. See Marion Le Roy Burton, *The Problem of Evil: A Criticism of the Augustinian Point of View* (Chicago: The Open Court Publishing Company, 1909), p. 216: "Sin becomes an attempt to destroy the essential unity of the universe."

7. St. Augustine, *Confessions,* R.S. Pine-Coffin, trans. (Baltimore: Penguin Books, 1961), p. 47.

8. Ibid., p. 49.

9. Ibid., p. 27.

10. Ibid., p. 28.

11. St. Augustine, *City of God,* p. 477.

12. It is important to bear in mind that the "two cities" is a metaphor for two human types and is not to be confused with any existing institutions. Such confusion was common in the later medieval period when the Church was frequently identified with the "city of God," an identification that St. Augustine never made. For St. Augustine there are members of the Church who belong to the "earthly city," just as there are those who play important roles within the state and other secular institutions who are members of the "heavenly city." The most that can be said in this regard is that the Church, as an institution, represents the values of the city of God, the State those of the earthly city.

13. See Herbert A. Deane, *The Political and Social Ideas of St. Augustine* (New York: Columbia University Press, 1963), p. 141: "The very sin of loving earthly goods thus supplies, to some extent, its own corrective and remedy." More than any other student of St. Augustine, Deane has shown how St. Augustine turns the problem (humankind's "sinful nature") into the solution (the consequent desire for social and political order). This analysis Deane applies not only to St. Augustine's conception of the state, but also to his theory of law and of political relationships generally. As will become apparent, Deane's analysis helps to explain the reason for, and the power of, St. Augustine's "political realism."

14. A distinction must be made here between state and society. St. Augustine follows the accepted Christian view that society is natural because human beings are by nature social creatures. The state, however, he interprets as a purely conventional institution necessary only because of humanity's fallen nature. Here, too, he follows the accepted Christian point of view, but he does so in a way that, contrary to the perspective of primitive Christianity, not only justifies the existence of the state, but that demonstrates its value to the Christian community.

15. St. Augustine does not deny that good Christians may, and do, engage in politics. It is clear, however, that he considers these to be a distinct minority, and that he rejects the classical view that political activity is a source of moral growth.

16. Deane, *Political and Social Ideas of St. Augustine,* pp. 11–12.

17. See R.A. Markus, *Saeculum: History and Society in the Theology of St. Augustine* (Cambridge: Cambridge University Press, 1970), p. 64: "In his image of the heavenly city Augustine had sketched the outline of the ideal form of human society. . . . What need was there to expound the precise status of the many imperfect forms of human association which, in all their variety, inevitably failed to measure up to this ideal? In this sense a 'political theory' . . . comparable with Aristotle's discussion of actual states . . . is absent from Augustine's work."

18. St. Augustine, *City of God*, p. 166.

19. Deane, *Political and Social Ideas of St. Augustine*, p. 222.

20. St. Augustine, *City of God*, p. 86.

21. Ibid., p. 112.

22. Ibid., p. 113.

6

St. Thomas Aquinas

St. Thomas Aquinas is generally recognized as the greatest thinker Catholicism ever produced. His philosophy is still influential in the Catholic Church. That St. Thomas attained such stature is not only a tribute to the quality of his mind but is also a measure of how successfully his philosophy met the needs of the Church in the late medieval period.

St. Thomas (1225–1274) was born into a noble family, dedicated himself to a religious life at an extremely young age, and eventually entered the Dominican Order. He received his advanced education at the University of Naples and, later, at the University of Paris where he studied theology. At Paris he became the student of Albert the Great, one of the greatest scholars of Aristotle in the Western world. Albert molded St. Thomas's whole intellectual life and thereby changed the course of medieval philosophy. For St. Thomas did no less than carry out a revolution in medieval thought; he integrated Aristotle's philosophy into the corpus of Christian faith.

But St. Thomas's grand synthesis of classical and Christian thought did not occur in a vacuum. Changes had occurred in medieval society that made this synthesis possible. The Church, to begin with, had changed radically since St. Augustine's time. It had become the central political and administrative institution of medieval society, and the spiritual, intellectual, and cultural center of the Western world. Yet, at the same time, new institutions were emerging that challenged the Church's supremacy. One of these new institutions was the university, which played such a crucial role in St. Thomas's intellectual development. Others, such as independent towns, craftsmen's guilds, and various other associations were also beginning to grow and to assert their autonomy. And the most important institution of all, the modern nation-state, which would eventually destroy the Church's political supremacy, was just beginning to emerge in outline form.

A kind of medieval populism, therefore, began to appear in the thirteenth century, and demands for self-governance and political participation began to be heard. People began to believe, although still quite inchoately, that government should in some sense originate with them. Thus, the theocratic top-down model of government that had been accepted by the Church since St. Augustine was beginning to be challenged by a more democratic conception of government.[1]

But perhaps the most important change, certainly in terms of political theory, was the recovery of Aristotle in the thirteenth century. This came by way of the Arab East, which, following the collapse of the Roman Empire, had become the repository of classical culture and learning. Throughout the early middle ages, up until the time of this recovery, what was known of Aristotle and of much classical thought was available only secondhand in works by other thinkers such as Cicero and St. Augustine. With the revival of Aristotelian studies, based now on firsthand knowledge of his works, there occurred a rebirth of Western consciousness that transformed medieval thought and laid the foundations of the modern world as we know it. And herein lies a paradox, for while Aristotle provided Christian thinkers with an intellectual system capable of dealing with the new social realities, his essentially secular philosophy would eventually be used to attack the spiritual supremacy of the Church. The leaders of the Church initially sensed the potential danger of Aristotelianism, and for a time they resisted its influence.[2] But so powerful were Aristotle's ideas, and so well suited to the emerging populism of the late medieval world, there was no holding them back.

Aristotle's thought fit well with this new populism because it legitimized the entire realm of politics as something natural to human beings and necessary to their complete development. Aristotle's defense of the small city-state and of citizenship was a ringing affirmation of the importance of the community and of self-governance. For these reasons, the adoption by St. Thomas of Aristotle's political science put the Church in step with the new social realities.

To be sure, even before Aristotle was recovered, changing social and political realities were compelling some modification of the more extreme Augustinian theocratic views. In the twelfth century John of Salisbury, the most important political thinker of his time, contemplated in his *Politicraticus* the possibility (under only the most extreme of circumstances) of tyrannicide. A major problem with the Christian theocratic model, as we noted in the last chapter, was that it allowed no way to constrain the ruler who violated divine and natural law. John's admission that extreme action must sometimes be allowed was one mark of a changing political consciousness.

Nevertheless, this was as far as John was willing to go. In other respects he conformed to the traditional theocratic view, and his whole mode of political reasoning was thoroughly informed by the Augustinian model. He followed the Church's emphasis upon its ultimate supremacy, patriarchical authority, and a rigid hierarchical ordering of social groups that, in a famous organic metaphor, John likened to a human body in which the ruler is the head and the peasants the feet.[3] Society was beginning to open up, but clearly not yet to the extent it did in St. Thomas's time, nor were Aristotelian ideas yet available to point to new political possibilities inherent in a more open social order. With these ideas, St. Thomas was equipped to stretch the boundaries of medieval political thought much further than John or earlier thinkers ever could.

St. Thomas's political theory closely parallels Aristotle's. In his most methodical political work, *On Kingship,* St. Thomas largely follows the *Politics.* He argues that the state is natural because "it is natural for man . . . to be a social and political animal, to live in a group."[4] Consequently, he insists that political activity is both necessary and good. Further, like Aristotle, St. Thomas roots people's political nature in their capacity to reason and to speak. And, like Aristotle, he argues that it is through reasoned action in the political sphere that we attain virtue and, therefore, happiness and fulfillment.

Like Aristotle, therefore, St. Thomas believes that the state is a moral community that has as its end the moral good of its members. Hence, St. Thomas argues that the state should be based upon justice, that the best should rule for the public good under the constraint of law. This leads directly to the problem of classifying constitutions and, again, St. Thomas follows Aristotle in using both quantitative and qualitative criteria. He classifies constitutions by the number of rulers and the quality of their rule.

St. Thomas also agrees generally, but not completely, with Aristotle on the best and best possible constitutions. While he agrees with Aristotle that monarchy is best, for example, his reasons are not strictly identical to Aristotle's. St. Thomas argues that since the universe is governed monarchically by God, we have a clear model of what is the best form of political rule. This is a uniquely Christian perspective that would have been quite alien to an essentially secular thinker like Aristotle. But St. Thomas is careful not to push his divine analogy too far. He understands that political rule is not strictly identical to heavenly rule. As an Aristotelian, St. Thomas knows that politics has its own worldly logic and dynamics, and that supernatural analogies cannot be carried too far. For this reason, he also defends monarchy on strictly secular grounds (as he does the mixed regime, which, again like Aristotle, he considers to be the best possible form of state).

St. Thomas also adopts Aristotle's larger philosophical system, which explains the similarities between *On Kingship* and the *Politics*. He agrees that form is immanent and that matter actualizes itself as it moves from potentiality to its completeness or perfection. Like Aristotle, St. Thomas is a teleologist; he conceives of the state as the highest end of people's social life, as the ultimate form or actualization of their communal existence. But there is this crucially important difference: St. Thomas grounds his teleology in a larger system that includes the spiritual dimension of human existence. He infuses Aristotle's teleological naturalism with a Christian spiritualism. Thus, he is able in good Christian conscience to adopt Aristotle's political theory and at the same time, as we shall see, to overcome that Augustinian dualism that would relegate people's political life to the world of sin, error, and confusion. This was of particular importance in St. Thomas's time, for in transcending Augustinianism he was able to work out not only the concrete political problem of how to establish the appropriate relationship of church and state, but the larger issue of how people's natural capacities could be made compatible with their spiritual destiny.

Let us take this larger issue first. St. Thomas's argument is that while human beings are at one level a part of nature, at another level they transcend nature. Within humankind nature and spirit are fused. Hence, St. Thomas argues, people's teleological development toward their end as natural beings cannot be conceived entirely apart from their development as spiritual beings. But, of course, it is not sufficient simply to assert that people are both natural and spiritual beings. St. Augustine admitted this much, yet he still perceived politics as an evil. What St. Thomas must further show is that people's natural and spiritual activities, while distinct, are yet joined in some higher unity. He must show that the natural and the supernatural are in some way united within humankind itself.[5]

The link between natural and supernatural, he argues, is reason. Of course, the ancients, the Stoics, and numerous other Western thinkers had argued that reason is the distinguishing characteristic of human beings, that it is this capacity that raises them above the beasts. In fact, so prevalent is this focus on reason that we should say it is the defining characteristic of Western philosophy. But St. Thomas gives reason a genuine spiritual content. He argues that reason raises humankind not only above the biological realm, as Aristotle had asserted, but above nature itself. According to St. Thomas, reason unites human beings directly with God. His argument for this thesis is contained in his theory of law, particularly in his theory of natural law, as developed in his greatest work, *Summa Theologica*.

The *Summa* establishes the existence of four levels of law, each distinct, yet each bound to the others in an underlying unity. This unifying agent is reason, for the defining characteristic of law for St. Thomas (as it had been for Aristotle) is that it is a rule based upon reason. What differentiates one form of law from another is simply the level of reason involved.

The highest and most comprehensive law, says St. Thomas, is eternal law, which is the divine reason operative in the universe as a whole. It is the natural and ethical order of things established by God. Next in order of importance is divine law. This is really a special category of eternal law; it is the revealed word of God in Scripture. But it is the next level—natural law—that is of decisive importance in understanding St. Thomas's expanded vision of human reason. (The final, and lowest level of law—human or civil law—we will discuss shortly.)

The idea of natural law, recall, goes back to the Stoics (St. Thomas is considered the greatest natural law theorist since the Stoics) and refers to moral law that is discovered by means of reason alone. It presumes that people have the capacity to use reason to arrive at certain ethical conclusions that ought to be binding upon them, whether codified in law or not. We do not need a criminal code to know that murder is wrong and to behave accordingly, for example.

What makes St. Thomas's theory of natural law unique, however, is that it establishes a link between the natural and the supernatural, between nature and spirit. Since right and wrong are determined by God's eternal law, "it is therefore evident," says St. Thomas, "that the natural law is nothing else than the rational creature's participation of the eternal law."[6] People's moral reason (natural law), in short, is an extension of a spiritual principle that transcends nature. Thus, when people follow the dictates of reason in their social and political relationships with others, their behavior involves both a natural and a spiritual dimension.

The political implications of St. Thomas's connecting nature and spirit in this way are far reaching. It allows him to argue not only that human law (what the Stoics called the "law of the city") is legitimate to the extent that it accords with the dictates of moral reason, but that to this same extent human law may be seen as a reflection of the ultimate justice of God's eternal law. Civil law is thus attributed an even greater importance in spiritual terms than it had previously enjoyed.

Most important, this link between nature and spirit made politics, from a Christian perspective, an important and worthy endeavor. For in St. Thomas's analysis, politics is something more than simply an activity natural to human beings as Aristotle had thought; it is something that is not entirely unrelated to people's spiritual welfare. This is why St. Thomas can argue that not only is politics compatible with human spirituality, but that it is conducive to it.[7] Being a good citizen now becomes part of being a good Christian. With this reasoning in mind, politics once again became an important activity, important in a way it had not been since classical times. So too, of course, did political theory. Certainly St. Augustine's question, "What does it matter under whose government a dying man lives?," would no longer be raised.

It is apparent that the real difference here between St. Thomas and St. Augustine lies in the realm of psychology. The defining characteristic of human beings for St. Augustine is sin. So ingrained is human evilness, so degraded are all human beings by Adam's original sin, that St. Augustine believes reason is powerless to raise people out of their natural condition. Indeed, he believes that human nature is so corrupt that people will use their reason for evil purposes.

St. Thomas cannot agree. He believes reason, not sin, to be the defining characteristic of humankind. To be sure, St. Thomas does not deny people's sinfulness. He is, after all, a Christian. But he does not believe that the capacity for evil is the full story of human nature.[8] People may sin, but they may choose not to, and reason aids them in directing their lives toward virtue and goodness. After all, St. Thomas might say, God has implanted reason in humankind; to reject its efficacy is to doubt the power of God's divine reason within us.

The practical effect of this expanded vision of reason was enormous. By linking reason to a larger spiritual dimension, that is, by uniting nature and spirit, St. Thomas was able, with a good Christian conscience, to apply Aristotle's political theory to the conditions of late medieval life. In this way, he found a means to defend the existence of the state and those subordinate associations that were beginning to demand autonomy. But while St. Thomas demonstrated the existence of an ultimate harmony between the natural and the supernatural, he nevertheless maintained that the supernatural dimension of human existence is higher than the natural—that spirit is superior to nature. While reason transforms natural activities such as politics into something higher or more important than Aristotle had supposed, reason in and of itself cannot attain the highest level of spiritual existence, says St. Thomas. Reason allows people to participate in the divine wisdom, it does not make them coequal with God.

Thus, St. Thomas was also able to defend the ultimate superiority of the Church—the sine qua non at that time for any political theory that expected a chance of being heard. The Church, after all, was a supernatural good: the repository of the faith and the spiritual center of medieval life. St. Thomas insists that on ultimate questions of moral and spiritual import the Church should be supreme. But at the same time, he argues, the state has its own legitimate realm of activity with which the Church need not interfere. The sacred and the secular each has its appropriate sphere, and each is sanctioned by the divine intelligence.[9]

St. Thomas applied this same logic to all of people's natural and spiritual activities, claiming that each had its proper and legitimate sphere. He shows, for example, that while faith is superior to reason, nevertheless reason is a legitimate and necessary corollary to faith. This was an important advance in medieval thought, for it must be remembered that much in the Christian tradition was hostile to reason. After all, the original sin had been to eat of the tree of knowledge, before which humanity had been innately good and innocent. This is why St. Augustine, who was the shaping influence on medieval thought until St. Thomas, distrusted reason. He argued that the emphasis upon reason led some prideful thinkers to suppose they could know as much as God. This Augustinian attitude persisted throughout the medieval period and led to much debate over the respective roles of theology (faith) and philosophy (reason). Some argued that faith was sufficient to the Christian believer; others insisted that reason was also necessary, that the truths of faith could, and should, be supported by philosophical proofs.

St. Thomas demonstrates that while faith is superior to reason (theology is superior to philosophy), each is an autonomous good ultimately linked with the other in a higher unity. Those who believed in the power of reason to explain all matters of faith were in error, but so too were those who utterly denigrated reason. Those who held up either of these judgments failed to see both the necessary distinction between faith and reason, and their ultimate harmony and unity.[10] But this failure was simply one part of a larger misunderstanding in which the appropriate relationship between the natural and the supernatural was misperceived.

In the broadest terms, St. Thomas once and for all liberated medieval thought from St. Augustine's metaphor of the two cities, not simply in terms of the dualism between church and state, but in terms of that larger dichotomy between people's spiritual and natural capacities. Politics, philosophy, science—the earthly city and all its activities—were incorporated by St. Thomas into a larger Christian framework.[11] The Christian needed no longer to reject this world in order to be saved, nor did the political thinker need to look to heaven for a political philosophy. It was only necessary to give formal recognition to the principle that spiritual values are higher than political values. Once this was done, the theorist was free to analyze politics from a secular point of view. This is why St. Thomas's defense of monarchy, while it involves a nonsecular analogy (God rules monarchically) employs a strictly secular argument at the same time.

We might say, therefore, that just as Aristotle freed political thought from Platonism, St. Thomas freed it from the constraints of Augustinianism. In uniting St. Augustine's two cities, St. Thomas performed the same task for the medieval political theorist that Aristotle had done for the classical thinker when he united Plato's "intelligible world of form" with the "sensory world of appearances." He made politics an important subject matter and freed the theorist from the spell of the ideal sufficiently to allow a comprehensive analysis of the "real world" of politics.

The advantages of St. Thomas's political theory were clear. It fit the conditions of late medieval life and opened new possibilities for the political thinker. But herein also lay a problem. St. Thomas's political theory is, as we have seen, an extension of philosophical principles that go beyond politics. Thomism is a combination of Christian spiritualism with Aristotelian naturalism. More than this, it is a synthesis of Christianity with the major trends of classical thought since Socrates. It is, as such, a grand and harmonious union of nature and spirit, sacred and secular, ethical and political. But the synthesis is essentially artificial. There was nothing to prevent the theorist from eliminating the Christian element and returning to a purely secular Aristotelianism once the power of the Church began to be challenged. Only so long as the state was constrained by the Church, only so long as the Church was perceived as a viable and necessary part of the medieval political order, would a political theory that united the sacred and the secular make sense.

Thus, the assault upon St. Thomas's philosophical system began almost as soon as it had triumphed over other modes of medieval thought. At first, political thinkers attacked the Church's political supremacy by interpreting Aristotle from a strictly secular point of view. They justified the supremacy of the state as the highest political community to which people may belong, and attacked the Church as an interference in the natural order of things.[12] But later the attacks became even more radical. Eventually Aristotelianism itself was rejected for reasons we will discuss in the next chapter. When this happened, the key theoretical assumption of ancient and medieval thought, that ethics and politics constitute an organic unity, no longer held.

CLASSICAL AND MEDIEVAL POLITICAL THEORY: A TRADITION OF DISCOURSE

St. Thomas's synthesis of classical and Christian thought indicates that throughout this section we have been discussing political philosophies that share in a common tradition of discourse. It was precisely because the major political theories of the classical and medieval periods shared certain assumptions in common that St. Thomas could combine them in one grand vision.

The essential element in that tradition of discourse is the presumed unity of ethics and politics. This presumption constitutes the defining characteristic of political thought from Socrates to St. Thomas and explains why all of the major classical and medieval political thinkers assumed politics to be an activity aimed at creating the conditions for an ethical and, therefore, a happy and fulfilled life. It was because of this underlying assumption, moreover, that they all believed political science to be the study of how people can best approximate within their collective lives the conditions of moral fulfillment. Political science was conceived, above all else, as a moral science.

To be sure, the early Hellenistic philosophies such as Cynicism and Epicureanism did not conceive of a unity of ethics and politics; most advocated withdrawal from political activity as the precondition for a virtuous life. But these were not really political philosophies—if anything they were antipolitical. They were important because they articulated certain ideals such as universal equality and cosmopolitan values that subsequently were incorporated into classical political thought, most notably into Stoicism and through Stoicism, and particularly Cicero's rendering of it, into Christianity. In this way the natural law tradition, clearly premised upon the classical ideal of the unity of ethics and politics, was developed and passed on to the medieval and ultimately modern worlds. However much primitive Christianity, later Roman Stoicism, or neo-Platonism may have returned to an antipolitical perspective, the sustaining fact was the persistence of the classical ideal.

The major exception to this, of course, is St. Augustine. That St. Augustine stands in some ways outside of the classical tradition of discourse is one reason he has been called the first "modern." But St. Augustine gives us only a fifth-century preview of what modern political theory will look like. He nowhere carries his political analysis to the radical conclusions that modern theorists do. Compared with them, St. Augustine does not stand as far outside of the classical tradition as it might at first appear. For example, although he largely denies that politics has a genuine ethical dimension, he does not question that the ultimate purpose of life is ethical or moral well-being in that sense of inner goodness of which Socrates first spoke. And it must always be borne in mind that St. Augustine's political philosophy reflected the crisis conditions of his time. In his day it was not easy to believe that politics had a moral purpose.

This belief in the unity of ethics and politics carried with it other assumptions that were commonly shared by the major classical and medieval theorists. The most important of these was the idea that reason is the defining characteristic of human beings, and that reason points to certain knowable ethical truths that humans ought to embody within themselves and within their societies and polities. From Socrates' discovery of the concept, to Plato's and Aristotle's theories of form, to the Stoics', Cicero's, and St. Thomas's natural law philosophies, the underlying theme has been people's capacity to reason to a moral end. All these theorists have been talking about the same thing from different perspectives. Socrates' ethical concept and St. Thomas's natural law are both theories of moral reason that differ only in detail, not in substance.

This idea that human beings possess moral reason carried with it other commonly held ideas, most importantly a psychology that asserted humankind's innate sociability. If people's reason leads them to ethical truths, and if ethics by definition deals with the moral relationships between people (that is, if ethics and politics are one), then human beings are by nature creatures who have the capability to organize themselves for socially beneficial purposes. Moreover, quite apart from this link between moral reason and sociability, until the modern period it was inconceivable to most thinkers that human beings could be understood apart from their social order. That no one is self-sufficing, as the ancient Greek theorists would say, was taken for granted by most of the major theorists from the moment Socrates rejected the individualistic power seeker praised by Callicles and Thrasymachus.

Finally, because of this emphasis upon people's sociability, classical-medieval theory is characterized by its focus upon the larger community. It is not the individual and his or her desires that are important to classical thinkers so much as the social and political order that surrounds people and shapes their behavior. For this reason, we typically find in classical-medieval political thought a focus upon social and political institutions and how those institutions can be shaped to improve the individual and to make life more complete and fulfilled. This focus reaches its zenith in the works of such thinkers as Aristotle, Cicero, and St. Thomas, but it is common to most of the important thinkers of the classical and late medieval periods. It is for this reason that political thinkers of these periods are so comprehensive in their political analysis, a comprehensiveness that attains its highest expression in Aristotle's theory of constitutions.

Of course, not all of these characteristics are shared equally by all thinkers in the classical-medieval tradition of discourse. But with some notable exceptions (St. Augustine in particular), they are shared to a surprising degree and had become accepted wisdom by the end of the medieval period.

The emergence of modern political thought marked no less than a full-scale assault upon this whole tradition of discourse. That assault, as we have said, opened with an attack upon St. Thomas's synthesis of the sacred and the secular. Modern thinkers first de-Christianized Aristotle and then attacked Aristotle himself. The result was the emergence of radically secular political theories that, in their own way, created a dualism between sacred and secular every bit as extreme as St. Augustine's—but in reverse. The heavenly city paled into insignificance, and for many modern thinkers disappeared altogether. The presumed unity of ethics and politics largely disappeared along with it. The consequences of this disappearance, and the changes in theoretical perspective that it entailed, are the subjects of Part II.

Notes

1. Walter Ullman, *Medieval Political Thought* (Aylesbury: Peregrine Books, 1965), pp. 159–64.

2. See Fernand Van Steenberghen, trans. Leonard Johnston, *Aristotle in the West* (Louvain: Nauwelaerts Publishing House, 1970), pp. 66–88, for a brief discussion of the debate that ensued within the Church over the increasing influence of Aristotle and the intermittent attempts to ban his works.

3. John of Salisbury, "The Statesman's Book of John of Salisbury," from John Dickerson, trans., *Politicraticus* (selections) (New York: Russell and Russell, 1963), pp. 64–65. The metaphor is more extensive than this. John calls the Church the soul of the commonwealth; the senate the heart; judges and governors the eyes, ears, and tongue; officials and soldiers the hands; and so on. Needless to say, the metaphor sustains a theocratic ideal: As the soul

is the most important element in the human person (it alone is immortal) so too, as the soul of the commonwealth, is the Church most important in the "body politic."

4. Dino Bigongiari, ed., "On Kingship," in *The Political Ideas of St. Thomas Aquinas* (New York: Hafner Press, 1953), p. 175. There is some dispute over the authorship of *On Kingship,* but it seems to be agreed that if not all of it was written by St. Thomas, it was likely written by a pupil influenced by his views. See Anthony Black, *Political Thought in Europe 1250–1450,* Cambridge Medieval Textbooks Series (Cambridge: Cambridge University Press, 1992), p. 22.

5. See Thomas Gilby, *The Political Thought of Thomas Aquinas* (Chicago: University of Chicago Press, 1958), pp. 107–11, for an excellent discussion of St. Thomas's treatment of the supernatural and the natural, and of its extraordinary importance in the development of a theoretical harmony between divine and natural law.

6. St. Thomas Aquinas, trans. Fathers of the English Dominican Province *Summa Theologica* (New York: Benziger Brothers, 1947), I, pt. 1–11, Art 2: p. 996.

7. F.C. Copleston, *Aquinas* (Harmondsworth: Penguin Books, Ltd., 1955), p. 242.

8. See Herbert A. Deane, *The Political and Social Ideas of St. Augustine* (New York: Columbia University Press, 1963), p. 234: Because St. Thomas "places less emphasis on the sinfulness and depravity of mankind after the Fall, he is not compelled, as Augustine was, to regard the State as primarily a negative, repressive instrument designed to hold in check the worst consequences of human sin."

9. See F. Aveling, "St. Thomas Aquinas," in F.J.C. Hearnshaw, *The Social and Political Ideas of Some Great Mediaeval Thinkers* (New York: Barnes & Noble, Inc., 1967), p. 103: "St. Thomas solved the apparent dualism . . . between the two orders of sovereignty temporal and spiritual. . . . [In Thomas's analysis] these orders were not mutually exclusive or incompatible; because, since the natural end of man is subordinated to the supernatural, it is completed and perfected—not destroyed—by the latter."

10. See Etienne Gilson, trans. Edward Bullough, rev. ed. G.A. Elrington *The Philosophy of St. Thomas Aquinas* (Freeport: Books for Libraries Press, 1937), p. 52: "Such . . . [are] . . . the distinctions between Reason and Faith in the system of St. Thomas. . . . Faith and Reason can neither contradict each other, nor ignore each other, nor be confused."

11. Alexander Passerin D'Entreves, *The Medieval Contribution to Political Thought: Thomas Aquinas, Marsilius of Padua, Richard Hooker* (New York: Humanities Press, 1959), pp. 20–21.

12. The most important early work to employ Aristotle's philosophy to defend the supremacy of the State over the Church is the *Defensor Pacis (The Defender of Peace)* written by Marsilius of Padua, an early fourteenth-century political thinker.

Part II

Modern Political Theory

The end of knowledge is power. . . .

—Thomas Hobbes,
De Corpore

7

Machiavelli

In Machiavelli's most famous political work, *The Prince* (written in 1513), the following passage ends irrevocably the classical and medieval traditions of political discourse and ushers in the age of modern political thought:

> My intention being to write something of use to those who understand, it appears to me more proper to go to the real truth of the matter than to its imagination; and many have imagined republics and principalities which have never been seen or known to exist in reality; for how we live is so far removed from how we ought to live, that he who abandons what is done for what ought to be done, will rather learn to bring about his own ruin than his preservation.[1]

There are a number of things about this statement that mark it as modern. In the most general sense we note a new spirit of realism and empiricism. Machiavelli is telling his readers that the appropriate way to understand politics is to eschew ideals and to look directly at the empirical reality of human behavior. For this reason, Machiavelli is considered one of the great theorists of realpolitik, so much so that his name has become almost synonymous with the term.

Machiavelli's new spirit of political inquiry was but one reflection of even deeper intellectual changes associated with the Renaissance, a period that lasted from roughly the late fourteenth into the seventeenth century. The

Renaissance, which marks the end of the medieval period and the beginning of the modern, involved a major transformation in the way people thought of themselves and of the world around them. In fact, the Renaissance produced an entirely new intellectual class: the humanists. Humanists were scholars and men of letters who attempted to revive the ideals of classical antiquity by reemphasizing the great literature of the past. These ideals were essentially secular; they glorified man and his works rather than God. Humanist ideals thus embodied that same spirit of empiricism and realism that Machiavelli brought to his political theory. Indeed, Machiavelli himself returned to the classical past, particularly to those political ideals of ancient Rome that emphasized the importance of the state and the practical political skills required to maintain it. As we shall see, however, at a deeper metaphysical and epistemological level, he rejected the whole classical heritage and, in the process, laid the foundations of modern political thought.

But there is much more to the Renaissance than a new intellectual vision. All social relationships underwent major transformations as the medieval order crumbled. In place of the old, static, and hierarchical society of the medieval world there emerged a new and dynamic social order. The beginning of modern capitalism, for example, can be traced back to the Renaissance when a new moneyed economy emerged in connection with the discovery of new markets.

Along with economic changes came a new sort of man: the entrepreneur, the self-made man who made his fortune through his own skill and effort. In fact, all spheres of society began to open up to those who in the medieval world would have been consigned by birth to a particular role or status. Corresponding to the new economic man of the Renaissance we find for the first time the "political entrepreneur," the self-made politician who by dint of his skill and daring could wrest a state for himself. At least this was possible in Machiavelli's Italy, which was divided into a series of small states, or principalities, that frequently changed hands.

We have already seen how this opening up of the medieval social order had begun in embryo form even in St. Thomas's time. This process involved the checking of the power of the Church by other emerging political units. By Machiavelli's time, the process, which culminated in the Reformation and the defeat of the Catholic Church as the key political unit in Europe, had greatly intensified. The defeat of the Church was but one reflection of the final decline of feudalism, a system of political organization that dominated Europe from about the ninth century A.D. up to the Renaissance. The feudal system was characterized by the existence of a host of different political communities: towns, principalities, baronies, and other small feudatory states, each claiming the right to rule its subjects. Exactly which community had ultimate authority, and exactly where the territory of one community ended and the other began, was no easy matter to determine. This is what made the Church so politically crucial prior to the Renaissance: It was the one organization capable of giving some kind of coherence to an otherwise fragmented social order.

Eventually, a new type of polity, the nation-state, would emerge from the wreckage of feudalism. We may define a nation-state as a form of polity in which people live within a legally defined territory and give their allegiance to one centralized government that has the power to enforce laws. The United States fits this definition, as does France, Great Britain, Sweden, and so on. Historically these political entities are quite modern. Indeed, some countries such as Germany and Italy were not fully consolidated into nation-states until the late nineteenth century, and many countries in the third world are still very much in the process of becoming nation-states.

In Western Europe the issue was resolved, more or less, by the end of the sixteenth century when the nation-state had emerged in clear form. This occurred under the leadership of absolute monarchs who, by appealing to new nationalist ideals, consolidated and centralized power at the expense of the Church and other institutions of feudal society. It is for this reason that the initial stages of the formation of the nation-state system have been called the *age of absolute monarchy,* an age that was bloody and violent in the extreme.

Machiavelli had some idea, albeit a very imperfect one, of this new emerging political order. In this sense Machiavelli's genius was the opposite of Aristotle's. Aristotle summed up the political experience of the polis, a form of political organization that was waning in his own day. Machiavelli, on the other hand, grasped the new forms of political action that would be required to found the modern state. Before Machiavelli, no thinker was able to take this step out of the feudal framework, although another Italian of the fourteenth century, Marsilius of Padua, came very close to doing so.

It is difficult to put Machiavelli's thought in historical perspective. He is a transitional figure standing midway between the medieval and modern eras. Thus, while he had a sense of what was to come, much of his thought was still tied to the past. He speaks of the state in an almost modern way yet possesses little idea of how it will be organized.[2] He recognizes that absolute monarchy will be required to unify the state into a coherent national entity, but he has little appreciation for the other factors that will be necessary for unification. And while he had a national vision (he desperately desired the unification of Italy, which was then divided into various small city-states), he was not yet fully a modern nationalist,[3] although he has traditionally been considered the first thinker to give expression to what we would now recognize as nationalistic ideals.

Despite these qualifications, we must nevertheless emphasize Machiavelli's essential originality. If he did not fully comprehend the emerging nation-state, or give unqualified expression to nationalist ideals, he went further in this regard than any of his contemporaries. And he most certainly grasped that the old order was crumbling and that new modes of political thought and action would be required to transform the chaotic, corrupt, and increasingly violent political order of Renaissance Italy into a stable and unified polity.

It is important to keep in mind this less attractive side of the Renaissance, for it is this side that interested Machiavelli as a political thinker. The social and political chaos of the times compelled him to approach his study of politics with a new spirit of empiricism and realism. Machiavelli's claim that "how we live is . . . far removed from how we ought to live" was never more true than during the Renaissance, so he was forced to look at politics without illusions and without the moribund ideals of the medieval world.

This lack of illusion was especially strong in Machiavelli because he was personally caught up in the conflicts and passions of the times. Born in 1469 in Florence, one of the five major Italian city-states, he became in 1498 a high-ranking official in the republican, or "democratic," government that had been formed four years earlier following the invasion by France. Prior to that time, Florence had been ruled by the tyrannical Medici family. In 1512 the Vatican (then a key city-state) drove the French from Italy and returned the Medicis to power in Florence. With the Republic ended, Machiavelli was not only expelled from his political post, he was accused of treason and tortured on the rack. Except for one brief period shortly before his death in 1527, he spent the rest of his days in exile from all political activity.

It was during the first year of exile that Machiavelli wrote *The Prince*. His other major political work, *Discourses on the First Ten Books of Titus Livius,* was published subsequently, as were *The Art of War, The History of Florence,* and several plays and other literary works. Almost all of his writings, his literary works included, have a political tone to them, for Machiavelli saw all human relationships as pervaded by politics. He was the most political of men in the most political of times and had he had the choice he would have preferred being in politics to philosophizing about it. But fate, or fortune as Machiavelli called it, determined that he would make his name as a political theorist rather than as a politician.

The Prince, because it is generally recognized as the first clearly modern work in Western political philosophy, and because it throws into bold relief the essential character of Machiavelli's political thought, is a good place to begin analysis of his political theory. We shall discuss it in conjunction with *The Discourses,* which serves as a corrective balance to some of the positions Machiavelli adopts in *The Prince,* most notably to the advocacy of monarchy. *The Discourses,* which expresses Machiavelli's real political ideal, calls for the creation of a republican, or "democratic," form of government. But Machiavelli understood that the conditions necessary for a republican system did not exist in the Italy of his time. What was required was stability and order, precisely what Italy lacked. Though medieval values had disintegrated, Italy had not yet become a nation-state and the political arena was thus open and chaotic. Italy's inability to unite into one political unit (into what we would now recognize as a nation-state), for example, made it subject to ceaseless invasions by more developed foreign powers that played off one city against the other.

Machiavelli grasped that a republican Italy required in the first instance a united or national Italy that could withstand the outrages of foreign invasion. But he further grasped that Italian unification would require the leadership of one strong man who possessed a new political vision and who had the political skills requisite to implement it. Thus, *The Prince* opens with a dedication to Lorenzo the Magnificent, the Medici ruler of Florence who had destroyed Machiavelli's beloved Republic, for Machiavelli was above all a political realist who understood that someone like a Lorenzo would be required to unite Italy. And what Machiavelli proposes in the dedication is to teach Lorenzo those political skills necessary to found a united Italy. He proposes, in short, to teach Lorenzo the rules of power politics.

It is this focus on power that in large part marks Machiavelli as the first genuinely modern thinker (and it is a focus intimately connected to the rise of the modern secular nation-state). Following Machiavelli, power becomes a key variable, indeed the prime variable, of political analysis. This is not to suggest that medieval or classical thinkers were unaware of the reality of power in politics. They were well aware of it. But they did not, with some rare exceptions such as St. Augustine, believe power to be the defining characteristic of political activity. Aristotle, for example, viewed politics as a key source of friendship and as an arena in which moral excellence could be acquired and displayed. He recognized the reality of power, to be sure, but he did not take it to be the defining reality of political life.

Now, because Machiavelli and so many political thinkers following him view power as the essence of politics, we need to define its meaning with some precision. *Power* may be defined as the ability to control others by compelling their obedience. The key word here is *compel:* to make people obey whether they want to or not. Clearly violence is a form of power, indeed the most extreme form, for it is the most extreme kind of compulsion. But power can be manifested in much more subtle forms as well. A threat of violence may be just as effective (Machiavelli believes in the long run that it is usually more effective) as its actual exercise. And even apparent acts of friendship, such as the granting of gifts and favors, may actually be a manifestation of power. Those who become dependent upon receiving favors from the political leader, for example, must constantly face the possibility that they will suffer the loss of their favored status if they cease to obey. This is why it is apparent that at bottom power, no matter how subtly applied, is a form of coercion. And this is why the essence of power, if it is not always violence in the strictest sense, is something very close to it.

It is clear that Machiavelli's emphasis on power implies a particular, and essentially modern, view of human nature. That view is that human beings are essentially self-interested and self-regarding. Clearly power would not be an effective influence unless self-interest were the defining character-istic of the human personality. Violence, for example, would not be capable of compelling obedience if it did not appeal to the individual's fear of death or bodily harm. And the same holds true for the subtler forms of power. In getting a person to obey by the promise of some reward (money, status, hon-ors, even simple flattery), the political leader has as surely appealed to self-interest as if violence had been threatened.

Of course, not all relationships based upon self-interest are power rela-tionships, but power is always based upon self-interest. If, like Socrates, human beings could transcend self-interest for some higher purpose, power relationships would not exist because neither the threat of death nor the granting of favors could compel obedience. Politics as we know it would dis-appear and Plato's Republic, or something like it, would become a real possi-bility. Machiavelli is convinced that no such possibility exists because his analysis of human behavior convinces him that self-interest is the essence of human nature. This is why he is so confident that power, if employed wisely, will work.

What makes Machiavelli's views genuinely modern, however, is the at-titude he adopts toward these "facts" of human nature and the corresponding reality of power politics. For unlike St. Augustine, who also focused on self-interest and the struggle for power, Machiavelli does not consider self-interested, self-regarding behavior to be sinful, anymore than he does the desire for, or the employment of, power. Machiavelli is an empiricist. His psychology is derived from observation of how people actually behave (as opposed to how they ought ideally to behave). Thus, when he asserts, as he often does, that people are "bad," he simply means to emphasize that people are inherently self-interested, and that as such they both desire and are sub-ject to the exercise of power. He means to make no moral or religious judg-ment. Being bad for Machiavelli does not mean being sinful; it simply means being what humans naturally are. There is no more sin involved in humans acting self-interestedly for Machiavelli than there is in the earth revolving around the sun. Both are simply following their "nature."

Given Machiavelli's view of human nature, his emphasis on power as the key variable in political behavior makes eminent sense. The political analysis that he employs to comprehend that behavior makes equally good sense. Machiavelli proposes to describe and explain the "logic of power," for he views power as something uniquely amenable to logical analysis. Power has to do with the manipulation of people's self-interest. To the extent that a political leader, such as Lorenzo, understands this and is able to determine what it is that people desire in any given situation, the kinds of actions neces-sary to maintain control of the situation can be logically deduced. This, at least, is Machiavelli's reasoning. Later thinkers who followed Machiavelli's pioneering efforts in this regard, most notably Thomas Hobbes in the seventeenth century, attempted to transform the logic of power into a comprehensive science of power.

For now, we need only recognize that *The Prince*'s most notable characteristic is that it is a technical manual on the logic of acquiring and maintaining political power. We should add that it was written essentially for a new type of monarch, for the "political entrepreneur" who was required to attain rulership by his own political skill in manipulating the levers of power, rather than for the hereditary leader who owed his authority to tradition. This new kind of monarch, who was becoming increasingly common in Renaissance Italy, lacked the support of tradition and was required, therefore, to rely upon the effective use of power in gaining and maintaining his political position. To be successful, he had to learn well the logic of power.

We cannot here discuss all of Machiavelli's rules of power politics. We can discuss the most important of them, however, and particularly those that best illuminate the basic structure of Machiavelli's theory of power and its uses. We will also discuss those rules that are particularly applicable to an understanding of *The Discourses*. As we shall see, Machiavelli's most basic assumptions about the nature of politics are the same in both works despite their advocacy of different political ideals.

In *The Prince,* Machiavelli advocates two intimately related rules of power politics that are clearly the most important of all because they are the basis for learning and applying all the other rules necessary to gain and maintain a principality. First, says Machiavelli, the prince must learn to think about politics in a new way. He must be strictly empirical in his political analysis, and cold-bloodedly logical in the conclusions he draws from that analysis. This requires that he eschew all ethical ideals, for it is precisely such ideals that blind the political leader to the reality of politics. And second, the prince must act as logically as he thinks, even if this means violating generally held moral values. For, recalling that "how we live is so far removed from how we ought to live, that he who abandons what is done for what ought to be done will bring about his own ruin," it follows, says Machiavelli, that "a man who wishes to make a profession of goodness in everything must necessarily come to grief among so many who are not good."[4] In short, if the prince expects to maintain his power, he cannot himself always behave "ideally"; he cannot approach his task as if he were conducting a Sunday school. The dictates of power require cold-blooded logic in action, no less than in theory.

The subsequent rules of power politics follow logically from these first two. Most important, says Machiavelli, the wise prince must keep power in his own hands, and he must never be the cause of another becoming more powerful than himself. Given the inherent workings of human nature, power that is shared or given to another will likely be turned against the prince. It is therefore logically imperative that, insofar as possible, power not be shared.

The problem, of course, is that it is impossible for the prince to keep power totally within his own grasp since he must rely upon others both in its creation and in its implementation. He must rely upon the police, the military, the population at large, his own advisors, and perhaps foreign allies if he is to be effective. Consequently, the prince must find mechanisms for maximizing his control over these various forces, for they are as much a potential threat to his power as they are the source of it. He must therefore keep others dependent upon him, and not the other way around, says Machiavelli, and this requires, he argues, that the prince be willing to either *caress* or *annihilate* men. He must be willing, in short, to employ power, whether in its extreme or subtle forms. In its most extreme form the prince may be called to kill his opposition, in which case he need no longer fear them at all, or he may manipulate ("caress") them with favors and thereby make them dependent and subject to his control.

We need go no further than this to see why Machiavelli has the reputation he does. It is not surprising that the Catholic Church put Machiavelli's writings on the index of forbidden books, or that generations of scholars, political leaders, and assorted thinkers have raised their voices against the "frightful Machiavelli." No charge has seemed too extreme. Frederick the Great of Prussia, for example, wrote a famous attack on *The Prince* in 1739 in which he called Machiavelli a criminal, a monster, and an enemy of humanity.[5] So intense has the opposition to Machiavelli been that the word *machiavellianism* has become a general term for the evils of power politics.

Frederick's attack upon *The Prince* is typical of much anti-Machiavellian literature in that it is based upon a misunderstanding of what Machiavelli actually says in that work, for nowhere does he praise the exercise of power for its own sake, nor does he advocate its unlimited use. Quite the contrary in fact. As we shall see, Machiavelli considers such behavior to be self-defeating. Nevertheless, we shall return again to this strain of literature, because it will help us to better appreciate what Machiavelli really says as opposed to what the popular imagination has always supposed him to say.[6]

Given the condition of the times, the idea that people must be caressed or annihilated is, logically at least, indisputable. If people will not obey willingly, then they must be forced or manipulated into obeying. This is a strictly empirical and logical conclusion for Machiavelli, not a justification of violence as an end in itself. The prince must exercise power in order to maintain his position, and violence is one of the tools for exercising power. As such, it must be employed when needed. The only real question for Machiavelli, then, is How can violence be used most effectively? not Is it ethical to employ it? Indeed, the wise prince must not even ask such a question, says Machiavelli, for to the extent that he concerns himself with ethical issues, he will fail to use violence appropriately, if at all, when needed. Ethical concerns induce moral squeamishness, a condition not conducive to the effective use of violence.

How then is the prince to employ violence for maximum effectiveness? Once again we may note some general rules. In the first place, it ought not to be used at all unless absolutely necessary because it tends to engender resistance and thereby pose a threat to the prince's security. In the second place, if violence must be employed, it must be used quickly and mercilessly. This is so, says Machiavelli, because people "will revenge themselves for small injuries, but cannot do so for great ones":[7] thus "the injury . . . we do to a man must be such that we need not fear his vengeance."[8]

Note the inexorable logic of what Machiavelli says here. If violence engenders resistance, then clearly it should be avoided if at all possible. And if it must be employed, then logically it should be done in such a way that it minimizes resistance. Clearly, killing one's enemy is in order since a dead man is by definition incapable of resistance. And anything short of killing must be sufficient to accomplish the same end: the utter destruction of one's enemy as a political force with which to be reckoned.

Machiavelli's analysis is based upon a crucially important insight into human nature: When people are subjected to violence short of being destroyed, they will seek revenge. This, says Machiavelli, is because violence has the unfortunate quality of engendering hatred, something, he emphasizes, that the prince should avoid at all costs, for hatred is a passion unlike any of the others, with the possible exception of love. Hatred transports people outside of themselves and causes them not to calculate their self-interest. People who hate are willing to sacrifice even their lives to gain revenge. Thus, the prince who has caused himself to be hated is in the unfortunate position of having to deal with people he can no longer control. As we have seen, power will be effective only so long as the prince is able to rely upon the normal workings of human nature.

This analysis of violence points out something about the nonviolent forms of power we have classified as manipulation. The rules of manipulation, Machiavelli argues, are exactly the opposite of the rules of violence, although the underlying principle is the same. That principle, to reiterate, is that the prince must appeal to the self-interest of others such that they remain dependent upon him and not the other way around. This means that violence must be used quickly and mercilessly. Nonviolent forms of power, on the other hand, such as giving gifts or granting favors, should be applied over a long period of time so as to maintain dependency upon the prince. Thus, Machiavelli concludes "injuries should be done all together so that being less tasted, they will give less offense. Benefits should be granted little by little, so that they may be better enjoyed."[9]

This brings us to the third rule of violence, which logically follows from the second rule that "injuries should be done altogether." (The first rule, remember, is to make every effort not to use violence.) Insofar as possible, says Machiavelli, the prince should get someone else to do the injuries for him. Any hatred that might arise will then be directed at the perpetrator of the violence, not at the prince. Moreover, once the violence has been committed, the prince may reap a further advantage by employing a particularly devious tactic that Machiavelli describes by way of an example drawn from the life of Cesare Borgia, his contemporary and his ideal of the wise prince. In the following example, Borgia had recently gained control of a small principality that had been poorly governed. Consequently, says Machiavelli:

> He . . . judged it necessary to give them a good government in order to make them peaceful and obedient to his rule. For this purpose he appointed Messer Remirro *de Orco,* a cruel and able man, to whom he gave the fullest authority. This man, in a short time, was highly successful in rendering the country orderly and united, whereupon the duke, not deeming such excessive authority expedient, lest it should become hateful, appointed a civil court of justice in the center of the province under an excellent president, to which each city appointed its own advocate. And as he knew that the harshness of the past had engendered some amount of hatred, in order to purge the minds of the people and to win them over completely, he resolved to show that if any cruelty had taken place it was not by his orders, but through the harsh disposition of his minister. And having found the opportunity he had him cut in half and placed one morning in the public square at Cesena with a piece of wood and bloodstained knife by his side. The ferocity of this spectacle caused the people both satisfaction and amazement.[10]

Even violence that generates hatred, then, may under certain circumstances work to the advantage of the prince if he uses it wisely. But, as the example clearly shows, the prince can use violence wisely only if he is utterly cold-blooded and unscrupulous, that is, only if he employs violence logically to attain his desired end without letting moral scruples cloud his judgment. This is quite different from using violence for its own sake. Cesare Borgia is not praised by Machiavelli because he was violent but because he used violence coolly and logically to attain his objective.[11] Once again, Machiavelli does not advocate the unlimited use of violence, but its very opposite.[12]

Machiavelli discusses a number of other rules of power politics in *The Prince,* all of which are grounded in the basic premise that the prince should, insofar as possible, keep power within his own hands and, short of this, keep others dependent upon him. To this end, Machiavelli tells the prince that it is better to be feared than loved, for "men love at their own free will, but fear at the will of the prince, and . . . a wise prince must rely on what is in his power and not on what is in the power of others."[13] With the same reasoning in mind, Machiavelli advises the prince, in what is perhaps his most famous metaphor, that he "being . . . obliged to know well how to act as a beast must imitate the fox and the lion, for the lion cannot protect himself from traps, and the fox cannot defend himself from wolves."[14] And the numerous other rules of power politics that Machiavelli discusses in *The Prince* are of a like kind. They are all logical rules deduced from empirical observation that aim at maximizing the prince's power.

One rule does deserve special mention, however. According to Machiavelli the prince should found his support upon the people rather than the nobility because "the aim of the people is more honest than that of the nobility, the latter desiring to oppress and the former merely to avoid oppression."[15] Since the people desire only to be left alone, they have no interest in acquiring power, nor do they have the political skills necessary to acquire it even if they did want it, says Machiavelli. And since they therefore pose no threat to the prince, it empirically and logically follows that it is among them that he should build his support. In *The Prince,* at least, it is not sentiment but the cool logic of power politics that dictates that the political leader rely upon the mass of average citizens.

Yet, there is more to what Machiavelli says about the people than mere considerations of realpolitik. He had made the momentous discovery that a state based upon mass support is more stable than one based upon an aristocracy. This discovery contradicted the popular assumption that, to use Machiavelli's own example, "he who builds on the people, builds on mud."[16] This belief in the political worthlessness of the masses goes back as far as Plato, and the aristocracy in Machiavelli's time (no less than elite groups in our own day) tended toward a kind of "Platonic elitism" based upon their belief in the lack of political sophistication of the average citizen.

Here we observe the real power of Machiavelli's empiricism. By carefully observing rather than basing his political judgment upon commonly held opinions, Machiavelli is able to show that lack of political sophistication is not the cause of instability but its very opposite. Careful observation shows that it is precisely the politically sophisticated nobility that is most likely to suspect the motives of the prince, to distrust his actions, and to look behind them for hidden meanings. As they are less trusting, so are they less manageable, and much more likely than the people to disobey the prince and to resist his rule. Moreover, along with political sophistication generally comes a love of power, and it is precisely this, according to Machiavelli, that is the source of political disorder and instability.

This is not to suggest that Machiavelli believes "the people" to be naturally "good." It is their social position that renders them placid, not any innate predisposition. Given the appropriate circumstances, Machiavelli recognizes that the people would behave no differently than the nobility. All people, he insists, are ready to show their "vicious" nature when it is to their advantage, and the wise leader must always bear this fact in mind. Nevertheless, unless the people themselves have become corrupted, says Machiavelli, their political naiveté and their desire for liberty rather than power make them the ideal group upon which the prince should found his support.

It is at this juncture that we must say something about *The Discourses,* because it is his discovery of the political worth of "the people" that leads Machiavelli to advocate a republican, or "democratic," form of government such as had existed in Florence before the return of the Medicis. Indeed, some would argue that Machiavelli provides us with the first glimpse (albeit no more than a glimpse) of the modern democratic nation-state whose stability rests precisely upon its capacity to generate mass support.[17] And while *The Discourses* stands as a corrective to *The Prince*'s promonarchism, it must be kept in mind that there is no fundamental disagreement between the two works. *The Prince* was written against a background of political corruption and instability. *The Discourses* was written with a more ideal situation in mind. Machiavelli's two treatises reflect different social conditions, not different assumptions about the nature of politics.

What then is Machiavelli's ideal republican system to look like? To begin with, it is to be "liberal" and "democratic," but, of course, it must be understood that Machiavelli does not have in mind liberal democracy in its contemporary sense. On the democratic side, he assumes a much more limited franchise than what we are accustomed to today. As for his "liberal" ideals, Machiavelli is no modern civil libertarian. He is not concerned about freedom of speech or press in the abstract; indeed, he expects fairly tight censorship of manners and morals. By *liberty* Machiavelli means the right of a people to live their day-to-day lives in relative freedom and to engage in the selection of their leadership without coercion or constraint.

Yet, for all this, Machiavelli's democratic and liberal ideals were quite advanced for their day. Not only does he advocate what for its time was an extensive level of popular political participation but, in regard to political liberty, he argues that the conflict between different groups professing different ideals will actually strengthen the state. Here Machiavelli was far ahead of his time, for conventional political wisdom had generally assumed that conflict is destructive of political order and should be avoided at all costs. But Machiavelli understood that political conflict, so long as it is not allowed to degenerate into violence, contributes to the strength and health of a republic and trains the citizenry in civic virtue. In many ways this idea of controlled conflict is reminiscent of Aristotle, but more importantly it brings to mind modern liberal democracies such as the United States that are premised upon political conflict between different social groups. Contemporary political scientists call this condition of group conflict *pluralism,* something that is now seen as the sine qua non of a free society.

Machiavelli recognizes that this republican ideal can exist only so long as the people remain uncorrupted. They must be trained in civic virtue, in love of country, else the natural tendency of human beings to maximize their self-interest at the expense of the whole society will become dominant. In these conditions, republican ideals will become hollow and people will eventually lose their liberty. Once the political sphere becomes corrupted by selfish interests, Machiavelli insists, control can be maintained only by the strong leader who is willing to wield power in the manner recommended to Lorenzo in *The Prince*.

In order to train the people in recognizing a larger public good, and thus to prevent their corruption, Machiavelli argues that the whole social order that undergirds his ideal republic must be structured in a particular way. To begin with, says Machiavelli, a republican government must be based upon an extensive equality, not only political equality, but social equality as well. For great inequality, Machiavelli emphasizes, is a fundamental cause of political discord between different groups in society and, consequently, of power struggles between them.

Machiavelli's emphasis upon equality as a necessary condition for a stable democratic system brings to mind Aristotle's discussion of polity as does his recognition that a stable and lawful republican regime requires a whole complex of viable social institutions to undergird the state and its laws. Like the classical thinkers, Machiavelli understands that a mere legal structure is not sufficient. A workable legal constitution requires a corresponding social constitution, that is, a network of social institutions that support the legal structure of the state. And of all these institutions, says Machiavelli, none is more important than that of religion.

Such a view seems at first surprising given Machiavelli's secularism and the fact that he was personally irreligious. But his interest in religion is political, not theological, and as a political realist Machiavelli is the first to recognize the political importance of religion. Religion, he says, gives a "divine sanction" to the laws without which the people would have no reason to obey. This is why he argues that

> the observance of divine institutions is the cause of the greatness of republics; . . . the disregard of them produces their ruin; for where the fear of God is wanting, there the country will come to ruin, unless it be sustained by the fear of the prince, which may temporarily supply the want of religion. But as the lives of princes are short, the kingdom will of necessity perish as the prince fails in virtue.[18]

From a political point of view, Machiavelli would wholeheartedly agree with Voltaire's statement that "if God did not exist, it would be necessary to invent him." Since the people lack sophistication, they require a supernatural agency to stand behind the laws and, indeed, behind all of their social institutions. But questions of precisely what form God takes, or how religious institutions are structured, are of concern to Machiavelli only in terms of the impact for good or evil upon the political sphere. It is for this political reason that Machiavelli insists that the state must control the church and its teachings.

Machiavelli criticized the Church of his day precisely for political, and not religious, reasons. He recognized that the existence of the papal state and its ceaseless struggle to dominate political affairs was a primary cause of Italy's inability to unite into one political unit. But Machiavelli's political critique of the Church went beyond a condemnation of its involvement in secular affairs. He was critical too of its teachings, again not for religious but for political reasons. And politically, Machiavelli was at best ambivalent about Christianity, for it taught the otherworldly virtues of meekness and humility rather than the political virtues of strength and courage, virtues that he insists are required to maintain the state, be it a principality or a republic. Christian principles, he argues,

> have made men feeble and caused them to become an easy prey to evil-minded men, who can control them more securely, seeing that the great body of men, for the sake of gaining Paradise, are more disposed to endure injuries than to avenge them.[19]

To the extent that Machiavelli did have a religious preference, it was for the pagan religion of antiquity, which, he says, "deified only men who had achieved great glory, such as commanders of armies and chiefs of republics, whilst ours glorifies more the humble and contemplative men than the men of action."[20] A religion of man, a theology of action—in short, a political religion—this was Machiavelli's ideal, an ideal that had not existed since the days of classical antiquity. In both Greece and Rome the pagan religion had been a state religion that glorified the state and the men of action who had created and defended it. In making the sacred superior to the secular, Christianity had subordinated the state to the church, so much so that not even St. Thomas could fully legitimize the state and that political activity necessary to maintain it. In returning to the classical ideal, Machiavelli rectified, if only theoretically, the modern divorce between religious and political ideals (but, of course, at the expense of the Christian idea that religious values are superior to political ones).[21]

Such then is Machiavelli's republican ideal: a "liberal" and "democratic" government, constrained by the rule of law and undergirded by deeply held social and religious values that encourage civic virtue and love of country. His ideal clearly is drawn from the Roman Republic to which he refers again and again in *The Discourses,* just as other Renaissance thinkers drew their ideals from classical antiquity. And while Machiavelli understood that his "Roman ideal" in no way corresponded to the actual conditions of Renaissance Italy, it was his hope that the great political leader might create the conditions for it. It was his hope that the rules of power politics he teaches in *The Prince* might provide the great leader with a way of "transcending" mere power politics.

Yet, no less than a principality, a republic requires excellent leadership, and Machiavelli is the first to recognize that the leadership of a republic can no more divorce itself from the realities of politics than can the leadership of a principality. Even coercive power will have to be exercised from time to time, and in some republics more so than in others, for there are various kinds of republics, Machiavelli argues, some of which are unstable and prone to corruption.

Moreover, no matter how ideal domestic conditions may be, the republic must exist among other states that are a constant threat to its existence. Those conditions that generate power politics, conditions discussed extensively in *The Prince,* are ever present in international affairs. As a consequence, the leader of a republic must exercise well the rules of power politics in his dealings with foreign countries even if he is able to modify those rules domestically.

Nevertheless, while power politics can never be transcended completely, especially in international affairs, Machiavelli clearly believes that in a well-founded republic obedience to the laws need not be coerced but should result almost naturally from the people's belief in their social order and those cultural traditions upon which it is based. As a consequence, the leader of a republic need not be ceaselessly coercing or manipulating. He is not chronically threatened by others who want only to seize power, for even if they exist they will be constrained by the people, who desire only their liberties and the survival of their beloved country. In short, the whole basis of obedience to law is more secure in a republic than in a principality. In a republic it is not primarily power that creates obedience (although power can never be entirely absent), but authority.

Authority, like power, is a term we use to describe how and why people obey their laws and support their political institutions. Unlike power, however, authority exists where people obey because they believe obedience to be morally appropriate, not because it is simply in their self-interest to obey. Unquestionably, most long-lived political systems are based upon authority. In those that are not, the leadership is driven to apply the rules of power politics that Machiavelli recommends in *The Prince,* for where internal moral controls are lacking the law can be enforced only by force.

Machiavelli clearly prefers authority to power, and for a very pragmatic reason: Power, particularly explicit-coercive power, is a terribly inefficient means by which to compel obedience. It requires enormous resources to hold a gun against the heads of an entire population: military personnel, police, domestic spies, and so on. Even then, raw power is frequently ineffective because it is simply impossible in most cases to hold a whole population in line by the use of force.

Moreover, Machiavelli emphasizes again and again that the excessive use of force is self-defeating. He shows that the more it is used the more resistance it engenders. And quite apart from this undesirable quality, the police and military forces that are required to exercise violence may turn against the prince himself. In *The Prince,* Machiavelli argues that the political leader must keep an eye even on his most trusted advisors; imagine how much more closely he must watch his own police forces where they have become the sole basis of his rule.

It is for these reasons that military regimes and many other forms of dictatorship are inherently unstable. They have behind them no real moral support, that is, no authority, and are incapable of using raw power efficiently and effectively. And the very mechanisms of control upon which the regime depends are frequently turned against it, making coups d'état common.

There is one other great disadvantage of power to which Machiavelli draws our attention in *The Discourses:* It lasts only so long as the prince survives or is able to maintain his position. But authority transcends the life or effectiveness of the prince because it is a moral predisposition on the part of the people to obey the law regardless of who is ruling or how effectively the prince enforces the law through threats of punishment. This is why Machiavelli argues that the primary function of the leadership of a republic, and insofar as possible even that of a principality, is to create the conditions for authority. As he notes:

> The welfare . . . of a republic or a kingdom does not consist in having a prince who governs it wisely during his lifetime, but in having one who will give it such laws that it will maintain itself even after his death.[22]

Here we can see perhaps more dramatically than before the importance of religious institutions for Machiavelli. Recall his statement that while the fear of a prince may "temporarily supply the want of religion . . . the kingdom will of necessity perish as the prince fails in virtue." Fear, a mechanism of power, is effective only so long as the prince is effective, but religion inculcates a moral predisposition to obey the law and to support the social order that transcends the life or effectiveness of the prince. Religion, in other words, is the primary basis of authority for Machiavelli. It is for this reason that he accords an even higher status to founders of religions than to founders of states.

But religion, remember, depends for its effectiveness upon the people whose essential naiveté leads them to accept uncritically certain "religious truths" and the moral appropriateness of their social order in general. Herein lies the real import of Machiavelli's discovery of "the people": A democratic regime is more stable than others because it is most capable of generating authority.

Thus, we conclude our analysis of *The Discourses* and its republican ideal with a picture of Machiavelli that utterly contradicts the popular image shaped by centuries of anti-Machiavellianism. Not only does Machiavelli reject unlimited violence, the most extreme form of power, he calls into question the ultimate value of power itself. Indeed, if we summarize the whole of Machiavelli's political theory, it would controvert the popular perception on almost every point. For it is perfectly accurate to say that Machiavelli was a democrat and a libertarian who believed the state should be bound by authority, based upon rule of law, undergirded by religious institutions, supported by an equality of citizenship, and ruled by those with a conception of the public good.

Why, then, the popular image and the long history of anti-Machiavellian literature that indicts Machiavelli for ideas he never held or advocated? The answer, at least in part, seems to be not that this literature has been wrong in its intuition that Machiavelli is saying something radically new and different, but in missing what that something is. What is genuinely new in Machiavelli is not that he justifies the unlimited use of power but that he stands opposed to the whole classical and medieval tradition of political discourse that had been summed up some two hundred years before by St. Thomas Aquinas.

Much anti-Machiavellianism has been based on an intuitive sense of this more radical aspect of Machiavelli's theory of politics, but it has failed to direct its criticism at this, the real issue. It has criticized his modernity indirectly by way of a superficial and quite mistaken analysis of what he says about power, violence, and the relationship of means to political ends.

The genuinely radical thrust of Machiavelli's political theory is best illustrated by returning to *The Prince* and a final rule of power politics (a rule that, as we shall see, has a direct bearing upon what Machiavelli says in *The Discourses* as well). According to Machiavelli, it is necessary for the prince to "learn how not to be good" while appearing to be the opposite.[23] Thus, Machiavelli argues, the prince

> should seem to be all mercy, faith, integrity, humanity, and religion. And nothing is more necessary than to seem to have this last quality, for men in general judge more by the eyes than by the hands, for every one can see, but very few have to feel. Everybody sees what you appear to be, few feel what you are, and those few will not dare to oppose themselves to the many, who have the majesty of the state to defend them; and in the actions of men, and especially of princes, from which there is no appeal, the end justifies the means. Let the prince therefore aim at conquering and maintaining the state, and the means will always be judged honorable and praised by everyone, for the vulgar is always taken by appearances.[24]

Now the first part of the rule, that the prince must "learn how not to be good," is really an encapsulation of the various rules of power politics that we have already discussed in some detail. Recall Machiavelli's argument that the prince must learn to play the beast—that he must actually learn how to be unjust. And this really is a quite modern perspective because it makes a virtue of necessity. To the extent that the medieval thinkers did discuss the fact that the political leader must on occasion act unjustly, it was taken as an exception to the rule that could be justified only as a terrible necessity. No medieval thinker would have suggested that one should, on principle, learn injustice.

But it is the second part of the rule that "the prince must appear to be good" that is genuinely revolutionary, for the implication is that what matters in politics is not the reality of any moral purpose, but only the appearance of one. Here Machiavelli reverses the whole Platonic order of things. In this sense, *The Prince* is the reverse image of the *Republic,* for Machiavelli's claim that what counts in politics is the appearance of justice rather than its reality is the very assertion that the *Republic* aimed at disproving. Recall Adeimantus's challenge to Plato that he demonstrate the intrinsic worth of justice; that he show why *being* just is in fact superior to simply *appearing* just. And recall further that Adeimantus was simply putting Thrasymachus's sophistical argument that might makes right into its most sophisticated guise.

It was quite clear to the disputants in Plato's *Republic* that if justice has no ultimate reality, if it is simply a word that the politician invokes for the sake of appearance, then indeed "might makes right" is the essence of "political ethics." In reducing politics to appearances, Machiavelli (and many political thinkers since) clearly returns to sophistic political principles. Not only does he emphasize the struggle for power, but he describes that activity in much the same way as did the Sophists of Plato's day. For the ability to successfully acquire and maintain power, an ability that requires appearing just while behaving unjustly, Machiavelli, like the early Sophists, calls *virtue!* Plato, you will recall, had devoted his life to demonstrating that what the Sophists called *virtue* is in reality evil.

Who is correct, Plato or Machiavelli? Once again we note the intimate connection between epistemology and political theory. If, like Plato, one accepts the existence of an objective moral order that people can know and incorporate into their lives, then clearly Machiavelli's prince is evil. But if, like Machiavelli, one does not accept the notion of such an order, there is nothing to "know" in the Platonic sense. What is knowable is nothing more than what we would now call the "real empirical world," what Plato had described as the cave world of appearances. In Platonic terms we could say that Machiavelli's virtuous prince is one who grasps that he is in the cave, that there is no leaving it, and that knowledge must be confined merely to using and manipulating those shadows and illusions that bind human beings and their societies together.

It follows that Machiavelli's rejection of the Platonic theory of knowledge applies equally to Aristotle and Cicero; while their political theories are secular and empirical, they presume a connection between the "real world" and a larger ethical purpose. Aristotle's empiricism, for example, is embedded in a teleological system. Machiavelli is antiteleological; he admits no larger purpose to human events than that which is observable. Indeed, in Machiavelli's political universe there is no form, no natural law, no teleology operating in the affairs of human beings. There is nothing but the empirical reality of politics as given to the observation.

This is the real import of Machiavelli's claim that it is useless to study "republics and principalities which have never been seen or known to exist in reality." His claim is a clear rejection of Plato and of that whole genre of classical and medieval political thought that was premised upon an ethical or "utopian" standard. It is not simply *The Prince*'s emphasis upon realpolitik, then, that makes Machiavelli a revolutionary thinker, for there is in this nothing new. St. Augustine had long before developed a theory of political realism. Rather, it is Machiavelli's insistence upon studying politics without any ethical standard at all (unless "reason of state" be considered such a standard) that makes him the first genuinely modern political thinker.[25]

What is dramatically new about Machiavelli's *Prince*, then, is not that it extols political immorality, as many anti-Machiavellians have supposed. What is new is that *The Prince* is a thoroughly amoral work. It is a book about the practical techniques of gaining and maintaining political power, techniques stripped of all moral (or immoral) considerations.[26] It must now be added, however, that *The Discourses* is an equally amoral work, for its basic epistemological assumptions are identical to those of *The Prince*. While *The Discourses* speaks of authority, civic virtue, liberty, and equality, these terms no longer possess ethical meaning in the classical sense. They are as ethically neutral as the rules of power politics discussed in *The Prince*.

What ultimately differentiates the republican ideal of *The Discourses* from the promonarchism of *The Prince*, therefore, besides the obvious differences of political structure, is not that a republic is based upon ethical principles and a principality is not, but that the character of appearances is likely to be different in a republic than in a principality. In a stable republic at least, people really believe in the "illusions" of justice and transcendent virtue because their religious and other social institutions give credence to them. Nevertheless, they remain illusions for Machiavelli, not ethical realities. Indeed, Machiavelli grasped what no medieval thinker did, or could—that for practical purposes it makes no difference whether there is an ethical order to things or not so long as people believe there is.

For Machiavelli, then, it is the illusion of an ethical order that creates authority in a republic, not the reality. In a principality of the kind that Machiavelli analyzes in *The Prince*, on the other hand, the illusion of such an order had disappeared because of the corruption of the Church and other key social institutions. Clearly the conditions to which *The Prince* refers are those of Machiavelli's own day and are the consequence not only of the corruption of the Church, but of the disintegration of all the major medieval traditions and institutions. In the Italy of his time, Machiavelli had no choice but to recommend the techniques of power, for the key ethical illusions of the medieval world no longer held.

It is part of Machiavelli's political genius to have recognized that the medieval world could not be put back together again, nor could the political ideals upon which it was based. He understood that the political reality of the modern world would require a new science of politics that would no longer conceive of politics from the perspective of ethical ideals. Exactly why this should be the case is the subject of the following chapters, but Machiavelli comprehended part of the reason from the beginning. The triumph of a purely secular state would inevitably generate purely secular theories of politics, theories that would go well beyond a mere separation of sacred and secular. The sacred itself would become secularized; it would become merely another illusion to be manipulated by those who, in Machiavelli's word, "understand." For those who understand, the classical unity of ethics and politics would no longer hold, either as a political reality or as a theoretical ideal.

Herein lies the genuinely revolutionary character of Machiavelli's political thought. In conceiving of ethical ideals as mere illusions he breaks asunder the classical unity of ethics and politics. In contemporary terms, we would say that Machiavelli attempts to study the empirical facts of politics in isolation from any consideration of ethical values. Or more precisely, to the extent that he does discuss values, he does so as if they were themselves merely facts. For example, Machiavelli's prohibition against excessive violence is not based upon any objective set of ethical values such as "divine law," but upon the strictly pragmatic consideration that, as a political fact, excessive violence is self-defeating.

Deriving values from purely factual or empirical considerations we may term *ethical naturalism,* and to the extent that modern political science deals with ethical considerations at all, it does so largely from a naturalistic point of view. In this, modern political science is heir to a way of thinking first initiated by Machiavelli. Indeed, from Machiavelli on the whole terminology of political philosophy changes, a terminology no longer premised upon the classical concept of ethical virtue, but upon the empirical facts of politics alone. And as we have seen, the key term of modern naturalism is *power,* a concept of minimal importance to the classical thinkers, but one that is central to almost all modern political thought down to our own day. Indeed, as we shall see in the following chapters, most of the key terms of modern political theory such as *sovereignty, natural right, individualism, consent,* to name but a few, are themselves framed within the larger conceptual context of power.

Here we may begin a brief critique of Machiavelli, for while he initiated the modern language of political theory, he was largely unaware of (or unconcerned about) those epistemological assumptions from which the language was derived. His empiricism and naturalism, for example, are the consequence of his interest in studying "real politics" firsthand, not of any philosophical principle. Whereas a Plato or an Aristotle began with metaphysical and epistemological concepts from which they derived their philosophies of politics, Machiavelli begins with politics and ends there, leaving his assumptions about the nature of reality and the basis of knowledge implicit in his political analysis.[27]

Because of his epistemological innocence, moreover, Machiavelli fails to appreciate or to question the revolutionary import of his new political science. A case in point is his belief that the secular state of his day—what would eventually evolve into the modern nation-state—was, in effect, its own justification; it did not need to be legitimized by some larger ethical principle. Indeed, Machiavelli seems to be suggesting, whether he is fully aware of it or not, that if people's loyalties could be shifted to the nation-state and made sufficiently intense, the state would become its own justification. (Here, perhaps, is the real task of Machiavelli's virtuous prince: to found the nation-state by manipulating the illusions of nationalism.) But the state can be its own justification only so long as we assume there is no broader ethical standard by which to judge it, an assumption that Machiavelli clearly holds to but never makes explicit. As such, he never offers any philosophical justification for the "state as an end in itself."

It is because of Machiavelli's failure to probe these deeper epistemological and ethical questions that he himself becomes an uncritical exponent of the emerging nation-state. The last chapter of *The Prince,* unlike the empirical and coolly logical chapters that precede it, is a strident and emotional appeal to Lorenzo the Magnificent to unite Italy. Machiavelli commits the fatal mistake of violating his own most fundamental rule of political analysis. Rather than stripping himself of all illusions, he uncritically accepts the greatest illusion of the modern age. Ironically, Machiavelli is a prisoner of the very nationalistic illusions he helped create, and that he believed, if only in an unformed and half-conscious way, were a sufficient justification for the state and for the actions of his virtuous prince.

Quite apart from these larger issues, there are some serious problems with the more concrete aspects of Machiavelli's political formula. For example, he seems to have a very imperfect notion of what would be necessary to create and maintain the modern state. It is *The Prince* that is most at fault here; *The Discourses* takes a broader view of the organizational necessities of the modern state. But even *The Discourses* fails adequately to outline the structure of such a state. Thus, while at times Machiavelli alludes to the necessity of new forms of administration and political organization, at others he speaks of his new Italy as if it were simply a larger and more comprehensive Florence, as if it were a kind of polis or Italian city-state writ large.[28]

When discussing his "ideal" republican form of government, for example, his pattern is drawn from pre-Medici Florence, or from the Roman republic, models that were not at all appropriate to a united Italy. Hence, he fails to discuss adequately the new role of citizenship in the modern state, mechanisms of representation, the limits of the central power, or conversely, the rights and liberties of the subjects, issues that would inform the whole debate over the nation-state in the centuries to come.

Indeed, Machiavelli failed even to see the outlines of that incipient debate that, as we shall see in the next chapter, revolved around the issue of church versus state, an issue raised to the highest importance by the Reformation. No doubt Machiavelli's ethical naturalism blinded him to the importance of religious questions.[29] But while he might treat religion simply as an illusion to be manipulated for political purposes, others were not disposed to treat it so lightly, as a century of religious conflict would amply demonstrate.

Yet, when all is said and done, the importance of Machiavelli as a political thinker is not to be denied. All of our criticisms have to do with the fact that he is a transitional figure in the history of Western political thought. Like the Renaissance itself, Machiavelli stands midway between the old medieval world and the new emerging order we call modern. And like most transitional thinkers, he is both prophetic and backward looking. This largely explains why Machiavelli has a vision of the future political order yet an imperfect understanding of what it will look like.

We should add, in conclusion, that Machiavelli's vision encompassed more than politics. It is a vision of humanity loosed from medieval traditions and constraints, including ethical constraints, freely shaping its own destiny. The great Renaissance historian Jacob Burckhardt noted that the thinkers of the Renaissance viewed the state as a work of art.[30] This is precisely how Machiavelli saw it, as something made by human beings and shaped to serve human purposes. And it is those qualities—boldness, audacity, courage, intelligence, foresight, in a word, *virtu* (virtue)—that allow human beings to shape and control events that Machiavelli praises.

Yet, on the other side of virtu, and standing opposed to it, is what Machiavelli calls *fortuna* (fortune). *Fate* perhaps comes closest to encompassing his sense of this term, for it comprises all those events that people can neither foresee nor control. Thus, while Machiavelli's new vision is optimistic, it is one that at the same time recognizes human limitations. But what is the extent of these limitations? To what degree can fortuna be controlled by virtu? These questions form the great underlying theme that runs like a thread throughout *The Prince* and *The Discourses*. And the general conclusion to which Machiavelli adheres is this: While the great political leader can to some degree control the effects of fortune by virtue, that is, by intelligent foresight and planning, the control is always imperfect. The human world can never be completely mastered; it will always be, at bottom, unpredictable. Like the classical thinkers, Machiavelli has a cyclical view of history that holds that societies periodically rise and decline. These cycles, and the chaos of events, are never within the power of human beings to control completely.

Such a limited view is not shared by Thomas Hobbes, a political thinker of the first rank who completes what Machiavelli began. Hobbes not only rejects the classical and medieval tradition of political discourse, he does so with the insights of modern science, insights that were not available to Machiavelli. In the name of science, and with the awesome power of the modern nation-state, Hobbes proposes to abolish the notion of fortuna altogether. He proposes to put politics, no less than the other aspects of people's lives, fully under human control for the first time in human history.

Notes

1. Niccolo Machiavelli, "The Prince," in *The Prince and The Discourses* (New York: Random House, 1950), p. 56.

2. John Plamenatz, "Machiavelli," in *Man and Society, Volume I: Machiavelli through Rousseau* (New York: McGraw-Hill, 1963).

3. See Max Lerner's "Introduction," in *The Prince and The Discourses*, pp. xxxiii–xxxiv.

4. Machiavelli, "The Prince," in *The Prince and The Discourses*, p. 56.

5. Frederick the Great, "Should a Prince Keep Faith?" in DeLamar Jensen, ed., *Problems in European Civilization, Machiavelli: Cynic, Patriot, or Political Scientist?* (Boston: D.C. Heath, 1960), p. 5.

6. On the other hand, there is some scholarly support for the idea that Machiavelli really was a philosopher of evil. See Leo Strauss, *Thoughts on Machiavelli* (New York: Free Press, 1958). Strauss's view constitutes a minority opinion.

7. Machiavelli, "The Prince," in *The Prince and The Discourses*, p. 9.

8. Ibid.

9. Ibid., p. 35.

10. Ibid., p. 27.

11. See Sydney Anglo, *Machiavelli: A Dissection* (New York: Harcourt Brace Jovanovich, 1969), p. 42. "The idealization [of Borgia] was simply of a method, not of a man."

12. See Sheldon S. Wolin, *Politics and Vision, Continuity and Innovation in Western Political Thought* (Boston: Little, Brown, 1960), chap. VII. Wolin argues that Machiavelli advocated an "economy of violence."

13. Machiavelli, "The Prince," in *The Prince and The Discourses*, p. 63.

14. Ibid., p. 64.

15. Ibid., p. 36.

16. Ibid., p. 38.

17. It bears repeating that Machiavelli is a transitional thinker. To argue that he provides a glimpse of the modern democratic nation-state is not to suggest that he was himself aware of what was to come. For a related discussion of Machiavelli's discovery of "the people," see Wolin, *Politics and Vision*, pp. 228–35.

18. Machiavelli, "The Discourses," in *The Prince and The Discourses*, p. 148.

19. Ibid., p. 285.

20. Ibid.

21. Yet Machiavelli was a realist. He understood perfectly well that Christianity would not be replaced by paganism, and to seriously suggest such a thing would be too extreme and shocking a position even for him to take. What he does advocate is a reform of Christian ideals such that they cease to affirm meekness and humility and begin to glorify love of country and to justify those actions that are necessary to defend the state.

22. Machiavelli, "The Discourses," in *The Prince and The Discourses,* p. 148.

23. Machiavelli, "The Prince," in *The Prince and The Discourses,* pp. 65–66.

24. Ibid.

25. Professor Isaiah Berlin, in his article "The Question of Machiavelli," in *The New York Review of Books,* 4 November 1971, argues another interpretation. According to Berlin, what is shocking about Machiavelli's political theory is not its denial of ethical values (he argues that Machiavelli possessed a pagan morality based upon the idea that the state itself constituted an ethical standard of value) but its assumption that there exists a multiplicity of ethical standards that are mutually exclusive of one another. Political ethics, in Berlin's analysis of Machiavelli, is thus different from, and exclusive of, private or Christian ethics. Such a perspective, Berlin argues, shattered the traditional Western assumption that ethical values are rooted in a common standard (natural law, for instance) and possess, therefore, a universal validity. In terms of our analysis, the consequences of this perspective could only be the loss of belief in the reality of ethical standards as such. Berlin, nevertheless, would insist that, whatever the consequences of Machiavelli's ethical dualism, he did not personally reject the existence of an ethical standard in politics.

26. Ernst Cassirer, *The Myth of the State* (London: Yale University Press, 1946), p. 153.

27. See Wolin, *Politics and Vision,* p. 211. Wolin argues that "one of the significant aspects of Machiavelli's political metaphysic was that it was unrelated to a systematic philosophy."

28. See Plamenatz, *Man and Society,* pp. 43–44, for a discussion of Machiavelli's inability to see beyond the confines of a small republic and the implications of this failure for his ideal of a united Italy.

29. See Federico Chabod, *Machiavelli and The Renaissance,* David Moore, trans. (New York: Harper & Row, 1958), p. 93. Machiavelli "shows little response to any spiritual movement that is not subordinate to a purely political idea; he is ignorant . . . of the eternal and the transcendent."

30. Jacob Burckhardt, *The Civilization of the Renaissance in Italy,* Vol. I (New York: Harper & Row, 1958).

8

Hobbes

Thomas Hobbes (1588–1679) was born prematurely when his mother was told that the Spanish Armada had been spotted off the coast of England. The Armada was defeated and England was saved, but his traumatic birth led Hobbes to exclaim that "fear and I were born twins."

But Hobbes's fearfulness stemmed from more than his traumatic birth: He was born into a time of violence and troubles. The Reformation, which had begun with Martin Luther's break from the Roman Catholic Church, had resulted in the establishment of a radically new religious doctrine that emphasized the authority of scripture and the direct, unmediated relationship of the individual to God. Luther's religion undercut traditional religious authority and pitted Catholic against Protestant in what was to become a general European civil war.

The Reformation was not, of course, simply a religious struggle. Its political implications were vast, and it was, in fact, the decisive factor in the emergence of the modern nation-state. Those European monarchs who wanted to free themselves from papal domination found an excuse in Protestantism. In the name of "religious truth" they broke from Rome, consolidated all political power in their own hands, and unified their respective domains into those large geographical units that define the modern nation-state.

Hobbes's England followed this general European pattern, although in a much more peaceful way than was typical of many other countries. The problem came later, in the post-Reformation struggles between the mainline Protestant groups who defended the absolute power of the monarch in religious affairs and the more radical groups who came to support the theory of limited monarchy. These latter groups, the Puritans, initially wanted no more than the "purification" of the organization and ceremonies of the Church of England to accord with scripture and conscience. But the logic of their religious position drove them not only to advocate limiting the power of the state in religious affairs, but also to argue for the right of resistance against "unlawful authority" as such.[1]

To make a long and complex story short, civil war broke out in England between the Royalists, who supported the king, and the Puritans, who supported Parliament. The Puritans won the day and for a short period established a republic under the leadership of Oliver Cromwell. But in 1660 the monarchy was restored. Nevertheless, the Puritan Revolution ultimately triumphed. In 1688, in what has come to be known as the Glorious Revolution, Parliament asserted its authority and the outline of a modern constitutional government was firmly established in England.

Hobbes took a very firm position on the politics of his time. He was a strong supporter of absolute monarchy and an implacable foe of the Puritan revolutionaries. Hobbes's political stance is only of historical interest now. But what is essential to our discussion is the complex philosophical system that underlay Hobbes's support of the monarchy, for it was not his political practice but his political theory that was to shape the future. More than any other thinker, Hobbes invented the modern theory of politics—its method, its language, and its concepts.

But in order to understand Hobbes's political theory, we must first turn to another revolution—the scientific revolution. To this revolution alone did Hobbes give his ardent and lifelong support, a revolution that began in outline form in the late sixteenth century and became an established fact by the seventeenth. We will analyze that revolution in some detail shortly, but broadly speaking it aimed at understanding the world from a strictly empirical point of view. The idea that knowledge could be found in the classics of the past was rejected in favor of direct observation and experimentation. In Hobbes's day this rejection took the form of an attack upon Aristotelianism and the whole classical tradition, which, as the result of the influence of St. Thomas and other thirteenth-century scholars, had become the basis of the European university curriculum.

As a student at Oxford, Hobbes came to dislike this standard curriculum intensely and increasingly adopted the new scientific paradigm, particularly that of Galileo, a thinker who came to be the decisive influence upon Hobbes. Galileo had not only demonstrated the correctness of Copernicus's discovery that the sun rather than the earth is the center of the solar system, he had also demonstrated that the earth and indeed the whole universe could be understood without recourse to theological or teleological explanations.

Hobbes simply applied Galileo's nonteleological method to the study of politics.

Seen from this perspective, we might say that Machiavelli was the Copernicus of political theory and Hobbes the Galileo who carried Machiavelli's revolutionary insights to their logical conclusion. And herein lies a historical irony. At the very time that Europe was being convulsed by religious revolutions, an intellectual revolution was occurring that would make the religious point of view irrelevant. Hobbes's works embody this irony. Not only did his defense of absolute monarchy offend the Puritans, but in employing the language of Galilean science he offended the Royalists as well. The Royalists claimed that the monarch rules by "divine right"; Hobbes claimed, on the contrary, that the monarch rules simply by the effective use of power. The new language of science had no room for such notions as divine right or the will of God, and Hobbes refused to employ them in his defense of monarchy.

Viewed historically, we can now see that the Royalists had more in common with their Puritan opponents than they did with Hobbes. Both argued their cases on the basis of religious assumptions. They were all essentially religious men whose mode of thinking was shaped by their particular reading of scripture. Hobbes's new scientific language utterly rejected religious forms of reasoning. It is not surprising, therefore, that Hobbes was widely believed to be an atheist (a most serious charge in the seventeenth century), particularly following the publication in 1651 of his major political treatise, *Leviathan*.[2]

Although Hobbes wrote other works in political theory (the most important being *De Cive*), his most mature and most exciting work is *Leviathan*.[3] Hobbes attempts to demonstrate in that work that Galilean physics provides a model of human psychology that in turn lays the foundations for a genuine science of politics.[4] To understand Hobbes's reasoning, we must first begin our analysis of *Leviathan* with a discussion of his metaphysical and epistemological assumptions, and from these move on to his physics, psychology, and finally his political science. Let us begin, then, with an analysis of the new science as it was understood by Hobbes and his contemporaries.

To begin with, the new science was premised upon a materialist metaphysics. Men such as Galileo took the universe to be a material reality that could be understood in its own material terms. They rejected teleological arguments or appeals to divine authority to explain why material events happen. Although most of them retained religious convictions of one sort or another, they excluded any religious explanations of physical reality. Their science was to be a strictly materialist science.[5]

It was the epistemology of the new science, however, that was most revolutionary. That epistemology was empiricism, but an empiricism of a quite different sort than that of Aristotle or even of Machiavelli. For the new empiricism, particularly that of Galileo, did not take the world of sensation (what people see, hear, and feel) at face value. Rather, it looked beneath this reality to something more basic. This something, according to Galileo (and consequently Hobbes), is body and motion.

Body and motion constitute the subject matter of physics for these two thinkers. *Body* refers to what we would today call mass, the basic structure of matter out of which all things are comprised. *Motion* refers to the fact that mass is energized—that bundles of matter move ceaselessly through space unless compelled to become stationary by the resistance of other bundles of matter. We are reminded here of Democritus, the pre-Socratic materialist, who claimed that the universe is reducible to material atoms moving through a void and combining in different ways to produce different elements.

It makes more sense, however, to link Hobbes with modern science than with pre-Socratic physics, for his underlying assumptions about the nature of reality have become the whole basis of modern science. Mass, energy, space, and time are those fundamental categories to which modern science reduces all sensory experience, categories that are simply more sophisticated versions of Hobbes's body and motion. Science relies upon these categories because they are common to all things that we perceive. Such a common denominator is the first requirement in the development of any scientific theory, for without it we would have no way to make any sense out of what we observe. In and of itself, what we observe is a world of infinite variety in constant change or, as Plato would say, in a ceaseless state of becoming.

For this reason, Plato himself assumed the existence of a common denominator. But Plato's common denominator was the nonmaterial principle of form, and it was precisely the introduction of nonmaterial principles that Hobbes and his contemporaries wished to avoid. They wanted to develop a strictly materialist science based upon strictly materialist assumptions. With a body and motion conception of reality, they claimed to have done just that. Without recourse to an "imaginary" perfect world of form, they claimed to have found the material common denominator by which to explain the universe in strictly scientific terms.

An example of how modern materialist science actually works will prove useful here. Let us suppose we wish to explain the phenomenon of color. So long as we remain at the crude empirical level of pure sensation, we will find it impossible to explain much of anything because we will have no common denominator of color. We will find it difficult even to get agreement on what is red versus what is pink, or reddish orange, and so on. This is why Plato rejected the sensory world of "becoming" as a valid basis for theory. He was compelled to posit a realm of pure unchangeable "being" in order to develop his physical and ethical doctrines. In the terms of this example, Plato would say that there is a pure ideal form of redness. The object and common denominator of Platonic science, then, is the ideal transcendent form of redness, rather than its imperfect empirical representation.

But suppose, like Hobbes and his contemporaries, we reduced all physical phenomena to body and motion. We would then inquire as to what kind of body and what kind of motion are involved in the phenomenon of color. Obviously color is visually perceived, which means it must be connected to the larger phenomenon of light. But what then, is light? Clearly it must be some kind of "body" that upon striking an object is reflected in such a way that it produces in us the sensation of redness. *Redness* is thus simply a word we use to describe a particular kind of body in motion.

The great theoretical advantage inherent in this way of thinking is that we can now explain the variations of redness as simply variations in the motion of minute material bodies of light. Put in the language of modern science, the property of redness, or of any other color, is simply a particular frequency of light particles (photons) or waves. Thus, with the language of body and motion we have reduced the phenomena of color to its most basic common denominator and, as such, no longer need worry about getting agreement on what is red versus what is pink. Red or pink are now simply subjective sensory experiences, what Hobbes calls *phantasms,* of an objective physical phenomenon. So long as we can describe that physical phenomenon, it does not matter what we think we see. If we agree that a certain wavelength of light shall be designated red, it is for scientific purposes red, even if we mistakenly perceive it as blue. Without recourse to a nonmaterial principle such as form, we have established a strictly material basis for "objective truth," no matter what we subjectively see, hear, or feel.

But something more than this new vision of reality was required for modern science to become genuinely theoretical. A language had to be invented that would describe the underlying physical reality of body and motion. Mathematics was the chosen language, for mathematics is a quantitative language and a body-motion conception of reality is at bottom a quantitative conception. Body can be described only in terms of height, width, depth, weight, density, and so on; motion only in terms of direction, distance, velocity, and time. These are all mathematical or geometrical terms. Precisely because of its materialist assumptions, modern science of necessity is a mathematical or quantitative discipline.

More important than their descriptive capabilities, however, the conclusions of mathematics and geometry are true by definition.[6] (It was this fact that most impressed Hobbes.) They are true precisely because they involve internally consistent definitions that we ourselves create. And because these definitions are internally consistent, their proper manipulation will produce new definitions or syllogisms that also are logically true. For example, given that we agree to define a circle as an infinite series of points on a plane equidistant from a common point, it logically and indisputably follows that any number of lines, or radii, drawn from the center to the circumference of any circle will be equal in length. And given our definition, we may further logically deduce that the circumference of any circle is equally proportionate to its radius, and so on. Consequently, to the extent that we can fit our mathematical or geometrical systems to the material world of body and motion, to that same extent we can deduce certain "truths" about that material world from those systems.

But here we must note something of crucial importance. From the perspective of modern science, when we deduce or predict something about the material world, the "truth" we produce is really a truth about our mathematical system, not about the material world as such. More generally, whatever symbolic language we use to describe that world, be it mathematics, geometry, or ordinary words, the truth of what we say is the truth only of our symbolic language. This is so because our language is simply a consistent set of symbols that we use to explain the physical world. These symbols are not identical to the world we are trying to explain. For this reason, Hobbes argues that science is nothing more than knowledge about how to use our symbolic language in logically coherent ways, that scientifically speaking, "true and false are attributes of speech, not of things."[7] That is, truth resides in our speech or symbolic language, not in the material world of things we describe with that speech or language.

This idea that truth is a function of language rather than of things is called *nominalism*. The nominalist maintains that words are merely arbitrary symbols that we use to classify things or ideas. Thus, according to the nominalist, when we say a flower is beautiful, the word *beautiful* is simply an abstract term or symbol we use to classify certain attributes of a flower. Beauty does not exist as a physical reality. Nor does it exist as a Platonic form. Thus, to understand beauty is simply to understand what we mean when we say beauty. It is not, as Plato would have it, to understand some larger reality called *beauty*.

Hobbes is a thoroughgoing nominalist. And it is this extreme nominalism that is the mark of modern science. Like Hobbes, modern science combines a materialist assertion that all that exists is the physical world with a nominalist theory of language that states that we can know that world only indirectly through the way we think and speak about it. It claims, along with Hobbes, that a scientific theory is nothing but a symbolic representation of the physical world.

Part of Hobbes's greatness as a thinker lies in the fact that he was one of the first to think of science in these terms. He grasped the importance of theory as a deductive or, as he would say, a geometrical means to understand the physical world. This key idea, which he got from Galileo, along with an understanding of geometry, opened a new world for Hobbes. He saw the possibility of literally deducing the structure of the universe from abstract-geometrical principles. He even imagined that it would be possible for the scientist to calculate the magnitude of the universe while sitting in a closet!

Even though we now recognize that Hobbes's notion of scientific method is not wholly adequate, it is important to understand how fundamentally correct his insight into the real nature of modern science was. Hobbes realized that even though science is an empirical discipline, its real value and power lie at the level of abstract theory. This is why Hobbes rejected the method of one of his famous contemporaries, Sir Francis Bacon. Unlike Galileo, Bacon stressed the accumulation of more and more empirical facts as the appropriate method of science, rather than the creation of increasingly comprehensive theories to deduce or predict the occurrence of physical facts.

In the final analysis, Hobbes and Galileo were more correct than Bacon, for contrary to what is generally assumed, the progress of modern science has been primarily the result of increasing theoretical sophistication, not of the accumulation of more and more physical facts. Thus, the great strides in seventeenth- and eighteenth-century science were closely linked to the development of new mathematical systems, such as calculus. And to the present day, the model of the great scientific thinker is not unlike that of Hobbes's theorist in the closet. The great advances in science have come, in other words, from those who had learned to think about the universe in new ways, who had developed new symbolic languages, not from those who simply collected new facts.

This brings us to Hobbes's psychology, or theory of human nature, for here the revolutionary implications of his scientific method are most apparent. Consistent with that method, Hobbes does not present us with new facts about human beings, but with a new way of looking at the "facts." Hobbes proposes to analyze humankind from that same materialist point of view, and with that same symbolic language, that Galileo employed in his study of physical nature. In short, Hobbes proposes to study human beings as a set of purely physical processes that are reducible to body and motion. As we shall see, it is from an analysis of these processes that Hobbes claims to have logically or "geometrically" deduced a scientific theory of politics.

Hobbes argues that we can note two kinds of physical motion that account for the totality of human life. The first he calls *vital,* or *involuntary motion,* by which he means those basic and unthinking life functions of inhalation, digestion, circulation, and so on. These comprise the purely physical aspect of human existence and are the subject matter of physiology. The second Hobbes calls *voluntary motion,* by which he means those forms of human activity that are willed, such as walking and speaking. Moreover, since these kinds of activities are usually done with others, Hobbes includes politics and other various kinds of social interaction in voluntary motion. Thus, Hobbes argues, voluntary motion (what the modern social scientist would call behavior) comprises the subject matter of political science.

But, Hobbes continues, since the outward forms of voluntary motion begin as psychological states, psychology must precede social and political science in the study of human behavior. Before we walk, we must first will to move our legs. Before we speak, we must know what we wish to say, and we must know how to use language to convey our intended meaning. Indeed, *knowing* and *willing* constitute the whole of our psychological processes, says Hobbes.[8] And these processes, he argues, are themselves simply internal voluntary motions. Knowing and willing are nothing more than physical "motions" within the brain caused by the stimulation of outer sensations. (If Hobbes had available to him the more sophisticated language of modern behavioral psychology, he would say that human behavior may be explained as the result of electrochemical functions within the brain that are triggered by the actions of the senses.)

Thus, knowing, says Hobbes, is a material or physiological activity by which we translate our sensations into words and then into language systems that can be manipulated to produce knowledge.[9] It begins when the organs of sensation receive the impressions of outer motion (such as the motion of air and light particles) and transmit them to the brain. The brain, in turn, absorbs and "reproduces" these grosser kinds of motions. These motions within the brain (Hobbes thought of it as the vibration of brain particles) lead to the experience or, in Hobbes's words, the *phantasm* of sensation. The brain then assigns names to our phantasms. For example, a particular wavelength of light (body) will stimulate a particular vibration or phantasm (motion) within the brain to which it assigns a particular name, such as *redness*. Once a sufficient number of primary names have been assigned to the variety of sensations that we experience, the brain can assign more abstract names to the primary names. For example, the word *red* can be subsumed under the more abstract term, *color*. In this way, the brain is able to evolve increasingly complex language systems that can be manipulated to produce knowledge. The word *black* and the word *white*, for example, can be manipulated by the brain to produce the indisputable truth that "the color black is not the color white."

Several points need to be made here. First, Hobbes's psychology of knowledge is an attempt to explain in scientific terms how human beings can think at a conceptual level, for it is this ability that distinguishes them from the rest of the animal kingdom, says Hobbes. A dog, he admits, will recognize its name when called. But only a human being is capable of assigning names to other names to create language systems that can be manipulated to produce knowledge. Thus, the seemingly trivial statement that "the color black is not the color white" turns out to be profoundly important. Animals are incapable of this kind of conceptualization. And further, the statement is a model of that same language—logic that we find in a more sophisticated guise in mathematics, geometry, and formal logic. These latter languages, geometry in particular, are preferred by Hobbes simply because they are the most abstract, inclusive, and logically coherent symbolic systems available to us. They are thus most capable of producing that "truth of words" we call scientific knowledge—truth that is indisputable because it is logically consistent.

Second, it must always be borne in mind that Hobbes has a strictly material psychology of knowledge. Behind our most complex and sophisticated scientific language, Hobbes insists, is a more basic material reality. All of our language may be traced back to initial physical motions in the brain. And it is these phantasms that we experience, not the material reality of body and motion that produces them. We do not, for example, see wavelengths of light; we "see" red. Nevertheless, behind the phantasm of redness is the reality of light particles and brain functions. Behind our most sophisticated language and conceptual knowledge lies the ultimate material reality of body and motion.

Finally, it must be kept in mind that this material psychology of knowledge carries with it a nominalist theory of language, for reasons that we can now perhaps grasp more clearly. Truth exists in words and not things, according to Hobbes, precisely because we cannot experience things directly. *Red* is simply a word we assign to a phantasm; it is not identical to the reality of light particles that produces that phantasm. Abstract words such as *color* or *beauty* are even further removed from our initial sensory experience. These are words that classify other words. And the language of geometry or mathematics is pure abstraction. Hence, we can know directly only our symbolic language. Truth, as a consequence, can only be defined as the logical consistency of that language.

Willing—the active, desiring side of the personality—works upon the same physical principles as knowing, according to Hobbes. The will comprises those internal motions called the passions, and they include not only the physical desires for food, sex, and so on, but the social desires for honor and status as well. But all of the passions are reducible to motions of physical particles that make up the human body. Moreover, says Hobbes, these motions (what the modern biologist would describe as physiochemical processes) are ceaseless, because life cannot exist in a condition of stasis. For this reason, Hobbes insists, no one "can anymore live whose desires are at an end, than he whose senses and imaginations are at a stand."[10] In short, the voluntary motions that cause us to desire things are as ceaseless as those that cause us to imagine and to acquire knowledge.

Yet, while we continuously will many things, from food to social status, all of our desires flow from the same internal physiological motions. All of our passions are part of the same life force. This Hobbes terms *endeavor,*[11] which he argues is nothing more than appetite and aversion, in effect, the desire to attain pleasure and avoid pain. What all human beings will in general, in other words, is the maximization of pleasure and the minimization of pain. Consequently, says Hobbes, it follows that the will is nothing more than "*the last appetite in deliberation*."[12] That is, the will is simply that pleasure or least pain a person finally selects after deliberating upon the variety available. The final act of deliberation—the choice we finally make—is what Hobbes calls the will.

Hobbes, in effect, had developed what we would now call a utilitarian psychology: He assumes that human behavior works upon the principles of pleasure and pain. Consequently it follows for Hobbes that the will is the determining factor in human behavior, not knowledge, as Socrates had maintained. In the Socratic system, knowledge is—or ought to be—prior to the will. That is, one must first know what is good before one actively desires something. In the Hobbesian system we first will something, that which we believe will bring us the greatest pleasure or the least pain, and use our knowledge accordingly. In Hobbes's view, in other words, we are driven by our passions and use our intellectual capacity simply as a means to determine what will bring us the greatest pleasure or the least pain. This, once again, is what Hobbes means when he says that the will is "the last appetite in deliberating."

Now given Hobbes's utilitarian psychology, it follows that human happiness or felicity can only be defined as the realization of pleasure. Felicity and pleasure, in other words, are identical terms for Hobbes. And since the biological makeup of the human species is such that the desire for pleasure is ceaseless, it follows, says Hobbes, that felicity "is a continual progress of the desire from one object to another; the attaining of the former, being still but the way to the latter."[13] Consequently, he concludes:

> The object of man's desire, is not to enjoy once only, and for one instant of time; but to assure forever, the way of his future desire. And therefore, the voluntary actions, and inclinations of all men, tend, not only to the procuring, but also to the assuring of a contented life; and differ only in the way: which ariseth partly from the diversity of passions, in divers men; and partly from the difference of the knowledge, or opinion each one has of the causes, which produce the effect desired.[14]

Note that Hobbes is careful to distinguish between our will and the objects of our will. It is perfectly true, says Hobbes, that different people desire different things, partly because of "diverse passions" (by which he means temperamental differences), and partly because of different opinions of what will produce pleasure. An Australian aborigine, for example, will not have entirely the same conception of what constitutes pleasure as a person from France. In other words, what people desire is socially or culturally determined. But the incessant desire for pleasure or felicity, however it may be defined, is a natural or biologically innate characteristic of all human beings according to Hobbes.

Yet, he argues, while different people will different forms of pleasure, we are compelled to recognize that all human beings do will or desire one thing in common: power. This is so because power is precisely the means by which to attain felicity, no matter how felicity is defined. And logically we cannot desire something without first desiring the means to attain it. Consequently, says Hobbes:

> I put for a general inclination of all mankind, a perpetual and restless desire of power after power, that ceaseth only in death. And the cause of this is not

always that a man hopes for a more intensive delight, than he has already attained to; or that he cannot be content with a moderate power: but because he cannot assure the power and means to live well, which he hath present, without the acquisition of more.[15]

Here is a perfect example of Hobbes's deductive or "geometrical" method. Given that all are by nature pleasure seekers, it must follow as logically as a geometrical demonstration that all are power seekers as well. And since the passions and desires are unlimited, it just as logically follows that the desire for power itself must be unlimited. Moreover, even if we add the qualifier that a person may be satisfied with a limited amount of pleasure, a qualifier that Hobbes accepts only for the sake of argument, logic still dictates that one must forever seek more power simply to ensure whatever "delights" one may currently possess. For so long as others continue to acquire power they will pose a threat to the felicity of those who do not continue to acquire it. As we shall soon see, this "logic of power" is central to Hobbes's political theory.

Here, then, is Hobbes's psychological profile of the species: a desiring, power-seeking animal that uses its intellectual capacity to further its ends. Hobbes thus regards human nature as utterly self-interested and self-regarding, hence innately antisocial. In this, he closely parallels St. Augustine, but with one terribly important difference. Hobbes is a materialist; hence, his psychology is strictly secular. He explicitly rejects any religious or moral judgments about human nature. "The desires and other passions of man are in themselves no sin,"[16] says Hobbes, and he refuses to use any language that would suggest otherwise, for scientifically it would make no sense to do so. To assign blame involves the supposition that human beings have a choice as to how they will behave. But scientifically they have no choice but to do that which maximizes their pleasure.

Herein lies the genuinely revolutionary character of Hobbes's theory of human nature. In reducing people's psychological life to those same principles of body and motion that govern the rest of the universe, he abolishes the Socratic, or classical, conception of freedom, a conception based upon the assumption of human choice. In other words, Hobbes denies the idea of free will, for as he says, "neither is the freedom of willing or not willing greater in man than in other living creatures."[17] We must bear in mind, therefore, that when Hobbes speaks of the will in terms of voluntary motion, he does not mean to suggest that there exists anything like a "free will." In point of fact, our voluntary actions are no more voluntary than the involuntary motions of our basic biological functions. We may think we make free choices, but ultimately our choices are determined by our "last appetite in deliberating." We will act upon what we think will produce the greatest pleasure or the least pain, for biologically we can act no other way. Thus, if we "choose" to be a "saint," Hobbes would argue, it is only because we believe it will bring us more pleasure in the long run than if we choose to be a "sinner."

Having examined the psychological states underlying voluntary motion, Hobbes is now prepared to discuss the outward forms of voluntary motion. Such a discussion constitutes political science for Hobbes. Not surprisingly, Hobbes's view of human nature has a profound impact on his political theory. His psychology of pleasure and pain greatly influenced his most important contribution to political thought—his theory of the social contract.

Although the concept of the social contract goes back to the Sophists and is briefly discussed in both Plato's and Cicero's *Republic,* it is really a modern idea. At least its articulation into full-scale theories of politics is modern. And while Hobbes is the first great modern contract theorist, contract theories persisted until the end of the eighteenth century as the dominant mode of political analysis. Locke and Rousseau, the subjects of the next two chapters, are both contract theorists.

The basic idea of the social contract is actually quite simple: The state is the result of a contract between human beings, and the scope and extent of the powers of government are to be determined by an analysis of the terms of the contract. It is as if a group of people were to form a business corporation by contracting with one another. The powers of the corporation and the respective rights and obligations of its members will be determined by the terms of the contract by which the corporation was formed. And just as a corporation is a fictitious person established by contract and given life by a board of directors, in the same way the state is a fictitious person given life by a "board of directors" we call government. The state, like the corporation, is an abstraction. Government is that body that gives the abstraction real life.

But if the basic idea of the social contract is simple, its implications are far reaching, for the contract theory claims that the state is created by the mutual agreement or consent of its members. As a consequence, government is legitimate only if it corresponds to what people have rationally consented to. This is a very modern notion that runs counter to medieval thought, which presumed that secular government exists by divine sanction. This idea was still prevalent in Hobbes's time and was employed by the Royalists, who argued that the monarch rules by divine right. The consent-contract theory flatly rejected this idea. It claimed, on the contrary, that government is legitimate only to the extent that people have consented to it.

Of particular importance to Hobbes is that the contract theory makes possible what he believes to be a strictly logical, "scientific" analysis of the state. Like all contract theorists, he reasons that human beings would consent only to that which rationally accords with their needs and desires (that is, with their human nature). It follows, then, that the state is a rational structure. Indeed, Hobbes goes so far as to conceive the state as a rationally constructed machine. As such, he argues, the state is amenable to scientific analysis, for what is rationally constructed may be rationally analyzed. We need only determine the essence of human nature, says Hobbes, in order to discover the logic behind the structure of the state.

But how to determine the essence of human nature? The theory of contract gives the answer, says Hobbes, for to assume that the state is created by contract is also to assume a precontract situation in which the state does not exist. More than this, it is to assume the nonexistence of what seventeenth- and eighteenth-century thinkers called *civil society,* by which they meant the whole socioeconomic and legal structure of society. This precontract condition they called the *state of nature,* a condition in which people are unconstrained by legal rules since there is no governing power to make such rules. And where human behavior is unconstrained, Hobbes argues, that behavior will reflect human nature as it really is. It follows, then, that we can discover the truth about human nature simply by "observing" the behavior of human beings in their natural condition.

Of course, Hobbes has already developed a theory of human nature by applying the first principles of Galilean physics to human behavior. This arguing from first principles Hobbes calls the *compositive method,* a method he has employed to demonstrate that the voluntary motions are ceaseless, that people's quest for pleasure is insatiable, and that, as a consequence, human beings are innately self-interested power seekers.

Hobbes's theory of the state of nature provides a corollary method for analyzing human behavior—the *resolutive method.* Where the compositive method begins with first principles, the resolutive method begins with the effects of things and deduces the first principles that must have caused the effects. By "observing" human beings in the state of nature, Hobbes employs the resolutive method, for he deduces from the effects of people's behavior their innate thirst for power, the ceaseless motion of the passions, and the underlying first principles of body and motion. The state of nature is thus a useful supplement to Galilean physics in the development of a scientific psychology. Taken together, Hobbes believes that the resoluto-compositive method provides a powerful demonstration of the validity of his theory of human nature.

The question, of course, is, Where is a state of nature to be found? The answer will at first seem perplexing, for Hobbes is much too sophisticated to believe human beings ever lived in a real state of nature. Even the most "primitive" peoples have a polity of some sort. For Hobbes, as for later contract theorists, the state of nature is nothing more than a mental construct. It is an intellectual act, a "thought experiment," in which the theorist imaginatively projects human beings into a prepolitical condition and, with the mind's eye, observes their behavior.[18]

Indeed, the whole idea of the social contract is an act of imagination. Hobbes does not really believe that civil society was formed at some determinate historical period by people sitting down and actually writing a contract, anymore than he believes in a real state of nature. For Hobbes, as for all the contract theorists, the social contract and the state of nature are simply ways of thinking about human beings and their politics, not real historical conditions or events.

Let us, then, begin with Hobbes's "experiment" into the imaginative state of nature and see if he is able to determine the truth about human nature. Hobbes's experiment is one into his own psyche, that is, a "thought experiment" in which he asks: "How would I and my fellow human beings behave if we were to find ourselves in a state of nature, and what does this behavior tell us about our innate predispositions?" And for us to participate in Hobbes's experiment, we need only to ask ourselves the same questions, but we can ask them even more pointedly: "How would I and those around me behave, and with what social and political consequences, if at this moment government disappeared, laws became inoperative, and the police force were abolished?"

The answer, Hobbes argues, is easily deduced from the conditions inherent in such a situation. By definition, the conditions would be those of absolute liberty and equality. Absolute liberty, since without laws to constrain individuals they would have a right to everything; absolute equality because human beings have roughly equivalent physical and intellectual capabilities. (It is not by nature but by arbitrary social conventions that people are rendered unequal in civil society, says Hobbes.) And given these conditions, Hobbes argues, there must inevitably be a ceaseless struggle for power. Since all have a right to everything, and since all are equal in their capability of exercising this right, all are subject to attacks from others. For the right to everything means the right to dominate and even destroy others. Remember that there are no laws to constrain behavior in the state of nature. Hence felicity, ultimately survival, dictates that we have a right to everything and that we use that right to acquire power over others lest they acquire it over us. The conditions inherent in the state of nature compel each person to engage in a parody of the golden rule, "to do unto others *before* they do unto you." Consequently, says Hobbes, we must conclude that "out of civil states there is always war of everyone against everyone."[19] The state of nature, in other words, is a state of war, and by war Hobbes means not only real violence, but the constant threat of violence.

Herein lies a paradox that, as we shall see, is crucial in understanding Hobbes's political theory. In the state of nature, the unending struggle for power is the very thing that makes felicity impossible. Since all are relatively equal, no one can ever get the upper hand. Yet, since there are no laws to constrain individuals, they all continue the struggle to dominate each other. Hence, in the state of nature everyone lives in constant fear of everyone else. And not only is life painful and unhappy in this chronic condition of war, but the simplest accoutrements of civilization are absent. Hobbes explains in some of the most famous lines ever penned by a political thinker exactly what this paradox of the state of nature means in real human terms:

In such condition, there is no place for industry; because the fruit thereof is uncertain: and consequently no culture of the earth; no navigation, nor use of the commodities that may be imported by sea; no commodious building; no instruments of moving and removing, such things as require much force; no knowledge of the face of the earth; no account of time; no arts; no letters; no society; and which is worst of all, continual fear, and danger of violent death; and the life of man, solitary, poor, nasty, brutish, and short.[20]

This is a brutally pessimistic view of human beings in their "natural condition." But there is no other view possible, Hobbes insists. Consequently, it must be concluded that human beings are by nature power seekers who, if not constrained, would annihilate each other. Human nature is thus proven to be innately antisocial. That it appears otherwise in civil society is merely a reflection of socialization and political control. Take these away, says Hobbes, and people's real human nature would quickly reassert itself.

Nevertheless, there will be those who refuse to draw Hobbes's conclusions. They will argue that human beings are not power seekers by nature. They will agree with Socrates and the classical tradition that humans are essentially ethical beings, and that they are naturally inclined to live together harmoniously. Those who hold to this Socratic view, of course, will claim that the state of nature is a state of peace. They might even go so far as some later contract theorists and argue that some form of civilization existed even prior to the contract into civil society. As a consequence, they will insist that human nature is innately social, and that it would remain so even outside the bounds of society.

Hobbes is well aware that these objections will be made, but he does not take them seriously. Those who draw Socratic conclusions, he argues, have not properly performed the thought experiment into the state of nature. More than this, they have failed to understand what the experiment is all about. For imaginatively to project human beings into a state of nature is to project oneself into that condition, to "observe" one's own behavior and, as a member of a common human species, to recognize oneself in others. "He that is to govern a whole nation," says Hobbes, "must read in himself, not this or that particular man; but mankind."[21] And to read mankind, one must read oneself accurately, that is, honestly. In other words, to understand the true condition of the state of nature, one must be scientifically dispassionate about one's own deepest feelings and motivations. In St. Augustine's words, each must judge naked his or her own heart, for it is here in the human heart that Hobbes's state of nature truly is to be found.[22]

But herein lies the problem, Hobbes argues: The Socrateses of the world are not honest about themselves. They do not want to admit the state of nature is a state of war because that would be an admission that they and their fellows are antisocial power seekers. They would have to face their own egotism, their innate selfishness and self-centeredness, their unlimited and unlawful desires that seethe beneath the outward appearance of civilized behavior. Like the patient on the psychoanalyst's couch, they resist the truth in order to maintain a good opinion of themselves. The "truth would set them free," but lies are more convenient and certainly more comfortable.

Yet, Hobbes argues that despite their dishonesty the behavior of his critics unwittingly confirms his view of human nature. Consider, he says, that when a man takes a journey

> he arms himself, and seeks to go well accompanied; when going to sleep, he locks his doors; when even in his house he locks his chests; and this when he knows there be laws and public officers, armed, to revenge all injuries shall be done him; what opinion he has of his fellow subjects, when he rides armed; of his fellow citizens, when he locks his doors; and of his children and servants, when he locks his chests. Does he not there as much accuse mankind by his actions, as I do by my words?[23]

It is thus indisputable, says Hobbes, that human beings are by nature antisocial power seekers. If we are honest with ourselves, there is no other possible conclusion to be derived from our thought experiment into the state of nature, a conclusion easily confirmed by anyone who bothers to observe how we daily behave toward one another. And for those with a philosophical bent, the compositive method of analysis leads to the same conclusion.

Knowing the true nature of humankind, it is now possible to "geometrically" deduce a scientific theory of politics, that is, one that is internally consistent and logically coheres to our psychological analysis. For the contract theorists, Hobbes included, this science of politics reduces itself to answering two fundamental questions: Why do human beings contract out of the state of nature to form the state? and What are the terms of the contract? The contemporary political scientist attempts to answer these same questions, but asks more directly: Why does the state exist? and What are the legitimate powers of government?

The answer to the first question, Why do human beings contract out of the state of nature to form the state?, is easier to provide given Hobbes's view that people are naturally in a condition of war. Clearly people create the state in order to secure peace, something they are logically compelled to do, says Hobbes, because it is the only way in which they can attain felicity. (Note here the similarity to St. Augustine's theory of the state, but bear in mind that Hobbes's theory makes no moral judgments.) In a state of war, life is "nasty, brutish, and short." In a state of peace, life is at least potentially pleasurable. At a minimum, people will not find themselves constantly threatened by each other. And since the object of people's wills is felicity, they have no choice but to contract out of the state of nature into civil society.

In contemporary terms, Hobbes is simply arguing that the state exists to provide security for people, not only security from other states, but most importantly security from each other. The other side of this argument, also reminiscent of St. Augustine, is that the state does not exist to engage in moral education as the classical thinkers claimed. And Hobbes is logically compelled to adopt this seemingly extreme view because it is the only view compatible with his idea that people's natural condition is a state of war. Clearly, if human beings are naturally rapacious and self-regarding, there is no way in which the state can better them through moral education. At best it can prevent them from unleashing their natural inclinations and hurting each other. In Hobbes's mind, the modern nation-state cannot be organized upon those political principles that Plato and Aristotle had taken for granted.

Yet, Hobbes does not seem perfectly consistent in his attack upon the classical conception of the state, for he seems to suggest that the contract is the result of a law of nature "to seek peace, and follow it."[24] In its traditional usage, a natural law is a rule of moral reason. It would seem, then, that we must conclude the state exists for other reasons than security alone, for if it were created under the impulse of moral reason, it must have a moral purpose beyond that of mere self-interest in survival.

There is, however, no inconsistency in Hobbes's position, for he fundamentally alters the classical conception of natural law to match his utilitarian psychology. He argues that a law of nature is nothing more than "a precept or general rule, found out by reason, by which a man is forbidden to do that which is destructive of his life, or taketh away the means of preserving the same."[25] In other words, a law of nature for Hobbes is nothing more than the application of reason to the problem of survival. In sum, it is a rule of reason that informs us how best to maximize our self-interest. Thus, morality and self-interest are one and the same for Hobbes, an idea that runs directly counter to what the great natural law theorists would have argued.[26]

What Hobbes has done is transform the classical theory of natural law into a naturalistic ethics. A naturalistic ethics, you will recall from our analysis of Machiavelli, is one that attempts to draw ethical precepts from people's actual behavior. It is an ethics based upon a "scientific" understanding of people's real psychological predispositions, rather than upon some supposed objective moral order or teleological principle. In this case, Hobbes has simply taken his utilitarian psychology of pleasure and pain and put it into the ethical language of natural law. People contract to "seek peace" in order to avoid the pain of war, not because peace is in some larger sense morally proper. And this naturalistic tendency intensified after Hobbes. For this reason, scholars speak of the disintegration of the natural law tradition following Hobbes, even though natural law theories abounded in the seventeenth and eighteenth centuries. By the end of the eighteenth century the natural law tradition was, for all intents, dead.

For practical purposes, then, we may dispense with Hobbes's reference to natural law. It is raw self-interest, not moral impulse, that explains the existence of the state. It is a basic, even primitive, desire for security that compels people to contract. And in showing that the contractual basis of the state is security, Hobbes has in effect already told us what the terms of the contract are. For if we say that people contract out of the state of nature for the purpose of security, it is clear that the powers of government must be sufficient to provide for it. And logically, Hobbes argues, this means that the powers of government must be absolute, since anything short of this would be insufficient to protect people from each other. Hence, the terms of the contract are that all power shall reside in the government, and the rights of the individual shall only be those allowed, or conversely those not circumscribed, by that power. In sum, there are no legitimate restraints that can be placed upon government.

That governmental absolutism logically follows from the desire for security can further be proven, Hobbes argues, by an analysis of what the "actual act of contracting" would look like. Clearly, it would be:

> as if every man should say to every man, *I authorize and give up my right of governing myself, to this man, or to this assembly of men, on this condition, that thou give up thy right to him, and authorize all his actions in like manner. . . .* And he . . . is called SOVEREIGN, and said to have *sovereign power;* and everyone besides, his SUBJECT.[27]

The state cannot exist, in other words, unless people lay down their right of governing themselves and turn it over to a common, or sovereign, power. And Hobbes is very explicit that to turn over the right of self-government people must confer "all their power and strength upon one man, or upon one assembly of men, that may reduce all their wills . . . unto one will."[28] It is not sufficient that they turn over just some powers or rights to government; they must turn over all of them. (For Hobbes *right* and *power* are equivalent terms; to have a right to something means simply to have the power to attain it.) Unless all powers or rights are turned over there can exist no common or sovereign will by which to unite people who otherwise would remain in a state of nature. The act of contracting, in other words, demonstrates that the state must be sovereign.

Here, then, is the heart of Hobbes's political thought: his theory of sovereignty. He was not the first to use the term *sovereignty* in its modern sense, however. A political thinker by the name of Jean Bodin used it in the late sixteenth century, and we find intimations of the idea even as far back as Marsilius of Padua. Clearly Machiavelli had a sense of it, although he could never quite articulate the concept because the political conditions of Renaissance Italy prevented him from doing so. What was required for the emergence of the modern idea of sovereignty was the consolidation of the nation-state, something that in Hobbes's time had come to pass. For the concept of sovereignty corresponds to the unified and centralized structure of the nation-state and is essentially incompatible with the decentralized political structure of feudalism.

Sovereignty means ultimate power, and when applied to a political unit such as the state, it means that the state possesses final and ultimate power over all other social and political bodies. Thus, when we say that the United States is sovereign, we mean that it has final political authority domestically and absolute political autonomy from other countries internationally. For this reason, it would not only be considered illegitimate for any other nation-state to invade its borders, would be considered equally illegitimate for any subordinate political unit within the United States to claim final authority.

It was the issue of internal sovereignty that particularly concerned Hobbes since the medieval church had traditionally claimed final authority. Moreover, numerous religious zealots in his own day were asserting the reformation philosophy that in religious matters the final authority is the individual's conscience. Hobbes, on the contrary, insisted that the state must control the church, and that it is supreme in matters of religious belief and dogma.

It is important to bear in mind that the term *sovereignty,* like the term *state,* is an abstraction. It is simply a word we use to describe that political unit with final authority. But the exercise of power ultimately requires real human beings who make real decisions. This is what we mean by government: It is a "board of directors" that is charged with the task of actually exercising the sovereign power of the "corporation" we call the state. If the government is effective, if it is able to assert final authority domestically and internationally, we engage in an intellectual fiction by saying that the state possesses sovereignty. In this sense, sovereignty is similar to the notion of horsepower. Horsepower is an abstraction that refers to the effectiveness of an engine, that is, its ability to move a vehicle. Sovereignty is a kind of "political horsepower" that refers to the effectiveness of a kind of "political machine" we call government.

But why does the creation of a sovereign power require the alienation of all of our powers or, what comes to the same thing for Hobbes, all of our rights? Why can we not simply alienate some of our rights to government and retain the rest for ourselves? It would seem to make sense, for example, to turn over to government the right or power of making and executing laws, but retain for ourselves such rights as freedom of speech, religion, and so on. Certainly this is an ideal to which the vast majority of people would subscribe. Does it not follow, therefore, that when each person agrees with every other to alienate the power of governing that certain rights or powers are retained? Are not the real terms of the contract, then, that some rights belong to government, others to the subjects?

This argument, of course, is that of the constitutionalist who believes that government must be limited by certain legal constraints. In the next chapter, John Locke will make just such an argument. But Hobbes immediately rejects it because he believes it to be based upon a fundamental misperception of human nature. The constitutionalists, he argues, fail to grasp that the state of nature is a state of war. They fail to understand, that is, that human beings cannot control their lust for power; that any power they possess will be used to acquire more. Thus, if individuals retain any power at all they will use it to subvert the power of government to their own advantage, just as in the state of nature they used it to subvert the power of others. In short, the constitutionalists fail to see that the sovereignty of the state cannot be ensured unless the act of contracting involves the total alienation of all individual rights and powers.

Now the objection might be raised that if human beings are as Hobbes describes them, they would never consent to these terms of the contract no matter how logically necessary they may be. If they are power seekers by nature, they would never contract to turn over their power to any man or assembly of men. But this objection fails to recognize that people have no choice, Hobbes argues. Their natural condition is so nasty and brutish that the creation of a sovereign power is their only means of escaping the horrors of pervasive fear and violence. The pain inherent in the state of nature, in other words, far surpasses the pain of alienating their rights and powers. And, as Hobbes has demonstrated, people always will choose the least painful course of action, since this is invariably the "last appetite in deliberating."

Note here a crucial fact about Hobbes's description of the contractual act. People do not contract with government at all. They contract with each other mutually to lay down their rights to everything and turn those rights or powers over to government. The contract is not a reciprocal agreement between subjects and sovereign. The government, in other words, is not a party to the contract, for if people contracted with government they would set limitations upon it, and limited government simply will not work. Given that human beings are incorrigible power seekers, the notion of a reciprocal contract is logically and scientifically indefensible, Hobbes argues.

It should be apparent that Hobbes holds a rather paradoxical notion of consent. It is true that people consent to government when they contract with each other, but once government has been created they "consent" to obey it because they have no other choice. Just as their self-interest compelled them to contract in the first place, once in civil society their self-interest compels them to obey the terms of the contract lest the power of government be exercised over them. Bluntly stated, people "consent" to obey government because it is in their self-interest to avoid the penalties of breaking the law. And this same logic holds true, Hobbes argues, whether sovereignty is created by force or by mutual agreement.[29] Whether we have in some sense formally contracted to create a governing power, or have had it imposed upon us by a conqueror, it remains in our self-interest to consent to any existing government by obeying the law.

This matter of law is crucial to Hobbes's political thought, for in his mind the problem of political order is ultimately a problem of law. How do you get people to obey the law when their natural inclinations are antisocial? Clearly, says Hobbes, by backing up legal rules with real sovereign power. "Law," he says, is "command,"[30] and the ability to command requires power. ("Covenants without the sword," says Hobbes, "are but words, and of no strength to secure a man at all."[31]) Given that the desires are the determining factor in human behavior, people will obey law only if compelled to do so. They will not obey simply because they think it morally correct to obey. It is for this reason that Hobbes does not believe natural law to be law at all, properly speaking. Natural law is law without the sword. It is incapable, therefore, of commanding obedience.

But it is precisely at this point that the key objection to Hobbes's political thought is raised. Once again, the objection is that of the constitutionalist who argues that Hobbes's theory of sovereignty makes it perfectly possible for government to pass immoral laws and compel obedience to them. Thus, the citizens in Hobbes's state may well be forced to live lives of injustice through the very act of obeying the law. For this reason, the constitutionalists argue, the legislative or sovereign power must be limited. (Most theorists of sovereignty agree that sovereignty ultimately resides in the supreme law-making body.)

The most readily obvious response to the constitutionalists' position we have already discussed. Given that the natural condition of humankind is a war of everyone against everyone, sovereignty is essential for any kind of political order, and sovereignty cannot be limited without being rendered ineffective. Hence, while the danger exists that absolute government may pass "immoral" laws, the danger is even greater that limited government will be unable to maintain any kind of law and order and society will disintegrate into civil war.

But Hobbes has a more fundamental criticism of the constitutionalists, one that takes us to the very heart of his political theory. That theory is based upon the new and revolutionary epistemological assumptions of modern science, and scientifically speaking there are no moral or immoral laws in any absolute or "Platonic" sense. Morality and immorality are but words people ascribe to different kinds of behavior, according to Hobbes. Thus, whether or not a law is just depends upon how we define justice, for justice is but a word. Recall here Hobbes's insistence that, scientifically, truth is in words, not things. Consequently, when the sovereign body legislates, its laws are by definition just because it has the power to define what is and is not just. And since we have contracted or consented to create the sovereign power, we cannot logically claim its decrees are unjust.

Hobbes is simply applying the same scientific epistemology in the political domain as Galileo had in the physical. Thus, *justice* for Hobbes is simply a word arbitrarily chosen to signify a particular phenomenon. To return to an earlier example, the word *justice* is in essence no different from the word *redness*. *Redness* is a word that signifies a particular wavelength of light; *justice* is a word that signifies a particular relationship between subject and sovereign. And since it has been shown that the sovereign by definition must have absolute power, it logically follows that justice must be defined as any decision the sovereign makes. Our definition of sovereignty, in other words, logically produces this definition of justice. Any other definition would violate the rules of logic (that is, the "truth of words") and would therefore be scientifically untrue, just as defining the radii of a circle as unequal lines would be untrue given the geometric definition of a circle. Thus, the constitutionalists' objection that Hobbes's political theory gives license to the sovereign to pass immoral laws is scientifically indefensible since, by definition, the sovereign cannot anymore pass immoral laws than can the radii of a circle be unequal in length.

Why then do the Puritan constitutionalists and their like claim that absolute monarchy is unjust? Why do they dispute an obvious scientific truth? In point of fact, Hobbes argues, their charge of injustice has nothing at all to do with truth. Rather, it has to do with their own self-interest, for the language of ethics, he notes, has "a tincture of our different passions."[32] And it is this that lies behind their political rhetoric, not philosophical principle. Thus, while the constitutionalists advocate limited government in the name of justice, what they really want, says Hobbes, is power for themselves. What they want is what all human beings want, "power after power that ceaseth only in death."

Hobbes's utilitarian psychology allowed him to see that human beings have an interest in misusing language to their own benefit. And he grasped that this abuse of language is not only the cause of political discord but is also the reason why a science of politics is so difficult to create. It is one thing to get agreement on the meaning of geometrical terms; it is quite another to get it on the meaning of political terms such as *justice, liberty,* or *equality.* In the former case no one has a personal stake in the definition; in the latter everyone does, for our definitions will have a real impact upon people's lives. If we define justice as the equalization of property, for example, the poor will clearly benefit at the expense of the rich. Consequently, the rich will refuse to abide by such a definition unless, of course, they are compelled to it by a sovereign power.

Thus the Puritan constitutionalists, the anti-Royalists, the advocates of limited government, and the champions of freedom of religion and expression, all were abusing the "truth of words" for their own political benefit as far as Hobbes was concerned. In the process, they were engendering that state of war that makes life "nasty, brutish, and short." And in Hobbes's mind, the only way to rectify the problem was to create a sovereign power capable of defining the meaning of words such as *justice* and, more importantly, capable of enforcing them. For at bottom, Hobbes argues, political concord requires that human beings work from a common set of premises, premises that do not exist objectively for all to discover, but that must be created and imposed by the exercise of real power.

We can now perhaps more fully appreciate Plato's and Aristotle's assertions that justice is not just a word, but an objective moral principle. This is what they meant when they said that justice is a form, and they realized that without the concept of form or an ethical equivalent such as natural law, the domain of politics would reduce itself to mere power. The modern theory that law is command, for example, follows inevitably from Hobbes's nominalism. If law does not correspond to objective ethical truths, then it can be nothing more than arbitrary rules—mere words—imposed by real power. Law cannot be a reflection of some larger ethical order as the classical thinkers believed.

For the same reason, other political variables in Hobbes's political thought, and in most political theory since Machiavelli, are also defined in terms of power. The absence of objective ethical truths makes power the key political variable. This is a prime reason why *power* has become such an important word in our contemporary political vocabulary, and why it had minimum import for the ancient thinkers. Thus, where Aristotle and the other classical thinkers conceived liberty as moral freedom, Hobbes conceives it as freedom from restraint, which is simply freedom to exercise one's power however one wants. This is why Hobbes insists that in a state of nature where there exist no legal restraints, people have a right to everything, a right limited only by the practical fact that they cannot amass sufficient power to exercise it. Their right is limited, in other words, only by the restraints inherent in their natural condition. And their rights in political society are restrained, not by ethical considerations, but by the law that is itself mere power or "command." There is, in other words, no ethical dimension at all to rights and liberties as defined by Hobbes. They are defined strictly in terms of power.

This same logic applies to the modern theory of equality, which, in great part, we also owe to Hobbes. Where Aristotle spoke of proportional equality, that is, of equality reflecting differentials in virtue, Hobbes speaks of the absolute equality of power that each individual naturally possesses vis-à-vis every other individual. We are all equal in our desire for pleasure, says Hobbes, and we are all naturally equal in our ability to exercise power over others in our pursuit of felicity. Once again, there is no ethical dimension in this conception of equality. As with liberty, law, or sovereignty, equality becomes merely another variable of power.

Such then is Hobbes's political theory—an ingenious combining of a materialist metaphysics, a utilitarian psychology, and a new scientific epistemology and theory of language. Taken together, this combination comprised a radical rejection of the classical vision of human beings and their politics. And so powerful was Hobbes's political thought that all manner of thinkers felt compelled to take up the pen against him. It is a mark of the greatness of his political thought that many political thinkers to this day still feel compelled to "refute" the mighty *Leviathan*. But more important, it is a mark of Hobbes's greatness as a political thinker that his ideas are still influential. Indeed, it was not until the nineteenth century that the real influence of Hobbes was felt, and not just in political theory. He has had a real impact on modern analytic jurisprudence, linguistics, and even behavioral psychology. But in his own time his arguments were too radical for most of his contemporaries to accept.

It is worth briefly reviewing here Hobbes's impact on contemporary political thought. This will not only help us to appreciate the depth of his influence, but also bring to life what is often seen as a highly abstract and remote political philosophy. And the influence of Hobbes's thought has been perhaps nowhere greater than in the field of international relations. The "realist" school of thought, in particular, is greatly indebted to Hobbes, for its basic vision of international politics is essentially Hobbesian.

The realists, for example, maintain that the international arena perfectly corresponds to Hobbes's description of the state of nature. There exists no sovereign authority, hence no overarching system of law. As a consequence, there is no way to constrain individual nation-states that are concerned only with their own national interest (just as Hobbes's "natural man" is concerned only with his own self-interest). Each state thus finds itself in a perpetual struggle of "power after power," with the result that each finds itself in a chronic condition of war.

The realists follow Hobbes as well in insisting that the international state of war could be eliminated only by nation-states mutually laying down all their rights and powers and turning them over to a common power that can unite their wills "unto one will." In Hobbes's terms, they agree that each nation-state would have to contract out of the state of nature and create a world sovereign power if lasting peace were to be attained.[33] Mutual disarmament would be the first step in the contractual act; turning over the means of violence to a common power would complete it. It follows from this analysis, say the realists, that unilateral disarmament will not work for those very reasons Hobbes originally indicated. If any one state disarms, others will attempt to take advantage of the situation and the state of war will continue unabated.

Moreover, while realists doubt that mutual disarmament will actually occur, apart from temporary and limited efforts, they agree with Hobbes that if states do disarm, it will be because of the fear and terror inherent in modern war, not because of any higher moral principle or "natural law." Those who believe that international concord will result from rational discussion and abstract appeals to justice, the realists argue, are simply misguided. An objective analysis of the international arena, they insist, demonstrates the truth of Hobbes's assertion that the essence of politics is power, not principle.

Furthermore, say the realists, the facts of international life bear out Hobbes's thesis that the ultimate power of any world government cannot be limited. In Hobbes's terms, they agree that the contract cannot be a reciprocal agreement between the world sovereign and the subject states. The United Nations has largely failed as a peacekeeping institution, they argue, precisely because each nation retains its powers or "rights." Hence, the United Nations does not possess sovereignty and, consequently, cannot translate its laws into commands. And until some world sovereign power is created, say the realists, we will continue to be in an international state of war, just as Hobbes's political theory would predict.

But there are an increasing number of thinkers, we shall call them the "neo-Hobbesians," who now argue that Hobbes's political theory is also borne out by the reality of domestic politics.[34] While the brute facts of political power may not be as easily perceived domestically because the state of nature has been abolished, they are still very real according to the neo-Hobbesians. For while our civilized order often hides these facts from us, that order can exist only so long as the state remains sovereign and the laws have the power to command.

This difficulty in recognizing the ultimate reality of power is particularly acute in liberal democracies such as the United States. Here the citizen feels a part of the governing system, if only indirectly through his or her representatives, and has available a whole range of civil rights and liberties. Under these conditions, it is difficult to believe that power is the ultimate reality of political order.

But it must be remembered that democracy refers to a specific form of government, sovereignty to the supreme power of the state. And so long as government, whatever form it may take, has the ability to enforce the law we must conclude that the state remains sovereign. Thus, while Hobbes believes a monarchical form of government is in practice best able to preserve sovereignty, he does not reject democracy as in any sense incompatible with it. And, as we shall see in Part III, many nineteenth-century thinkers came to argue that democracy is, in fact, not only the surest guarantee of sovereignty, but that it involves forms of social and political control surpassing anything imagined by Hobbes.

Moreover, from a Hobbesian perspective, it is mere pretense to believe that "constitutional rights" really limit the power of government. These rights and liberties are granted by government and can be taken away whenever government sees fit, although our constitutional mythology supposes otherwise. In the meantime, the contemporary Hobbesian will argue, the existence of extensive rights and liberties is simply a reflection of the fact that the power of the state is sufficiently secure that freedom of expression poses no threat to the effective functioning of government. Once these conditions cease, as they often do during times of crisis, the real power of government becomes manifest. Then we see civil rights and liberties go by the board. We have seen in our own history, for example, that it is not atypical for civil liberties to be severely circumscribed, if not outrightly abolished, during times of war when the sovereignty of the state is at issue.

Finally, it is worth noting that many contemporary political thinkers are beginning to employ a Hobbesian analysis in response to the crisis of modern industrial society. They are suggesting that the relative affluence of the Western nations is now coming to an end and that conditions of scarcity are upon us. In such a condition, where people can no longer attain felicity because real limits must be placed upon their limitless desires, conflict and dissension are sure to emerge. The state of nature will be upon us, they argue, and civil rights and liberties will have to be curbed in the name of order. Then the veil will be lifted from people's eyes and they will see the truth of Hobbes's analytical system: Power is indeed the ultimate reality of politics, and its effective organization is humanity's only salvation.

Yet, here we must conclude our discussion of Hobbes with what seems to be a contradiction. Hobbes himself did not advocate the extensive exercise of power over the individual that some now say is necessary. Quite the contrary, in fact. Hobbes argued that the sovereign power need not interfere in most spheres of life, and that in most circumstances people should have the liberty

> to buy and sell and otherwise contract with one another; to choose their own abode, their own diet, their own trade of life, and institute their children as they themselves think fit; and the like.[35]

Clearly Hobbes is in no sense the father of modern totalitarianism as he is sometimes, quite mistakenly, said to be. Ironically, the great proponent of absolute sovereignty laid the foundations for the liberal theory of the negative state. We shall discuss that theory in the next chapter. For now, it is sufficient to note that the theory claims that the state's functions ought to be confined to maintaining law and order, and that the other spheres of life ought to be left free from political constraint. For Hobbes those other areas comprise for the most part the economic aspects of human activity, what Aristotle referred to as the household or private domain. And it was part of Hobbes's political insight to recognize not only that the state need not interfere in people's private lives in order to maintain control, but that people would be less likely to meddle in affairs of state if they were left free to pursue their economic interests.

Herein lies a paradox of the first order. Hobbes at one and the same time advocates a sovereign state with negative functions—that is, a state possessing ultimate power yet limiting the exercise of that power over the individual. But he was perhaps the first to have understood that the enormous centralization and consolidation of political power that is the essence of the modern nation-state is actually conducive to the liberation of the individual from social and political constraints. For to consolidate power into one unit is to take it from others and thus leave the individual free from the control of subordinate powers.

Historically, the formation of the centralized nation-state involved just this, for it not only destroyed the church as a political power, but the whole range of feudal entities that had theretofore constrained the individual. Thus, just as Hobbes's concept of sovereignty is the theoretical reflection of the new nation-state, so too is his idea, paradoxical though it may seem at first, that the state's functions ought to be essentially negative and the individual granted a large measure of social and economic liberty.

Viewed from this perspective, we can now see that while power is the basis of Hobbes's nation-state, it is not power in the narrow sense of force or violence. Hobbes expects very little actual force to be used by the sovereign power, except against the criminal class that exists in every society. Rather, the Hobbesian system is to be held together by the mutual self-interest each individual has in maintaining that system. Each will have an interest in obeying the law, since disobedience will result in some form of punishment. But even more important, each individual will have a personal stake in maintaining a system of governance that grants extensive liberty to pursue private social and economic interests. The negative state, in other words, allows individuals to pursue their self-interest in a way that would have been impossible in the feudal system, yet it ensures that political control will be maintained.

In the same way, it is in the self-interest of the sovereign body to limit the scope of its power in order to maintain the continued support of the subjects. If government were to abuse its powers by violating people's lives and liberties, the whole purpose of the contract would be vitiated. Carried to its logical extreme, the abuse of power might lead people to revolt in the false belief that a condition of war could be no worse than their present condition. Thus, in limiting the exercise of power, particularly in the economic domain, the sovereign authority actually ensures its continued existence.

Here we may begin our critical analysis of Hobbes's political theory. The problem is that Hobbes is such a complex and provocative thinker that there is hardly an aspect of his thought that does not invite a challenge. Down to our own day political theorists have attempted to refute him on almost every point. We cannot here discuss all of the criticisms that have been directed at him. We can, however, look at what is potentially the most devastating criticism that has been made of his political theory: that he renders his mighty sovereign weak and ineffective by divesting it of any real authority.

Both *power* and *authority,* you will recall, are terms we use to describe forms of political obedience. Power in the narrow sense is that which compels obedience by the use of force or by the threat of its use. In the broadest sense, however, power is based upon an appeal to self-interest. Thus, as we saw in the chapter on Machiavelli, "caressing" people is no less a form of power than is "annihilating" them. And while it is clear from our analysis that Hobbes's sovereign is much more a caresser than an annihilator, his caress is still very much an expression of power.

Authority, on the other hand, is that form of obedience that is inwardly willed because the citizen feels he or she ought to obey the law. It is not self-interest, but a moral predisposition to obey. And, Hobbes's critics argue, it is precisely the lack of this form of obedience that renders his sovereign ultimately weak, because mere power and self-interest are incapable of holding together any polity.[36]

It is worth reconsidering here Machiavelli, who, along with Hobbes, is perhaps the greatest exponent of power politics in the Western tradition of political thought. Yet Machiavelli was the first to recognize the necessity of authority regardless of the type of state, whether principality or republic. It was for this reason that he would instill in the people a love of country and a deep sense of ethical purpose. And this Machiavelli would do despite his own belief that ethical purposes and religious values are essentially illusions.

Hobbes, of course, is in perfect agreement with Machiavelli that ethical values, in the sense most people think of such values, are illusions. If justice is but a word, and natural law merely another term for self-interest, we are no longer speaking of ethics as an objective reality. But Hobbes goes one step further than Machiavelli; he strips not only the political leader of ethical illusions, something that Machiavelli considers essential, but the people themselves. For to organize the polity strictly upon the basis of self-interest is to train the citizens to view their relationship to the state in these same terms. Thus, in Hobbes's state, the subject obeys largely because of the felicity that can be attained by being left free to pursue pleasure in the social and economic domains. Obedience does not derive from any deeply felt moral purpose.

Herein lies the problem, say Hobbes's critics. His sovereign retains the ability to command only so long as it can continuously create the conditions for felicity. Should these conditions cease, as in times of extreme and protracted economic hardship, for example, resistance to the sovereign is inevitable because people will have no stake in the system or each other beyond their own individual self-interest. And the sovereign will be incapable of calling the people to a higher public purpose because the sovereign power itself is not based upon a higher purpose and is incapable of even creating the illusion of one.

This criticism is not merely academic. Quite the contrary; it goes to the very heart of our modern politics. It touches one of the deepest problems inherent in the Western industrialized nation-states. For to an amazing degree we have come to accept the basic political assumptions that lie behind Hobbes's theory of sovereignty, even though we do not accept his monarchical conclusions. Thus, if Hobbes's critics are correct, our modern democratic state, despite its outward appearance of awesome power, is in reality internally weak because it cannot create real authority.[37]

Applied to this country, the argument is that we have gone a long way toward replacing a public spirited community with a collection of self-interested individuals held together only by contractual ties and legal constraints. Thus, what binds our country together is merely the self-interest each has in supporting a political order that allows for an extensive degree of economic gratification. So long as we are able as a nation to continue expanding the gross national product, thus perpetuating the satisfaction of "desire upon desire" for material things, we support the political order. But if the condition of affluence should end, it is argued, support will be withdrawn and the country may well break into that "war of everyone against everyone" that Hobbes so feared. It is precisely this possibility that lies behind the neo-Hobbesian argument that the implementation of state power, that is, power in the narrow sense of force or violence, will be increasingly necessary as affluence declines.

All of this, of course, is speculative. What we should note in conclusion, however, is that the problem of authority in Hobbes's political theory, a potentially real problem in industrialized countries such as the United States, arises from a more fundamental issue inherent in all contemporary political thought. It is an issue intimately connected to the epistemology of modern science, and it can best be summarized by the following question: If the universe is nothing more than body and motion, if what exists is simply the result of the accidental combining of atoms, if our language can posit no ultimate truth, wherein then is to be found that larger principle of order and harmony from which to derive those ethical principles necessary to found a theory of authority? Wherein is to be found Plato's Good or its equivalent? Given Hobbes's framework, it does not exist. As Hobbes puts it, "there is no . . . *finis ultimas,* utmost arm, nor *summum bonum,* greatest good, as is spoken of in the books of the old moral philosophers."[38] In Platonic terms, there is no ethical purpose beyond the cave world of appearances.

In short, the scientific revolution in political thought that begins with Hobbes has virtually eliminated those ethical concepts that had heretofore been the heart of all classical theories of authority. It is not surprising, therefore, that Hobbes conceives of the state as a machine. A machine has no more ethical purpose than a stone. Further, it cannot be maintained that human beings whose will is seen as nothing more than "the last appetite in deliberating" have any ethical purpose either. Such views inevitably will speak of body and motion, of pleasure and pain, but not of virtue, at least not in the classical sense. And where the language of virtue is abolished, the creation of theories of authority becomes, if not impossible, clearly problematical.

It would not be too great an oversimplification, then, to say that the dilemma of political thought since Hobbes, indeed since Machiavelli, has been to find some way of deriving a theory of authority from the metaphysical and epistemological assumptions of modern science. The dilemma is to reunite ethics and politics within the intellectual framework bequeathed to us by these two thinkers. John Locke, Hobbes's contemporary and the subject of the next chapter, wrestled with this very dilemma and, in the process, gave us many of the political ideas upon which this country was founded.

Notes

1. See William Haller, *Liberty and Reformation in the Puritan Revolution* (New York: Columbia University Press, 1955), for a classic discussion of the revolutionary logic of the Puritan position.

2. Parliament, believing that Hobbes's "atheistical philosophy" had called down God's wrath, went so far as to cite his doctrines as a likely cause of the Great Fire of London in 1666. For a thorough and fascinating discussion of the controversy that surrounded Hobbes's alleged atheism, see Samuel I. Mintz, *The Hunting of Leviathan* (London: Cambridge University Press, 1969).

3. Other key works of Hobbes include *De Corpore; De Homine;* and *De Corpore Politico,* which was originally part of a larger work entitled *The Elements of Law, Natural and Politic. The Elements* included "Human Nature," a famous psychological treatise. Also deserving mention is *Behemoth,* a history of the English Civil War from its inception in 1640 to the Restoration in 1660.

4. This, at least, is the usual interpretation of Hobbes's thought. For a contrary view on the scientific status of Hobbes's views, see Leo Strauss, *The Political Philosophy of Hobbes: Its Basis and Its Genesis* (Chicago: The University of Chicago Press, 1963).

5. On the Continent, the philosopher Descartes divided the universe into material and spiritual realms. This Cartesian dualism became the basis of modern philosophy, and it had the "advantage" of maintaining a spiritual reality for those materialists who were unwilling to give up their religious convictions altogether. Hobbes rejected Descartes's philosophy.

6. Hobbes thought geometry superior to other forms of mathematics and to algebra in particular. For our purposes, however, Hobbes's distinction is no longer important. What matters is that he grasped the importance of mathematical thinking in understanding material reality.

7. Thomas Hobbes, "Leviathan, or The Matter, Form, and Power of a Commonwealth, Ecclesiastical and Civil," in Sir William Molesworth, Bart, ed., *The English Works of Thomas Hobbes of Malmesbury* (London: John Bohn, 1966), III:23.

8. "Of the powers of the mind there be two sorts, cognitive . . . and motive," says Hobbes. See Thomas Hobbes, "Human Nature," in ibid., IV:2.

9. Hobbes posits two kinds of knowledge. *Knowledge of fact* is simply mem-

ory of sensation. *Scientific knowledge* is knowledge of the logical connection between words. Since mathematics is the most abstract and logical language available to us, Hobbes considers it to be the foundation of all scientific knowledge. We are concerned only with what Hobbes calls scientific knowledge since it is the basis of his political theory.

10. Hobbes, "Leviathan," p. 85.

11. *Endeavor* is a term Hobbes employs to describe the smallest conceivable motion of body in space. In his words, endeavor is "motion made in less space and time than can be given." Thus, when applied to human psychology, endeavor refers to those infinitesimal and ceaseless motions of brain particles that cause us to desire and to act upon those desires. See Thomas Hobbes, "De Corpore," in Molesworth, ed., *English Works of Thomas Hobbes,* I:206.

12. Hobbes, "Leviathan," p. 49. (Emphasis in original.)

13. Ibid., p. 85.

14. Ibid.

15. Ibid.

16. Ibid., p. 114.

17. Hobbes, "De Corpore," p. 409.

18. Contract theorists were not always consistent in treating the state of nature as a hypothetical condition, however. (It was not uncommon, for example, to argue that the American Indian lived in a state of nature, although nothing could be further from the truth.) Nevertheless, the major contract theorists all understood that, at bottom, the state of nature was nothing more than an imaginative construct.

19. Hobbes, "Leviathan," p. 113. This is Molesworth's marginal synopsis of Hobbes's argument. Hobbes's words for the state of war are "every man against every man."

20. Ibid.

21. Ibid., p. xii.

22. See Norman Jacobson, *Pride and Solace: The Functions and Limits of Political Theory* (Berkeley: University of California Press, 1978), p. 56, who argues that Hobbes's state of nature is neither a historical condition nor primarily an analytic tool, but "a metaphorical description of what moves us all as creatures."

23. Hobbes, "Leviathan," p. 114.

24. Ibid., pp. 117–18. There are actually two laws of nature that Hobbes considers the basis of any civilized order, but the second (which is to lay down one's "natural right" to everything) is really comprehended in the first "to seek peace and follow it." It is impossible, in Hobbes's scheme, to seek peace without laying down one's "natural rights." For this reason, it is sufficient for our purposes to discuss only the first "law of nature." Other sub-

ordinate natural laws, and Hobbes discusses a number of them, are not relevant to our analysis of his contractual theory of the state.

25. Ibid., pp. 116–17.

26. See Howard Warrender, *The Political Philosophy of Hobbes: His Theory of Obligation* (Oxford: Clarendon Press, 1957), for a contrary and greatly debated analysis of Hobbes's theory of natural law, and for a more general argument in favor of the thesis that Hobbes does possess a moral theory of obligation.

27. Hobbes, "Leviathan," p. 158. This giving up of one's "natural rights" corresponds to Hobbes's "second law of nature."

28. Ibid., p. 157.

29. Ibid., p. 185. A commonwealth (state) created by force Hobbes calls "commonwealth by acquisition." That created by contract—that is, by mutual agreement—he calls "commonwealth by institution." But, in either case, Hobbes argues, the absolute rights of the sovereign are identical.

30. Ibid., p. 251.

31. Ibid., p. 154.

32. Ibid., p. 28.

33. Most international theorists of the realist school severely doubt the possibility of creating a world sovereign power. At best, they believe a balance of power possible, which means the ever present possibility of violence. In Hobbes's terms, they doubt that the international state of war can ever be transcended completely.

34. Unlike the realists of international theory, those whom we would call "neo-Hobbesians" are an inchoate group of thinkers from many different disciplines who, for the most part, are unaware of the Hobbesian element in their thinking. Perhaps the most outstanding example of this unconscious neo-Hobbesianism is the now famous essay by Garrett Hardin, "The Tragedy of the Commons," *Science,* 13 December 1968, pp. 1243–48.

35. Hobbes, "Leviathan," p. 199.

36. See, for example, Sheldon S. Wolin, *Politics and Vision, Continuity and Innovation in Western Political Thought* (Boston: Little, Brown, 1960), p. 285, for a related critique of Hobbes. "In the last analysis, [says Wolin] the Hobbesian conception of political power was a grossly oversimplified, even hollow, one. The power to act required only the elimination of hindrances rather than the active enlistment of the private power and support of the citizens."

37. See John H. Schaar, "Legitimacy in the Modern State," in Philip Green and Sanford Levinson, eds., *Power and Community* (New York: Random House, Inc., 1969), for a discussion of the Hobbesian basis of the diminution of authority in the contemporary democratic state, and particularly in the United States.

38. Hobbes, "Leviathan," p. 85.

9

Locke

John Locke (1632–1704) was a contemporary of Thomas Hobbes. Locke's confrontation with the events of his time, however, led him to political conclusions very different from those of Hobbes. Where Hobbes was the great exponent of absolute monarchy, Locke has traditionally been considered the most important advocate of what we now call *liberal democracy*. As such, Locke's ideas have become a heritage in all Western constitutional democracies, particularly in the United States. Indeed, most of our political ideals and social values are essentially Lockean, although there has been some debate over how directly we have derived these ideals and values from Locke.[1]

The political differences between Hobbes and Locke can in part be traced back to the differing influences that came to bear upon them. Locke came from a well-to-do Puritan family that was intimately involved in the English revolution and civil war. His father was a captain in the parliamentary army. Moreover, Locke was influenced by the Levellers, a radical wing within the army that advocated what was for its time an extensive level of democracy and individual liberty.[2] Unlike Hobbes, he was thus predisposed to a "liberal" and "democratic" point of view.

Locke was as intellectually advanced as he was politically progressive. He was educated at Oxford and became thoroughly disenchanted with the Aristotelian curriculum of the universities. Like Hobbes before him, Locke found an alternative in the new science that aimed at rejecting traditional ideas for a more direct and empirical understanding of the world. While at the university, Locke was fortunate to meet some of the new scientific thinkers. But it was not until Locke made the acquaintance of Lord Ashley, who was later to become the Earl of Shaftesbury and in 1672 Lord High Chancellor to Charles II, that he had the opportunity to meet the finest minds of his day, not only in science but in politics as well. Locke's greatest philosophical work, *An Essay Concerning Human Understanding,* was the result of a series of discussions with some of the thinkers he had met through Shaftesbury.

It was also through Shaftesbury that Locke confronted the hard realities of seventeenth-century politics. In 1682 Shaftesbury began plotting with others to overthrow James II, successor to Charles II, because of his Catholic sympathies, but Shaftesbury was discovered and forced to flee England. Locke by this time had become an intimate of the Shaftesbury family—he was the earl's secretary and advisor—and was implicated in the plot, although there is no evidence that he had had any part in it. As a result, Locke left England and in 1683 took up residence in Holland. He returned after the Glorious Revolution of 1688, which, you will recall, enshrined the principle of limited constitutional government by making Parliament "supreme" and thus checking the absolute power of the monarch. He remained in England until his death in 1704.

The Glorious Revolution was the first step toward liberal democracy in Great Britain, and many of the ideas behind the revolution were similar to those expressed in Locke's major political work, *The Second Treatise of Government.* It is for this reason that Locke has traditionally been considered the father of liberalism, a political doctrine that, as we have said, undergirds the structure of Western democratic states such as the United States. Yet, Locke is less liberal and less democratic than has often been supposed. Even the "revolutionary" Locke of *The Second Treatise* is certainly no liberal democrat in the modern sense. For example, while he advocates an elected legislature based upon majority rule, his majority is to be composed of men of property, not the people as a whole.[3]

Yet, there is no question that later liberals used Locke's works as a sourcebook. They may have read too much into him, but they nevertheless found in his *Second Treatise* the basic outline of their own political values. For this reason, we shall view Locke as his followers saw him, as the father of modern liberal democracy. And since liberalism did not fully emerge until the nineteenth century (it was not until then that the term was even used) we shall have to look some one hundred years beyond Locke to get some sense of the revolutionary implications of his political philosophy.

In the broadest terms, we may define liberalism as a political philosophy—in Part III we shall call it an ideology—that espouses a radical individualism on the one hand, and a theory of the negative state on the other. The individualistic aspect of liberalism, at least until the middle of the nineteenth century, encompassed the social and the economic as well as the political dimensions of people's lives. Thus, the early liberals argued that individuals ought to have liberty to acquire property and to order their lives as they see fit, as well as an extensive liberty of conscience and opinion.

The theory of the negative state was simply the other side of the liberals' radical individualism. Clearly, the liberals argued, unless government is constitutionally limited and its functions kept to a minimum, the civil rights and liberties of the individual cannot be ensured. For this reason, liberalism is best known for its various schemes for limiting the power of government, some of which we will discuss later in our analysis of *The Second Treatise.*

Moreover, liberalism came to advocate a democratic system of government (hence the term *liberal democracy*), although not all the early liberals were particularly pro-democratic and, as we have noted, Locke himself had a very limited view of democracy. But the logic of liberal individualism was such that the democratic point of view came to prevail. In the first place, the emphasis upon individual rights and liberties inevitably led liberal theorists to include the right to vote among other rights. And second, they just as inevitably came to argue that the vote is the surest guarantee of limited government since it provides for a popular check upon the potential abuse of power. (As we shall see in Part III, however, later nineteenth-century liberals began to question the premise that democracy is the surest guarantee of limited government.)

Clearly the thrust of these ideas is anti-Hobbesian. Yet, Locke and later liberals shared certain assumptions with Hobbes. We note in Locke's case, for example, that his theory is framed within the same intellectual universe as Hobbes's. Both thinkers are consent-contract theorists. Thus, like Hobbes, Locke assumes that the state is conventional rather than natural. Moreover, both Locke and Hobbes take as a given that the nation-state is the best form of polity for the satisfaction of human needs, although they disagree on how it ought to be structured since they have differing interpretations of the "terms of the contract."

Further, both thinkers agree in broad terms on basic metaphysical and epistemological issues. Locke was greatly influenced by the new science and, like Hobbes, he too rejected the Aristotelian curriculum of the seventeenth-century university. Thus, Locke is a materialist who believes that reality can be explained in material terms and, again like Hobbes, Locke's epistemology is empirical. The "great source of most of the ideas we have, depending wholly upon our senses, and derived by them to the understanding," says Locke, "I call SENSATION."[4]

This is not to say that there are not some very real metaphysical and epistemological differences between the two thinkers. For our purposes, however, these differences are not relevant. Let us just say that Locke does not carry his materialism to the extreme that Hobbes does. While he believes the physical and social worlds can be explained in material terms, he does not claim that body and motion are the only reality. Thus, whereas Hobbes probably doubts the existence of God, or at least the traditional view of God, Locke was a devout Christian who attempted to provide a rational defense of Christianity in his major theological work, *The Reasonableness of Christianity.*

But for all practical purposes Locke is a materialist, an empiricist, and a nominalist. His point of view, no less than Hobbes's, is that of modern science. For this reason, Locke rejected those philosophies that presumed the existence of an a priori truth. Since Locke believes that knowledge for the most part is rooted in sensation, he concludes that there are no pre-experiential truths that the human mind can know. The mind can know only that which it has first experienced through sensation. Thus, like Hobbes, Locke argues that experience ought to be our real source of knowledge, not tradition or the authority of antiquity.

In his *Essay Concerning Human Understanding,* Locke employs what has become a famous analogy to explain his experiential psychology of knowledge. The mind, he says, is like a piece of blank white paper upon which experience writes. Elsewhere in the *Essay* he compares the mind to an empty cabinet, or to an empty closet that experience fills up with the material of ideas. Locke's idea that the mind is blank until experience "writes upon it" or "fills it up" came to be known by his later followers as the *tabula rasa* theory of mind (*tabula rasa* is a Latin term meaning blank slate).

The tabula rasa theory was employed by Locke against the doctrine of innate ideas then current in the universities. This doctrine presupposed that certain ideas, the idea of god for example, are present in the mind from the moment of birth. It presupposed, in other words, that the mind is not a blank sheet, but a repository of certain key ideas that exist prior to knowledge attained through experience.

The doctrine of innate ideas was a carryover from the ancient and medieval epistemological tradition. Socrates' notion that knowledge is within us and must simply be brought to light by dialectical reasoning is a case in point. But the whole mode of reasoning from Socrates to St. Thomas involved a similar idea. Almost all classical theories of moral reason, from ethical forms to natural law, either explicitly or implicitly employed the concept of innate ideas.

Locke rejects the doctrine of innate ideas, not only because he considers it to be unscientific, but because he believes it leads to intolerance. In his own day, the university schoolmen, as they were called, employed their so-called innate ideas to suppress other points of view. They simply deduced the "truth" from these "ideas," ideas that were largely Aristotelian in origin, and refused to grant any validity to other points of view. And many of these scholastic schoolmen were quite willing to employ the power of the state to enforce their views and suppress those of others, particularly in the realm of religion.

Locke's notion that knowledge is rooted in experience, on the other hand, means that truth is not absolute but something that must be modified and expanded as new experience is gained. Thus, the suppression of ideas stands in the way of the expansion of our knowledge. Scientific truth requires toleration, and toleration requires that the power of the state be limited, Locke argues, lest it lead to a tyranny over the free expression of ideas. Thus, despite his own religious convictions, and contrary to both Hobbes and the religious zealots of his day, Locke is a strong advocate of religious toleration and in his *A Letter Concerning Toleration* (he wrote three letters on toleration) he lays much of the intellectual groundwork for the great liberal principle of separation of church and state. Indeed, it is at this point that the similarities between Locke and Hobbes end and the political differences begin.

These differences are to be found in Locke's *First* and *Second Treatise of Government.* The *Two Treatises* constitute the basic source of his political thought, the essence of which is the liberal principle that the power of government over the individual must be limited. Locke's advocacy of intellectual and religious toleration, then, is but one part of a larger political argument against Hobbes's justification of absolute monarchy and unlimited governmental power.

Yet the *Two Treatises* were written to refute not Hobbes's *Leviathan,* but Sir Robert Filmer's *Patriarcha or The Natural Power of Kings,* a work that defended the principle of absolute hereditary monarchy. In line with the divine right tradition, Filmer argued that the power of the monarch is a paternal power such as that exercised by a father over his child, a power that he maintains is by its very nature absolute and a form of personal property that the monarch has a right to pass on to his heirs.

Filmer based this argument on scriptural grounds, tracing back the absolute power of the monarch to "God's grant of dominion" to Adam. As a consequence, Locke's own argument in the *First Treatise* is heavily laced with biblical exegesis. But despite the traditional form of argumentation, Locke's complaint against Filmer's doctrine reveals a modern liberal temperament. Filmer's theory of paternal power, says Locke, does nothing "but flatter the Natural Vanity and Ambition of Men, too apt of itself to grow and increase with the possession of power."[5] The men Locke has in mind here, of course, are the monarchs and princes of seventeenth-century Europe, including the British monarchs prior to the Glorious Revolution of 1688.

In specific terms, Locke's argument is that Filmer had engaged in a false analogy. He had assumed that paternal power is the same as political power when in fact, says Locke, they are quite different. Paternal power, he argues, is legitimate in those cases in which the subject is not capable of reasoning. The father's power over the child is a case in point. But where the subject is a rational adult, power must be exercised in accordance with what the subject reasonably consents to. And power by consent, that is, political power, is by definition limited, Locke argues, because rational adults would not consent to or contract for an absolute power over them.

It is clear that while Locke's argument is directed at Filmer, it is actually anti-Hobbesian. Filmer is a "traditionalist" who bases his defense of absolutism upon history and scripture rather than upon the consent-contract theory of politics that Locke and Hobbes share. Why then does Locke fail even to mention the name of Hobbes, though there are obvious allusions to him in *The Second Treatise?*

The answer is not entirely clear. Most probably Locke chose Filmer as his intellectual opponent because he, rather than Hobbes, was used by the Royalists to defend the principle of absolute monarchy. Even though Hobbes was a far better theorist than Filmer, no one in the seventeenth century wanted to be charged with atheistic Hobbism, and this was particularly true for the Royalists. But why Locke does not even mention Hobbes where his argument is clearly anti-Hobbesian is less clear. Indeed, the whole relationship between Locke and Hobbes is obscured in *The Second Treatise,* and perhaps for good reason. Despite his rejection of Hobbes on one level, he may well agree with him on another.

Some scholars have even suggested that *The Second Treatise* is actually a form of "secret writing" in which Locke intentionally obscures the Hobbesian elements in his thinking.[6] As we shall see, this issue is crucially important, since how we interpret Locke and subsequent liberal thought will depend in large part on how we interpret his real relationship to Hobbes. For now, it is sufficient to note that not only is the structure of Locke's political analysis closer to Hobbes than to Filmer, but that the underlying metaphysical and epistemological assumptions are much closer as well. For this reason, we shall from this point on contrast Locke's defense of limited-democratic government with Hobbes's secular justification of absolutism rather than with Filmer's traditional justification of paternal power.

Locke's defense of constitutionally limited and democratic government is based, of course, upon his analysis of the "terms of the contract," terms he argues that Hobbes had misconstrued. For Locke, it is inconceivable that human beings would consent to any absolute form of government, whether it be Filmer's paternal ruler or Hobbes's secular sovereign. This is why he insists that political power is by its very nature limited. But to suggest that Hobbes had misconstrued the terms of the contract, Locke must demonstrate that he had misunderstood the conditions of the state of nature as well. And here we run into a very troublesome problem. Locke actually presents us with two contrary views of the state of nature and, therefore, with two differing conceptions of human nature. One view is the opposite of Hobbes's, the other nearly identical. As we shall see, Locke's ambivalence on this issue imparts an ambiguity to his interpretation of the contract and, indeed, to his political thought as a whole.

The first view, the one Locke most desires to implant in the reader's mind, is the opposite of Hobbes's. While Locke agrees that the state of nature is a condition of perfect freedom as well as of perfect equality, he does not agree that people use their natural freedom to destroy each other. Thus, Locke states early in *The Second Treatise* that while the state of nature

> [is] a State of Liberty, yet it is *not a State of Licence . . . ,* [because] . . . The *State of Nature* has a Law of Nature to govern it, which obliges every one: and Reason, which is that Law, teaches all Mankind, who will but consult it, that being all equal and independent, no one ought to harm another in his Life, Health, Liberty, or Possessions.[7]

In other words, the state of nature is a state of peace because human beings are rational creatures capable of discovering moral truths and obeying them. In line with an ancient tradition, Locke calls this rational capacity *natural law.*[8] Thus, even though in a state of nature there are no positive laws to constrain people, they know they have an obligation not to hurt or destroy another's life, health, liberty, or possessions. Natural law, in short, means that human beings are social creatures capable of rising above sheer self-interest. For this reason, in an obvious rejoinder to Hobbes, Locke insists that there is a

> plain *difference between the State of Nature and the State of War,* which however some Men have confounded, are as far distant, as a State of Peace, Good Will, Mutual Assistance, and Preservation, and a State of Enmity, Malice, Violence, and Mutual Destruction are one from another.[9]

The state of nature, says Locke, is simply a condition in which there exists no common authority, that is, no government. A state of war, on the other hand, exists wherever there is "Force without Right upon a Man's Person."[10] Hobbes's mistake, according to Locke, was to assume that want of a common authority would inevitably lead to illegitimate force upon a man's person. He failed to understand that in the state of nature people are constrained to obey natural law. It does not follow, therefore, that the absence of government necessarily means a "war of everyone against everyone."

But the more serious mistake, Locke argues, is Hobbes's assumption that a state of war is necessarily eliminated with the creation of government. He fails to see that government itself is perfectly capable of exercising force without right. In fact, Locke suggests, a state of war is more likely to occur within political society in which the concentrated power of government is easily abused than in the state of nature in which power is dispersed among many individuals. Consequently, Locke argues, the object in contracting out of the state of nature is not to institute absolute government at any cost, as Hobbes maintains, but to create a common authority that is incapable of abusing its powers. It is with this logic in mind that Locke proposes a radically different view of the act of contracting than that of Hobbes, and an entirely different reading of the terms of the contract.

Although Locke is not entirely clear about the nature of the contractual act, it is evident from a careful reading of *The Second Treatise* that, for analytical purposes at least, it occurs in two stages. The first stage is the social contract that forms society; the second stage is the political "contract" that creates a common authority. The social contract, Locke argues, requires the unanimous consent of every party to the contract. The political "contract" to form a government requires only a majority decision, and the subsequent actions of government are legitimate, says Locke, so long as they are based upon the will of the majority.

The reason the social contract must be made by unanimous consent is, upon a moment's thought, fairly obvious. No society could exist unless there were universal recognition of its necessity. The political "contract," on the other hand, does not require unanimous consent because it is not so fundamentally important. For this reason, Locke does not consider the political contract to be strictly speaking a contract at all, but rather a fiduciary agreement (*fiduciary* means to hold in trust). Government is instituted only as a trustee of society, according to Locke, and can therefore act only upon what the majority of that society desires. Of course, Locke admits that unanimity would be the ideal, but in real life it is seldom attained. Practicality, not philosophical principle, dictates the principle of majority rule for Locke.

It should be added that Locke probably conceives the two contracts as occurring simultaneously. It is for analytical purposes that he separates the social contract from the establishment of a common authority. Locke wants to make very clear that government is not to be confused with society, and that it exists merely as an agent and trustee of society, not as its overseer and master as Hobbes would have it.

It is with this distinction between the two stages of the contract in mind that the terms of the political "contract" or trust now become clear. Since government is merely a trustee of societal values, its powers cannot be absolute. It is limited by rights and liberties the citizen carries into society. Unlike Hobbes's political contract, then, the terms of Locke's "contract" are: Some rights must be turned over to government; others remain with the individuals who comprise society. Specifically, Locke argues, the members of society turn over to government the right or power of executing the laws of nature that in their natural condition they were required to execute for themselves. They turn over, for example, the right to punish those who have harmed them. But other rights and liberties, such as those embodied in the first amendment of the United States Constitution, remain with the individual.

There are a number of important political principles that flow from Locke's two-stage theory of the contract, principles that have by now become an integral part of liberal political thought. Among the most important of these is that government must be limited since the relationship between itself and the citizen is reciprocal. While the citizen is obligated to obey legitimate laws, government is obligated to respect the rights of the citizens. This is contrary to Hobbes's theory that there is but one contractual act that government is not a party to and that therefore creates no reciprocity between sovereign and subject that would limit governmental power.

Moreover, implicit in Locke's two-stage theory of the contract is a radically new conception of sovereignty. Whereas Hobbes's sovereign is identical to government, since in Hobbes's mind the state could not survive if government did not have final and ultimate authority, Locke roots sovereignty within society. He is an advocate of what we would now call *popular sovereignty*. Final authority, in other words, remains with the people or, more accurately, with a majority of the people since the real contract for Locke is the social contract, not the political trust that creates government.

Finally, Locke's two-stage theory of the contract, with its implicit recognition of popular sovereignty, logically carries with it a theoretical justification of revolution. Clearly, Locke argues, if government should violate its trust by using illegitimate force, it stands in violation of the social contract and, consequently, the people have a right to revolt. Indeed, Locke is quite explicit that the cause of revolution is governmental rebellion against the terms of the social contract, not any tendency on the part of the people to anarchy or violence. Like Machiavelli, Locke believes the people to be essentially conservative, and that only a long train of abuses by government would spark a revolt.

Indeed, Locke's two-stage theory of the contract is inherently revolutionary because it undercuts Hobbes's objection that revolution will destroy that very social order that the contract was to create in the first place. The two-stage theory means that even if an illegitimate government is temporarily eliminated, society remains intact; social accord is maintained; and the locus of sovereignty is retained.

This brings us back to Locke's theory that the state of nature is a state of peace, for the two-stage contract is simply an affirmation that human nature is innately social and cooperative. Without this, a two-stage contract would be impossible. If people were as Hobbes describes them, the creation of a social contract as distinct from a political trust would simply not work. Given Hobbes's view of the state of nature, only a one-stage political contract that creates an absolute government with sovereign power over the individual would be capable of maintaining social order.

But Locke has another, and seemingly contradictory, interpretation of the state of nature. We may surmise this fact by asking ourselves, Why, if as Locke maintains human beings possess a social and ethical capacity, is it necessary for them to create government at all? Obviously because they are not as ethical or as social as Locke's initial view of the state of nature would have us believe. His later view is less optimistic:

Civil Government is the proper remedy for the Inconveniences of the State of Nature, which must certainly be Great, where Men may be Judges in their own Case, since 'tis easily to be imagined, that he who was so unjust as to do his Brother an Injury, will scarce be so just as to condemn himself for it.[11]

According to this view, human beings are not so peaceful in their natural condition as Locke would initially have had us believe, since they clearly do have a capacity to use illegitimate force against one another. Hence, without a common authority, one that judges disputes impartially, people will tend to violate the rules of justice laid down by natural law. Does this mean, then, that human beings are as Hobbes describes them and that the state of nature is indeed a state of war? Or does Locke mean to suggest that only some people fit the Hobbesian description and that government must be instituted to protect the majority of decent people from the violence of an antisocial minority?

Locke is not entirely clear about what he does mean to say. Lockean scholars have been unable to agree among themselves how best to interpret him. Yet, there are unquestionably Hobbesian elements in Locke's second interpretation of the state of nature, although to what extent he agrees with Hobbes is not certain. But in Chapter 5 of *The Second Treatise,* Locke provides certain clues that give us some sense of his connection to Hobbes. This is the chapter on property, the most famous in *The Second Treatise,* and it is in his analysis of property that Locke most clearly reveals his real view of human nature and, in the process, throws new light on the terms of the contract.

Locke's starting point in his analysis is a familiar one. Human beings are rational creatures, he argues, and "*Reason* . . . tells us that Men, being once born, have a right to their Preservation, and consequently to Meat and Drink, and such other things as Nature affords for their Subsistence."[12] Rational people, in other words, must concede that every human being has a right to life, and therefore to those things necessary to preserve life.

This right to life, and those things necessary to preserve it, Locke calls property. The right to life, he argues, means that "every man has a *Property* in his own *Person.* This nobody has any Right to but himself."[13] In other words, every person owns himself, an idea Locke borrowed from the Levellers. And, logically, the right to property in person means that all human beings have a right to property in those goods and possessions acquired through labor that are necessary to preserve their person. Thus, Locke argues, we must conclude of any man that

The *Labour* of his body, and the *Work* of his Hands . . . are properly his. Whatsoever then he removes out of the State that Nature hath provided, and left it in, he hath mixed his *Labour* with, and joyned to it something that is his own, and thereby makes it his *Property.* It being by him removed from the common state Nature placed it in, hath by this *Labour* something annexed to it, that excludes the common right of other Men. For this *Labour* being the unquestionable Property of the Labourer, no Man but he can have a right to what that is Once joyned to, at least where there is enough, and as good left in common for others.[14]

To this point, Locke's argument seems straightforward enough. Since human beings have property in their persons and hence a right to life, it follows that they have property in those possessions that they have legitimately labored to obtain. In other words, property, in both person and possessions, is a right that belongs to every human being as human being. It is a right all people possess whether they be in a state of nature or in political society. Thus it follows, says Locke, that "the great and *chief end* . . . of Men's uniting into Commonwealths, and putting themselves under Government is the Preservation of their Property."[15] Consequently, "Government has no other end but the preservation of Property,"[16] which means, says Locke, the preservation of people's "Lives, Liberties, and Estates."[17] (Liberty is a property right for Locke because to have property in one's person implies the right to think, speak, and act freely.)

It is now apparent why Locke believes government must be constitutionally limited and based upon majority rule. This is the only way to ensure that government does not violate people's property rights—their lives, liberties, and possessions. And since it is precisely to protect these rights that people contract out of the state of nature, any theory such as Hobbes's or Filmer's that justifies governmental absolutism is, in Locke's view, simply illogical. Rational human beings would not logically consent to any form of government that would threaten their basic property rights.

Put another way, Locke is asserting that property rights are natural rights. (Although the concept of natural right goes back to the ancients, Locke is its greatest modern exponent.[18]) A natural right is precisely what it says: It is natural rather than conventional. Consequently, it can neither be created nor taken away by government. In the language of contract theory, natural rights are those that belong to human beings even in the state of nature. Hence, they cannot contract them away as Hobbes maintains.

It is apparent that natural right has much in common with natural law. Both are known by moral reason, and both are prior to government and civil law. The difference is that natural laws are constraints; natural rights are liberties. They are opposite sides of the same coin. Consequently, for every natural right there will be a corresponding natural law. If, for example, I have a natural right to life and liberty, I must logically recognize a natural law to respect the lives and liberties of others. Moreover, civil laws and civil rights must accord with their natural counterparts. Any government that passes laws that violate the principles of natural law or natural right is by definition illegitimate.

This matter of the relationship between natural right and natural law raises a crucial question in our analysis of Locke. At what point is the natural right to acquire property in possessions limited by natural law? We have already seen part of Locke's answer. He has argued that in the state of nature property is held in common until people mix their labor with it at which point it becomes their private property. And, Locke has told us, a person has a right to appropriate as much common property as desired so long as "there is enough and as good left in common for others." But how is this to be determined?

Locke's basic rule of thumb is that enough and as good has been left so long as what has been appropriated does not spoil. To use Locke's own example, if a person were to gather a hundred bushels of apples and half of them spoiled before they could be eaten, then, "he took more than his share, and robb'd others."[19] He overstepped the bounds of natural law by violating other people's natural rights.

Clearly, Locke believes that natural law severely limits the amount of private property an individual may appropriate. Just as clearly, Locke had to find some way around this limitation. Bear in mind that his political theory is a justification of the modern nation-state that emerged along with and was dependent upon a new-monied economy that vastly increased competition for more and more private property. For this reason, Locke's theory of property not only justifies appropriating more from the common than is necessary for survival but, in light of the availability of new money, condones the unlimited acquisition of property.[20]

Locke's argument is as follows: In the state of nature people come to give their tacit consent to the use of money or currency of some kind if only shells or pebbles. (By *tacit consent,* Locke means the informal agreement to something through its use.[21]) Since money does not spoil, once people have consented to its use it becomes possible to acquire more than one can personally use by selling the products of one's labor for a nonspoiling commodity. Indeed, Locke argues, one can acquire an unlimited amount of money, hence property, without violating the precepts of natural law.

Of course, once money is introduced common property will be rapidly replaced by private property since money gives people the right to take as much as they desire for private use. The apple tree held in common, for example, will now become part of a privately owned orchard from which trespassers will be excluded. But Locke insists that this exclusion of others will not cause them to be denied the necessities since privately owned property is capable of producing much more for everybody than property held in common. This is so, he argues, because the owner of private property has an interest in improving it in order to acquire more money. The owner of the apple orchard, for example, will wish to increase the yield of apples because it will increase the size of his estate. Money, in a word, is a spur to productivity, and increased productivity will ensure that more of the goods of this world are available to people even though property held in common disappears.

The objection might be made, however, that the right of unlimited accumulation will mean that some will acquire more property than others and thereby destroy humanity's natural equality by producing social classes. Locke concedes as much, although he never explicitly mentions social class in *The Second Treatise*. But, he argues, this is as it should be, for

> God gave the World to Men in Common; but . . . it cannot be supposed he meant it should always remain common and uncultivated. He gave it to the use of the Industrious and Rational (and *Labour* was to be his *Title* to it); not to the Fancy or Covetousness of the Quarrelsome and Contentious.[22]

Locke's idea that the world belongs to the "industrious and rational" is what the sociologist Max Weber termed the Protestant ethic.[23] It was an ethic that emerged amongst the Puritan middle class in Locke's time and corresponded to the beginnings of modern capitalism. The essence of the ethic was that those who use their heads and work hard deserve more than those who do not, and that it is entirely up to the individual alone to succeed—or fail—economically. What we now call the American work ethic is simply a modern version of these ideas. This is simply one example of how profoundly Locke has influenced our most basic attitudes and beliefs.

While Locke does not deny that his theory of property is a justification of social division, he has in mind a modern class system that is open, in theory at least, rather than the closed and rigid class system of the feudal period. Under such a system he assumes implicitly the existence of what the nineteenth-century liberals called "equality of opportunity," that is, all people have the same opportunity to shape their economic fate. Thus, regardless of the inequality of property in their possessions, people retain their natural equality of property in person and have thereby an "equal right" to determine their own class position. If the poor wish to be rich, they need only exercise their natural right to acquire more than they now have, Locke argues. They need only determine to be "industrious and rational."

What had begun as a strictly political critique of Filmer and Hobbes has gone considerably beyond the bounds of political theory narrowly conceived. Locke's theory of property rights is, in fact, as much social and economic as it is political. Along with his advocacy of a particular form of government, Locke wishes to justify certain kinds of social and economic behavior. His analysis of property rights clearly glorifies the emerging economic entrepreneur just as Machiavelli's analysis of power glorified the new political entrepreneur of Renaissance Italy.

In short, Locke's claim that the legitimate function of government is the preservation of property means not just that government must protect people's lives and possessions, but that it must ensure the right of unlimited accumulation of private property. Some scholars, therefore, have argued that Locke's *Second Treatise* provides not only a theory of limited government, but a justification for an emerging capitalist system as well.[24] And while we must be very careful about making too facile a connection between Locke's theory of property and modern capitalism, it is true that after Locke liberal-democratic ideas became inextricably joined to pro-capitalist and free-enterprise economic doctrines. The result was, and still is in this country, that such "natural rights" as freedom of expression were seen as not distinctly different from the "right" to make money and acquire property. More than this, it became an article of early liberal faith that capitalism is the only sure guarantee of political liberty. Such was the consequence of Locke's linking property in person with property in possessions.

But we shall return to these larger issues of Locke's thought shortly. At this point it is sufficient to recognize that property is the foundation of rights for Locke and consequently the basis of his claim that the terms of the contract call for a constitutionally limited and, for its time, democratic form of government. Yet, property is more than a right for Locke; it is also a source of conflict. And this brings us back to his second interpretation of the state of nature. Recall that Locke had admitted the existence of certain "inconveniences" in the natural state, namely the violence that at least some would employ against others. It is now clear what the cause of the violence is: property, both in person and in possessions. Without some common authority to make and enforce laws, murder and robbery will be commonplace.

Yet, the problem goes much deeper than this. A close analysis of Locke's theory of property indicates that it is not just a "criminal class" that makes the state of nature inconvenient, but humankind itself. This follows from Locke's argument that the invention of money allows people to circumvent the natural law limitation on the accumulation of property. For the argument implicitly admits that people's desire for property is unlimited and that, as a consequence, the state of nature is indeed a state of war. As Hobbes amply demonstrated in his *Leviathan,* where desires are unlimited the state of nature is inevitably a "war of everyone against everyone." Consequently, Locke does admit that "to avoid this State of War . . . is one great *reason of Men's putting themselves into Society,* and quitting [that is, contracting out of] the State of Nature."[25]

Despite Locke's disagreement with Hobbes's defense of absolutism, then, we note an underlying area of agreement between the two thinkers. Locke's second interpretation of the state of nature is remarkably similar to that of Hobbes. And since the *state of nature* is in essence a seventeenth-century term for human nature, it follows that Locke's psychological views must closely parallel those of Hobbes as well. The implications of Locke's second interpretation of the state of nature, in other words, is that the unlimited desire for pleasure and the avoidance of pain is the determining factor in human behavior, not moral reason or the capacity to know and obey natural law, as he had initially argued. In Locke's case, pleasure is closely identified with the accumulation of property, pain, with its absence.

But what is only implicit in *The Second Treatise* is made explicit in the

Essay Concerning Human Understanding. Here Locke openly espouses a utilitarian psychology and, most importantly, follows Hobbes in attempting to derive an ethical theory from it. Thus, Locke claims that "the cause of every less degree of pain, as well as every greater degree of pleasure, has the nature of good, and vice versa."[26]

Does this then mean that Locke's theory of natural law, like that of Hobbes, is actually a rejection of the natural law tradition? Is Lockean natural law simply a utilitarian-naturalistic ethics in the guise of a classical ethics? The answer is both yes and no. In one sense no, because Locke attempts to show in *An Essay Concerning Human Understanding* that pleasure and pain accord with the higher moral standard of God's "divine law." Locke would argue, for example, that while most human beings do not steal because they fear the pain of divine retribution in the next life, it is nevertheless this fear that makes them conform to that higher moral standard we call natural law.

In the long term, however, it became clear that Locke's naturalism was incompatible not only with the classical tradition of natural law but with that of natural right as well. Once it was admitted that moral rules could be founded upon the psychological "facts" of pleasure and pain, any notion of an ethical standard beyond utility became redundant. Thus, no sooner had Locke's ideas traveled to France than his Continental followers began to drop the older ideas of natural law and natural right and replace them with a strict utilitarian standard. They argued that both the rights and the obligations of the individual should be determined on the basis of pleasure and pain alone. They thus made explicit what in *The Second Treatise* is only implicit: Government must protect property as a right because property produces pleasure, and the powers of government must be limited so that it cannot inflict pain by violating those rights.

In effect, Locke's followers erected his liberal-democratic political theory upon Hobbes's psychological and ethical insights. In the nineteenth century, liberal thinkers called *utilitarians* completed this link between Hobbes and Locke. (It is for this reason that many scholars believe Hobbes to be the real, though unwitting, founder of liberalism.) But here we confront a seeming contradiction. Hobbes had shown that a utilitarian psychology is incompatible with limited government. He had demonstrated, he thought conclusively, that self-interested pleasure seekers whose desires are unlimited require an absolute power over them lest society disintegrate into a state of war. How, then, could Locke's followers link his political theory to Hobbes's psychological and ethical assumptions? And how could Locke himself, given the Hobbesian implications of his second interpretation of the state of nature, advocate constitutionally limited government?

The real genius of liberal thought was to find a way around Hobbes's political objections to constitutionally limited government while retaining his psychology. For Locke and later liberals insisted that there is a fatal flaw in

Hobbes's political logic, a flaw summed up in Locke's claim that *"Absolute Monarchs* are but Men."[27] As mere mortals, monarchs are all too likely to violate the natural rights of others unless constrained—a conclusion that logically follows from Hobbes's own psychology. All human beings, monarchs included, are self-centered pleasure seekers who, given sufficient power, will not hesitate to inflict pain upon others if it will maximize their own pleasure. It is for this reason that Locke insists that a state of war can exist as certainly in political society as in the state of nature. Consequently, says Locke, it is wrong to assume that the terms of the contract call for absolute government since people would not logically consent to a condition that is no better—in fact he believes worse—than the state of nature.

Yet, given their utilitarian psychology, Locke and later liberal thinkers could not deny Hobbes's assertion that human beings need political controls over them. If monarchs need to be constrained, so too do the subjects who are themselves only human. Thus, they had to find some way to give government sufficient power to govern lest society disintegrate into a state of war, yet at the same time ensure that it be constitutionally limited so that it could not itself enter a state of war against society. The liberals had to discover ways by which to put real control in the hands of government, yet find some mechanism to control the controllers. And this is precisely what they did. Following a line of reasoning that begins with Locke, they argued that government can at one and the same time be made both effective and limited if it is appropriately structured.

Let us look first at the ways in which Locke proposes to limit the power of government; we can then better understand how he gives government sufficient force to perform its tasks. Bear in mind, however, that Locke's analysis became the touchstone of all subsequent liberal thought. Thus, what follows is a theory of governmental structure that, in outline form, is held by liberal thinkers to this day.

Most important in terms of limiting the power of government is the democratic principle itself. The legislature is to be periodically elected by the people. It could be no other way, in fact, since legitimate government must be based upon the consent of the governed according to Locke, and direct election of representatives to the legislature makes consent a reality. And since elected representatives depend on popular support for their tenure in office, they have every interest in staying within legal bounds.

A further limitation upon the legislative power recommended by Locke is a limiting of the duration of legislative sessions because, he argues, "constant frequent meetings of the Legislative. . . . could not but be burthensome to the People."[28] In Locke's mind, the less frequent the meetings of the legislature the fewer the laws passed and, consequently, the less chance that mischief will be done. Implicit in this analysis is an idea that became the rallying cry of early nineteenth-century liberalism: "The less government the better."

Moreover, when the legislature is not in session the representatives revert to ordinary citizens who are then subject to the very laws they have made. It is therefore unlikely, says Locke, that they will make laws that have the effect of violating their own "natural rights."

Another crucially important structural principle in limiting the power of government is the separation of powers between the executive and the legislature. The logic behind this principle, says Locke (and note here his implicit agreement with Hobbes's view of human nature), is that "it may be too great a temptation to human frailty apt to grasp at Power for the same Persons who have the Power of making Laws, to have also in their hands the Power to execute them."[29] What better way to correct this problem, therefore, than to separate power into distinct departments such that no one person or group of persons is capable of amassing sufficient power to abuse the citizen's rights.

Locke, however, does not go so far as to make the separation of powers an absolute condition for limited government. And, in fact, the British parliamentary system upon which he partially modeled his theory was not, nor is it today, based upon the separation of powers.[30] Nevertheless, Locke is one of those thinkers who illuminates the future by expressing ideas that later become doctrines. Such is the case with the separation of powers, for it is an idea that was taken up and further developed by later liberal thinkers, particularly in the United States where it was formally embodied in the structure of the Constitution. Moreover, implicit in Locke's theory of the separation of powers is a series of ideas that are wholly modern.

To begin with, there is the idea that political power is not unlike power in the physical sense in that it can be separated, combined, or balanced to produce a particular result. Certainly, this is how later thinkers who followed in Locke's footsteps came to conceive of it. For this reason, while Locke's idea of the separation of powers is reminiscent in certain ways of Aristotle's idea of the mixed constitution, in reality it is something quite different. Aristotle had in mind mixing together different political principles such as oligarchy and democracy to produce a just and stable system. Locke has in mind not so much a mixing of different political principles, but a breaking of power into distinct quantities as if constructing a machine. He has in mind a conception of power not unlike that employed by Galileo and Newton in their study of the physical universe. For this reason, some scholars have argued that the American Constitution owes as much to Newton as to Locke.[31] And while we discussed the American separation of powers from the point of view of the mixed constitution in the chapter on Aristotle, in truth Newton's system makes a better analogy here.

Second, implicit in Locke's idea of the separation of powers is a very modern idea that while human nature cannot be changed, its effects can be controlled by "scientifically" structuring government. Thus, rather than speaking of improving people morally as did the classical thinkers, Locke takes as a given that people are incorrigible power seekers and is concerned only with controlling the effects of human nature. In suggesting the separation of powers he does not mean to alter people's desire for power, he simply means to ensure that they will not be successful in acquiring too much of it.

Later thinkers in the Lockean tradition developed this idea of controlling the effects of human nature even further. In a classic work of American political thought, *The Federalist Papers*, James Madison speaks of separating powers between various branches of government such that "ambition [will] be made to counteract ambition."[32] He proposes to separate powers so that the natural inclination of the president to acquire power will be checked by the same inclination on the part of the legislators. In this, Madison goes much further than Locke, but he is following a mode of thinking implicit in the work of his predecessor. To find an equivalent line of reasoning before the modern era, one would have to return to St. Augustine's idea of using people's sinful lust for power to control its effects. Unlike St. Augustine, however, Locke and Madison are moderns who do not consider the "lust for power" a sin, but rather an objective description of human nature.

Finally, the theory of the separation of powers is modern insofar as it implicitly accepts conflict as something that is not necessarily destructive of public order, an idea first expressed by Machiavelli. Clearly if you divide power between executive and legislative branches of government, you create the possibility of conflict between them. By the same token, if you separate church and state or, as Locke advocates, you prevent the state from interfering in religious matters, you create different bodies with different and often conflicting interests. And if you advocate a large degree of individual freedom in the realm of speech and conscience (recall that Locke is one of the great theorists of toleration), conflicts of political opinion are inevitable. Later liberals carried this emphasis upon conflict to its logical conclusion, advocating diversity and pluralism at all levels: economic, social, and political.

Herein lies a key problem of modern liberal-democratic theory, however. To the extent that powers are separated and decentralized and institutions and individuals are left free to pursue their own interests, to that same extent governing becomes increasingly difficult. Logically, it would seem that the best way to ensure rational and effective political decisions would be to put absolute power in the hands of one person. This, of course, was Hobbes's solution, for he could not imagine effective government that was not absolute. He sacrificed limited government for political effectiveness.

Locke and later liberals, as we have said, claimed to have found within the structure of government a means to make government both limited *and* effective. Thus the separation of powers and other limiting structures of which Locke speaks are to be counterbalanced by a strong executive. At the same time, of course, Locke believes that in keeping the legislative function distinct from the executive, the powers of the executive will not become so extensive as to destroy limited government.

The executive combines two distinct powers for Locke: executive and federative. The executive power has to do with domestic policy, the federative with foreign affairs. We no longer make this distinction, however, since what we call the executive is charged with both domestic and foreign responsibilities, and Locke himself notes that the executive and federative powers are almost always united in the same person. Thus, we shall employ the term *executive* alone rather than follow Locke's distinction between the two powers.

The power of the executive rests upon the fact, says Locke, that it must always exist, because while "there is not always need of new Laws to be made . . . [there is] . . . always need of Execution of the Laws that are made."[33] In other words, political leadership is a constant necessity; lawmaking is not. Hence, the powers of the executive will necessarily be quite extensive relative to those of the legislature, which meets for limited periods of time.

Thus, in line with the parliamentary tradition with which Locke was familiar, the executive is to have the power to call legislative sessions at times when the constitution does not specify regular meetings. Moreover, Locke argues, the executive ought to have the power to periodically restructure electoral districts to ensure fair and equitable representation in the legislature. But the truly fundamental power of the executive is *prerogative* which, in Locke's words, is the "power to act according to discretion, for the public good, without the prescription of the Law, and sometimes even against it."[34]

This is an enormous power that Locke concedes to political leadership. Not only does he grant the executive the right to make decisions where the law does not explicitly constrain him from doing so, but he is willing to grant the executive the right of breaking the law where circumstances justify it. An example of such a circumstance would be a wartime crisis, and in our own history we have had some notable examples of the president acting against "the prescription of law."

Coming from the pen of one of the great theorists of limited government, this doctrine of executive prerogative seems, at first glance, incomprehensible. Yet, as a political realist, Locke is quite correct in his emphasis upon a strong executive. This is all the more necessary, paradoxically, in the kind of political system that Locke advocates. Where the powers of government are limited by their separation and decentralization, and where social pluralism is condoned, there more than anywhere else strong leadership is required to check the centrifugal forces inherent in such a system. Locke understands very well the need for some kind of centralizing and unifying force in his ideal democratic state. And while he asserts the primacy of the legislature since that body represents the "consent of the people," Locke is the first to acknowledge that the legislature cannot provide the kind of political leadership required in a modern nation-state. This really is what is behind his argument that the executive must always exist, and that it must have an extensive prerogative.

Such, then, is Locke's answer to Hobbes: Government can be both limited and effective if it is structured appropriately. And, as we have noted, herein lies the real genius of liberal thought: It developed and elaborated that structural analysis of government that Locke began and added immeasurably to our knowledge of how effectively to channel political power. For this reason, Locke has had a great influence upon the constitutional structure of all Western liberal democracies.

But, as we noted at the beginning of this chapter, nowhere has Locke had greater influence than in this country. The American Revolution was carried out, if only indirectly, in the name of Lockean ideals. The *Declaration of Independence,* for example, not only speaks the language of natural rights, but implicitly conveys the idea that George III had violated the terms of the social contract. Moreover, Locke's economic and social theories have by now become an American ideology. His emphasis upon the importance of private property, the Protestant work ethic, and individual rights has been profoundly influential in this country. And, of course, the impact of Locke's structural analysis upon American constitutional theory has been enormous.

It is precisely because of Locke's influence that American students find it difficult to criticize his political theory. To criticize Locke is to criticize their own most cherished ideals. Yet, it is exactly for this reason that we should make every effort to be critical, for this is the first step toward a critical understanding of our own political ideas. Let us begin our critique of Locke, then, by returning to his theory of governmental structure; we can then go on to some of the deeper issues inherent in his political thought.

Perhaps the key problem with Locke's theory of government is that it fails to provide adequate means to control the vast reservoirs of power that exist in his new liberal state. For example, his doctrine of executive prerogative extends enormous powers to the executive, powers that may pose a real threat to limited government. It is Locke's assumption, of course, that the legislature and the people as a whole will effectively resist any illegitimate encroachments of political power by the executive. But such an assumption is not necessarily warranted, at least not from the perspective of this century, which has seen the executive become increasingly dominant in all Western constitutional states.

Another source of power that Locke fails to recognize as a potential danger to limited government inheres in the democratic principle itself. Locke assumes that majority rule is the surest guarantee against the abuse of power by either the legislature or the executive. But what Locke does not consider is that the majority may become so dominant and so powerful that minorities will be abused. A legislature that represents a powerful majority, for example, is perfectly capable of passing laws that violate the rights of the minority. In our own history there have been innumerable cases in which racial, ethnic, and intellectual minorities have been tyrannized by democratically elected representative bodies reflecting the will of the majority.

There are deeper problems with Locke's political theory that go beyond the strictly governmental, however. These problems are rooted in the economic dimensions of his political thought—that is, in his theory of property. And clearly the most serious problem is that in making property a natural right Locke puts severe limitations upon the power of government to regulate or control it, for a natural right is one that no government can legitimately deny or alter.

Of course, so long as the right to property means simply the right to life and to the necessities of survival, as initially it does for Locke, there is no problem. No serious thinker would want to argue that government has a legitimate power to deny people their lives or their means of subsistence. There is a problem, however, with Locke's argument that the unlimited accumulation of property is also a natural right or, more precisely, that the invention of money makes it equivalent to a natural right. Such an argument means that government must not only protect property in the limited sense of protecting life and liberty, but that it must not interfere in the competitive and unlimited struggle among individuals to accumulate property in possessions. The result, particularly in this country, has been that various problems of urban industrial society too often go unattended.

For example, where the unlimited acquisition of property is protected and even encouraged, the assault upon the natural environment will be severe. As Locke himself shows, the creation of property requires the destruction of something in nature. To build a house, for example, requires cutting down trees, and when home building becomes a venture in the accumulation of more and more capital, the number of trees cut down grows exponentially. Yet, we have found it politically difficult to prevent this destruction of woodlands since limiting the number of trees cut down means standing in the way of the individual's right to accumulate property.

Now extend this dilemma to the whole range of urban and environmental problems. You can see how difficult it is for government to deal with them without violating our most cherished ideals of individual rights. The tendency, particularly in this country, has been to preserve property rights and let the problems go unattended. This is precisely what the neo-Hobbesians now argue cannot continue, and they are at least in part correct. The extensive growth of executive prerogative that Locke did not anticipate is due in large measure to the need for increasingly powerful and centralized leadership to deal with the problems generated by the unregulated exercise of individual property rights.

Another problem rooted in Locke's economic philosophy has to do with the issue of social class. Recall Locke's claim that all individuals are equal in their right to accumulate property in possessions, and that so long as they are industrious and rational they have an equal opportunity for economic success. For this reason, Locke perceived no contradiction between people's natural equality and their social inequality. We now know, however, that there is indeed a contradiction. Social scientists have shown, rather conclusively, that the existence of social classes is incompatible with equality of opportunity as Locke and later liberals conceived it. The class system is much more rigid than Locke suggests. Few people are able to climb out of their class position, and this is particularly the case for the lower classes. And the reason is that the very attitudes and skills required to be "industrious and rational" are class determined. They are, by and large, attitudes and skills that belong to those in the middle class. Hence, it is class position—that is, the amount of property one has in possessions—that most often determines one's economic success. It is not, as Locke believed, the other way around.

There is, further, a serious psychological problem that attends this emphasis upon the individual rather than social class although, in fairness, Locke could hardly have anticipated it; for inasmuch as he puts the burden of economic and social success upon the individual, the lower classes will not only be viewed as irrational and lazy by others, they will view themselves in the same light. Indeed, in a society as Lockean as the United States, many people suffer from a pathological fear of economic "failure," not because of any likely possibility of real economic distress but because their dignity as human beings rests upon the amount of property they possess. Should they "fail" economically, they would be proven essentially lazy and irrational. Such great American literary works as Miller's *Death of a Salesman* are really treatments of these psychological dilemmas inherent in our Lockean society.

Finally, we note certain political problems connected with Locke's theory of property, in particular the disenfranchisement of the poor. In the nineteenth century, for example, all Western liberal democracies imposed a property qualification on voting. In this they simply followed the lead of Locke himself who assumed that the democratic vote would be extended only to men of property, even though this involved the violation of his premise that all humans have property if only in the limited sense that they can be said to own themselves. In this country, this same premise was violated as well in the case of African Americans who, while formally attaining the right to vote after the Civil War, did not in fact acquire it in many states until the Voting Rights Act of 1965. Later liberals, in any case, soon forgot Locke's full meaning of property and rooted political rights in the ownership of estate rather than in the simple fact of being a member of the human species.

This same forgetfulness, it should be added, applied to women who were also disenfranchised until well into this century, and in their case there were specific legal limitations on the right to own and control property. In this, women were even in a worse situation than propertyless males who could at least stake a legal claim to acquire property however much the reality of nineteenth-century capitalism made it unlikely they would ever do so. What is particularly interesting in this case is that while women were "citizens" of a Lockean liberal democracy premised upon the notion of consent, they were excluded from the vote, that is, from full citizenship, on the basis of an explicit patriarchal ideology. Men's control of property "justified" their control of women and, at the same time, "justified" excluding women from the voting booth.

But it was not simply a misreading of Locke that allowed men to deny women the vote. The fact is that Locke himself accepted their exclusion from the franchise and, despite his rejection of paternal power as a legitimate form of political authority (recall his dispute with Filmer on this very issue), he accepted it as a matter of course in regard to women. This was possible only on the assumption that the patriarchal family is natural, that it existed even in the state of nature, and that as a consequence women never possessed that property in either person or possessions that would have made them equal participants with men in the act of contracting.

This would seem to be what Locke does assume, but it is an assumption that raises the most serious difficulties for his whole theory of contract. For example, it posits the existence of a precontract social order that legitimizes paternal authority rather than a state of nature comprised of equal and freely consenting individuals. This obviates the whole idea of contract since a non-contractual theory of political society could be derived from this perspective, as indeed Filmer originally did. It is not surprising, therefore, that feminist theorists have pointed to this and other inconsistencies in Locke, as well as in the other contract theorists who, in different ways, also legitimize patriarchy. As one feminist critic bluntly put it, "contract is far from being opposed to patriarchy; contract is the means through which modern patriarchy is constituted."[35]

Needless to say, women ultimately challenged patriarchy and their resultant disenfranchisement, but for the most part they did so in Lockean-liberal terms. In this they simply followed the logic inherent in the concept of consent and contract—that as free and equal individuals, as they ought to be, they would never consent to patriarchal domination and political disenfranchisement.

Today, of course, universal suffrage is the norm in all Western liberal-democracies. Yet, this has not resolved all of the problems that the previously disenfranchised groups have faced, and this in part is also connected to Locke's theory of property. The economically deprived, which includes a disproportionate number of women and minorities, have neither the education nor other advantages that make for full political and legal equality. Because of their class position, they do not in reality have the full human rights that Locke at least initially claimed to be those of every human being as human being.

But all of these problems, from the structural and political to the economic, reduce themselves to a more fundamental issue: Locke's ambivalence about the state of nature. Clearly, Locke's emphasis upon structurally limiting the exercise of political power is connected to his second, or "Hobbesian," interpretation of the state of nature. Why worry about limiting the exercise of power unless, as Hobbes maintained, human beings are insatiable power seekers? And Locke's justification of the unlimited accumulation of property makes sense only if we consider human beings to have by nature an unlimited desire for property, a view connected to Locke's thesis that the state of nature is indeed a state of war. But Locke's initial thesis is that the state of nature is a state of peace, a thesis that would imply a quite different political theory than that we have just been criticizing. How, then, do we interpret Locke's ambivalence? There are at least two possible approaches.

The most favorable interpretation is that Locke's theory of the state of nature is ambivalent because human nature itself is ambivalent. We observe most human beings to be both loving and cooperative as well as selfish and competitive, and Locke's differing views of the state of nature may simply be objective and realistic assessments of the way human beings actually behave. Granted, Hobbes's view of the state of nature is logically more consistent, but humans seldom fit logical categories. Locke may be less consistent, but perhaps he is more realistic.

The least favorable interpretation of Locke's ambivalence we may call the "ideological interpretation." In this context, *ideology* means a set of social or political ideas that reflect socioeconomic or class interests. Some scholars, many of whom are Marxists, argue that Locke's political theory is really a hidden justification of capitalist society and bourgeois rule.[36] They claim that Locke's theory of property rights is not so much a justification of liberal democracy as it is a defense of the unlimited appropriation of property and an emerging capitalist class. From this perspective, then, Locke's real view of the state of nature is the second, or Hobbesian, view, which claims the state of nature to be a state of war. For in order to justify the unlimited appropriation of property, Locke must demonstrate that the human desire for property is itself unlimited. He must demonstrate, that is, that capitalism is justified by the facts of human nature.

Here we return to the crucial question of Locke's relationship to Hobbes. If the ideological interpretation of Locke is correct, it is apparent that Locke does agree with Hobbes's view of the species. By the same token, it becomes clear why, at the same time, Locke disagrees with Hobbes's defense of absolutism based, as it is, upon the theory that people lay down all their rights in the act of contracting. Clearly if all rights are given up, the right of property exists at the whim of the sovereign power. Under these conditions the right of property and its unlimited accumulation could not be absolutely secured, and the continued existence of the emerging capitalist class could not be guaranteed. By making property a natural right, and by limiting the power of government such that it could not interfere in the exercise of that right, Locke ensured the continued existence of the capitalist class. From this perspective, it is clear that Locke had made the discovery that liberal democracy is the political form most compatible with capitalism, a point of view held by Marxists to this day.

Which interpretation of Locke's ambivalence is correct? No definitive answer is possible. As we have seen, scholars disagree among themselves about how to interpret *The Second Treatise,* and there are other interpretations besides the two extremes we have given here. What we can note, however, is that Locke's ambivalence puts his justification of constitutionally limited government upon very shaky grounds. For to the extent that he adopts the Hobbesian interpretation of the state of nature, Locke cannot avoid sharing with Hobbes his utilitarian psychology, his rejection of natural law, and his nominalism. And, as we have seen, Hobbes uses these very psychological and epistemological assumptions to destroy the constitutionalists' argument that there are certain objective and universally applicable rights beyond the power of government to deny or alter.

Yet, for our purposes, it makes no difference which of the various interpretations of Locke is most accurate. We can safely leave that debate to the scholars. What is of real interest to us is that Locke's ambivalence has had a paradoxical effect upon our own political consciousness, as it has upon liberal thought in general. For on the one hand we expect the community to be organized for social ends, and government to rule for the public good, as if human beings were social and ethical creatures. On the other, we praise and encourage self-interested individualism and demand that government refrain from intervening in the competitive struggle for material possessions and social status, as if human beings were by nature the way Hobbes describes them. In other words, our own political values embody Locke's ambivalent view of human nature as expressed in his differing interpretations of the state of nature.

It is clear that Locke's ambivalence plays a real function for us, although a very dangerous one. It allows us to continue to speak of our political order in ethical terms while justifying forms of liberalism that imply something quite different. It allows us to believe, as did the classical thinkers, that ethics and politics are united, while in reality we work upon the presumption that they are not. In other words, Locke's ambivalence comfortably deceives us, for it prevents us from seeing the "unpleasant" Hobbesian elements in our most cherished political and social values. It prevents us from seeing that mere power and self-interest may be what hold our polity together rather than any genuine authority.

But if Locke's ambivalence deceives us, it failed to deceive the last of the great contract theorists. Long before his fellow thinkers had sensed any difficulties with Locke and the new science of politics, Jean Jacques Rousseau laid bare the "fatal flaw" in all political thought since Machiavelli. In the process, he called into question the validity of the nation-state itself, whether organized on Hobbesian or Lockean premises.

Notes

1. The debate over Locke's influence in this country is not really relevant here. Whether or not Locke has had a direct impact upon our political consciousness, the fact remains that our ideals and values are thoroughly Lockean.

2. The Levellers, however, were more radical than Locke in this regard. See Julian H. Franklin, *John Locke and the Theory of Sovereignty* (Cambridge: Cambridge University Press, 1978), p. 125.

3. See C.B. Macpherson, *The Political Theory of Possessive Individualism: Hobbes to Locke* (Oxford: Oxford University Press, 1962), for an analysis of Locke's views on the franchise.

4. John Locke, "Essay Concerning Human Understanding," in *John Locke: Works* (Germany: Scientia Verlag Aalen, 1963), I:83. The other source of knowledge is what Locke calls reflection, by which he means ideas produced by the internal activity of the mind itself.

5. John Locke, "The First Treatise," in Peter Laslett, ed., *Two Treatises of Government* (New York: New American Library, 1965), p. 183.

6. See Richard H. Cox, *Locke on War and Peace* (Oxford: Oxford University Press, 1960), for one example of the "secret writing" thesis.

7. Locke, "The Second Treatise," in *Two Treatises of Government*, p. 311.

8. There are certain difficulties with Locke's use of "natural law," for natural law had traditionally been connected with the concept of innate ideas, which Locke rejects. In *An Essay Concerning Human Understanding*, therefore, Locke insists that "there is a great deal of difference between an innate law and a law of nature," (p. 31), and goes on to argue that natural law is learned, like most other things, by reasoning from sense experience. Yet, in "The Second Treatise," Locke uses the authority of Hooker to defend his concept of natural law. Hooker was a sixteenth-century divine and political thinker who traced his ideas back to St. Thomas Aquinas and the traditional concept of natural law. See John W. Yolton, *Locke and the Compass of Human Understanding* (Cambridge: Cambridge University Press, 1970), for a more thorough discussion of Locke's concept of natural law and related epistemological issues.

9. Locke, "The Second Treatise," p. 321. (Emphasis in original.)

10. Ibid.

11. Ibid., p. 316.

12. Ibid., p. 327. (Emphasis in original.)

13. Ibid., p. 328. (Emphasis in original.)

14. Ibid., p. 329. (Emphasis in original.)

15. Ibid., p. 395. (Emphasis in original.)

16. Ibid.

17. Ibid.

18. There is a fundamental difference between classical and modern theories of natural right, however. The former is rooted within a larger ethical system; the latter is not. See Leo Strauss, *Natural Right and History* (Chicago: University of Chicago Press, 1953), for a thorough discussion of this difference.

19. Locke, "The Second Treatise," p. 342.

20. See Macpherson, *The Political Theory of Possessive Individualism,* who has been most responsible for advancing this thesis. There is a great deal of scholarly debate over Macpherson's argument. However, while other of Locke's writing may indeed modify the idea of a right to unlimited accumulation, it is difficult to interpret the argument in "The Second Treatise" as anything other than a claim to that right.

21. Locke, "The Second Treatise," p. 392. In the same way, Locke argues, we tacitly consent to government by acquiring property or simply by enjoying the benefits of living within society. Express consent, on the other hand, is that given via a formal contract.

22. Ibid., p. 333. (Emphasis in original.)

23. See Max Weber, *The Protestant Ethic and The Spirit of Capitalism,* Talcott Parsons, trans. (New York: Charles Scribner's Sons, 1958).

24. See, for example, Macpherson, *Political Theory of Possessive Individualism.* For a contrary point of view, see Peter Laslett's "Introduction to John Locke," in *Two Treatises of Government,* p. 119.

25. Locke, "The Second Treatise," p. 323. (Emphasis in original.)

26. Locke, "An Essay Concerning Human Understanding," p. 263.

27. Locke, "The Second Treatise," p. 316. (Emphasis in original.)

28. Ibid., p. 417.

29. Ibid., p. 410.

30. Parliamentary systems are based upon a fusion of powers in which the executive is a part of the legislature. The judiciary never has been a separate department in Great Britain, and Locke does not treat it as such in his discussion of the separation of powers.

31. Locke's principle of majority rule is also based upon a "Newtonian" or physical conception of power. In Locke's words "it is necessary the Body should move that way whither the greater force carries it, which is the *consent of the majority*" (Locke, "The Second Treatise," p. 375. Emphasis in original.)

32. James Madison, "Federalist Paper No. 51," in *The Federalist Papers,*

Alexander Hamilton, James Madison, and John Jay (New York: New American Library, 1961), p. 322.

33. Locke, "The Second Treatise," p. 415.

34. Ibid., p. 422.

35. Carole Pateman, *The Sexual Contract* (Stanford, Calif.: Stanford University Press, 1988), p. 2. Pateman, however, distinguishes between patriarchal and paternal power. See Chap. 1.

36. See, for example, Macpherson, *Political Theory of Possessive Individualism,* whose interpretation is similar, though not identical, to the ideological interpretation. Macpherson's analysis of Locke's ambivalence or, in his words, Locke's ambiguity, has reshaped contemporary Lockean scholarship.

10

Rousseau

Jean Jacques Rousseau was the intellectual "father" of the French Revolution, as well as the last and perhaps greatest of the modern contract theorists. He was in some sense aware of his own importance, for he claimed to have resolved what he believed to be the most fundamental issue of modern political life. In his major political work, *The Social Contract,* he frames the issue as follows:

> Man is born free, and yet we see him everywhere in chains. Those who believe themselves masters of others cease not to be even greater slaves than the people they govern. How this happens I am ignorant; but if I were asked what renders it justifiable, I believe it may be in my power to resolve the question.[1]

At first glance, this statement seems extravagant. Despite the continued existence of hereditary monarchy, had not the trend since the Renaissance been an expansion of freedom, and had not modern political theorists given increasing attention to the question of liberty? John Locke, for example, had made the language of consent and popular sovereignty common currency among eighteenth-century intellectuals. Where then lay the problem? How could Rousseau seriously claim that men are "everywhere in chains"?

If these questions rise immediately to the mind of the modern reader of Rousseau, they rose even more dramatically to the minds of his contemporaries. We at least have come to question some of the more optimistic political assumptions of Locke and his followers. But in the eighteenth century, no serious intellectual was prepared to deal with the possibility that men were in chains. This was the age of the Enlightenment, a period of time that stretches roughly from Locke to the beginning of the nineteenth century. It was a time in which supposedly the "light of reason" fully illuminated human affairs for the first time. And it was this light of reason that Enlightenment thinkers such as Voltaire believed to be the cause of human liberation and the source of human progress. Just as Galileo and Newton had used reason to liberate humanity from superstition, John Locke and his followers had used it to liberate people from false political doctrines such as those propounded by Filmer and other pre-Enlightenment defenders of absolutism.

Seen in this context, it is not difficult to imagine how shocking Rousseau's claim appeared to his contemporaries. It was a claim that not only ran counter to their optimism in the progress of liberty, but also challenged their unquestioning faith in reason itself. And such radical thinking is not to be explained in intellectual terms alone. It must be seen in part as an expression of a deeper emotional and temperamental reality. This is particularly the case with Rousseau, for perhaps more than any other thinker we have studied, Rousseau's political philosophy is a direct reflection of the man himself. Just as his political thought was out of joint with the generally accepted assumptions of the times, so too was the man out of joint with the society in which he lived. He was, in fact, an intensely unhappy and neurotic person whose life ended in madness and despair.

Rousseau (1712–1778) was born in Geneva to an artisan family. His mother died of complications arising from his birth, a tragedy that filled Rousseau with a lifelong sense of guilt and in all probability lay behind much of his neurotic behavior and personal unhappiness. As a young man, he was apprenticed in several trades, and in 1728 he set out for a period of travel during which he engaged in an extensive process of self-education. He was not, like Hobbes and Locke, formally trained in the university, nor did he consider himself a philosopher in any formal sense.

In 1742 Rousseau set out for Paris where he met the leading cultural, scientific, and philosophical luminaries of Enlightenment France. Among them was Diderot, a leading *philosophe* (as the major French Enlightenment thinkers were called) and the founder of the *Encyclopedie,* a multivolume work that aimed at encompassing all knowledge. Rousseau contributed several articles to the *Encyclopedie,* the most important of which was the *Discourse on Political Economy.* This work, along with the *First and Second Discourses,* and, most importantly, *The Social Contract,* constitutes the basic source of Rousseau's social and political thought, although he wrote several other minor political works, such as *The Government of Poland.* In addition, Rousseau wrote several novels and numerous essays, and he produced three autobiographical works, the most important of which is *The Confessions.* In 1761, the same year that saw the publication of *The Social Contract,*

Rousseau published *Emile,* perhaps the most famous work on education ever written.

Emile marked a disastrous turning point in Rousseau's life, for so shocking was the book to Rousseau's contemporaries that it was publicly burned in Paris and Rousseau was threatened with arrest. Worst of all, both *Emile* and *The Social Contract* were confiscated in his beloved Geneva, a city that he frequently referred to as his political ideal. Rousseau had no choice but to flee. He became for the last years of his life a wanderer and an outcast. Many of his former friends abandoned him, the philosophes attacked him, and Rousseau found it increasingly difficult to establish or maintain friendships with anyone. Always a neurotic and unhappy man, he became increasingly so near the end of his life. His last years were marked by psychotic depression and paranoia.

Apart from the tragic condition of his birth, the precise reason for Rousseau's personal unhappiness is not known, and normally it would not really be important in itself. We want to know what a theorist said, not why he said it, except insofar as the theorist's motivations and inner conflicts help us to grasp the substance of his argument. Because the connection between this man and his thought is so intimate, Rousseau is such a theorist. His inner and essentially neurotic conflicts have a direct bearing upon his political theory.[2] And the essence of Rousseau's problems lay in the inconsistency between his behavior and his beliefs. If ever there was a man who could say in all sincerity "Do as I say, not as I do," it was Jean Jacques Rousseau.

In *The Confessions,* for example, he tells us that he feels for his fellow human more deeply and genuinely than others, yet he could not maintain friendships with anyone, and he thoroughly mistreated his mistress (eventually his wife) of many years. He tells us in *Emile* that the education of the child requires the total attention of the tutor, yet he sent all of his illegitimate children to a foundling home and never saw them again. He complains of the superficiality and immorality of the theater and other forms of "civilized" entertainment, yet he was an avid theatergoer, and his novels contain the kind of excessive romanticism and sentimentality that he elsewhere indicts as the "degrading influence of civilization." He argues that the intellectual life is the unnatural product of civilization (in the *Second Discourse* he goes as far as to say that "the man who meditates is a depraved animal"),[3] yet he was a thoroughgoing intellectual and frequented the salons and other intellectual gatherings that he says he so heartily detests. And while he insists that the desire for fame and other forms of ego gratification are civilized perversions, he himself desperately sought fame and recognition.

Rousseau was not unaware of his own inconsistencies. Quite the contrary. He was not only aware, he was puzzled, for he was convinced that despite his outwardly bad behavior he was a good man. In contrast to *The Confessions* of St. Augustine, which aimed at demonstrating their author's essential depravity, Rousseau, addressing his fellow man in the opening pages of his *Confessions,* exclaims "let them groan at my depravities, and blush for my misdeeds. But let each one of them reveal his heart . . . with equal sincerity, and may any man who dares say 'I was a better man than he.' "[4]

This inconsistency between Rousseau's outer behavior and his inner life is the key to his political philosophy, for he insists that the inconsistency characterizes all civilized peoples and is to be explained only by the absence of liberty. If men were not everywhere in chains in European society, says Rousseau, they would not behave as they do. For where real political control had been taken from the people, he argues, there is not simply the loss of liberty in the narrow political sense, but loss of inner freedom to express one's innate decency and goodness as well. That people behave as other than the loving and cooperative creatures they naturally are is proof that neither outer political nor inner personal liberty is a reality.

But what causes this loss of liberty? Rousseau's claim in *The Social Contract* that he is ignorant of how men came to be in chains is not entirely valid. In his *Second Discourse on the Origin and Foundations of Inequality Among Men,* a work written some years before the publication of *The Social Contract,* he attributes the loss of freedom to the inequality produced by the emergence of private property. Primitive people had no property, says Rousseau, and hence each was as equal and as free as everyone else. Civilized people, on the other hand, have developed social classes based upon extreme inequalities of property, and along with social inequality has come a loss of liberty in both the political and the personal sense.

Political liberty is destroyed because the propertied classes possess the power to dominate others. But this same inequality of property destroys as well the freedom to express one's innate goodness, Rousseau argues, because it produces competition for economic goods, the struggle for political power, and strivings for honor and status. All these unnatural social desires create conflict rather than cooperation, envy and malice rather than love and affection. Human beings began to calculate their own self-interest rather than thinking first of their fellows, and in the process they became what the sociologist David Riesman has termed *other directed.* Rather than being true to themselves, they act in ways calculated to gain praise or to elicit flattery. They do anything to raise themselves above others.

Worst of all, says Rousseau, with the emergence of inequality reason itself becomes perverted. Not only do people begin to use their reason to calculate their own advantage at the expense of others, reason becomes merely another source of vanity. Learning and philosophy are acquired, not for their own sakes, but to demonstrate one's intellectual superiority. Most seriously, civilized people use their reason to produce philosophies that actually justify loss of political and personal liberty.

This latter point Rousseau first developed in his *First Discourse on the Question: Has the Restoration of the Sciences and Arts Tended to Purify Morals* (1750). The question was posed for an essay contest by the Academy of Dijon, a scientific institution comprised of the leading French Enlightenment intellectuals. Rousseau's *First Discourse* won the prize and made him famous, for not only did he dispute the Enlightenment's optimism in the power of reason to liberate humankind, he insisted that reason had contributed to the loss of freedom by blinding men to their actual condition of slavery. In a full-scale assault upon the Enlightenment, Rousseau claimed that

> The sciences, letters, and arts . . . spread garlands of flowers over the iron chains with which men are burdened, stifle in them the sense of that original liberty for which they seemed to have been born, make them love their slavery, and turn them into what is called civilized peoples.[5]

Rousseau believes there are certain obvious political conclusions that follow from his analysis of Enlightenment civilization (an analysis, incidentally, that can be applied to our own contemporary society). Clearly, European society and polity must be reconstituted such that political liberty and inner freedom are returned to "the people." Indeed, the two must be united, says Rousseau. Political liberty must be made a reality so that people can shape their social order to encourage the expression of that natural goodness that is the essence of inner liberty. It is not sufficient that people individually reform themselves, as St. Augustine proposes, nor is it even a second best alternative, as Plato suggests. Rousseau's own life had demonstrated to him that human freedom and fulfillment cannot exist apart from a polity that makes them possible. Apart from this, human beings will behave badly despite their innate goodness.

Since Rousseau believes that inequality is the source of the problem, one might reason that his reforms will include the elimination of private property. Such is not the case. While he clearly disagrees with Locke that property is the source of rights and liberties, he is in no sense a proto-Marxist, although his critique of private property in the *Second Discourse* clearly had a great impact upon Marx. Indeed, much of what Rousseau proposes will at first perplex the reader, for his political theory runs essentially contrary to our normal political assumptions. Indeed, scholars have not themselves been able to determine how best to interpret his political thought, and he has been labeled everything from a liberal to a totalitarian.[6]

But if Rousseau's meaning is not always easy to discern, the manner in which he must be interpreted is clear. Rousseau is the last of the great contract theorists. As such, his political thought must be understood within the context of his theory of contract, which is developed most clearly in his major political work, *The Social Contract*. Yet even in *The Social Contract* Rousseau presents difficulties in interpretation, for he need not have employed the idea of the contract at all. Indeed, there are elements of his political thought that contradict the notion that political society is the result of an express agreement as opposed to an unthinking historical evolution. But, in certain important respects, the theory of contract corresponded to Rousseau's most fundamental assumptions about the nature of social and political order. Moreover, he understood that a political theorist must speak in a language familiar to his readers if he expects to change their political opinions, and in his day the contract theory had become the dominant mode of political analysis. For these reasons, he chose to employ that theory.

What is unique about Rousseau's political analysis is that he combines elements of Hobbes's and Locke's theories of contract in a way that challenges both. This is true as well in his interpretation of the state of nature, which, of course, is the starting point for all contract theorists. In the case of Rousseau, however, the state of nature is treated more as an actual historical condition than it is by his predecessors, although the basic mode of reasoning he employs in thinking about the state of nature and the contract is still essentially that of logical imagination. What Rousseau does unequivocally concede to Hobbes and Locke is that, whether the state of nature is conceived historically or imaginatively, people's natural condition is one of absolute liberty and equality. From this point on Rousseau selectively accepts, rejects, and modifies Hobbes's and Locke's contractual analysis.

To begin with, he agrees with Hobbes that in the state of nature human beings lack any social capacity, but he goes much further than Hobbes. He not only claims that human beings are naturally isolated individuals, he argues that they are utterly amoral as well.[7] Hobbes had conceded that humans in the state of nature could, in the abstract, conceive of something like natural law, but according to Rousseau they cannot even imagine it, much less behave according to its dictates as Locke believes.

Rousseau's insistence that human beings are naturally amoral (not immoral) and asocial (not antisocial) is based upon an insight that never occurred to either Hobbes or Locke. Language, Rousseau argues, is an invention of civilization. "Primitive peoples" are without it; they can therefore neither reason nor speak. As such, they are incapable of knowing those moral rules necessary to create a viable community. Like Aristotle, Rousseau insists that without speech politics is impossible for speech is the necessary precondition for human sociability.

Despite his agreement with Hobbes that people are innately asocial individualists, however, Rousseau does not conclude that the state of nature is a state of war. Rather, he agrees with Locke that human beings are essentially decent creatures and that, as a consequence, their natural condition must be one of peace and concord. But, as we have seen, he cannot accept Locke's contention that this peace is the result of people's ability to know and obey natural law. Without language and the capacity to reason, human beings are incapable of knowing moral truths.

What then inclines people to peace? Feeling, says Rousseau. Hobbes did not notice, he argues, that "savage man . . . tempers the ardor he has for his own well-being by an innate repugnance to see his fellow man suffer."[8] This innate repugnance Rousseau calls *pity,* the only natural virtue that human beings posses (all other virtues, says Rousseau, are socially created, or conventional). And pity, he continues, is "all the more universal and useful to man because it precedes in him the use of all reflection; and so natural that even beasts sometimes give perceptible signs of it"[9]

Simply put, Rousseau believes the state of nature is a state of peace because people are naturally "good" in the sense that they have a natural empathy for their fellow creatures. (Bear in mind, however, that this is not in the strictest sense moral goodness since morality requires the ability to speak and reason.) This natural "goodness" is easily confirmed, says Rousseau, because we see it in ourselves as well as in others. No normal person wants to see others suffer, and there are many examples of people risking their lives to prevent others from being hurt. Even the beasts, as he says, give perceptible signs of pity or compassion, and he gives as an example the tendency of a horse to avoid trampling underfoot another living creature.

It follows from this analysis that pity or compassion is the foundation of all human virtue and goodness for Rousseau since it is a universal and prerational tendency to be concerned about our fellow beings. (This natural concern, however, is not interpreted by Rousseau as an indication of a natural sociability.) Without this, other virtues would either not exist or would be little more than hollow rules of behavior. Indeed, this is precisely Rousseau's complaint about Enlightenment civilization: It had lost its capacity to feel and, as such, its purported virtues were little more than vanities. Worse, he believes that Enlightenment virtues are actually destructive of human goodness.

It is clear that Rousseau's description of the state of nature is not simply a metaphor for human nature, as it is for Hobbes and Locke. It is a thoroughgoing critique of contemporary civilization, for it vividly illustrates that civilization has had the effect of repressing human goodness. And it is apparent, therefore, that for Rousseau the fundamental flaw in both Hobbes's and Locke's conceptions of the state of nature is that they had read into it civilized man and civilized conditions. In Rousseau's words "they spoke about savage man and they described civil man."[10]

Locke, for example, speaks of natural man's ability to know natural law when the capacity to reason, says Rousseau, is clearly a civilized trait. Worse, Locke and the other Enlightenment thinkers impose a form of reasoning on people in the state of nature that is already perverted by a diseased social order. The kind of social and political structure that Locke assumes people would rationally consent to is one that only a "civilized" mind would find agreeable.

But Hobbes made the more fundamental mistake in reading the real conditions of the state of nature. Locke merely imposes the civilized capacity to reason upon natural man; Hobbes imposes the passions produced by civilization. The desire for power after power that he ascribes to human nature is in fact a product of civilization, says Rousseau. Moreover, he argues, the state of war that Hobbes claims is the consequence of the struggle for power is first observed in nascent society, not in the state of nature. In short, Hobbes did not look deeply enough into his own heart. He did not recognize his own underlying goodness. Precisely because he was a civilized man he assumed that his desires and passions were innate in human nature rather than the unnatural by-product of social inequality.

Given Rousseau's argument that both Hobbes and Locke failed to grasp the real essence of human nature, we can expect his view of the contractual act to differ considerably from those of his predecessors. Yet the reason why human beings contract out of the state of nature Rousseau does not make entirely clear. He simply tells us that the contract is made at that point where "the strength of each individual is insufficient to overcome the resistance of the obstacles to his preservation."[11] But what are these obstacles? Clearly they cannot be those discussed by Hobbes or Locke: the war of everyone against everyone or, what comes to the same thing, the insecurity of property. Such views are contrary to Rousseau's theory that the state of nature is peaceful and that humans have a natural regard for one another.

The obstacles Rousseau seems to have in mind are purely physical in nature, for in his *Essay on the Origin of Languages* he tells us that "human associations are due largely to accidents of nature,"[12] such as floods, earthquakes, and the like. People unite to help protect themselves from natural catastrophes. Yet, in Rousseau's case, it is more relevant to ask what benefits accrue from contracting than what impels human beings to enter political society. And here Rousseau is both clear and explicit:

> The passing from the state of nature to the civil state produces in man a very remarkable change, by substituting justice for instinct in his conduct, and giving to his actions a moral character which they lacked before.[13]

It is clear that for Rousseau the act of contracting has an effect far surpassing anything imagined by either Hobbes or Locke. For these thinkers, human beings remain the same before and after the act of contracting. The contract simply makes them more secure than they had been in the state of nature. For Rousseau, on the other hand, the act of contracting transforms what are little more than dumb animals into human beings by "substituting justice for instinct." Upon entering society people learn to relate to one another on the basis of moral rules rather than mere feeling. As such, they become truly free for the first time. In Rousseau's words, the contract creates "moral liberty, which alone renders a man master of himself."[14]

Rousseau is in no sense, therefore, a primitivist. He does not prefer the "noble savage" to civilized humanity as many have mistakenly believed. Quite the contrary in fact. The superiority of civilized people, at least their potential superiority, is clear: They alone have risen above mere animal existence to become moral beings who are capable of making moral choices. In Aristotle's words, they have become capable of reasoned action and thereby free. Thus it is clear that Rousseau's critique of Enlightenment people is not that they are civilized as such, but that the form of their civilization is perverse. And his claim in the *First Discourse* that the arts and sciences have corrupted and enslaved them is not to be interpreted as an attack upon reason in and of itself, but upon a perverted form of reason.

It also bears repeating here that Rousseau's contract is, at bottom, an imaginative construct; it is not to be taken literally. Unless this is kept in mind, what Rousseau says about the contractual act makes little sense. Certainly no mere agreement to enter into society can create language or turn people into reasoning creatures. To be perfectly precise, human beings could not contract at all without the ability to reason or speak. (It is probably for this reason that Rousseau sometimes treats the state of nature as a historical condition in which human beings evolve over time sufficiently to allow them to acquire those social and linguistic skills necessary to "contract out" of the state of nature.)

If we take what Rousseau says metaphorically, however, we find that he is agreeing with some of the profoundest insights of modern social science. For what Rousseau means to say in his theory of the contractual act is that language and reason are acquired in society. Consequently, all of our moral rules are social products; they are conventional rather than natural. Moreover, what we are ethically and in fact in every other way is largely the result of socialization. Beyond our natural capacity for pity, there is no innate human nature. "Human nature" is itself a social product.

What Rousseau really wants to do in his analysis of the contract, therefore, is to demonstrate that people can be genuinely free and happy only when human nature has been socially structured such that reason is made moral. Reason must become ethically based; it must be made to be something other than mere calculation of one's self-interest. But how is this to be accomplished? Rousseau has in fact already given us the answer: Reason must be united with feeling, with people's natural and prerational tendency to have compassion for their fellow beings. And such a unification requires a society in which gross inequalities are not allowed to debase people and make them self-interested and rapacious rather than public-interested and loving. Ideally conceived, this is the kind of society that the contract is supposed to create according to Rousseau.

It is at this point, however, that Rousseau confronts what he considers to be the major theoretical problem inherent in the contractual theory of society. He has agreed with the other contract theorists that people must contract out of the state of nature because of the obstacles to their preservation. Yet, it is apparent that the terms of the contract specify that they must give up their natural liberty and agree to live by society's rules. There is no other possible reading of the contract that makes any logical sense, says Rousseau. How, then, is the liberty of the individual to be made compatible with the necessity of social order? The problem is summarized by Rousseau in the following way:

> Where shall we find a form of association which will defend and protect with the whole common force the person and the property of each associate, and by which every person, while uniting himself with all, shall obey only himself and remain as free as before?[15]

Hobbes's response to this dilemma was to conclude that people have no rights in society but those granted by government, a conclusion that Rousseau cannot accept since the enhancement of liberty, both political and personal, is the whole intent of the contract. Without liberty, people could not exercise that moral autonomy that it is the purpose of the contract to create in the first place. Yet, Rousseau cannot accept Locke's solution of limiting the exercise of sovereign power over the community either. Like Hobbes, he conceives of people in the state of nature as essentially isolated individuals. He absolutely rejects Locke's thesis that they possess a natural social capacity. Thus, unless the sovereign power is absolute in all spheres, as Hobbes claims it must be, Rousseau concedes that society would disintegrate into an individualistic state of nature.

Rousseau's greatest claim to fame as a political thinker is that his analysis of the contract resolves this apparent contradiction between the liberty of the individual and the requirements of social order. He had found a way to create a sovereign power as absolute as Hobbes's yet which, at the same time, allows individuals to maintain their liberty in an even more absolute sense than Locke would have it.[16]

Before we consider precisely how Rousseau accomplishes this, it is worth noting the enormous importance of what he proposes to do. Rousseau claims to have resolved a paradox that not only confounded the great contract theorists but has lain at the heart of Western political thought from the beginning. One might even say that this contradiction between individual liberty and the imperatives of social order has been the defining issue in Western normative theory since Socrates. Indeed, Socrates founded Western political thought around this very issue when he refused to sacrifice his liberty to teach yet died in order to affirm the necessity of law.

The Socratic solution Rousseau does not find acceptable. Death may be an appropriate means to overcome the contradiction for the philosopher, but not for the average person. In practical terms, a political rather than a philosophical solution is required. The state must be so constructed that both liberty and social control are possible. And the political principles that must be employed to accomplish this task can only be determined by a radically new interpretation of the contract, Rousseau argues.

To begin with, says Rousseau, the act of contracting must, as Hobbes maintained, involve "the total alienation of each associate and all his rights."[17] Anything short of this would not work. But, he continues, this alienation of rights is from the individual to the whole community, not simply to one man or assembly of men who, as Hobbes held, are not a party to the contract. In other words, each individual must contract with all others to turn over their natural rights to every other individual. In this way, says Rousseau, the locus of sovereignty remains within the whole community of which each individual is a part. It follows, therefore, that while all are subject to the sovereign power of the community, at the same time all share a portion of that power in their capacity as citizens. If, for example, the state is composed of ten thousand citizens, then, says Rousseau, "each has . . . a ten-thousandth part of the sovereign authority, though he is entirely subjected to it."[18]

What this analysis points to in political terms, Rousseau argues, is that the legislative power must belong to the entire community of citizens, and each citizen must have an equal voice in the legislative process. This is the only way in which the individual can be made subject to the sovereign authority of the community yet retain a legitimate share of that authority. And that this reading of the contract is correct, Rousseau insists, is proven by the political results that follow.

Recall that the purpose of the contract is to create a form of association in which "every person, while uniting himself with all, shall obey only himself and remain as free as before." This, says Rousseau, is precisely what occurs when the legislative authority is given to the whole community. Each is united with all to form a sovereign authority, yet in obeying the law the individual obeys rules he himself has had a share in making. Sovereignty and liberty, social order and freedom, are thus rendered compatible. More than this, the one becomes the necessary condition for the other.

It should not be thought that Rousseau is simply propounding Locke's doctrine of popular sovereignty in a new guise. He is most surely a theorist of popular sovereignty, and he therefore agrees with Locke that government is merely a trust or, in his words, merely a law, by which he means that it is created by a legislative act of the sovereign community.[19] But Rousseau's theory of popular sovereignty is not only different from Locke's, it is in fact a thoroughgoing critique of the whole tradition of Lockean liberal democracy. For while Locke recognizes the principle of popular sovereignty in theory, he rejects it in practice, says Rousseau. In point of fact, he argues, Locke's contract does not give the legislative power to the people, but to a representative legislature. As such, sovereignty belongs to the elected representatives, or more precisely to a majority of representatives, rather than to the community as a whole. Thus, Locke actually puts sovereignty in the hands of a very small minority, thereby denying to the people that political liberty that a correct reading of the contract shows they rightfully ought to possess.

One might contend that liberty is in fact no more assured in Rousseau's ideal state than in Locke's, since the community may pass laws to which particular members will object. Each, after all, has only a small part of the sovereign authority, only one vote among many. And there is no more guarantee that the citizen will agree with laws passed by the whole community than with laws passed by a representative legislature. It would seem, therefore, that in obeying the law citizens in Rousseau's state do not necessarily obey themselves.

This argument, while seeming unassailable on the surface, really misses the point, says Rousseau. Admittedly, some members of the community may object to a particular law, but this does not mean that they will not willingly and freely obey it. If society and polity are appropriately organized, the "dissenters" will recognize that the laws were made for their own good and will freely grant their obedience. And if the citizen should refuse to obey the general will, he "shall be compelled to it by the whole body,"[20] says Rousseau, and he concludes in what is arguably the most controversial statement ever made in Western political theory: "This . . . only forces him to be free[!]"[21]

The obvious objection to this line of reasoning is that to be forced to be free is a contradiction in terms. Rousseau anticipated the objection; indeed, *The Social Contract* is, in a sense, an extended answer to it. For unless Rousseau can demonstrate that in his ideal polity there is no contradiction between force and freedom (as there is, he would argue, in Hobbes's or Locke's state) he will have failed to accomplish his major theoretical objective. He will have failed to demonstrate that there is no incompatibility between absolute sovereignty and absolute liberty, for there will obviously be times, although Rousseau believes they will be infrequent, in which the subject must be forced to obey the law.

The key to Rousseau's answer is to be found in his statement that those who shall be forced to be free are those who refuse to obey the *general will*. The concept of the general will is Rousseau's major contribution to Western political thought, and any comprehension of his political theory requires a thorough grasp of it. Actually, we have already gone a long way toward explaining the concept without explicitly using the term, so we should be able to grasp the idea of the general will fairly readily.

The general will is Rousseau's term for the sovereign power. When the community as a whole meets in legislative assembly, says Rousseau, it expresses in law the *will* or moral sense of the *general* or whole community. By *moral*, of course, Rousseau means that which is in the public interest (from

Socrates on, the public interest has always been defined as the essence of justice or political morality). And what makes the general will a moral will is precisely its generality. Since members of the community must legislate for the whole (general) community including themselves, they have every personal interest in making law in the public interest. Remember that the creation of the general will requires the alienation of the rights of each to all others. Consequently, says Rousseau, "the condition of every person is alike; and being so, it would not be to the interest of anyone to render that condition offensive to others."[22] By the simple expedient of putting the sovereign legislative power in the whole community, in other words, it becomes the self-interest of each to promote the public interest of all.

On the opening page of *The Social Contract,* Rousseau says that he "shall endeavor to unite what right permits with what interest prescribes, that justice and utility may not be separated."[23] This merging of justice, or the public interest, and utility, or self-interest, is the essence of the general will and may be said to be the key organizational principle of Rousseau's ideal state. For when self-interest, as Hobbes believes, is opposed to the public interest, sheer power must be exercised to maintain social order and real liberty is thereby destroyed. When self-interest is identical to the public interest, on the other hand, as is the case says Rousseau when each citizen has a share of the sovereign legislative power, the need to exercise power is dramatically decreased and liberty is maintained. Under most circumstances people will willingly obey laws that they themselves have made and that they believe reflect a genuine public good.

More than this, the recognition that one's self-interest lies in the public interest (a recognition that can occur only when each has a share in the sovereign legislative power) generates over time a larger love of one's fellow citizens, says Rousseau. To grasp that one's self-interest is the public interest is to recognize that self-love can only be expressed by love of country. Thus, in connecting justice and utility, the general will gives political expression to people's natural virtue of compassion, of concern for others. In this way, reason is united with feeling, and political decisions thereby become moral decisions.

In real life, of course, it is not quite this simple, as Rousseau is well aware. There will always exist the danger that the citizen legislators will fail to see that it is in their self-interest to vote the public interest. They may come to support laws that reflect their own narrow or short-term self-interest, what Rousseau calls their *private will,* rather than those that reflect the public interest or general will. Indeed, the danger is that the community will disintegrate into nothing more than a collection of private or corporate wills. Reason and feeling will become disjoined and people will begin to act as amoral and self-regarding individuals. For this reason, as we shall see, Rousseau advocates a complete restructuring of society and polity to prevent the emergence of any type of particular will in the community. But making each citizen a member of the legislative body is the first and absolutely necessary condition for the existence of the general will. Without this, the general will could not possibly be expressed, since it would clearly not be in the self-interest of each to be concerned with the public interest of all. Justice and utility, in short, could not be united.

For now, it is sufficient to recognize that so long as the general will is not alienated to a legislative assembly and is not allowed to disintegrate into a collection of particular wills, it remains by definition general, hence moral.[24] As such, Rousseau concludes, the general will is "always right," that is, always right in the moral sense of reflecting the public good. It may happen, of course, that the sovereign community will misjudge the real public interest, but this Rousseau considers a technical problem that can in large measure be resolved by effectively structuring society and state. But it cannot happen that the general will, so long as it remains general, would ever consciously pervert the public good. "The people are never corrupted," says Rousseau, "but they are often deceived, and only then do they seem to will what is bad." [25]

It is now clear why the citizen can be "forced to be free" in Rousseau's ideal state. Inasmuch as the general will is always morally right, refusal to obey the law would clearly be wrong. And since the whole purpose of the contract is to give human beings that "moral liberty which alone renders a man master of himself," it cannot logically be maintained that to do moral wrong, that is, to disobey the general will, is an act of moral liberty. By definition moral liberty is always conformity to the general will. Hence, were some inclined to disobey the general will, their freedom could be maintained only by being compelled to obey. Real liberty is always obedience to the law because the law reflects a genuine moral will.

Rousseau's analysis is perfectly logical once it is recognized that he holds a positive theory of liberty.[26] The idea of positive liberty is that freedom cannot be discussed apart from some moral end. To be free means to be free *for* something. In Socratic terms, for example, real freedom means seeking that which enhances virtue and order within us. In much the same way, Rousseau believes that genuine liberty comprises only those actions that enhance us as moral beings. Hence, conformity to the general will, even if coerced, is clearly an expression of liberty since the general will is always moral.

The contrary view of liberty, the negative theory, supposes that liberty means simply the absence of external restraints. There is in this no moral dimension at all. People are free so long as there is nothing to prevent them from doing what they want to do. One is not free *for* something, only *from* something. This is the view propounded by Hobbes and, less bluntly, by Locke. For this reason, the notion of positive liberty seems to us to be a contradiction in terms. We have been influenced so greatly by Lockean liberalism that we automatically assume people ought to have liberty to do anything not specifically circumscribed by law. The idea that freedom involves certain moral constraints is simply alien to our mode of political thinking. And the logical extension of this idea in Rousseau's claim that the state can force its members to be free seems to us not only erroneous but, in application, totalitarian.

Yet, there is nothing illogical or even necessarily totalitarian about the positive theory of liberty, even when carried to the extreme of forcing people to be free. As we have seen, the positive theory rests upon political assumptions that are perfectly coherent even if we do not share in those assumptions. And, as we shall see, the totalitarian implications of the theory are mitigated by the kind of polity Rousseau advocates. But the best way to come to terms with Rousseau's theory of positive liberty is to apply it to a real situation. In application, it will be seen to make as much practical as theoretical sense.

For the sake of argument, let us take an extreme case. Let us suppose that certain citizens in Rousseau's ideal state have become addicted to drugs. We may safely assume that the community is opposed to the abuse of drugs and has expressed itself as such in the law. Now, given the nature of drug addiction, those addicted will surely attempt to break the law if left to their own devices. In the process, they will become increasingly enslaved to their addiction and will likely rob from others in order to continue supporting their habit.

Clearly, the behavior of our hypothetical citizens is unethical since it is a violation of the general will. It reflects their short-term "self-interest" rather than the public interest or moral will of the whole community. Moreover, as members of the sovereign community our citizens almost surely voted for the prohibition of drugs knowing that their use would be as damaging to themselves as to the community. Thus, when the community forces them to give up the use of drugs it really forces them to do that which they themselves desire to do because, as ethical beings, they desire to do that which is right for themselves and others. The community merely "forces them to be free." And if our citizens have become so corrupted that they no longer care what is right or wrong, this only indicates that they have become utterly enslaved to their addiction. Eliminate the enslavement, even if by force, and you set them free.

Of course the prohibition against drug abuse exists in all modern liberal states. But the prohibition is simply that, a prohibition. The act of obeying the law carries with it no positive notion of free moral choice, only the negative idea that breaking the law will meet with punishment. Certainly the idea that those who break the law will be "forced to be free" is unthinkable from the liberal perspective. Either you are free or you are not, and the scope of law determines how much or how little freedom you have.

It is, in fact, this negative conception of liberty that lies behind the liberal's theory of the negative state. In order to enlarge individual liberty there was no choice but to severely delimit the scope of state power. If, as Hobbes maintains, liberty is nothing other than the absence of law, then the rights and liberties of the individual could be ensured only by reducing the scope of law. This was to be done both by limiting the number and extent of laws ("the less government the better") and by erecting more fundamental laws or constitutions that would set parameters around the kinds of laws that could be made. A case in point is the First Amendment to the American Constitution, which states that "Congress shall make no law respecting an establishment of religion . . . ; or abridging the freedom of speech, or of the press," and so on.

Rousseau would certainly not accept such constitutional limitations in his ideal state. He expects religion, speech, and press to be carefully regulated and controlled for reasons that should by now be obvious. Clearly Rousseau's conception of liberty requires that the citizens of his republic be trained in moral virtue. They must learn to think first of the public interest rather than their narrow self-interest (or, more precisely, they must learn to recognize that the public interest is their self-interest). In other words, the state must play the role of moral educator. Rousseau is an advocate of the positive state (that is, of the state actively involving itself in regulating the community) as a necessary corollary to his theory of positive liberty, just as on the opposite side the liberals supported the negative state as the corollary to their theory of negative liberty.

As products of the liberal tradition, it is difficult for us to imagine preserving individual liberty and preventing the abuse of state power from any other than this negative point of view. Rousseau thus remains essentially hostile to our most basic political assumptions. But it is important to recognize that Rousseau's defense of the positive state and positive liberty is not only logically coherent but that it embodies much practical political sense as well. For Rousseau is quite correct in his insistence that a political community cannot be simply a collection of self-interested individuals who have no concern for the larger public good. Without some sense of the general will, no society could exist, for it would quickly disintegrate into Hobbes's "war of everyone against everyone."

Indeed, it is with Hobbes in mind that we can now see the real value of Rousseau's general will. It is in essence a moral concept that illuminates what he believes to be the fundamental flaw in all modern states organized on Hobbesian or Lockean premises. They lack any genuine ethical basis and, as such, the citizens have no inner reason or self-imposed duty to obey the law. Law then becomes in Hobbes's words "command," that is, a civilized form of force or coercion. Thus, obedience to law ceases to be an act of freedom and genuine liberty is destroyed. The concept of the general will indicates that it is the liberal state that is based upon force and coercion, not Rousseau's ideal polity where if force is employed it actually enhances freedom.

This brings us to Rousseau's principles of political organization, for it should be apparent at this juncture that his political ideals require a unique political structure. And quite clearly the basic organizational principle is that the state must be constructed so as to maintain and promote the general will. Unless this principle can be realized in practice, the state will rest upon sheer power, the laws will be little more than coercion, and real liberty will be destroyed. And while Rousseau discusses a number of ways to preserve the general will, two considerations are of particular importance: The state must be relatively small, and the underlying social order must be essentially egalitarian.

The most important and obvious reason for a small state is that it allows the people to gather into a sovereign lawmaking assembly. Smallness is thus the necessary precondition for the existence of the general will. In extremely large states it becomes necessary to elect representatives, which, as we have seen, subverts the general will. Moreover, the larger the state the smaller the proportion of sovereign power that each individual possesses. This is why, Rousseau insists, "that liberty is diminished by the enlargement of the state."[27]

Moreover, a small state contributes to an intense sense of community, and this encourages citizens to care for one another. It thus evokes within them that natural virtue of other-regardingness that undergirds the general will. Rousseau would agree with Aristotle that a primary function of political life is to engender friendship, and that without friendship and concern for each other people would be incapable of giving expression to the general will.

Finally, a small state contributes to a simplicity of manners that prevents the people from being misled about what constitutes the real public interest. This is so, says Rousseau, because "men of integrity and simplicity are difficult to deceive because of their very simplicity: Lures and refined pretexts do not impose upon them, and they have not even cunning enough to be dupes."[28] For this reason, a small state discourages those political subterfuges on the part of special interests that might deceive the people as to what constitutes the real general will. It is precisely "sophisticated" people who are most easily deceived by the appeals of special interests, and large complex states tend to produce sophisticated people. Hence, Rousseau concludes in one of the more famous passages in *The Social Contract:*

> When we see, among the happiest people in the world, groups of peasants directing affairs of state under an oak, and always acting wisely, can we help but despise the refinements of those nations which render themselves illustrious and miserable by so much art and mystery?[29]

Equality is even more essential to the maintenance of the general will than smallness and simplicity for "liberty cannot subsist without it,"[30] says Rousseau. The reasons behind his claim we have already examined in our discussion of his *Second Discourse.* Inequality means that some will be dominated by others and that, as a consequence, the people will lose that moral autonomy that is the essence of liberty and the very foundation of the general will. But, Rousseau hastens to add:

> Equality . . . must not be understood to mean that power and riches should be equally divided between all; but that power should never be so strong as to be capable of acts of violence, or exercised but in virtue of the exerciser's station, and under direction of the laws; and that in regard to riches, no citizen should be sufficiently opulent to be able to purchase another, and none so poor as to be forced to sell himself. This supposes on the side of the great, moderation in wealth and position, and, on the side of the lower classes, moderation in avarice and greed.[31]

Clearly, Rousseau is no fanatical egalitarian, nor does he condemn the existence of private property as one might suppose from a reading of the *Second Discourse.* It is not necessary that everyone be absolutely equal to everyone else; it is sufficient that no one group be so rich or so powerful that it can dominate others. Relative, rather than absolute, equality is Rousseau's goal. To this end, he argues in his *Political Economy,* it is government's function to prevent extreme inequalities by removing the means of accumulating too much wealth.[32] And rather than raising taxes to accomplish its ends, says Rousseau, government should strive to limit needs. He is convinced that increases in taxation are a mark of social disintegration. They imply that unnecessary social needs are increasing and along with them that complexity and social inequality that subverts the general will. And for Rousseau the first principle of political economy is precisely the maintenance of the general will, not the unlimited accumulation of wealth.

Note here the dramatic difference between Rousseau's economic views and those of Locke and modern economists. Like the classical thinkers, Rousseau takes as a given that economic considerations, no less than political ones, are in essence moral concerns. Economic decisions have as their object the preservation of a larger public good. Thus, Locke's notion of the unlimited right to accumulate property is alien to Rousseau, as is the contemporary idea that economic health resides in an ever-expanding gross national product. Both ideas conceive economics to be an end in itself rather than part of a larger ethical whole. And both ideas have become the theoretical underpinnings of the modern industrial state with all those complexities and inequalities that Rousseau insists destroy the public good. For this reason, Rousseau's insistence that the economy must exist within certain ethical constraints carries with it an ideal of a small, simple, and essentially agrarian state.

Apart from this, there are several political or quasi-political institutions that Rousseau recommends as further supports to the general will. Interestingly, he follows Machiavelli's lead and returns to the experience of the Roman Republic. Like Machiavelli, Rousseau believes the Romans to have been the most political of all peoples and to have devised the most excellent of political institutions. Their example, therefore, he believes to be of great value to the theorist.

We need not discuss all of the institutions that Rousseau recommends except to note their Roman origins as a review of the chapter on Cicero will make clear. Two of them, the dictatorship and the tribuneship, have to do with certain technical constitutional considerations that need not concern us here. And Rousseau's analysis of the Roman *Comita,* or assembly, shows how his ideal sovereign assembly is to function, a matter we will discuss shortly. Two institutions, however, deserve special mention because they illuminate Rousseau's more fundamental political ideas.

The first of these is the censorship, an institution, says Rousseau, established "to preserve morality by preventing the opinions of men from being corrupted."[33] For Rousseau, opinion is really the most fundamental law of the state. It is the law "written" within the human heart without which civil laws can have no meaning. As such, morality is subverted and the state ceases to express the general will if opinion is allowed to become corrupted, if, for example, people come to believe their individual interest is superior to the collective interest. The censorship is thus crucial to the maintenance of the public good.

We, of course, are rather shocked by the notion of censorship since freedom of opinion is one of our most cherished values. But it bears repeating that Rousseau holds a positive view of liberty and a positive theory of the state. To his mind, it is precisely the object of the state to engage in moral education so that the liberty of the subject will conform to the general will. Absolute freedom of opinion can no more exist in his ideal state than can an absolute right to the unlimited accumulation of property.

This same logic lies behind Rousseau's argument for the institution of civil religion. Clearly, religious opinions, as with any opinions that have social or political import, must be fixed in Rousseau's ideal state. Hence, he argues, there must be a purely civil profession of faith on the part of the citizens, the articles of which are to be determined by the sovereign. And while he is willing to tolerate other religions so long as they do not contradict the tenets of the civil faith (the most important of which is the sanctity of the social contract), it is clear that Rousseau prefers the civil religion to others.

Rousseau's preference is again reminiscent of Machiavelli. Like Machiavelli, he criticizes Christianity and other such universalistic religions, what he calls the "religion of man," because their otherworldly orientation directs people's attention away from the political community and makes them concerned only with "the purely internal cult of the supreme God."[34] Civil religion, or the "religion of the citizen," on the other hand, is an intimate part of the state and thus makes religious and political values compatible.[35] Where Christianity teaches otherworldliness and humility, civil religion glorifies the state and teaches those political virtues that contribute to its survival.

If we now take these various institutions as a whole and recall

Rousseau's basic principles of smallness and equality, it becomes apparent that the whole social infrastructure of his ideal polity is such as to direct the citizen's attention almost totally toward the state. Love of country is the inevitable result, and this is precisely what Rousseau intended, for the prime political virtue, indeed the absolutely necessary virtue, he argues, is patriotism. For patriotism, says Rousseau, combines "the force of egoism with all the beauty of virtue!"[36]

We come full circle back to Rousseau's starting point. Recall his basic principle of political organization: Justice and utility, moral rightness and self-interest, must be united. Rousseau has already shown that in making each citizen a part of the sovereign body it does become the self-interest of each to be concerned with the public interest of all. But patriotism absolutely ensures this unity, says Rousseau, because it is the very embodiment of justice (virtue) and utility (egoism). Patriots are those who cannot distinguish between their own interests and those of their country. Patriotism thus unites self-love with love of others. As such, it evokes people's natural goodness and makes them concerned above all else with the public good. For this reason, patriotism is the very foundation of the general will.

It is at this juncture that we must analyze the structural and organizational principles of the two most crucial political institutions in Rousseau's ideal state: the sovereign and the government. The sovereign, of course, is the more important of the two. We shall, therefore, discuss it first. But it must be kept in mind that what makes the sovereign work, what makes it give expression to the general will, is the patriotism of the citizenry. And patriotism, in turn, is the result of those organizational principles and political structures we have just discussed.

Rousseau's sovereign, of course, is the legislative assembly of all citizens constituted to give expression to the general will. To this end, there are certain obvious rules that apply. The citizens must meet in legislative assembly periodically, and they must be able to assemble during crises or emergencies. Rousseau does not provide us with any precise schedule, but he does state a general rule: The more powerful the government the more frequently the general will must meet. The logic behind this rule will become evident shortly. For now, it is sufficient to note that government has a tendency to usurp the prerogatives of the lawmaking body. As the power of government increases the danger of usurpation also increases, thus necessitating more frequent meetings of the assembly to guard against the increased danger.

Now the task of the legislative assembly is not burdensome, nor is it complicated, says Rousseau, because a small egalitarian state "requires but very few laws."[37] If this were not the case, as it usually is not in large and complex industrial states, the general will could not be expressed since the legislative task would be beyond the average person. In fact, Rousseau argues, the sole object of the legislative assembly "is the maintenance of the social treaty" [that is, the social contract].[38] Consequently, it is primarily laws of constitutional stature, what Rousseau terms *political* or *fundamental laws*, that concern the assembly. As for subordinate civil or criminal laws of a more complex and detailed nature, government may promulgate the requisite rules. Rousseau is insistent, however, that only those decisions made by the legislative assembly are, properly speaking, laws, since they alone embody the moral sense or general will of the whole community.

There are, however, two decisions that Rousseau argues the legislature must always make at the beginning of its deliberations. The first deals with the fundamental constitutional issue of whether or not the existing form of government should continue. The second deals with the less fundamental, but still crucially important issue of whether or not the existing administration should remain. The latter, of course, is routinely dealt with in all liberal-democratic states in election years. This, however, is the only issue generally dealt with by the people as a whole since real decision making rests with the elected deputies once the election is over. It is for this reason, says Rousseau, that the people of England are free "only during the election of members of parliament: For as soon as a new one is elected, they are again in chains and are nothing."[39]

Now, despite the fact that the general will is absolute, "it neither will, nor can, exceed the bounds of general conventions,"[40] says Rousseau. That is, while the general will is sovereign, the legislative assembly cannot pass laws that contravene the generally accepted values held by the society, the most important of which, he concedes, is the right of property. Indeed it is precisely because Rousseau considers property to be the most sacred of conventions that he does not advocate its total elimination in the name of equality. And while it may seem a contradiction that the sovereign is absolute yet limited by the conventions of society, Rousseau in fact is stating a truism. Since the general will is the moral will of the whole community, it can neither legislate that which is contrary to its will, nor could it possibly enforce such laws even if it did pass them.

But if it is an obvious fact that the general will is constrained by general conventions, it is a fact premised upon the structure of Rousseau's sovereign. Where the sovereign power resides in Hobbes's man or assembly of men, or in Locke's chamber of deputies, there the very real danger does exist that the sovereign power will exceed the bounds of general conventions. For, if Rousseau's analysis is correct, wherever ultimate power resides in a minority of the community, there the possibility always exists that the minority will act independently of the wishes of the community as a whole.

How, then, is the sovereign assembly to actually make laws that express the general will? Quite simply, says Rousseau, by voting until a simple majority is reached.[41] Like Locke, Rousseau insists that only the social contract that creates political society need be decided by unanimous consent; all subsequent decisions require only a majority.

The objection will almost surely be raised here that a majority is not the whole community. Yet, there is no inconsistency in Rousseau's argument. To begin with, Rousseau roots his majority in the whole community rather than in a minority of legislators as does Locke. Hence, Rousseau's majority is much more likely to reflect the real interests of the community. But, more important, Rousseau nowhere suggests that the majority is identical to the general will. It is perfectly possible, although if the state is appropriately structured Rousseau believes improbable, that the majority will merely reflect the self-interest or individual wills of the larger number of citizens. Yet this is equally true of the "will of all," says Rousseau. A unanimous decision may reflect nothing more than the self-interest or private will of each voting citizen. For this reason, he argues, there is often a great difference between the will of all and the general will.

> The latter regards only the common interest; the former regards private interest, and is indeed but a sum of private wills: But remove from these same wills the pluses and minuses that cancel each other, and then the general will remains as the sum of the differences.[42]

In other words, the general will cannot be determined simply by counting votes. Even if the votes are unanimous, this does not in and of itself guarantee a moral decision, that is, a decision in the public interest as opposed to one reflecting a collection of individual self-interests. The entire assembly, for example, may refuse to increase taxes it knows to be in the public interest simply because each member's selfish interest in paying lower taxes predominates. Thus, the general will is expressed only when the votes, whatever their number, reflect the general or public interest of the whole community, a condition that Rousseau describes rather mechanically when he speaks of subtracting from each other the pluses and minuses of self-interest.

All that can be said about the number of votes, and this is all Rousseau does say, is that the larger the majority the greater the probability that it is an expression of the general will. And the only general rule of number that Rousseau provides is that the more important the issue at stake the larger the majority should be, and the more immediately serious the issue—a crisis situation for example—the smaller it need be.

The point is that majority rule is perfectly legitimate for Rousseau so long as it is understood that a majority decision is not necessarily a moral decision. Rousseau is thus a good corrective to the popular notion that a majority decision is necessarily a "correct one." Where the state has only negative functions, and liberty is simply the absence of restraints, it cannot be expected that majority decisions will be more than the sum of self-interests, Rousseau would argue. Within the liberal-democratic framework proposed by Locke, he insists, a majority will rarely assert the public interest because it is largely incapable of expressing the general will. This, and not majority rule as such, is the problem.

Such, then, are the basic organizational principles of Rousseau's sovereign assembly. But the issue of government still remains: What is the appropriate relationship of the government to the sovereign, and what is the best form of government in maintaining this relationship? Put simply, what form of government is most compatible with the maintenance of the general will? There are two points that must be made before we get to these specific issues.

First, Rousseau makes a great point of distinguishing government and sovereignty, a distinction that he believes some thinkers (Hobbes rather obviously) have confounded. For Rousseau, *government* refers to the executive power in the state, not the legislative or lawmaking power that belongs to the sovereign assembly alone. And, technically speaking, government does in fact refer to the executive. We have a tendency in this country to subsume under government the executive, legislative, and judicial functions. But in European parliamentary systems the term *government* is reserved for the executive power.

Second, Rousseau insists that the existence of government in no way violates the basic principle of sovereignty that the general will is inalienable because, as he argues, "the power may well be transmitted but not the will."[43] In other words, the essence of the general will is precisely its will or moral capacity. This it cannot alienate without ceasing to be a general will. In political terms, the legislative function of the whole community cannot be transmitted to any other body such as Locke's assembly of representatives. But power or the ability to enforce the laws can and must be transmitted, says Rousseau, since it would be undesirable, not to mention impossible in most cases, for the people as a whole to enforce the laws. The exercise of power, in other words, properly belongs to government.

This is not to suggest that government does not pose a potential threat to the sovereignty of the general will. Quite the contrary—this is precisely the danger according to Rousseau: "Just as the private will continually acts against the general will, so the government makes an unremitted effort against the Sovereign"[44] until the social contract is broken. And he continues, "this innate and inevitable vice tends, from the birth of the body politic, to destroy it, as old age and death do in the human frame."[45]

In other words, while government is necessary, it inevitably subverts the general will. This is so because the government is itself a particular will, what Rousseau calls a *group will,* that stands as a constant threat to the general will. But unlike the private will of the individual, or the corporate will of an interest group, the group will of government has real power behind it. Hence, of all the particular wills in the community, government is the most dangerous because it is most capable of asserting its prerogatives against the public interest.

Surely Rousseau presents us with a troublesome paradox. Government is necessary, yet it is the prime cause of social disintegration. But this is the same paradox that Plato raises in *The Republic:* The ideal state must inevitably decline because the principle of decay is built into all human affairs. And, like Plato, Rousseau argues that the best that can be done is to forestall the inevitable for as long as possible. This is to be done, he says, by fixing "the exact point where the force and the will of government . . . can be combined in the manner most advantageous to the state."[46] That is, the point must be found where the power of government and its own group will are so balanced that government will act as an agent of the general will rather than as its master.

The founder of a state, says Rousseau, must strike this appropriate balance.[47] And the general rule is this: The larger the number of magistrates or officials in government, the weaker its group will and the less able it is to abuse its power. Conversely, the smaller the number of officials the stronger its group will and the more powerful it will be. Thus, the most powerful government is monarchy because the group will is identical to the private will of the monarch. The weakest is direct democracy because the group will is confounded with the general will of the whole community.

A moment's thought will reveal the logic behind Rousseau's reasoning. As the size of government increases "the more . . . force [it must] employ on its own members, [and] the less there . . . remain[s] to expend on the whole people."[48] Simply stated, the larger the government the more difficult it is to get internal agreement upon policy or to execute decisions once they have been made, hence the more energy that must be expended to accomplish these objectives and the less available to expend on the citizenry. The smaller the government, the easier these tasks become. Clearly where one person rules there can be neither dissension over policy nor over execution so long as the monarch is secure upon the throne. The monarch is thus free to employ all his power upon the citizenry.

What, then, is the best form of government? Although Rousseau does have a clear preference, the answer in the final analysis depends upon how strong the government needs to be under existing circumstances. Rousseau's basic rule of thumb is that the larger the state the stronger government must be, the smaller the state the less so. Hence, larger states require smaller governments since small governments are most powerful; smaller states are more compatible with larger governments.

Once again, the logic behind Rousseau's analysis is obvious. As the state increases in size so too does inequality, complexity, and the emergence of special interests, all those social ills that subvert the general will. And, as Rousseau has already demonstrated, where the general will is weak or nonexistent, force or power becomes the basis of political control. Hence, large states require powerful governments. They are thus most compatible with monarchy, which, for reasons we have just discussed, is the form of government most likely to subvert the general will. This, among other reasons, is why Rousseau dislikes large states and monarchical governments.

On the other side, an extremely small state does not require a powerful government because it is easy to govern and less likely to develop those diverse private interests that threaten the general will. Hence, an extremely small state is most compatible with direct democracy, a very weak form of government precisely because it is so large. Yet, says Rousseau, democracy is not the ideal form of government either. In the first place, it confounds the legislative and executive powers since the citizen is both legislator and executor of the laws. This poses a threat both to the purity of the general will and to the appropriate functioning of government. Second, it is not, he insists, in the natural order of things "that the greater number should govern, and the smaller number be governed."[49] And it is rare to find a state small enough and a people sufficiently simple to make democracy a very practical possibility in any case, he argues.

Rousseau's ideal is elective aristocracy, a form of government most compatible with middle-sized states. Here is a government neither too large to be effective nor too small to be overly powerful. Moreover, it is comprised of the best elements in society leading the rest. Hereditary aristocracy, on the other hand, Rousseau dislikes as much as monarchy since the heredity principle makes popular control of government more difficult. And while he does not explicitly say so, it is clear that he also dislikes it because it does not ensure rule by the excellent.[50]

Most students are perplexed to discover that the "father" of the French Revolution is a defender of aristocracy. But it must be remembered that it is an aristocratic government that Rousseau prefers, not an aristocratic state. The sovereign general will belongs to the whole people and it is expressed within the legislative assembly by a democratic vote. Thus, Rousseau's ideal state remains thoroughly democratic despite its aristocratic form of government.

A final type of government Rousseau discusses is the Aristotelian mixed form. And while in theory Rousseau prefers a simple rather than a mixed government "because it is simple,"[51] in truth he admits that all governments are in some sense mixed. Moreover, he argues, there are times when a proper balance between the various constitutional elements of the state requires consciously mixing different forms of government to produce a desirable result.

Indeed, Rousseau agrees with Montesquieu, an important eighteenth-century political thinker, that "liberty not being a fruit that every climate will produce, it is not within the abilities of all peoples."[52] A country's geography, natural resources, historical circumstances, and other such factors determine to a great extent what form of government is possible, and it is the task of the wise political leader to produce the best government possible under existing circumstances. As a general and by now obvious rule, however, Rousseau notes that "monarchy . . . is suited to none but opulent nations; aristocracy to those states which are moderately rich and extensive; and democracy to such states as are both small and poor."[53]

We can now see that much in Rousseau's analysis of government is reminiscent of Aristotle. Like Aristotle, Rousseau's ideal is aristocracy and, again like Aristotle, Rousseau recognizes that creating the best possible state depends upon a host of circumstances that the wise statesman must take into account. For both thinkers, the object is to approach the ideal within the framework of what is possible. *The Social Contract* essentially establishes Rousseau's ideal. (In this sense it is similar to Plato's *Republic*.) Rousseau's other political works deal with the best possible state that can be established under existing circumstances. In *The Government of Poland*, for example, Rousseau suggests employing the federal principle to create a condition of smallness and simplicity within a larger nation-state that otherwise would be much too extensive to allow for the expression of the general will.

Such, then, is the political philosophy of Jean Jacques Rousseau. But there is more to this philosophy than is immediately apparent. As we have seen, Rousseau wanted a theory that would expose the fallacies of Enlightenment civilization and the inadequacy of modern political values. As such, he was not simply interested in constructing a logically coherent political theory; he wanted to construct a theory that, when taken as a whole, would stand in direct opposition to the political ideals of the modern world, ideals that he believed actually destroy human freedom. This is precisely what Rousseau's political philosophy accomplishes, for it is a thoroughgoing reaffirmation of classical ideals.

We have seen this in Rousseau's distinction between the best and the best possible states. He is following the classical mode of political analysis, which distinguishes between the ideal and the real. We have seen this same connection to classical thought in the other striking similarities between Rousseau and the classical thinkers. But it is Rousseau's concept of the general will that most clearly and directly connects his philosophy to the classical tradition, for the general will affirms on a new basis the classical ideal of the small state or polis engaged in moral education and the Aristotelian concept of citizenship as direct involvement in political affairs.

More than this, the general will is a reaffirmation of the classical belief in the unity of ethics and politics. Without this assumed unity, Rousseau's distinction between the best and best possible state would make no sense, nor would any of his other political ideals. And, most important, without it Rousseau would have been unable to affirm what he believed to be the prime political virtue of classical political thought, namely, its emphasis upon authority; or to demonstrate the corresponding defect of modern political analysis, its focus upon power.

Rousseau understood very well the philosophical genesis of the modern emphasis upon power. The naturalistic view of the universe had in Hobbes, and even in Locke, led to a strictly mechanistic and utilitarian vision of humankind that replaced the classical language of ethical virtue with the language of pleasure and pain. The general consequence of this was that political scientists came to assume that power alone is sufficient to control human beings. This is seen most clearly in Hobbes, of course, but this emphasis upon power begins as far back as Machiavelli and has continued as a general trend down to our own day. Even Locke and the later liberals took power to be the essence of politics and were concerned, not with eliminating it, but only with controlling its effects.

But Rousseau also understood what few of his contemporaries could: It was precisely the exercise of power and all that goes with it that transforms people into practicing utilitarians. It is not because human beings are pleasure-pain machines that power becomes necessary. It is power that transforms what are otherwise compassionate creatures into self-interested pleasure seekers. Modern political theorists had mistaken the effect for the cause.

Viewed from this perspective, Rousseau's emphasis upon authority involves much more than that strictly political critique of power relationships that we have discussed in previous chapters. It is not merely the fact that power is an insufficient basis to hold the state together that troubles Rousseau; Machiavelli admitted this much, and even showed the advantage of authority, or at least the appearance of authority. Rousseau is also concerned with the effect power relationships have upon individual human beings. Clearly, where individuals are coerced to obey the law in a situation where there exists no general will or conception of the public good, they lose their moral autonomy. Once this happens, they cease to act as free agents and become calculating and self-interested individuals lacking any genuine concern for their fellow creatures. Vanity and egotism become rampant as people attempt to gratify their desires at the expense of others. Psychologically, human beings become increasingly alienated from their own "natural goodness." They lose their inner freedom to be as they truly are as surely as they lose their political freedom to determine their collective destiny.

Authority, then, is not only more politically effective than power for Rousseau, it is the necessary precondition for human integrity and happiness. This is what the classical thinkers understood, and this is why Rousseau returns to classical ideals. Yet, paradoxically, the genuine importance of Rousseau as a political thinker lay precisely in the fact of his modernity. His ideal polity may have had a classical form, but his underlying theoretical assumptions were thoroughly modern. It is for this reason that Rousseau could not be easily dismissed by his contemporaries. He used their own underlying assumptions to challenge their explicit political beliefs.

For example, Rousseau adopts the modern position that the state is contractual or conventional in origin. This sharply distinguishes him from the classical thinkers who believed the state to be natural. But Rousseau also distinguishes himself from the classical thinkers when he speaks of the moral basis of the state, for the general will is a product of the contract. Hence, the general will itself is purely conventional; it is an expression of subjective, even arbitrary, values held by a particular community of human beings. It is not an expression of objective universal standards such as form or natural law.

We have already noted that the natural law tradition was in a state of disintegration from the seventeenth century on. This disintegration reflected a deeper set of epistemological changes in which modern thinkers began to reject the notion of the existence of any kind of universal ethical standard. Rousseau clearly reflects these changes, so much so that he goes further than many of his contemporaries in his rejection of the natural law tradition.[54] All moral values, at least those expressed in the political domain, are conventional for Rousseau; they are human-made values that reflect attitudes and opinions of a particular culture.

For the same reason, Rousseau rejects the concept of natural right. He does not accept the Lockean notion that rights are rooted in a universal standard that applies to all peoples at all times. As with any other set of ethical values, rights are conventional expressions of a particular culture. Rousseau denies, for example, that property is a natural right. It is, he argues, a strictly conventional right granted by society. And while he considers the right of property to be the most sacred of conventions because it is recognized as such in most societies, it nevertheless remains a convention. It remains a right granted by society and not, as Locke would have it, a right that all societies must recognize as a matter of course. And it certainly is not true that people have a natural right to the unlimited accumulation of property. As we have seen, Rousseau expects the community to set definite limitations upon the amount of property any citizen may possess.

In sum, Rousseau believes the laws and rights that pertain in any given society are socially determined. In this he agrees with the basic insights of modern social science, which argue that ethical values are not a reflection of the word of God or of other such standards external to society. But unlike modern social science, and in contradistinction to the Hobbesian-behavioralist school of political thought, Rousseau does not employ these insights to deny the reality or validity of ethical values. Rather, he attempts to reaffirm them on a new basis. Hence, the unity of ethics and politics that characterizes Rousseau's political thought is classical in form but modern in substance. His concept of the general will, in other words, is a thoroughly modern idea in the guise of a classical ideal.

Here we may begin our critical analysis of Rousseau's political theory, for while the concept of the general will is Rousseau's rightful claim to fame, it is also the source of the most important theoretical criticisms that have been leveled against his political thought. There is, however, a frequently made criticism of a more practical nature with which we should first dispense, namely, that Rousseau's ideal polity would not work given the size and complexity of the modern nation-state. Some scholars have gone so far as to argue that Rousseau's political theory is irrelevant because his ideal state is a throwback to the Greek polis, a form of polity that simply does not fit modern political conditions.

This criticism largely misses the point. As we have seen, Rousseau follows the classical distinction between the ideal political order and the real, and the purpose of the ideal is to establish a standard by which to judge existing states. The point, then, is not the practicality of Rousseau's ideal, although, as he himself suggests, even in practical terms it might be possible to modify the modern state in the direction of his ideal. The point is that Rousseau's ideal polity may well have been intended to demonstrate the inadequacies of the nation-state,[55] and, whether intended or not, *The Social Contract* makes quite clear what those inadequacies are. In its largeness and impersonality the nation-state fails to develop the conditions for the existence of the general will. As a consequence, authority is replaced by power and human beings are thereby debased. Read in this way, Rousseau's critique of the nation-state is the political side of his intellectual assault upon Enlightenment civilization and modern values.

What we can say with some assurance about the practical applications of Rousseau's ideals is that given the nation-state as it now exists, they would likely prove disastrous. In a large modern state with its bureaucratic impersonality on the one hand and its lack of any deep sense of community on the other, any attempt to evoke more than a very limited expression of the general will would likely have totalitarian implications. It is one thing to attempt moral unanimity to the point of "forcing men to be free" in a small state with an intense sense of community. It is quite another in a large state that encompasses many diverse interests. In such a situation unanimity is well-nigh impossible, and any attempt to create it will necessarily involve forms of almost total political control over a recalcitrant citizenry. For this reason, most of us find Locke preferable to Rousseau. On the other hand, those Lockeans who insist that Rousseau's political ideal is totalitarian forget that he had in mind a radically different form of polity than the nation-state.

Beyond these considerations, criticisms of the practical viability of Rousseau's political schemes do not take us very far. The more important criticisms are those that challenge the validity of the general will at a theoretical level. And perhaps the most fundamental theoretical criticism we might make is that the general will is too ambiguous as an ethical ideal. This is because it is an ideal that lacks any real substance or content. We know that the general will is derived by a majority vote of the sovereign community. We do not know, however, whether a vote really gives expression to it. Even complete unanimity is no guarantee that the general will has been found. Thus, the moral underpinnings of Rousseau's ideal state are not very clearly defined.

There are two fairly evident reasons for this. The general will is, as we have seen, an expression of a particular community at a particular point in time. The general will, in other words, is socially relative. As such, it cannot be given a definite content. (Paradoxically, Rousseau's attempt to affirm the importance of ethical standards upon a modern basis leads, as it does in most modern thought, to ethical relativism.) And second, the general will is ultimately a subjective standard. It is incapable, therefore, of being fully expressed in logically coherent terms. Remember that the general will is rooted in what Rousseau believes to be our natural capacity for compassion. It is thus based, in the final analysis, upon feeling rather than reason. And feeling, however real or intense it may be, is a purely subjective experience.

Yet, we should temper this criticism by crediting Rousseau with having recognized that the ethical underpinnings of the state cannot be based upon reason alone. Quite apart from the validity of such strictly rational systems as natural law, they reflect only one aspect of people's ethical capacity. We feel as well as reason, and our moral sense surely includes both. We do not, for example, refrain from hurting others on rational terms alone, but because we feel for our fellow creatures. This really is what Rousseau wished to emphasize when he claimed that we all have the natural virtue of pity or compassion. And his claim was based upon what he rightly perceived to be a disregard for the emotional dimension of human experience by modern science and Enlightenment philosophies. The complaint one hears today about the impersonality and coldness of modern technological society echoes a concern first expressed by Rousseau.

On the other hand, Rousseau perhaps is too pessimistic about the power of reason to establish the ethical basis of the state and too optimistic about feeling and emotion. Feeling, as we have noted, can produce only a subjective, hence ambiguous, ethical standard. The great advantage of such rational standards as form or natural law, conversely, is that they are explicit, logical, and therefore unambiguous. As such, rational standards are capable of producing a knowable body of rules that apply universally. It was this optimism in the power of reason alone to shape the human community for beneficial ends that lay behind the emergence of Western political thought. With Rousseau this optimism is shattered.

It must be kept in mind, of course, that theories of form or natural law may be philosophically invalid. Rousseau thought so, as do most modern social scientists. Hobbes may be quite correct when he says there is no knowable *summum bonum,* or "greatest good." But, in and of itself, feeling does not adequately replace rational ethical systems, and Rousseau does not seem fully sensitive to this fact. Moreover, the emphasis upon feeling and subjective experience carries with it the danger of encouraging irrationalism. As a matter of fact, this is precisely what occurred in certain strains of nineteenth-century romantic thought that were heavily influenced by Rousseau. Those same strains of thought contributed to the development of various fanatical ideologies later in the century.

When all is said and done, however, Rousseau has the mark of a truly great political thinker: Our criticisms take us to the very heart of his political theory and raise the perennial political issues. It does not really matter whether or not we agree fully with Rousseau. What matters is that his political analysis raises all the important political issues and makes us think about them from fresh perspectives.

Most important, Rousseau alerts us to the contradictions inherent in Western political thought, contradictions that he alone had the insight to recognize were reflected in his own personality and the personalities of all European peoples. Ethics versus politics, sovereignty versus freedom, the individual versus the state, and classical ideals versus modern ideas, all are encompassed in Rousseau's political thought. And while we may or may not agree that he overcomes these contradictions, we cannot deny that in his attempt to do so Rousseau raises the key issues in the long tradition of Western political thought and makes us think about them anew.

MODERN POLITICAL THEORY: THE REJECTION OF THE CLASSICAL TRADITION

In our concluding remarks in Part I, we noted that the unity of ethics and politics was the defining characteristic of classical and medieval political thought. We also noted that modern political thought is characterized by a breakdown of that unity, and for reasons that should now be clear. Beginning with Machiavelli there emerge new metaphysical and epistemological assumptions that call into question the reality of ethical absolutes, and new visions of the human condition that raise serious doubts about the moral and social basis of human behavior.

In political theory, the obvious consequence of this separation of ethics and politics has been an emphasis upon power as the organizational basis of the state. But, as we have seen, the concern with power is based upon a more fundamental political fact: the emergence of the modern nation-state. The nation-state is premised upon the consolidation and centralization of power, more so than would have been even imaginable in the medieval world, and political theory inevitably gave paramount importance to this fact. The modern concept of sovereignty, to take the most obvious example, would have been inconceivable without the reality of the nation-state.

The role of the nation-state in the formation of modern political thought points out, once again, that directly or indirectly political theories are reflections of a given form of polity. Classical political thought took for granted the unity of ethics and politics precisely because the small and socially unified *polis* was by its very nature a moral community. Thus, the political condition of the city-state inevitably led theorists to think in terms of community and moral responsibility. An Aristotle could claim that the essence of politics is friendship because his polity gave credence to his claim. Hobbes's insistence that the essence of politics is power reflected an entirely different set of political circumstances. He was not speaking against the background of a small unitary community but against that of a large and impersonal political structure that, precisely because of its largeness and impersonality, was incapable of acting as a moral community. He was dealing with a condition in which the unity of ethics and politics in the classical sense had, in political fact, disintegrated.

Initially, modern political theorists perceived no problem inherent in the rejection of the classical tradition. To their minds the modern state need not be based upon ethical absolutes because nationalism, self-interest, or the effective implementation of power were believed to be sufficient to maintain social and political unity. They believed, in other words, that they had found social and political surrogates for ethical absolutes. But with Rousseau this belief is challenged, for he not only reaffirms the ethical basis of political order, he shows that in ignoring the ethical dimension the modern state may actually damage the human personality.

Rousseau's challenge essentially lays the foundation of contemporary political thought. On the one hand, his criticism foreshadows the contemporary concern with the centralization of power and bureaucratic impersonality that typifies the modern state. On the other hand, Rousseau's critique has led to an equal concern with the psychological consequences of the new political order. In this century in particular, increasing numbers of political thinkers speak of modern people as creatures lost and unhappy within the very civilized order they have created. They pursue a line of reasoning first articulated by Rousseau.

But this pessimistic side of contemporary political thought carried with it, at least until this century, a fundamentally optimistic point of view. If Rousseau had shown that modern society was debasing humankind, he also demonstrated the innate goodness of the human personality. For subsequent radical thinkers this was a uniquely important insight, for it meant that with the revolutionary overthrow of those conditions that suppress humanity's natural goodness the good society would emerge almost automatically.

In point of fact, the nineteenth century was an age of rampant optimism, despite the warnings of some of the more sober thinkers. It was not just radical thinkers in the tradition of Rousseau who felt that the good society was at hand; almost all thinkers saw the future in terms of unlimited human possibilities. Following the French Revolution, doctrines of unlimited progress and the perfectibility of the species abounded, for the majority of thinkers shared with Rousseau a fundamental belief in the ability of human beings to better themselves by altering their society, however much they may have disagreed with him in other matters. These new doctrines came to be called *ideologies*. In Part III we will be examining in detail three of the most intellectually important of them: liberalism, conservatism, and Marxian socialism. And we will conclude with an analysis of modern nationalism, for nationalism has ceased to be merely that ardent form of patriotism preached by a Machiavelli or a Rousseau. Nationalism has itself become an ideology, indeed the most influential ideology of our time, so influential that the other major ideologies must now be understood within the context of national ideals.

Notes

1. Jean Jacques Rousseau, *The Social Contract*, rev. by Charles Frankel (New York: Hafner Press, 1947), p. 5.
2. See Ernst Cassirer, *The Question of Jean Jacques Rousseau,* in Peter Gay, ed./trans. (Bloomington: Indiana University Press, 1963), p. 39: "The man and the work are so closely interwoven that every attempt to disentangle them must do violence to both."
3. Jean Jacques Rousseau, "The Second Discourse," in Roger D. Masters and trans. Roger D. Masters, and Judith R. Masters, eds., *The First and Second Discourses* (New York: St. Martin's Press, 1964), p. 110.
4. Jean Jacques Rousseau, *The Confessions,* J.M. Cohen, trans. (Baltimore: Penguin Books, 1954), p. 17.
5. Jean Jacques Rousseau, "The First Discourse," in Masters et al., eds., *First and Second Discourses,* p. 36.
6. See Joan McDonald, *Rousseau and the French Revolution: 1762–1791* (London: The Athlone Press, 1965), pp. 11–21, for a good, if brief, survey of the variety of interpretations of Rousseau's political thought.
7. Rousseau does concede that the family constitutes a precontract form of simple society. Indeed, he argues that the family is the only natural society that exists; all others being contractual or conventional. But he hastens to add that "the children remain attached to the father no longer than they have need for his protection. As soon as that need ceases, the bond of nature is dissolved. The child, exempt from the obedience he owed the father, and the father, from the duties he owed the child, return equally to independence." (Rousseau, *The Social Contract,* p. 6.)
8. Rousseau, "The Second Discourse," p. 130.
9. Ibid.
10. Ibid., p. 102.
11. Rousseau, *The Social Contract,* p. 14.
12. Jean Jacques Rousseau, "Essay on the Origin of Languages Which Treats of Melody and Musical Imitation," in John H. Moran and Alexander Gode, trans. *On the Origin of Language* (New York: Frederick Ungar, 1966), p. 40.
13. Rousseau, *The Social Contract,* p. 18.
14. Ibid., p. 19.
15. Ibid., pp. 14–15.

16. See Charles Frankel's Introduction to *The Social Contract*, p. xxii.

17. Rousseau, *The Social Contract*, p. 15.

18. Ibid., p. 52.

19. Indeed, Rousseau is even more emphatic than Locke that government is not contractual in origin. "There is," says Rousseau, "but one contract in the state, I mean that of association [that is, that which creates political society]: all others are excluded by it." (ibid., p. 88.)

20. Ibid., p. 18.

21. Ibid.

22. Ibid., p. 15.

23. Ibid., p. 5.

24. The fundamental characteristics of Rousseau's sovereign general will may be summed up as follows: it is inalienable, indivisible, absolute, and general [moral]. (Ibid., pp. 23–30.)

25. Ibid., p. 26.

26. T.H. Green, a nineteenth-century political thinker we will discuss in Part III, was the first to employ the term *positive liberty*. The term has now gained general currency and is clearly applicable to Rousseau's conception of liberty.

27. Rousseau, *The Social Contract*, p. 52.

28. Ibid., p. 92.

29. Ibid.

30. Ibid., p. 46.

31. Ibid., pp. 46–47.

32. Jean Jacques Rousseau, "Discourse on Political Economy," in Roger D. Masters, ed., and Judith R. Masters, trans., *On the Social Contract with Geneva Manuscript and Political Economy* (New York: St. Martin's Press, 1978), p. 221.

33. Rousseau, *The Social Contract*, p. 114.

34. Ibid., p. 118.

35. A third form of religion, what Rousseau terms the religion of the priest (and he has in mind Roman Catholicism in particular), he absolutely rejects because it divides people's political loyalties between the church and the state.

36. Rousseau, "Discourse on Political Economy," p. 218.

37. Rousseau, *The Social Contract*, p. 92.

38. Ibid.

39. Ibid., p. 85.

40. Ibid., p. 30.

41. The election of members of government, which is a key function of the

sovereign assembly, is to be by choice, says Rousseau, not lot. Election by lot was a common practice in ancient Greek democracies.

42. Rousseau, *The Social Contract,* p. 26.

43. Ibid., p. 23.

44. Ibid., p. 76.

45. Ibid.

46. Ibid., p. 57.

47. Rousseau uses the term *legislator* rather than *founder.* We employ the latter term, however, in order to avoid confusing the legislator with the sovereign legislative assembly.

48. Rousseau, *The Social Contract,* p. 55.

49. Ibid., p. 59.

50. Rousseau posits natural aristocracy as a final type, but he argues that it is suitable only for very simple peoples.

51. Rousseau, *The Social Contract,* p. 69.

52. Ibid.

53. Ibid., p. 70.

54. Rousseau does sometimes refer to natural law. See, for example, Jean Jacques Rousseau, *The Government of Poland,* trans. Willmoore Kendall (New York: Bobbs Merrill, 1972, p. 29), but it is clear that he is simply connecting to a tradition of thought familiar to his contemporaries. In his insistence that the general will and moral values are conventional, Rousseau unequivocally rejects natural law as a valid form of moral reason.

55. Whether or not Rousseau intended his political theory to be a critique of the nation-state is a matter of scholarly dispute. One point of view, represented by Willmoore Kendall, is that Rousseau did indeed intend an attack upon the nation-state but feared the ridicule that would follow if he were too explicit about it. (See Rousseau, *The Government of Poland,* pp. ix–xxxix.) For contrary points of view see Robert Nisbet, *The Quest for Community* (New York: Oxford University Press, 1969), pp. 140–52, and Alfred Cobban, *Rousseau and the Modern State* (London: George Allen & Unwin, Ltd., 1964), pp. 165–66. Whatever his intent, his political theory in fact constitutes a fundamental critique of the nation-state.

Part III

Contemporary Political Theory

The philosophers have only interpreted the world in various ways; the point, however, is to change it.

—Karl Marx, *Theses on Feuerbach*

11

Conservatism

We have seen that modern political thought traces its origins back to Machiavelli and the Renaissance. But modern political ideas remained essentially ideas in most of Europe until the fateful year of 1789. Then, in the great French Revolution, the old order or ancien regime was finally swept away, not only in France, but in much of Western Europe. Ideas that had been expounded only by small groups of Enlightenment intellectuals were finally put into practice.

The French Revolution, like its earlier American counterpart, was carried out under the banner of liberal ideas. The notion that human beings are inherently equal, that they possess certain natural rights that no government may legitimately violate, and that "democracy" is the only valid form of government were the ideas upon which the French Revolution was based. But unlike the American revolt, the French Revolution led to some very illiberal consequences, a fact that lies behind the development of the counter-liberal philosophy of conservatism.

To understand that philosophy we need briefly to reconstruct the events of the French Revolution. In 1789, the king of France was compelled to convene a session of the French legislature—the States General—which had not met since 1614. Its failure to meet was a clear reflection of the triumph of absolute monarchy in France and, indeed, it would not have been called into session at all had France not been on the verge of bankruptcy.

The States General was comprised of three different legally recognized classes called estates: the nobility, the clergy, and the people at large represented by the bourgeoisie or middle class. Each estate formed one chamber of the States General, but not all chambers were equal in representation or power. The nobility and clergy were dominant and, not without reason, they supported the existing order of things. The nobility enjoyed a host of privileges not granted to the rest of society, and the Catholic Church was the officially recognized state religion. Only the third estate, the new emerging commercial class, was fundamentally dissatisfied with the status quo.

What had begun merely as an attempt to secure new revenues rapidly turned into a revolutionary upheaval of the whole society. Through adroit political maneuvering, the third estate increased its representation and unified all three chambers into a new legislative body called the National Assembly. Under the control of the third estate, the new National Assembly passed into law the *Declaration of the Rights of Man and of the Citizen,* which "sounded the death-knell of the Old Regime"[1] and, in theory at least, replaced it with a society based upon liberal values. Equality before the law, equality of taxation, and an equal right to obtain political office were assured, as were the liberal ideals of the right to property, freedom of expression, and so on.

In order to implement these new liberal reforms, the third estate attempted to restructure the whole social and political order of France. The aristocracy was eliminated as a privileged and legally recognized class. The power of the Church was broken, and its vast property holdings were confiscated. The whole political structure, from local to national government, was fundamentally altered. Most important, the power of the monarch was severely circumscribed, and that of the legislative body was vastly increased.

So radical were these measures of the newly constituted National Assembly, and so contrary to the traditions and interests of the ancien regime, that the revolutionary third estate became increasingly isolated from major segments of French society. Moreover, other European powers, frightened by the specter of the Revolution and the possibility that it might spread to their countries, united militarily against France. Faced with increasing domestic and international hostility, the more militant members of the third estate, the Jacobins, formed an oligarchical faction to rule the country. Under their rule the monarch was beheaded, as were a number of other "enemies of the revolution," and what has come to be known as the "Reign of Terror" engulfed France. Although the tyranny of the Jacobins was eventually eliminated and their leader, Robespierre, guillotined, the Revolution failed to return to its original ideals. Unable to settle upon a final and workable constitutional arrangement or to resolve its political problems, France ultimately fell under the dictatorship of Napoleon Bonaparte.

Napoleon came to power initially as the savior of the Revolution, but he quickly became an absolute dictator and, eventually, emperor. Under Napoleon, French armies swept abroad, destroying once and for all the ancien regime of old Europe and, despite the dictatorial means employed, introducing liberal reforms in the newly conquered territories. Without Napoleon, ironically, liberal-democratic Europe as we understand it would not exist.

Nevertheless, old Europe did not willingly accede to the new order of things. With Napoleon's defeat in 1815, a period of reaction set in. The nations that had defeated Napoleon formed the "Holy Alliance," a concert of European powers dedicated to monarchical rule and the illiberal ideals of the old order. But the Holy Alliance was unable in the long run to stop the tide of liberal democracy. What the French Revolution and Napoleon had accomplished could not be undone.

It is at this point that the key thinker of this chapter emerges as an important political philosopher, for the political reaction of the Holy Alliance was mirrored by a theoretical reaction against the French Revolution and the tenets of liberalism. This reaction came to be called *conservatism,* and its first and most important exponent was a British parliamentarian of Irish extraction named Edmund Burke (1729–1797). In a classic of polemical political theory entitled *Reflections on the Revolution in France,* published in 1790 while enthusiasm for the Revolution was still high, Burke utterly rejected the Revolution and its ideals. The *Reflections* became the bible of the Holy Alliance and of all those who rejected the liberal philosophy. It remains the bible of conservatism to this day.

Yet, Burke had no intention of creating a political doctrine. He was by inclination and occupation a practicing politician, not a political philosopher. It was the events of the French Revolution that compelled him to write the *Reflections.* Indeed, all of his conservative writings were produced in response to particular events or issues. For this reason, the student of Burke must search through his parliamentary speeches, letters, and occasional pieces in order to reconstruct the basic outlines of his conservative philosophy.

We may begin our analysis of that philosophy by noting that it is the very opposite of what the popular idea of conservatism would lead one to believe. To begin with, Burke spent his parliamentary career defending what he thought to be the genuine principles of the Whig faction in Parliament. Paradoxically, the Whigs had been established to uphold the principles of the Glorious Revolution of 1688, which embodied many of the "liberal principles" espoused by John Locke.

Moreover, Burke was known as a great reformer. Perhaps his most notable effort in this regard was his attempt to reform British rule in India. It must be kept in mind that Great Britain was at this time a major imperial power and did not always treat its colonies benevolently. In India, British rule was particularly harsh, and no more so than under the governorship of a man named Warren Hastings. Because of Hastings's violation of what Burke took to be elementary human rights, he attempted to have the man impeached. What particularly infuriated Burke was Hastings's assertion that the Indians were slaves, subhumans, and that he could therefore do as he pleased with them. In his impeachment speech to Parliament, Burke asserted against

Hastings a principle that any Lockean or modern-day liberal would commend. Says Burke, "the laws of morality are the same everywhere . . . and there is no action . . . of oppression in England that is not an act . . . of oppression in Europe, Asia, Africa, and all over the world."[2]

This same attitude about the universality of moral law led Burke to defend the Irish Catholics from what he believed to be unjust British laws directed against them. And, again like Locke, he defended the right of nonestablishment Protestant dissenters to exercise their beliefs as they saw fit. Indeed, Burke went even further than Locke, for he stated that he "would give full civil protection . . . , and a power of teaching in schools, as well as Temples, to Jews, Mahometans and even Pagans."[3]

But Burke is best known for his defense of the American Colonies. Taking an apparently "Lockean position" (actually a pragmatic position), he "agreed" with the colonists that Parliament had no right to tax them without their consent. And when America declared its independence, he counseled his countrymen against engaging in a war against the Colonies. He was convinced that such a war could lead only to the suppression of liberty in America with the inevitable devaluing of liberty at home.[4] For this reason, Burke supported American independence and advocated peace with the revolutionary Colonies.

The inevitable question is How could a Whig, a reformer, and a friend of the American cause possibly be the father of modern conservatism? But in fact the question is misplaced, for it is based upon the popular view of conservatism rather than upon what we will call the philosophical conservatism of Edmund Burke. The popular view equates conservatism with antiliberal and antireform values. But Burkean or philosophical conservatism is neither antireformist nor is it even illiberal. Burke's argument with the liberal cause lay not so much with its explicit ideals, many of which he accepted and even cherished, as with the way in which those ideals were philosophically derived and, most importantly, politically applied.

The best way to grasp Burke's philosophical disagreement with liberalism is to deal with it in the context of his attack upon the French Revolution, for what Burke understood better than any of his contemporaries was that the liberalism of the French Revolution was radically different from the liberalism of the American Revolution or that of the Glorious Revolution of 1688. Whereas most viewed 1789 as simply the logical sequel to 1776 and 1688, Burke saw an unbridgeable chasm. For unlike their predecessors, Burke argued, the French revolutionaries were attempting to impose strictly rational a priori standards of natural right without any consideration for the real nature of society and the real needs of human beings. The consequences of this folly, Burke predicted, would be to produce a very illiberal society if, indeed, society managed to survive at all.

We shall return to Burke's dire predictions at a later point. We want first to understand his argument against the doctrine of natural rights as interpreted by the French revolutionaries. In essence it is quite simple. Rights, Burke argues, are inherently social rather than individual because human beings are by nature social creatures. They are not, as the Enlightenment contract theorists would have it, individualists who leave the "state of nature" and enter society simply for purposes of securing their "natural rights." Indeed, says Burke, it is a myth to suppose that human beings could even exist as mere individuals outside of society, and a danger to rational political thought to base a doctrine of rights upon such a supposition.[5] In point of fact, he insists, "the state of civil society . . . is a state of nature."[6] Society is people's natural state, and any doctrine of rights, says Burke, must be premised upon this fact.

What then makes any right legitimate for Burke (and indeed any political institution) is that it is recognized as such by the society at large. Such socially recognized rights and institutions Burke calls *prescriptive* because they are given or prescribed by society. And, of course, what makes any right or institution prescriptive is tradition. If a society has, over historical time, evolved rights and political practices that are recognized as legitimate, then they are usually so, Burke argues, no matter how much they may seem to contradict the logic of natural rights. For given people's innate sociability, no right or practice can be recognized as legitimate unless socially condoned. Thus, speaking of his own political system, Burke states that "Our Constitution is a prescriptive constitution; it is a constitution whose sole authority is that it has existed time out of mind."[7]

Now this is not to suggest that Burke is unwilling to concede that there exist, in the abstract, certain universal rights. Recall that his indictment of Warren Hastings appealed to just such rights. It is simply that Burke recognized that rights do not exist a priori or abstractly, but concretely in society.[8] As such, Burke argues, so-called natural rights, as they actually exist in society, "undergo such a variety of refractions and reflections, that it becomes absurd to talk of them as if they continued in the simplicity of their original direction."[9]

That all people, for example, have a natural right to life is philosophically true, Burke would concede, as he would agree in the abstract that all have a natural right to property. But he would also insist that to assert these truths is to state the obvious on the one hand and to wholly miss the point on the other. The point is not whether people have a right to life and property, but how these "rights" actually exist in society. In fact they have undergone all kinds of social "refractions and reflections." They have been utterly modified by society and no longer exist in their theoretically pure form. No one, for example, has an absolute right to property under every condition, nor for that matter even to life. It is therefore absurd, says Burke, to speak of any right, even the most basic, as an abstract natural right that belongs to every individual in its pure "state of nature" form.

But to Burke's mind it is more than just absurd; it is downright politically dangerous, for in proportion as "natural rights" are "metaphysically true," he insists, "they are morally and politically false."[10] The more precisely a right can be stated in absolute philosophic form, the more politically and morally destructive it will be when put into political practice. Why? Because the more abstractly true a right is, the more it can be stated in "the simplicity of its original direction," the further removed it is from how it actually exists prescriptively. Hence, any attempt to apply an abstract right to society can only destroy that right as it actually exists, and the more abstractly true the asserted right the more destructive it must be.

We might, for example, conclude with the French revolutionaries that all human beings ought to enjoy the same rights because they are all created equal. But precisely to the extent that our philosophy of equality is true, Burke would argue, our theory of rights must be politically false. For while it is true in the broadest philosophical sense that human beings are created equal, it does not follow in political terms that they should enjoy equal rights. The rights people enjoy in society, their real existing prescriptive rights, are not equal, never have been, and never will be. If, then, one attempts to impose an equality of rights by political means, the existing rights, which are not distributed equally, will be destroyed. And since rights can exist only prescriptively, the result must be the loss of all rights and indeed the destruction of all the social orders and institutions that give those rights reality.

As we shall see, Burke saw with almost uncanny foresight that the French Revolution would produce just these consequences. For this reason, his *Reflections on the Revolution in France* is an extended polemic against what Burke believed to be the absurd and dangerous attempt on the part of the French revolutionaries to apply in practice the doctrine of natural rights. In the name of that doctrine the revolutionaries were destroying the prescriptive rights of the aristocracy, the clergy, and as a consequence, he argues, the rights of the people as a whole.

Burke had made the important discovery that the principles of natural right, when carried in their pure form into political practice, contradict the principles of prescriptive right. But inherent in his discovery was an insight of even deeper significance, an insight that has its origins in Aristotle and that now constitutes the very core of serious conservatism. Burke understood that the political domain is destroyed whenever it is made to conform to purely abstract philosophical principles. Pure reason and absolute rationality have no place in politics, Burke argues, for society simply does not conform to philosophical abstractions, and it cannot ever do so without destroying itself.

There are two other crucially important reasons why Burke rejects the application of pure philosophy to the political realm. In the first place, he argues, prescription "is accompanied with another ground of authority in the constitution of the human mind, presumption. It is a presumption in favor of any settled scheme of government against any untried project, that a nation has long existed and flourished under it."[11] Support for traditional institutions and values, in other words, is inherent in human nature. It is part of the very structure of the human mind. It thus follows that any attempt to apply the doctrine of natural rights or any other abstract philosophical system is manifestly contrary to the facts of human nature and, as such, unworkable.

In the second place, says Burke, to respect the prescriptive structure of society is to exercise the highest form of political rationality, a political rationality higher than that of any individual no matter how philosophically profound he or she may be. Burke calls this higher rationality *prejudice,* and he explains its meaning in the following famous quotation from the *Reflections:*

> Instead of casting away all our old prejudices, we cherish them . . . ; we cherish them because they are prejudices; and the longer they have lasted, and the more generally they have prevailed, the more we cherish them. We are afraid to put men to live and trade each on his own private stock of reason; because we suspect that this stock in each man is small, and that the individuals would do better to avail themselves of the general bank and capital of nations, and of ages. Many of our men of speculation, instead of exploding general prejudices, employ their sagacity to discover the latent wisdom which prevails in them. If they find what they seek, and they seldom fail, they think it more wise to continue the prejudice, with the reason involved, than to cast away the coat of prejudice, and to leave nothing but the naked reason.[12]

Inherent in this concept of prejudice is a philosophy of political reason, reminiscent of Aristotle and Cicero, that states that social and political knowledge is essentially historical rather than individual; that it is the result of the ideas and practices of many generations. It is a philosophy, in short, that conceives history to be rational. It is therefore to history, and not pure philosophy, that we must turn if we want to know what is really politically appropriate, whether we are speaking of rights, forms of government, or any other political matter.

Contrast this with the Enlightenment philosophies that had seen political reason as entirely an affair of the individual mind and had counterposed it to the irrationality of the historical evolution of institutions. The theory of contract, for example, was frequently employed to demonstrate the irrationality of existing political institutions by arguing that rational beings would never have consented or contracted for them. The contract theory was essentially ahistorical; it denied the past and took into consideration only what was rationally agreeable to the individual in the present.

In rejecting this liberal individualistic view of political reason, it is important to keep in mind that Burke is in no sense defending irrationality. This is crucial, for the popular view is that conservatism is an unthinking defense of tradition simply because it is tradition. The opposite is the case. Conservatism is a defense of tradition because it is presumed to be historically rational, more rational than any political scheme proposed by an individual thinker.

Burke's critique of liberalism to this point has involved concepts that revolve around his key underlying assumption that human beings are inherently social creatures and that their rights, political institutions, and indeed their very mode of thinking are determined by the society in which they live. At bottom, this view presumes the classical or organic conception of society—that society itself is not unlike a living organism to which human beings are intimately connected. It conceives of society as a mutually interdependent set of institutions and traditions that encompass the individual and that are connected to each other in much the same way as are the various organs of a living body. And just as any alteration in one organ of the body must cause changes in all the rest, by analogy the same results occur when alterations are made in the social body. Changes in one part of society alter the whole, and in ways that seldom can be anticipated, Burke argues.

It was this that the liberals failed most to comprehend, Burke believed. Their inability to understand the importance of presumption, prescription, and prejudice was due to their inability to grasp the real organic nature of society, for these terms are but different expressions of this same basic social fact. In the liberal's mind, society was nothing more than a collection of property- and power-seeking individuals, hence nothing more than the mechanical sum of its various individual parts. (For this reason, early liberal thinkers have rightly been called *social atomists*.) Indeed their theory of contract, from which the doctrine of natural rights was derived, took for granted that the individual is prior to and higher than society. It is no wonder, Burke argues, that they could not perceive the pernicious effects of their political philosophy. In eliminating the unequal prescriptive rights of the aristocracy, for example, they thought that they were simply affecting a definite and limited number of individuals. They could not see, given their atomistic vision of society, that the aristocracy was a social institution intertwined with all those other institutions and traditions of French society that are the sole basis for the existence of rights (prescription), the legitimacy of government (presumption), and the rational ordering of society (prejudice). They could not comprehend, therefore, that their philosophy of abstract equal rights, once applied in practice, must inevitably destroy the whole social order.

How then does Burke propose that the revolutionary leadership of France ought to conduct itself? This is, in fact, the real issue for Burke, not the philosophical inadequacies of liberal thought as such. Burke's answer constitutes the last key element of modern conservative thought and may be briefly summarized as follows: For reasons that should now be clear, political leaders cannot approach their task as academic philosophers. Pure philosophy and metaphysics do not belong in the domain of political decision making. Rather, Burke argues, the leaders must derive their political principles from society itself, which means that they must rely upon history and prejudice as the source of their political knowledge. This, the true art of statesmanship, Burke calls *prudence*. The following quotation illustrates his meaning:

> Pure metaphysical abstraction does not belong . . . [in political] . . . matters. The lines of morality are not like the ideal lines of mathematics. They are broad and deep as well as long. They admit of exceptions; they demand modifications. These exceptions and modifications are not made by the process of logic, but by the rules of prudence. Prudence is not only the first in rank of the virtues political and moral, but she is the director, the regulator, the standard of them all. Metaphysics cannot live without definition; but Prudence is cautious how she defines.[13]

Here we confront an issue that we have thus far held in abeyance. The statesman's art lies in the exercise of *prudence,* that is, in the reliance upon the "reason of prejudice" in the process of lawmaking. But prejudice is not always reasonable. In this country, for example, *prejudice* has led to the *presumption* that certain *prescriptive* rights enjoyed by whites, and denied to African Americans, ought to be maintained. Few people today would want to defend such a point of view. Certainly Burke would not. He had shown in his defense of the American cause that it is not possible to deny basic human rights to one group without threatening the rights of all. For this reason alone, he would never suggest that prudence is always and in every case a slavish respect for prejudice. What he does argue is that it is the task of statesmanship to maintain prejudice where it is rational, and to alter it where, as in the case of racial prejudice, it is clearly irrational. In Burke's words, "a true politician always considers how he shall make the most of the existing materials of his country. A disposition to preserve, and an ability to improve, taken together, would be my standard of a statesman."[14]

The real question for the conservative statesman, then, is not, How shall I maintain the status quo under all circumstances? but, given the existing materials of my country, When and how shall I improve? To begin with, says Burke, improvement should be made only when there is a specific and concrete grievance, and the grievance must be such that resolving it will make for a greater good (or a lesser evil) than ignoring it. As to how the statesman should improve, the answer is more problematical, but Burke does provide a basic rule of thumb by way of a distinction between change and reform. Change, he argues,

> alters the substance of the objects themselves, and gets rid of all their essential good as well as of all the accidental evil annexed to them. Change is novelty. . . . Reform is not change in the substance or in the primary modification of the object, but a direct application of a remedy to the grievance complained of.[15]

Although his language is opaque, Burke is actually stating a very simple idea. Change is that which attempts to eliminate grievances by altering the whole structure of society. As such, it actually causes more harm than good because most of the institutions of society are more rational than the scheme of any individual politician. Reform, on the other hand, attempts to eliminate grievances without altering the basic structure of society. In this way the good is maintained while the evil is eliminated. Clearly, Burke's conservative statesman is to improve existing conditions through reform and not, as did the French revolutionaries, through wholesale change.

Burke provides no absolute, clear-cut rules of reform. As should by now be apparent, he is opposed to any absolute rules in politics. It was the assertion of just such absolute rules on the part of the French revolutionaries that Burke objected to. Nevertheless, there are certain guidelines that may be gleaned from his writings that may be said to constitute the basic legislative philosophy of conservatism.

First, says Burke, "to follow, not to force, the public inclination—to give a direction . . . to the general sense of the community, is the true end of legislature."[16] In other words, make laws that reflect changes in society, rather than change society by making laws. This is the true art of reform, for it corresponds perfectly to the rule of prudence. The legislator should follow "the general sense of the community" rather than "force the public inclination" because the community embodies a higher kind of wisdom than does the individual.

Second, Burke argues, reforms should be early and temperate, because

> it is the interest of government that reformation should be early, it is the interest of the people that it should be temperate. It is their interest, because a temperate reform is permanent, and because it has a principle of growth. Whenever we improve, it is right to leave room for further improvement. It is right to consider, to look about us, to examine the effect of what we have done.[17]

Clearly reforms must come early, otherwise grievances will intensify until wholesale change, even revolution, becomes inevitable. Burke wishes to avoid this at all costs, for reasons that should now be clear. But reforms must be temperate as well because temperate reforms alone are permanent. This is so because they have a "principle of growth"; they leave room for improvement. They allow the legislator to examine their effects, to modify where necessary, and to make improvements over time. Radical change, on the other hand, has none of these characteristics. For this reason, Burke insists radical change is rarely permanent. No sooner is it made than it is undone as people come to realize its defects.

Finally, in making reforms the statesman must represent the whole nation and not just the constituency that elected him. This is so, says Burke, precisely because society is an organic whole, and not simply a collection of individuals as the liberals would have it. Politicians who neglect the whole for their own particular constituency, like doctors who treat only a part of the body with no concern for its impact on the whole organism, will produce a deformity. Conversely, voters who elect representatives simply because they cater to their own narrow interests fail to understand what their real political duty is. They ought to be electing people who have the skill, the courage, and the integrity to look to a larger public good.

There is a deeper issue involved here, for if it is possible for the representative to represent the whole nation, there is no inherent reason why voting districts should be equal or, for that matter, why everyone should have the right to vote. People, in Burke's words, are *virtually* represented in any case. It was this logic that led him to resist an attempt to reform representation in Parliament, which, at the time, was unrepresentative of the voting population.

To the American mind, influenced as it has been by the liberal doctrine, the Burkean theory of *virtual representation* (the term has now passed into general usage) is a heretical idea. How, the American will ask, can one be represented without the vote, or without a vote equal to everyone else's? The answer is that one cannot given the liberal assumption that society is simply a collection of self-interested individuals. Clearly, in this view, only by giving each person an equal vote can the interests of each be protected. But Burke does not share the liberal perspective. To his mind society is an organic whole and, as such, can be and should be represented as a whole.

Such then, is the political philosophy of Edmund Burke, a philosophy that has remained the touchstone for all subsequent conservative thought. It is a philosophy that was consciously developed in opposition to revolutionary liberalism. And it has remained the major alternative, not only to liberalism, but to all political theories that call for the revolutionary transformation of society in the name of abstract principles.

Yet we confront here an apparent contradiction that has been with us from the opening pages of this chapter. Burke is a Whig who attacks the very "liberal" principles that the Whigs, following Locke, had defended: natural rights, individualism, and the contractual theory of the state. The contradiction, however, did not exist for Burke, because in his mind Locke was associated with the Glorious Revolution of 1688, a revolution that he understood as a reaffirmation of traditional British values.[18] Thus, for Burke and most other Whig politicians, Locke's doctrine of natural rights (and indeed the whole of his political theory) was not seen as a rejection of the idea of prescription. Locke had shown, for example, that property is the source of rights, and the Whigs took this to mean, as did Locke himself, that the propertied classes have a "natural right" to rule. But this natural right corresponded precisely to their prescriptive right, that is, to a right that had always been extended time out of mind to the propertied classes.

Moreover, Burke was not so much opposed to Locke's political theory as to the extremes to which the French revolutionaries took it. Part of their problem, Burke was convinced, was that they had read, or rather misread, Rousseau. They had come to believe Rousseau's claim that "man is born free, yet everywhere in chains" and had proceeded in the name of natural rights to remove them.[19] They failed to recognize that those "chains" are the bonds of society, and that what was needed was reform, not the radical destruction of the whole basis of social authority.

At the deepest level, this was Burke's most fundamental criticism of the French revolutionaries and the key reason for his distinction between the revolution of 1789 and those of 1688 and 1776. In their eagerness to change the whole social structure of the ancien regime, the French revolutionaries were destroying the sole basis of authority, namely, the prescriptive and traditional structures that had existed time out of mind. And the consequences of this, Burke insists, must be the increasing use of force or raw power in French society and, along with it, the end to liberal ideals of justice and equality for all.

Burke, as it turned out, was correct. He was more than correct; he was prophetic, for he saw in almost intimate detail the form this new power would take. It will be a military dictatorship, said Burke, under the leadership of one all-powerful leader who shall "draw the eyes of all men upon himself . . . [and become] . . . your master; the master of your king, the master of your assembly, the master of your whole republic."[20] The man Burke describes is none other than Napoleon.

Burke's apparently uncanny foresight was, in fact, based upon hardheaded political analysis. He recognized that the destruction of prescriptive rights and institutions would inevitably cause people to turn to an all-powerful leader. Without any traditional or presumptive basis of authority, people would have no other option. Moreover, Burke understood that these institutions—classes, groups, religious orders, and so on—check the central power because each of them possesses its own authority. Each resists encroachments upon its prescriptive rights, something no lone individual is capable of doing. As such, says Burke, each "composes a strong barrier against the excesses of despotism."[21] Thus, with the inevitable breakdown of social distinctions that must follow the destruction of prescriptive institutions, the centralization of power must become equally inevitable, Burke insists.

Burke also recognized that the various associations that make up society not only resist encroachments upon their prerogatives, but they act as well as a buffer between the central power and individual citizens. When, therefore, these associations are eliminated, individuals stand utterly alone. They become a multitude of faceless entities, in Burke's terms a "homogeneous mass." In such a mass society individuals are not only powerless, they lose along with their group identification the ability even to imagine other alternatives to existing reality. Given such a society of isolated, lonely, and demoralized human beings, the central power finds nothing in the way of implementing the most extreme despotism.

Unwittingly, of course, the creation of mass society is precisely what the revolutionaries aimed at since their doctrine of natural rights was inherently opposed to social distinctions. Burke recognized, however, as did Karl Marx later in the nineteenth century, that the revolutionaries' doctrine of the "rights of man" was not at all opposed to the advancement of bourgeois property rights and bourgeois values. But what the revolutionaries did not comprehend, says Burke, is that the possibility of tyranny is vastly increased with the elimination of social distinctions. They wrongly presumed that their assault upon prescriptive rights and institutions was the necessary condition for the elimination of tyranny rather than the essential condition for its existence.

Burke's analysis of the destruction of authority following the French Revolution was profoundly important in the development of later political thought, both conservative and liberal. For Burke was not only the first to note the emergence of mass society, he was the first to see the link between it and the centralization of power. This latter point was particularly important to nineteenth-century liberals, for they came to see the danger inherent in their individualistic philosophy. The more they emphasized individual rights the more they cut the individual loose from the constraints of other social groups. Thus, their emphasis on rights encouraged the development of mass society and the specter of a centralized tyranny that could only make a mockery of those rights. Nineteenth-century liberals found themselves caught in a paradox that Burke was the first to grasp and to which, as we shall see, they devoted much theoretical work attempting to resolve.

For now it is sufficient to grasp Burke's distinction between the French Revolution and the earlier English and American revolts. The French Revolution aimed at the elimination of prescriptive rights rather than their reform, the destruction of the psychological and sociological basis of authority, and thus the erection of an all-powerful military tyranny. It was this that led Burke to distinguish sharply the French Revolution from those of 1688 and 1776 despite certain common liberal ideals. Many of his fellow Whigs, seeing only the common ideals, failed to grasp these very real differences. It was not until much later, when the Revolution had worked itself out to its tyrannical conclusion, that the importance of Burke's position became clear. Until then, many idealists saw Burke as a traitor to the Whig position and to the liberal cause.

In the final analysis, of course, Burke's political theory really was not compatible with that of Locke and the Whig faction. Under a different set of circumstances, he would himself have recognized that his objection to the revolutionaries did not lie simply in their taking the theory of natural right to socially destructive extremes. His objection would have been that their whole form of political reasoning is false. And indeed, this fundamental difference between liberalism and conservatism was eventually recognized by Burke's followers. His political philosophy ultimately became the heritage of the Tory or conservative movement in England rather than of the Whig or liberal party. But it bears repeating that while this philosophy is antiliberal it is not in content illiberal.

Clearly, it is Cicero and, most notably Aristotle, not Locke that Burke most closely resembles as a political thinker. Like Aristotle, he wishes to derive political philosophy from the existing feelings and opinions of the citizenry, not from philosophical abstractions. Again like Aristotle, Burke conceives of humankind as innately social and of the social order as an organic structure of traditions and institutions. Moreover, he thinks of state and society in the same teleological terms as did Aristotle. In Burke's words, the state is a "moral essence"; it is a repository of values and institutions that have evolved over generations and that represent historically given rational-ethical ideals.[22] It is for this reason that Burke praises prejudice, much as Aristotle and Cicero praised the "experience of the ages." And Burke's ideal of the statesman as one who employs prudence, who draws upon the "sense of the community" and "works with existing materials" in the act of legislating, conforms precisely to Aristotle's and Cicero's idea of the political actor.[23]

How, in conclusion, shall we judge the political philosophy of conservatism? As a theoretical response to liberalism its importance is clear. To this day, Burkean conservatism constitutes one of the most important criticisms of liberal ideas. But even more important, it constitutes a critique of all modern revolutionary ideologies. We can see in retrospect that his critique of liberalism is a critique of ideological thinking as such, for Burke grasped that liberalism, or at least revolutionary liberalism, involved more than just a set of political ideals. He understood that it involved an entirely novel, and he believed an extremely dangerous, form of political thought and action that we now recognize as characteristically ideological.

To appreciate this broader critique of ideology, we need to define and explain its meaning. The term is derived from the works of a group of French thinkers of the revolutionary period who wished to employ the insights of Enlightenment science to develop an understanding of social and political affairs. They were called ideologues and their new "science" was termed ideology. Through a series of historical events, which included the conservative reaction against Enlightenment philosophy, the term took on a quite different meaning.

This meaning Burke first articulated in his criticism of revolutionary liberalism, a meaning we now recognize as common to various systems of modern thought that in every other substantive way are quite distinct. Unfortunately, ideology is one of those words used in the social sciences that seems to be almost inherently plastic. The term continued to undergo a series of definitional transformations, one of the most important of which we shall examine in the chapter on Marx. Nevertheless, there are two basic characteristics of all ideologies that Burke first noted in his critique of the liberal doctrine and that have been generally accepted as the key elements of ideological systems of thought.

First, Burke grasped in that critique the "worldview" character of ideological thinking. A worldview is an all-encompassing intellectual system based upon social and political principles that are believed to be universally valid. Liberalism, as Burke noted, possessed just these characteristics. The "rights of man" constituted for liberal thinkers universally valid principles upon which they erected an all-embracing theoretical system. Having determined that all men possess certain inalienable rights, liberal thinkers deduced a philosophy that attempted to account for the totality of social and political phenomena. In a different way, as we now recognize, Marxism asserts these same universalistic principles and attempts to evolve an all-embracing theoretical system from them, as does fascism and nationalism in yet other ways.

Burke saw very clearly the flaws inherent in this mode of political thinking. In place of a realistic assessment of what is politically possible, ideologies are invariably utopian and fanatical, invariably because the complexity of human societies is forgotten whenever we apply without careful reservations universal abstractions to real human beings. Only carelessly applied abstraction could produce the unrealistic notion that all would be well once governments were compelled to respect natural rights. And only such a notion could produce a fanatical belief in the utter rightness of the liberal doctrine and the assumption that those who opposed it were evil.

The assertion of abstract-universal principles does not in and of itself, of course, constitute a basis for utopianism or fanaticism, nor does the comprehensiveness of political vision. In its own way, classical and medieval thought possessed a universal and comprehensive perspective, yet was neither fanatical nor utopian (at least not utopian in the modern sense). Indeed, not even all ideologies initially possessed these undesirable characteristics. Liberalism, for example, is in many ways a sophisticated theory of politics. As we have seen, it remains one of the best analyses of power and of how to constitutionally channel it that is available to us. And Marxism in its original formulation is anything but utopian or fanatical. It is, in fact, a profoundly sophisticated social science.

The problem is that whatever original sophistication these systems of thought may have initially possessed, they all eventually took on these undesirable ideological characteristics because—and this brings us to the second key element of modern ideologies—they all became the theoretical basis of mass revolutionary movements. They became radical impetuses to mass action (as Burke clearly recognized in the case of liberalism) and not simply theories about the nature of politics. And whenever political ideas become the source of revolutionary mass action they are inevitably reduced to utopian political slogans that encourage fanaticism rather than sober thought.

Radical ideas premised upon abstract principles cannot be made popular without appealing to people's unsophisticated and often emotional view of the world.

Herein lies the essence—and danger—of ideological thinking for Burke: the combining of philosophical abstraction with revolutionary passion. Such a combination, he recognized, transforms otherwise harmless and often useful abstractions into those utopian and fanatical political principles that are characteristic of modern ideologies. Moreover, he grasped the underlying sociological basis of this phenomenon. Almost every modern government, says Burke, has become "in its spirit almost democratic."[24] This Burke attributes to the emergence of the modern press, which is able to disseminate political ideas to large masses of people. He recognizes, quite correctly, that modern means of communication have "democratized" ideas without which ideologies would have remained the province of a small group of intellectuals. Modern communications, Burke argues, have for the first time in history made it possible for the intellectuals to communicate their political ideals to the masses of people.

Had ideologies remained simply the ideals of an intellectual class, Burke would not have been so violently opposed to them. They would, after all, have remained no more than ideas. But once "democratized," once put in the hands of the mass of the people, Burke believed that civilization itself is threatened, for his experience with revolutionary liberalism had demonstrated that ideologies are used to overturn the very basis of society, not simply to alter the existing political structure. As Burke notes about the French Revolution, "it is not a revolution in government. It is not the victory of party over party. It is a destruction and decomposition of the whole society."[25]

Burke's statement contains a crucially important insight into the nature of modern revolutions based, as they are, upon ideological worldviews. They are essentially social in nature, not primarily or only political. What the revolutionary liberals wanted was not simply the elimination of monarchy, a particular form of government, but the complete reorganization of social classes, the church, the economic system, and so on. The Marxist movement, which was to emerge in the nineteenth century, aimed at no less.

Today we take for granted the social character of modern revolutionary movements, but Burke was the first to see their true nature and to grasp the intimate connection between social revolution and the popularization of ideological worldviews. It is because of this connection that we speak of the period from the French Revolution to the present time as both the "age of ideology" and the "age of revolution." Burke possessed the insight to see the seeds of this new age in the ideas and actions of the French Revolution. It is not without reason, then, that his opposition to the Revolution was so militant. He believed he was not simply fighting a localized problem but a set of ideas that had the capacity to overturn the basic values of Western civilization itself. Says Burke, "we are at war with a principle, and an example, which there is no shutting out by Fortresses, or excluding by Territorial Limits."[26]

The war has continued down to the present day. Indeed, we no longer even think of war as limited engagements for the purpose of conquering territory, anymore than we think of revolutions as limited political engagements. We have come to view wars as essentially ideological. They are ostensibly fought to preserve the world for democracy, communism, fascism, or nationalism. The whole globe has become a political battleground in which wars are fought in the name of abstractions and which aim at no less than the total transformation of the human condition. Burke saw all this at a time when most of his peers viewed the French Revolution as nothing more than the logical culmination of the events of 1688 and 1776.

At the same time, Burke must be criticized, for there was much he did not see. He vastly underrated the abuses of the ancien regime in France. As the famous liberal polemicist Thomas Paine said about the *Reflections,* Burke "pities the plumage, but forgets the dying bird."[27] He appreciates the aristocratic glitter of the old order, but fails to see the underlying social disintegration. As a consequence, he is unable to grasp that mere reform would have been insufficient, that revolution would have come sooner or later in any case.

Moreover, although Burke understood that ideologies depend for their existence on modern mass communications, he did not fully grasp the implications of his insight. Modern mass communications are simply one part of that whole process of massive social change engendered by the industrial revolution. For this reason, it is generally recognized that modern ideologies are the intellectual reflections of industrial society. This Burke did not fully grasp. Indeed, he was a supporter of the economic ideas of emerging capitalism, ideas that were not only a crucial component of industrial progress but that did much to shatter the belief in those traditional values that Burke wished to maintain.[28] In fairness, he probably could not have foreseen the full implications of the emerging industrial society. But in failing to foresee this larger dimension of social change, Burke attributed much too much importance to ideas and political events as the basic cause of revolutionary change and upheaval, and much too little to the underlying sociological and economic factors involved.

Apart from Burke's inability to see the full dimensions of the coming age, there are several other criticisms we might make of conservatism as a political philosophy. We might ask, for example, whether or not conservatism really fits the conditions of the modern nation-state. It would seem not.[29] Conservatism is akin to Aristotelian or Ciceronian ideals, ideals that can be realized only where the polity is sufficiently small for a genuine sense of community to exist. Clearly the nation-state does not, and probably cannot, fit these conditions, as Rousseau had indicated. And in Burke's day the problem was compounded by the fact that England held an empire so vast that little if any community of interest was possible. This is why, despite his attempt to reform relations with the colonies, Burke could muster little support for his proposals.

Another criticism has to do with Burke's concept of statesmanship. He provides precious few ground rules for the statesman to follow, other than that it is necessary to employ prudence in the act of legislating. Indeed, Burke has a very incomplete political philosophy. He has no explicit metaphysical and epistemological system, no abstract theory of the state, no distinction between ideal and real states, and no theory of forms of government. Of course, given his belief that philosophical abstraction has no place either in politics or in political philosophy, this is precisely as he intended. The problem, nevertheless, is that the conservative statesman can find in Burke few hard rules to rely upon when having to make decisions. "To reform or not to reform" is his dilemma, and with so little to go on besides an intuitive sense of prudence, he is likely to take the latter course when the former is required.

A final difficulty inherent in conservatism is what we might call the "historical problem." The conservative derives his political values from history, from traditional values. The problem is that once these values must be made explicit, once people must be told to respect their traditions, it is in most cases already too late. The power of prejudice, after all, lies precisely in its inarticulateness, its unthinkingness. That power is lost when it becomes necessary to "intellectualize" it, for this is a sure indication that prejudice is no longer viable. The moment conservatives feel it necessary to defend historically given values, history has in most cases already passed them by.

Yet, it must be admitted that there is at the same time an advantage inherent in the historical problem. In defending values that are in a state of decline, conservatism acts as a powerful indictment of existing ones. Even though conservative values may no longer conform to present reality, those values alert us to what we have lost and what we will lose if we continue our present course. As such, the conservative philosophy stands as a constant and necessary reminder that there exists much potential evil even in our most idealistic political schemes.

Before we conclude our discussion of Edmund Burke, a summary of what became of Burke's political theory is in order. It is important to realize that Burke took what had always been an intellectual tendency and turned it into a concrete set of political ideas. He founded a distinct school of political thought that we now call conservatism, and as with any school of thought it grew in directions its founder could hardly have anticipated.

Burke's philosophy, for example, had a great impact upon the Romantic movement of the early nineteenth century. Like Burke, the Romantics stressed the feeling and emotional side of the personality as opposed to the often narrow emphasis upon rationality we find in Enlightenment philosophies. Also like Burke, the Romantics emphasized the importance of community and of traditional values, but they went well beyond Burke in this regard. Many of them romanticized the·medieval past and counterposed it to the evils of modern society since the French Revolution.[30]

In political theory, Burke's influence was more direct, but often contrary to what he would have wished. His most famous disciple, for example, a French political thinker named Joseph de Maistre (1793–1821), took Burke's political philosophy to reactionary conclusions. Unlike the conservative, the reactionary is one who wants to return to the past rather than use the past as a set of guidelines to enable the statesman to make decisions in the present. Burke, you will recall, was a proponent of reform and would have utterly rejected de Maistre's idea that the past could be recreated.

Most unlike Burke, de Maistre was an extremist. He detested the French Revolution and the Enlightenment philosophy upon which it was based. He wanted a return to absolute monarchy, the preservation of the aristocracy, and the utter subordination of the individual to the state. The great respect for constitutionally limited powers that marks Burke's thought, the "Lockean" or "Whig" element, is utterly alien to de Maistre.

A contemporary of de Maistre, Louis de Bonald, shared his peer's extremism and made many of the same kinds of political arguments. Others followed suit, although reactionary political thought never gathered large numbers of converts. It remained, nevertheless, a distinct tendency throughout the nineteenth century despite its obvious flaws. While we today find it hard to imagine someone actually making these kinds of arguments, it must be remembered that the specter of the French Revolution loomed large in the minds of those with conservative tendencies, much as the Russian Revolution did in the minds of conservatives during much of this century. Given this, it is not difficult to see how conservatism could be transformed into a reactionary doctrine and its proponents into fanatical "utopians" of the past.

If we take these various developments of Burke's thought as a whole, a crucial and paradoxical fact emerges. Conservatism began to take on all the characteristics of an ideology. For the Romantics, conservatism became a backward-looking utopianism. For de Maistre and other political thinkers of that tradition, conservatism was transformed into a reactionary and often fanatical worldview. Others took Burke's emphasis upon the traditions of a people to nationalistic conclusions. And some extremists even claimed to have discovered behind the idea of the nation and its traditions and institutions a more basic biological reality of race or blood. This group (which influenced later fascist thought) concluded that the existence of supposedly "national-cultural superiorities" must be the result of some form of "racial superiority."

These modes of reasoning were, of course, utterly alien to Burke. He was neither romantic nor reactionary, and he would have found the concept of racial superiority repugnant. Even the idea of cultural superiority he would have rejected. His conservatism, on the contrary, was based precisely upon an appreciation of the value and uniqueness of all cultures. It was this appreciation that led him to indict British rule in India and to defend the legitimacy of the American colonists' complaints against the British Crown.

The paradox in all of this is that Burkean conservatism aimed at eliminating ideological thinking in political affairs, not in creating new ideological systems. That Burke's ideas were twisted by some for ideological reasons is not his fault. He was simply the first victim of a very modern phenomenon: The founders of the modern systems of political thought have almost invariably been misinterpreted by their followers.

Notes

1. George Rude, *Revolutionary Europe 1783–1815* (New York: Harper & Row, 1964), p. 108. This book provides a good general overview of the period of the French Revolution up to Napoleon's defeat.

2. Edmund Burke, "Speech on Impeachment of Warren Hastings," in *The Works of The Right Honorable Edmund Burke*, 12 vols. (Boston: Little, Brown, 1866), IX:448.

3. Edmund Burke, "Letter to William Burgh, February 9, 1775," in Thomas W. Copeland, ed., *The Correspondence of Edmund Burke*, 10 vols. (Chicago: University of Chicago Press, 1958), III, *July 1774–June 1778*, ed. George H. Guttridge: 112.

4. See Frank O'Gorman, *Edmund Burke: His Political Philosophy* (Bloomington: Indiana University Press, 1973), for a thorough discussion of Burke's position on the American cause, and British imperial relations generally.

5. Actually, Burke never explicitly repudiated the concept of a state of nature, but simply refused to take it seriously as a description of the human condition or as a valid mode of political analysis.

6. Burke, "Appeal from the New to the Old Whigs," in *Works*, IV:175.

7. Burke, "Speech on Reform of Representation of the Commons in Parliament," in *Works*, VII:94.

8. See Francis P. Canavan, S.J., *The Political Reason of Edmund Burke* (Durham: Duke University Press, 1960), p. 114. Burke "in fact . . . never denied the state of nature or original rights, and was content to say that they were irrelevant to a discussion of the rights of man in civil society."

9. Edmund Burke, "Reflections on the Revolution in France," in Edmund Burke and Thomas Paine, *Reflections on the Revolution in France and The Rights of Man* (Garden City, N.Y.: Doubleday, 1961), p. 74.

10. Ibid., p. 75.

11. Burke, "Speech on Reform of Representation of the Commons in Parliament," in *Works*, VII:94.

12. Burke, "Reflections on the Revolution in France," pp. 100–01.

13. Burke, "Appeal from the New to the Old Whigs," in *Works*, IV:80–81.

14. Burke, "Reflections on the Revolution in France," p. 172.

15. Burke, "Letter to a Noble Lord," in *Works*, V:186.

16. Burke, "Letter to the Sheriffs of Bristol," in *Works*, II:225.

17. Burke, "Speech on the Plan for Economical Reform," in *Works*, II:280.

18. See Burleigh Taylor Wilkins, *The Problem of Burke's Political Philosophy* (Oxford: Clarendon Press, 1967), p. 252. Burke "affirmed that in certain contexts, in England especially, most historic rights could safely be presumed to satisfy the requirements of natural law and natural rights."

19. Burke despised Rousseau and saw in the excesses of the French Revolution the inevitable consequences of this thinker's "perverse philosophy." Yet, scholars have long recognized that in many respects the two share much in common (for example, their emphasis upon community and their recognition of the social basis of rights). See David Cameron, *The Social Thought of Rousseau and Burke: A Comparative Study* (Toronto: University of Toronto Press, 1973) for a thorough analysis of their similarities.

20. Burke, "Reflections on the Revolution in France," p. 237.

21. Ibid., p. 202.

22. Such ideals had traditionally been defined as natural laws. Burke holds to this definition, but he conceives of natural law within a historical context. For Burke, the principles of natural law evolve teleologically out of the historical progress of society. Such a perspective does raise some perplexing theoretical problems, however, because natural law had traditionally been understood to be rules of moral reason transcending history. See Wilkins, *Problem of Burke's Political Philosophy*, for an analysis of Burke's relationship to the natural law tradition. For a brief synopsis of Burke's "Aristotelianism" (and "Thomism") see Canavan, *Political Reason of Edmund Burke*, pp. 205–11.

23. Burke's frequently stated dictum that "art is man's nature," that is, that man shapes and constructs the given materials of his environment, is thoroughly Aristotelian and conforms precisely to his ideal of statesmanship.

24. Burke, "Letters on a Regicide Peace: Letter II," in *Works*, V:380.

25. Burke, "Letters on a Regicide Peace: Letter I," in *Works*, V:325.

26. Burke, "Letter to the Comte de Mercy-Argenteau, August 6, 1793," in *The Correspondence of Edmund Burke*, V, ed. P.J. Marshall and John A. Woods: 387.

27. Thomas Paine, "The Rights of Man," in Burke and Paine, *Reflections on the Revolution in France and The Rights of Man*, p. 288.

28. Burke largely agreed with his friend Adam Smith, author of *The Wealth of Nations*, a book generally conceded to be the first explicit defense of a laissez-faire or nonregulated, individualistic, economic system. Indeed, he

went so far as to argue that "the laws of commerce . . . are the laws of Nature, and consequently the laws of God." Burke, "Thoughts and Details on Scarcity," in *Works,* V:157.

29. Ironically, Burke was probably the first to give explicit expression to nationalist ideas. See Alfred Cobban, *Edmund Burke and the Revolt Against the Eighteenth Century* (London: George Allen & Unwin Ltd., 1960), pp. 97–130.

30. See ibid. for a discussion of Burke's influence on the Romantic movement.

12

Classical Liberalism

Burke's conservative criticism of the liberal ideology did not, of course, bring an end to the liberal tradition of political thought. Quite the contrary— the nineteenth century was very much the age of liberalism. But the underlying philosophical assumptions of the doctrine were radically altered in the early part of the century by the utilitarians or, as they were sometimes called, the philosophical radicals, and altered once again near the end of the century by an anti-utilitarian group of thinkers called the Oxford Idealists. Both groups, be it noted, were British; liberalism from Locke's time on was almost entirely an Anglo tradition of political thought.

The thinker most responsible for first changing the philosophical underpinnings of liberalism, although he himself was no liberal, was David Hume (1711–1776), a theorist whose impact upon modern thought extends well beyond the boundaries of political philosophy. It was Hume's moral philosophy, in particular, that had such a profound influence on liberal political thought. This philosophy was based upon a "new" (really ancient) insight into the psychology of human behavior. That which people claim is morally good or bad, according to Hume, is really nothing more than sentiment. Sentiment, in turn, is simply a reflection of what we find agreeable or disagreeable. That which is agreeable we call good; that which is disagreeable, bad.

In short, our moral rules are utilities. Hume, however, does not derive from his utilitarian psychology Hobbes's selfish theory of behavior. Hume simply wished to emphasize that people's moral sense is based upon sentiment, that people naturally support values that they find agreeable to them.[1]

Hume's utilitarianism was directed against the whole natural law tradition of ethical discourse. In place of that tradition, Hume wanted to create a strictly naturalistic ethics that could be scientifically validated, for he demonstrated quite effectively that there is simply no way to prove scientifically the existence of natural law or of any other a priori ethical standard. "Natural law," Hume insists, is simply a moral sentiment, a utility, that people have mistakenly taken to be an objective moral standard.

This same argument applies to the corollary principle of natural right. Rights and liberties are moral sentiments no less than laws and obligations. They exist as utilities plain and simple, not as a priori moral truths. Nor do they exist because people have rationally consented to them. For Hume the doctrine of contract or consent is neither historically accurate nor is it validated by the facts of human nature.

This criticism of the natural law—natural right tradition profoundly influenced the theoretical development of early nineteenth-century liberalism. The founder of this new liberal doctrine, what we now call classical liberalism, was a man named Jeremy Bentham (1748–1832). Bentham read Hume and proceeded to revolutionize the epistemological underpinnings of the liberal doctrine by substituting the principle of utility for that of natural right and the theory of contract. Actually, Bentham's utilitarianism is much closer to that of Hobbes and to the later Lockean school than to the softer and more subtle version we find in Hume. But it was Hume who provided the initial insights necessary to eliminate from liberal thought a language of politics that had its roots in the medieval past.

Indeed, herein lies the real importance of the utilitarians. Following Hume, they finally introduced clarity into modern political discourse. No longer are we confused, as we were with Locke, about whether natural right is an a priori rule of moral reason or a naturalistic ethics in the guise of such a rule. With Bentham and the utilitarians, we know we are dealing strictly with a naturalistic ethics of utility. The language of natural right and of natural law as well is finally eliminated from political discourse.[2]

Yet, for all of this, Bentham and his fellow utilitarians were not at heart political philosophers at all. They were practical men interested in initiating practical liberal reforms. Their philosophy, as far as they were concerned, was put forward primarily for the purpose of giving their political activities direction, and of justifying their proposed reforms. This was certainly the case for Bentham who was neither a political philosopher in spirit, nor initially even a liberal. He began his career as a legal reformer interested only in replacing what he believed to be an incoherent British legal system that stood in the way of social progress with a new legal order based upon the "scientific" principle of utility.[3]

We, however, are interested in the larger dimension of Bentham's thought. We want to know what the principle of utility implies for his political theory in general, not just for his legal philosophy. In fact, it was another utilitarian, James Mill, who most consistently drew out these implications. But Bentham did elaborate the basic framework for the development of utilitarian political thought. His most important work in this regard in his *An Introduction to the Principles of Morals and Legislation,* published in 1789. The opening page of that work states the basic principle of utilitarianism, a principle from which Bentham logically deduces the basic outline of a moral and political theory. Says Bentham,

> Nature has placed mankind under the governance of two sovereign masters, pain and pleasure. It is for them alone to point out what we ought to do as well as to determine what we shall do.[4]

Note that the principle embodies both a psychological and an ethical dimension (as it did, recall, for the hedonistic philosophy of Epicurus). It not only tells us "what we shall do," but "what we ought to do." What we shall do is behave so as to maximize pleasure and minimize pain, for psychologically we can act in no other way. (This is what Hobbes meant when he said that "the will is the last appetite in deliberating.") It follows, then, that what we ought to do is to recognize our inherent psychological predispositions and act accordingly. We ought to act, in other words, as we must act, the basic statement of any naturalistic ethics. Any other ethical principle, says Bentham, is false by definition, for scientifically speaking it is impossible to act in ways that are contrary to human nature.[5]

Given this logic of utility, it is now possible to determine the essential function of government. Since human beings do, and therefore ought to, desire pleasure or happiness (the two terms are identical for Bentham as they had been for Hobbes), it follows that government ought to maximize pleasure and minimize pain for the greatest number possible. In Bentham's famous formulation, the principle of utility applied at the political level must be "the greatest happiness of the greatest number."

The greatest happiness principle constitutes the utilitarian conception of the public interest. But note the full implications of this conception. Contrary to Burke's view, the public interest is not defined in terms of some community that transcends the individual. It is defined strictly in terms of number of individuals. In Bentham's words, the public or community interest is nothing more than "the sum of the interests of the several members who compose it."[6] Hence, the community itself can be nothing more than the sum of its individual parts. This is such a radically individualistic view of community that, for all practical purposes, it is a denial of it. As we shall soon see, this has some profound implications for other areas of liberal political theory.

Note also the principle of majoritarianism inherent in this conception of the public good. The "greatest happiness of the greatest number" is, or in almost all circumstances will be, the happiness of the greatest possible majority. As with the emphasis upon the individual, this focus on the majority is a key element of liberal thought. It takes no great imagination to see how easily this becomes connected to the liberal ideal of democratic rule. Less obvious are the problems majoritarianism would eventually present to the integrity of the liberal doctrine, a matter we shall examine in the next chapter.

For now, it is sufficient to recognize that, given Bentham's greatest happiness principle, the task of government is to promote the public interest by legislating the happiness of the greatest possible majority. But what precisely is the greatest happiness? It is not enough simply to assert that it is the greatest possible maximization of pleasure, for that which constitutes pleasure must first be determined.

Bentham claims in his *Principles* to have developed a genuinely scientific comprehension of the nature of pleasure. Pleasure, he argues, may be said to be of lesser or greater value depending upon certain measurable variables such as intensity, duration, fecundity, and so on. One pleasure, for example, may be more intense than another, but of shorter duration. Another pleasure may be of great duration, but lack fecundity, that is, the capacity to generate other subordinate pleasures. Moreover, as Epicurus had also noted, pleasures are often accompanied by pain (the pleasure of eating, for example, may be followed by the pain of stomachache) and some pleasures are more apt to be accompanied by pain than others.

Knowing these variables (and Bentham analyzes them in great detail) we are able to determine whether any act is good simply by adding up the various variables of pleasure produced by the act and subtracting the accompanying pains. If the sum of pleasure is greater than the sum of pain, and greater than the sum of any pleasure produced by a different act, the act is good; if the sum is less, the act is bad. And just as we can apply this form of analysis to any individual act, so too can we apply it to political or legislative acts that affect the whole community. We need only add to our "calculus of pleasure" the extent, or number, of people affected by the act.

Clearly, Bentham had reduced ethics to mathematics; indeed he called his method the *felicific calculus*. But it is important to recognize that Bentham's calculus works only so long as two assumptions hold. We must assume first that the ethical is identical to the pleasurable, and second that the pleasurable can be defined in strictly quantitative terms such that any pleasure can be mathematically compared to any other. As we shall see in the following chapter, modern liberalism evolves out of a rejection of these two assumptions. The idea that all pleasures are equally quantifiable is rejected first and, eventually, the principle of utility itself is jettisoned.

But Bentham had no doubts at all about the principle of utility or about his "mathematical ethics." Here, he thought, we finally have a genuine science of ethics, a mathematical science to rival those of physics and chemistry. And since this science can be applied to the community as a whole, we have for the first time a genuine science of politics as well, one that is capable of determining the public good or the "greatest happiness of the greatest number."

Needless to say, Bentham's new science of pleasure had radical implications for political thought. Law, for example, ceased to be Aristotle's "rule of moral reason"; it became nothing more than a set of conventional rules designed to control behavior by creating pleasure or, in the case of criminal law, by inflicting pain. Indeed, Bentham defined law as "artificial consequences," for in his legal system law simply establishes consequences of pleasure or pain in order to produce desirable behavior. In effect, this theory of law corresponded to that of Hobbes, who defined law as command, or power. In Bentham's system, as in Hobbes's, law is simply the power to create pleasure or inflict pain, not, as in the natural law tradition, the reflection of some larger ethical order.

Even more radical in its implications is the role the legislator must play given this theory of law. Bentham's legislator is nothing less than a social scientist who employs the techniques of social engineering.[7] His object is the scientific restructuring of society for the greatest happiness of the greatest number, and his instruments for doing so are pleasure and pain. He is, therefore, the precise opposite of the Burkean legislator who employs prudence, follows the "sense of the community," and respects the "experience of the ages." Bentham's ideal legislator does none of these things. It is science, not prudence, upon which he relies. He certainly has no respect for the ages since he views the past as nothing but a collection of errors. And since the community to his mind is simply the sum of self-interested individuals, there can be no "sense of the community" to follow.

But here it will be asked, "In what possible way can Bentham's political vision be called liberal?" What is liberal about giving power to social engineers who manipulate the public for its own good? Where in this vision is to be found the liberal ideal of the free individual, the elimination of state power, and democratic rule? As we have noted, Bentham was initially not a liberal at all. He quite frankly espoused the idea of ruling society through a benevolent despotism. And many contemporary students of Bentham admit that his idea of rule by social engineers describes the modern bureaucratic state more than the negative and decentralized state defended by the early liberals.

Yet, since Bentham, one persistent strain of thought within the liberal tradition has been a belief in the efficacy of social engineering despite the illiberal implications. As we shall see, this belief is more prevalent in modern liberalism than it was in the early utilitarian doctrine. But for Bentham, there was no incompatibility between social engineering and liberal-democratic values. When he adopted, finally, the liberal position, he continued to think in terms of engineering society to produce "desirable consequences."

It was James Mill (1773–1836), Bentham's most devoted and important disciple, who convinced his mentor that his proposals for legal reform could succeed only within a liberal-democratic framework. For Bentham had discovered, as had every reformer since Plato, that simply having a better idea is no guarantee it will be put into practice. What is first required is a political leadership that is willing to enact reform, and this means that the most important reform of all must be of the political structure within which decisions are made.

For the utilitarians, the most important reform of this type involved the attempt to restructure representation in Parliament by expanding the franchise. The purpose of this was to diminish the power in Parliament of the wealthy landholders. This group was interested in protecting its "feudal interests" rather than paving the way for Britain to become a modern industrial state. They resisted, for example, a policy of promoting international free trade, a policy that was essential to the development of Great Britain as a modern industrial-capitalist power.

Despite this resistance, however, Great Britain was continuing to develop along these lines. This process included the emergence of a new middle class whose wealth depended not upon land but upon capital accumulation. Clearly the interests of this class lay in the development of a modern capitalist system, not in the preservation of a moribund economic order. Needless to say, the utilitarians considered this new class, to which they themselves belonged, to be the repository of all that was progressive and enlightened. In their minds, therefore, it followed that the extension of the franchise to increasing numbers of this class, and even to certain elements of the working class, would break the power of the antiprogressive landed interests in Parliament. In short, the creation of a modern liberal-democratic state would assure the possibility of reform, not only of the economic order, but of the whole social and political system.

It was James Mill who most consistently employed Bentham's principle of utility to urge the liberal-democratic ideal. His major work in this regard is *Essay on Government,* a short treatise that attempts to demonstrate that representative democracy is the only legitimate form of government since it alone conforms to the principle of utility.

Mill's analysis revolves around a crucial assumption shared by all the utilitarians and, indeed, by all liberals since Locke, that property is the chief source of pleasure. It thus follows, says Mill, that "the greatest possible happiness of society is . . . attained by insuring to every man the greatest possible quantity of the produce of his labor."[8] The ideal form of government, therefore, is that which allows for the greatest possibility of accumulating property. In the utilitarian scheme, only this form of government is ethically defensible.

Of course, the ideal would be to eliminate government entirely. In a condition of anarchy individuals theoretically could acquire as much property as they desired without any limitations at all. The problem, as Hobbes and Locke both demonstrated, is that the unlimited desire for property is precisely what makes government necessary. Without it, people's ceaseless quest for property would put them in an unending state of war over each other's lives and possessions. Under these conditions, property would constitute a chronic source of pain rather than an object of pleasure. Framed in the language of utilitarianism, Mill explains the dilemma as follows:

> That one human being will desire to render the person and property of another subservient to his pleasures notwithstanding the pain or loss of pleasure which it may occasion to that other individual, is the foundation of government.[9]

The problem for Mill, then, as it had been for Locke, is how to create a government that is effective politically yet at the same time is incapable of abusing its powers. Bear in mind that the very principle of utility that makes government necessary is the same one that makes it susceptible to the abuse of power. Simply because human beings become government officials does not change the fact that they are human beings who, given the opportunity, will use power to their own ends "notwithstanding the pain or loss of pleasure it may occasion others."

Mill's solution is to identify the interest of those in government with the interests of the community as a whole. If such an identity could be created, the interests of the government would be in promoting the good of the community rather than in the abuse of power. How is this to be accomplished? Clearly, Mill argues, it requires that government cease to be a minority standing opposed to the vast majority of the population, for given the psychology of utility any minority, including that political minority we call government, will pursue its own interests at the expense of the majority unless it is in some manner checked.

Given these considerations, it follows that monarchy and aristocracy are not legitimate forms of government. They constitute distinct minorities whose interests are not identical to those of the community as a whole. And Mill rejects as well the Aristotelian mixed form of government since he thinks it inevitable that one element within government will come to dominate the others.[10]

Clearly, direct or classical democracy would be the ideal since such a government would constitute the whole community. Here the interests of government and the people would be "perfectly" identical (although it is important to recall here Rousseau's criticism of this assumption). But just as clearly direct democracy is a practical impossibility. The nation-state is much too large an entity to allow for the direct political participation of each individual.

We are thus left with representative democracy. A representative legislature is a minority of the community, to be sure, but it is a democratically elected minority. We may presume, therefore, that its interests are not remote from those of the community.[11] But Mill recognizes that the democratic element in the representative system is not, in and of itself, sufficient. He therefore offers a proposal that now forms a part of the general stock of liberal constitutional wisdom: Legislators must be limited in the duration of time they actually exercise power. In this way, they will have less time to promote their own "sinister interests." Most important, and here Mill pursues an idea first suggested by Locke, limiting the legislators' tenure means that they must return periodically to the community as ordinary citizens. Thus, the short term pleasure they derive from misgoverning in their own interest will soon turn to the long-term pain of being subject to their own legislation.

But there is a more fundamental issue here, says Mill, namely "who the persons are by whom the act of choosing ought to be performed."[12] Who, in other words, are to choose the representatives? This is the crucial question, for no matter what else we may do to constrain the legislators, they will represent only the interests of those who have the power to elect them, for the electors alone are capable of inflicting the pain of turning them out of office. Thus, we derive a principle of representation that corresponds precisely to our basic principle of government. Just as we must reject any form of minority government, we must for the same reason reject any form of minority representation.

With this basic philosophy of representation in mind, Mill goes on to criticize various forms of representation that were then favored by many but that, from a utilitarian point of view, he believed to be scientifically indefensible. To begin with, Mill rejects the argument that a property qualification ought to accompany the right to vote. Clearly, Mill argues, those with property form a minority of the community and, as such, are incapable of electing representatives whose interests are identical to the whole community. Unfortunately, Mill is not entirely consistent on this matter since he allows for exclusion from the franchise of the very poorest elements of the population. But, for his time, Mill was well in advance of most in his argument to delimit the scope of property qualifications.

Mill also rejects what we now call functional representation, that is, representation based on class, profession, or some other such identifiable group. Those advocating such a system realized, of course, that it would be impossible, not to mention undesirable, for all groups to be directly represented. But they argued that those not directly represented would be represented virtually and that, as a consequence, the interests of the community as a whole would be taken into account.

Mill was not persuaded by these arguments. Functional groups, he insists, are minorities with interests distinct from, and often hostile to, those of the community. As such, they are incapable of electing representatives who reflect anything but their own particular group interests. They cannot, therefore, virtually represent anyone. As was evident in the chapter on Burke, virtual representation can work only where there is a community of interest, a general will, that transcends the particular interest of any group, a condition that cannot exist given the basic principle of utility.

It would seem to follow, then, that the only legitimate form of representation for Mill is direct representation of all adults or, as we would say today, "one man (woman)–one vote." In a direct representative system each individual in society would be represented, and the legislature would be compelled to take into account the interests of the entire society, not just a particular group or social class.

But, amazingly, Mill equivocates, and not just in regard to property qualifications. While he quite naturally excludes from the franchise children "whose interests," he argues, "are involved in those of their parents,"[13] he also considers women in this category, "the interest of almost all of whom," he says, "is involved either in that of their fathers or in that of their husbands."[14] And Mill adds to these excluded groups young men whose interests he also considers to be involved in that of their fathers and older males. Who then are the electors to be? All males forty or older, says Mill, because they have "an interest identical with that of the whole community . . . [and] . . . may be regarded as the natural representatives of the whole population."[15]

Given his utilitarian assumptions, how could Mill seriously claim that males forty years or older could represent everyone? Indeed, his position comes close to that Burkean notion of virtual representation that he rejects as incompatible with the principle of utility.[16] The answer may in part be that Mill believed that any realistic reform of the franchise, given the current conventions of his society, would require the exclusion of certain groups.[17] Surely were he alive today he would not advocate excluding women and those under forty, anymore than Aristotle would advocate slavery. This is all the more the case given that his views on representation and the franchise were extremely progressive for his time.

But there may be a deeper reason for Mill's inconsistency, one that raises a key theoretical issue about the classical liberal tradition. Almost invariably those who insist that human behavior is strictly self-interested will, at some point, assert the opposite. And this is because it is impossible to conceive of any society actually functioning that does not possess some sense of community interest that transcends the self-interest of the individual. Thus, while Bentham's and Hobbes's assertion that society is nothing but the sum of its individual parts is accepted by Mill in theory, in practice he too assumes the existence of community, if only of a very limited kind. In arguing that older males can represent their wives, daughters, and sons, he implicitly asserts a commonality of interests, at least within the family.

Later liberalism, as we shall see, breaks from the classical liberal position precisely over this question of community. Unlike the classical doctrine, it emphasizes humankind's essential sociability and is therefore explicit in its recognition of community. Until then liberal thinkers followed the lead of Bentham and Mill. They gave no explicit recognition to the idea of community and therefore continued to justify extending the franchise strictly in terms of protecting the interest of the individual.

It is no wonder, then, that historically the principle of "one man–one vote" has been advocated by every disenfranchised group in Western liberal democracies. They have demanded direct representation precisely on the basis that they alone are capable of representing their own interests. In this country the suffragettes were adamant on this point, as have been young people in more recent years. The argument on the part of many young males that "if we are old enough to fight we are old enough to vote" is a case in point. Quite clearly they did not believe that on the issue of war and peace they shared a community of interests with older males who were too old to fight.

We may conclude here our analysis of the political theory of classical liberalism. One point of a general historical and theoretical nature needs to be stressed, however. Viewed from the broadest perspective, it is apparent that Bentham and Mill united Hobbes's utilitarian psychology with Locke's liberal-democratic theory. This unification, described in the chapter on Locke, had begun long before the emergence of classical liberalism. But just as they made the final and explicit break from the tradition of natural law and natural right, the utilitarians completed the process of uniting Hobbes with Locke. From Bentham until the beginning of modern liberalism, the liberal argument in its essentials held that Locke's political theory is validated by Hobbes's utilitarian psychology. The argument, in other words, was that the unlimited desire for property necessitates a liberal-democratic political structure.

The classical liberal tradition encompassed more than a theory of politics, however. It also contained an economic philosophy that closely paralleled its political theory. Not surprisingly, the common element that united the political and economic components of the liberal doctrine was the emphasis upon property. From the political point of view, property was understood as the source of individual rights. From the economic side, the right of property was considered the necessary precondition for a viable economy. The evolution of these economic ideas may be traced to a group of eighteenth-century thinkers called *physiocrats*, who argued that economic health is best assured when individuals are left free to pursue the acquisition of property without governmental constraint.

What the physiocrats had begun was completed by the British thinker Adam Smith (1723–1790). In 1776 Smith published his famous *The Wealth of Nations,* a book that laid the foundation of classical or liberal economics. The essence of Smith's argument in that work is that *laissez-faire capitalism* is the ideal economic system. It is one in which government does not interfere in the free and competitive struggle for wealth and property. Prices are set by the market mechanism rather than by governmental regulation, and the processes of production and consumption are left strictly to the individual.

The great advantage of laissez-faire capitalism, Smith argues, is that it generates enormous productive forces and thus produces the maximum economic progress. This is so, he contends, because a free market unleashes the desire for property and thus encourages initiative, inventiveness, and the willingness to work and produce.

There is another great advantage to laissez-faire capitalism, says Smith: It is self-regulating. In his now famous metaphor, Smith claims that the market is regulated as if by an "unseen hand," for the law of supply and demand automatically produces rational prices and the rational distribution of goods and services. Moreover, Smith argues, a free market encourages both an increase of goods and a lowering of prices, for given market competition the entrepreneur must lower prices in the hope of selling and must therefore increase production in order to make a profit.

Smith's new economic ideas enjoy such wide currency today, particularly in this country, that it is difficult for the student to appreciate their revolutionary implications. But it must be borne in mind that, historically speaking, capitalism is a quite modern phenomenon. You will recall from the chapter on Machiavelli that the basic outline of modern capitalism did not even begin to appear until the Renaissance. Indeed, it was not really until the nineteenth century that capitalism emerged as anything like a distinct economic system. Hence, Smith's ideas, which are the theoretical reflections of these economic changes, are as radically novel in historical terms as are the changes themselves.

Perhaps the best way to see the revolutionary import of Smith's economic theory is to contrast it with medieval economic values. In the medieval world there was no free market in the modern sense. Products and prices were regulated by productive units called guilds. A shoemaker's guild, for example, would determine the price of shoes and the remuneration a shoemaker could receive. This same determination would be made by all other guilds that constituted the productive structure of medieval society. And corresponding to this structure was a set of economic beliefs that was the very opposite of Smith's. To the medieval mind, property and wealth were of course to be regulated for a larger public good. The notion that one would sell property for individual profit seemed unnatural, and contrary to the interests of the community.

Behind these medieval ideas lay the deeply held belief that unleashing one's self-interest is sinful, whether in economic or any other terms. To make profit, to compete for economic advantage, to center one's life on the acquisition of property and wealth, these were all sinful activities. The object was to constrain self-interest for the spiritual good of the individual as well as the secular good of the community, not to freely express it.

Herein lies the genuinely revolutionary character of Smith's economic theory: He rejected the idea that self-interest is sinful and opposed to the larger public interest. Self-interest is not a sin for Smith; it is simply a fact of human nature. And it certainly is not contrary to the public good, for he had demonstrated that if individuals are allowed to maximize their economic interests, a larger economic good is produced as if by an "unseen hand." Indeed, in Smith's economic system self-interest is virtuous rather than sinful, for it is the source of the community's economic well-being. For this reason, Smith speaks of economic self-interest as "enlightened self-interest," a term that has become commonplace in our society but one that would have utterly perplexed the medieval mind.

It is in contrast with medieval values that we can now see the connection between Smith's economic theory and classical liberal political thought. Smith and his nineteenth-century followers (Ricardo and Malthus, to name the two most important) were, in effect, all utilitarians. They all asserted the basic principle of utilitarian psychology that human behavior is by nature self-interested. Moreover, they took for granted the utilitarian assumption that property is the chief source of pleasure and thus the dominant drive in human behavior. Finally, their economic theory led them to political conclusions quite in harmony with utilitarian political thought, namely, that the powers of government must be limited and that the functions of the state must be negative.

Taken together, the classical economists and the early utilitarians provided a powerful defense of liberal ideals. And, as we have seen, for both groups this defense was ultimately based upon the "right of property." For the liberal political thinkers, property was the foundation of civil rights and democratic government. The classical liberal economists saw property in narrower economic terms, of course, but their advocacy of laissez-faire capitalism carried with it a defense of these other key liberal values as well. By the middle of the nineteenth century, classical liberalism embodied a set of economic and political ideals that logically reinforced each other, and that taken together constituted an all-embracing worldview. Beginning in Locke as a basic outline of ideas, classical liberalism had become a full-blown ideology.

This ideology did not, of course, end with James Mill and the classical economists. Numerous thinkers in the nineteenth century carried on this liberal tradition of thought, and it still enjoys some popularity today, particularly in this country. (That many Americans still equate capitalism with democracy is a case in point.) But perhaps the most important figure in the further evolution of classical liberalism was yet another British thinker named Herbert Spencer (1820–1903).

Spencer went one step further than Mill and the liberal economists by adding the forces of evolutionary biology to the justification of the laissez-faire state. Spencer took for granted that human beings are by nature self-interested property seekers, but he added the idea that the competitive struggle for property is governed by the biological processes of natural selection. Those who are not able to compete successfully—those who in Locke's words are not "industrious and rational"—are, Spencer argues, genetically inferior, at least in regard to those survival traits crucial in a capitalist society. For this reason, Spencer concluded that any attempt on the part of government to aid the poor could only have the effect of maintaining an unfit element within the population and of ensuring that ineffective traits would be passed on to later generations. Thus, viewed from the perspective of the species as a whole, Spencer argued that government has no business becoming involved in social welfare. The more government helps people, the more it upsets the process of natural selection to the detriment of the species and the betterment of society.[18]

Spencer's argument, which came to be known as *Social Darwinism,*[19] became the rage among classical liberal thinkers. For with Spencer it was possible to demonstrate not only that a capitalist system fits the facts of human nature, but that it accords with the science of biological evolution as well. Apply Darwin's analysis to the social and political sphere, the classical liberals argued, and we have irrevocable proof of the validity of capitalism, individualism, limited government, and the negative state.

Needless to say, Spencer and the Social Darwinists were enormously popular with the new capitalist class and with the rising middle classes. Here was a doctrine that not only justified their desire for property and wealth, but also told them not to worry about the increasingly impoverished working class spawned by the industrial revolution. In an even more radical sense than Adam Smith, Spencer had asserted that self-interest is in reality socially beneficial, and that altruism is actually contrary to the public good. Such a doctrine was bound to be popular with the economically successful. No wonder that in his day Spencer was enormously influential, and that he could make the extreme arguments he did only confirms how powerful liberal-capitalist ideas had become by the middle of the nineteenth century.

Today, however, Spencer is not taken seriously as a political theorist. Among other reasons, few contemporary political thinkers would agree that society is equivalent to a natural environment in which different species struggle for survival, much less that there is a genetic basis to economic success or failure. These facts are readily explainable in sociological terms: a person's class position, educational opportunities, and so forth. Nevertheless, Social Darwinist ideas, in this country particularly, have never entirely died out, even if Spencer's theory has, and there is presently a revival of these ideas on the part of various thinkers largely outside the discipline of political science.

We need not at this point devote a great deal of time to a critical analysis of the classical liberal ideology. Most of the important criticisms were developed in the chapter on Locke, for the social and political problems inherent in Lockean liberalism are essentially identical to those found in the classical doctrine. This is the case despite the clear-cut philosophical differences between the two, for in conceiving property and its acquisition as the dominant motive force of the personality, it makes little difference in practical human terms whether property is defined as a natural right or as a utility. The consequences are the same in either case.

The most serious consequence of the liberal defense of property—the increasing impoverishment of the industrial working class—does deserve special note, however, because it compelled some important liberal theorists to rethink their premises. They were forced to recognize that laissez-faire capitalism and the industrial revolution were producing an exploited and brutalized working class. Not everyone was benefiting from Smith's "unseen hand," and people of good will—as most of the liberals were—were unwilling to accept Spencer's neglect of the poor in the name of an abstraction called "property rights."

A related issue also encouraged liberals to rethink their premises. It was becoming increasingly evident that the new middle class was not using the franchise to reform and elevate society. Although it should have come as no surprise to the utilitarians, the newly enfranchised groups were pursuing their own economic interests with precious little regard for any larger public good. The middle class, and indeed every other group in the new industrial society, was behaving precisely like good Benthamites. They were all practicing utilitarians, maximizing their own class interest with little thought for the rest of society, and with almost none for the condition of the working class.[20]

What made these facts so particularly troublesome to the liberal reformers was their expectation that the middle class would act as the leader and exemplar for those in the lower ranks of society. Bear in mind that the ideal of a universal franchise inherently followed from the utilitarian theory of representation, and this meant the eventual inclusion of the working class into the political process. Given that class's lack of political experience and its general cultural deprivation, liberal democracy could not survive unless it was led by those who did have the requisite experience and values. It was just this belief in the leadership capabilities of the middle class that led James Mill to assert at the end of his *Essay on Government* that "there can be no doubt that the middle rank . . . is that portion of the community of which, if the basis of representation were ever so far extended, the opinion would ultimately decide. Of the people beneath them a vast majority would be sure to be guided by their advice and example."[21] Their example, it was becoming apparent, was not at all what Mill and his fellow liberals had hoped for.

Indeed, as the century progressed, liberal-democratic societies seemed to move inexorably toward a kind of mindless self-centeredness extending to all ranks of society. Thus, the liberal ideal of majority rule increasingly meant rule by those whose concerns extended no further than their own economic advantage. Under these conditions, those who deeply appreciated the ideals of liberty and democracy—those, in other words, who were most capable of leading society—found themselves an ever diminishing minority unable to resist the overpowering weight of a politically ignorant and socially unconcerned majority.

This came to be known among liberal thinkers as the problem of majority tyranny, a problem never anticipated by Locke and the early classical liberals. And it was a problem that raised a profoundly troubling paradox. Not only did it appear that democracy was perfectly compatible with tyranny, but that every extension of democracy (a key plank in the liberal platform) would simply extend the majority's tyranny over the minority of progressive and enlightened people.

In major part, modern liberalism evolves out of a critique of those elements of the classical doctrine that justified the debasement of the working class and that contributed to the problem of majority tyranny. Broadly, the critique took the form of a reexamination of the principles of economic individualism and of majority rule. In the next chapter, we shall examine that critique in some detail, beginning with the issue of majority tyranny, which is, in fact, theoretically the prior issue. For even if the working class could be incorporated into the political process, and its economic conditions improved, all would be lost in terms of liberal ideals if its political contribution would be nothing more than perfecting the tyranny of an unenlightened majority.

Notes

1. Hume argues that one of the strongest components of sentiment is benevolence or concern for our fellows and that therefore "the voice of nature and experience seems plainly to oppose the selfish theory." David Hume, *An Inquiry Concerning the Principles of Morals,* Charles W. Hendel, ed. (New York: The Liberal Arts Press, 1957), p. 44.

2. See John Plamenatz, *The English Utilitarians* (Oxford: Basil Blackwell & Mott Ltd., 1958), pp. 159–60. Plamenatz states this fact in its broadest context. "It is to the English utilitarians . . . that we owe our liberation from the political vocabulary inherited from the Middle Ages." Plamenatz's book remains one of the best introductions available to the history of utilitarian thought.

3. Bentham's new legal theory is developed in *A Fragment of Government,* a work written to refute the legal ideas of Blackstone, the most influential legal thinker at the time and a defender of the existing—and Bentham believed unscientific—common law tradition.

4. Jeremy Bentham, "An Introduction to the Principles of Morals and Legislation," in *The Utilitarians* (Garden City, New York: Anchor Press, 1973), p. 17.

5. Here, clearly, Bentham had misread Hume. See R.P. Anschutz, *The Philosophy of J.S. Mill* (Oxford: Clarendon Press, 1963), p. 11: "Hume offers the principle of utility as a description of received morality, Bentham as a standard by which it should be judged."

6. Bentham, "An Introduction to the Principles of Morals and Legislation," p. 18.

7. Here Bentham anticipates the tendency toward social engineering characteristic of such contemporary thinkers as the behavioral psychologist B.F. Skinner. See Douglas G. Long, *Bentham On Liberty: Jeremy Bentham's Idea of Liberty in Relation to His Utilitarianism* (Toronto: University of Toronto Press, 1977), pp. 216–20. Long points to some of the dangers inherent in what Bentham and his modern "representatives" propose to do.

8. James Mill, *Essay on Government,* Currin V. Shields, ed. (New York: Bobbs Merrill, 1955), p. 49.

9. Ibid., p. 56.

10. Mill does not consider the British Constitution of Crown, Lords, and Commons to constitute a mixed form of government, at least not when Commons, the elected representative body, remains sovereign. For this reason he does not recommend, as one might initially expect given his constitutional theory, the elimination of Crown or Lords.

11. To be precise, Mill's analysis employs the parliamentary model that reserves the term *government* for the executive body. Hence, in his scheme the people check the legislature, which, in turn, checks the government.

12. Mill, *Essay on Government,* p. 72.

13. Ibid., p. 73.

14. Ibid., pp. 73–74.

15. Ibid., p. 74.

16. Mill's position comes close, but of course is not identical, to Burke's idea of virtual representation. It is not identical because the theory of virtual representation presumes a community of interest that transcends the self-interest of the various individuals that make up society. This Mill does not presume, at least not explicitly. His assertion that the interest of others is involved in that of older males is to mean only that they all share an identity of individual self-interests. Yet, if only implicitly, there seems to be in Mill's advocacy of a limited franchise some notion of a community of interest beyond that of the individual.

17. See C.B. Macpherson, *The Life and Times of Liberal Democracy* (Oxford: Oxford University Press, 1977), pp. 37–42, for a discussion of Mill's ambivalence about a universal franchise and of his position generally in regard to those groups he would exclude from the vote.

18. See Herbert Spencer, *The Man Versus the State,* Donald Macrae, ed. (Baltimore: Penguin Books, 1969), for an example of these kinds of arguments and for a basic overview of his political theory.

19. Spencer, however, did not initially derive his ideas from Darwin.

20. See Guido de Ruggiero, *The History of European Liberalism,* R.G. Collingwood, trans. (Boston: Beacon Press, 1959), p. 138: "Liberalism had fought the aristocracy in the name of the general interest. But its actions showed itself attached to its own interest alone."

21. Mill, *Essay on Government,* p. 90.

13

Modern Liberalism

In 1831 Alexis de Tocqueville (1805–1859), a French aristocrat, was sent by his government to study prison conditions in this country. De Tocqueville accomplished his task and published his findings in 1833. Two years later he published the first volume of a work of substantially greater importance, *Democracy in America*. This work, the second volume of which was published in 1840, is now recognized as a classic study of the sociological and political structure of democracy.

The major thesis of *Democracy in America* is that the spread of democracy is a "providential fact." De Tocqueville stresses that every social, economic, and political development of the modern world confirms it to be so. He sees no contrary tendencies of sufficient power to impede its inexorable triumph. For this reason, de Tocqueville concludes that "to attempt to check democracy would be . . . to resist the will of God."[1] It would be, at best, an exercise in futility.

De Tocqueville's analysis was just what was required at the time. The excesses of the French Revolution still loomed large in the consciousness of many and the reaction of the Holy Alliance was still very real. Many held the unrealistic hope that the movement toward liberal democracy could still be halted, and the ideals of the ancien regime somehow reinvigorated. De Tocqueville's analysis compelled a more realistic assessment of the situation and directed attention to the real issue: how best to reform democracies, not how to prevent them.

But de Tocqueville's analysis was needed as well by those on the other side of the political spectrum. If he showed the conservatives the "historical inevitability" of democracy, he showed liberal democrats its potential evil— its inherent tendency to degenerate into a tyranny of the majority. So powerful is this tendency, de Tocqueville argues, and so great the evil, that unless means can be found to check it, liberal democracy will become a contradiction in terms.

Clearly, given de Tocqueville's analysis, liberal theory would have to be revised, for its assumption that democracy is the surest guarantee of liberty no longer could be accepted uncritically. In and of itself, extending the franchise would simply compound the problem. But de Tocqueville was not himself interested in revising liberal thought. He was interested in showing the potential dangers inherent in democracy through an analysis of an actually existing democratic regime, not in attempting to modify a political philosophy. Nevertheless, de Tocqueville's analysis of democracy in America was an important landmark in the evolution of liberal theory, for it influenced others to rethink some of liberalism's most basic assumptions. This was most notably the case with John Stuart Mill, a thinker whose work we shall discuss shortly.

The root cause of majority tyranny, de Tocqueville argues, is the overweening desire on the part of democratic peoples for equality, which, carried to its logical extreme, destroys liberty. This is so because equality and liberty are not entirely compatible. In the case of equality, the value of being like others is stressed; in the case of liberty, that of being different. Where all are exactly the same, liberty in any meaningful sense cannot exist. Hence, where equality is taken to an extreme, liberty will of necessity be destroyed. And it is precisely a capacity to go to this logical extreme that is inherent in democracy, says de Tocqueville. In the name of equality, the majority is willing to destroy the liberty of people to be different.

The source of this emphasis on equality is not difficult to find. Democracy by definition implies a certain equality of political participation and, therefore, an egalitarian value structure. And, it must be remembered that liberal democracy arose in reaction against the aristocratic structure of the ancien regime. With the aristocracy eliminated or in retreat, the social and economic order was thrown open to people who would have heretofore been consigned to a particular class or status. Invariably, this process was accompanied by a new egalitarianism in the social and economic spheres. In this way the democratic revolution intensified egalitarian ideals and made equality the supreme and, if de Tocqueville's analysis is correct, extreme value of democracies.

This is not to suggest that a democratic people have no desire for liberty. On the contrary, says de Tocqueville, they have a natural love of it. But, he hastens to add, "liberty is not the chief and constant object of their desires; equality is their idol . . . and they would rather perish than lose it."[2]

What makes this ideal so extraordinarily dangerous, de Tocqueville argues, is its pervasiveness. It is not simply political (for instance, "one man–one vote") but social, economic, and cultural as well. The natural inclination of democratic peoples is to level all distinctions, not just political ones. Most frighteningly, says de Tocqueville, they apply the principle of equality to the intellect itself. The majority expects others to think exactly like itself and will pressure minorities, and particularly intellectual minorities, to conform to its opinion. For in a democratic nation, those whose opinions are different from the majority will implicitly violate the principle of equality, which proclaims they ought to be the same. This the majority will not tolerate.

It is this pervasive opinion of the majority, in short, public opinion, that constitutes the real essence of majority tyranny for de Tocqueville. Its danger resides in the fact that it possesses the power to tyrannize irrespective of constitutional protections guaranteeing liberty of thought and expression. Legal rights to freedom of opinion may continue to exist, but they will be of no avail to those who do not agree with public opinion, for such people will be pressured socially to conform and ostracized if they refuse. Legal or physical coercion will be unnecessary; the psychological pressures will be sufficient. "Fetters and headsmen were the coarse instruments which tyranny formerly employed," says de Tocqueville, but "in democratic republics . . . the body is left free, and the soul is enslaved."[3]

This is a chilling view of majority tyranny. But there are even deeper and more disturbing implications to this picture. Unless checked, says de Tocqueville, majority tyranny may become a form of despotism that extends beyond the majority itself. Imagine, he says, that in the name of equality the majority has established complete control. It not only rules public opinion, but has established a government that perfectly reflects its wishes. In such a condition (and given the inordinate desire for equality, it is a perfectly possible condition, de Tocqueville emphasizes) the tyranny of the majority will lead to an entirely novel form of despotism. The majority will not merely tyrannize the minority, it will actually enslave itself! In perhaps the most famous—some would say prophetic—lines in *Democracy in America,* de Tocqueville describes what he imagines this new species of oppression will look like:

> The first thing that strikes the observation is an innumerable multitude of men, all equal and alike, incessantly endeavoring to procure the petty and paltry pleasures with which they glut their lives. Each of them, living apart, is as a stranger to the fate of all the rest—his children and his private friends constitute to him the whole of mankind; as for the rest of his fellow-citizens, he is close to them, but he sees them not;—he touches them, but

he feels them not; he exists but in himself and for himself alone; and if his kindred still remain to him, he may be said at any rate to have lost his country.

Above this race of men stands an immense and tutelary power, which takes upon itself alone to secure their gratifications, and to watch over their fate. That power is absolute, minute, regular, provident, and mild. It would be like the authority of a parent, if, like that authority, its object was to prepare men for manhood; but it seeks, on the contrary, to keep them in perpetual childhood: it is well content that the people should rejoice, provided they think of nothing but rejoicing. For their happiness such a government willingly labors, but it chooses to be the sole agent and the only arbiter of that happiness; it provides for their security, foresees and supplies their necessities, facilitates their pleasures, manages their principle concerns, directs their industry, regulates the descent of property, and subdivides their inheritances: what remains, but to spare them all the care of thinking and all the trouble of living?[4]

What is this novel form of despotism to which de Tocqueville refers? Clearly it is the despotism (or the potential despotism) of the modern bureaucratic welfare state. And such a despotism, unlike that of any past tyranny, is both absolute and mild. Indeed, it is absolute because it is mild. Democratic people are willing to grant to government an almost total power when that power is used to make them forever happy and content. And the principle of equality proclaims, does it not, that all have an equal right to happiness and contentment.

It is important to note here that the "immense and tutelary power" of this bureaucratic state corresponds strikingly to Bentham's political vision. Bentham, you will recall, believed that the function of government is to manipulate pleasures and pains to produce the greatest happiness of the greatest number. This is why many thinkers argue that Bentham's political theory is actually more compatible with the modern bureaucratic state that de Tocqueville describes than with the negative state advocated by the classical liberals.

But note also that the social conditions that de Tocqueville argues give rise to bureaucratic despotism closely corresponds to Bentham's and the early utilitarians' view of the nature of society. Had they not claimed that society is simply a collection of self-interested individuals ceaselessly striving to maximize their pleasure? And is this not precisely de Tocqueville's unattractive description of the democratic social order, as one in which there "is an innumerable multitude of men, all equal and alike, incessantly endeavoring to procure the petty and paltry pleasures with which they glut their lives?"

De Tocqueville had discovered a crucial connection between liberal individualism and bureaucratic despotism. Within a democratic society, the more individuals are set free to pursue their own interests, the more intense the desire for equality becomes. This is so because the logic of individualism in a democratic society is such that individuals believe their right to satiate their desires ought to be equal to everyone else's. But such an equality of rights can be maintained only where there is a central bureaucratic authority to ensure an equality of happiness for all. This was de Tocqueville's great discovery. In democratic society, individualism leads not to an expansion of liberty, but, unless special precautions are taken, to the "happy and willing" enslavement of the majority itself, indeed of the whole population, to an "immense and tutelary bureaucratic power."

But de Tocqueville had discovered something else of equal importance. It is not just that the utilitarian and individualistic psychology of democratic people encourages them to willingly submit to bureaucratic despotism; that same psychology actually creates the social conditions in which the despotism can effectively function. Recall in the previous quotation de Tocqueville's statement that democratic man "exists but in himself and for himself," and that "as for the rest of his fellow citizens, he is close to them, but he sees them not;—he touches them, but he feels them not." His point, simply, is that liberal individualism isolates people from each other. People are so interested in pursuing their own "paltry pleasures" that they are unable to establish any real community with their fellow citizens. The consequence of this, says de Tocqueville, is a tendency in democratic societies for groups and associations to disintegrate, leaving the central authority free to act without resistance. Paradoxically, the more democratic individualism is stressed, the more associational life declines and the greater the power of the central bureaucracy to suppress the liberty of the individual.[5]

Carried to its logical extreme, de Tocqueville argues, democratic society degenerates into a mass society in which individuals stand alone, isolated from their fellows, and therefore utterly dependent upon the central bureaucracy for their protection, their happiness, their very life. This analysis brings immediately to mind Edmund Burke's criticism of the French Revolutionaries. (Recall that Burke was the first to comprehend this trend toward mass society.) The revolutionaries were so intent upon granting to each individual certain abstract rights that they were willing to destroy those traditional institutions and associations that, in their minds, stood in the way of the exercise of those rights. But it was these very associations, Burke argued, that preserved rights by checking the power of the central authority, and that made despotism inevitable once they were eliminated. De Tocqueville perfectly agrees with Burke's analysis and for this reason insists that "there are no countries in which associations are more needed . . . than those which are democratically constituted."[6] What is needed, in other words, is a pluralistic society to act as a bulwark against the central power.

Herein lies the great advantage of the American system according to de Tocqueville: It has a rich associational life and, as such, is less likely than other democratic nations to succumb to bureaucratic tyranny. There are in the first place, he notes, highly developed legal associations such as townships, municipalities, and counties that check the power of the national government. These associations not only draw people into local political affairs and thus prevent their political isolation, they also decentralize the process of administration. In the United States, de Tocqueville emphasizes, it is the local authority that collects taxes, implements the laws, and descends to the details of carrying out the decrees of the federal government. Thus, he argues, no matter how powerful the federal government becomes, or how much it reflects the will of the majority, the townships and municipalities prevent it from fully administering the tyranny of the majority. Even "if an oppressive law were passed," says de Tocqueville, "liberty would still be protected by the mode of executing that law."[7]

But even more important than these legal associations, says de Tocqueville, are the voluntary associations, political and otherwise, that abound in American society. "In the United States," he says, "associations are established to promote the public safety, commerce, industry, morality, and religion."[8] More than this, he argues, Americans tend to form extemporaneous associations to handle even the most mundane matters. This habit of association, says de Tocqueville "may be traced even in the schools, where the children in their games are wont to submit to rules which they have themselves established."[9]

Like the permanent legal associations of local government, these voluntary associations act as a check upon the central authority. They attempt to maintain their prerogatives and thus to resist governmental coercion. But apart from this explicit political role, voluntary associations also stand in the way of the tendency of the majority to compel submission to its opinions. One of the key functions of voluntary associations, de Tocqueville argues, is to provide its members with a common opinion that will act as a check upon the otherwise overwhelming power of public opinion. A non-Christian religious association, for example, will provide its members with a common belief system contrary to that of the majority and will morally support its members in the exercise of those beliefs. Without the association, the average individual would lack the moral strength to exercise his or her beliefs publicly. In real life the individual needs the support of others if the power of public opinion is to be resisted.

The right and practice of association is by no means the only factor that de Tocqueville discusses in mitigating the tyranny of the majority in the United States. It is, however, the most important. But the existence of a rich associational life, important as it is, is ultimately dependent upon something even more basic. The fact is, says de Tocqueville, the United States has derived from its historical connection with England a whole complex of ideas and values that support not only the liberty of association but a variety of other liberties as well, such as liberty of the press, religion, and so on. In the final analysis, it is this underlying cultural factor that secures liberty against the potential tyranny inherent in any democratic system.

Herein lies de Tocqueville's real contribution to liberal-democratic theory. In his analysis of democracy in the United States, he had demonstrated that a liberal-democratic government cannot exist apart from a liberal-democratic society.[10] He had shown that it is not sufficient merely to create the legal structure of liberal democracy; it is equally necessary to create a corresponding social structure, and an underlying set of cultural attitudes that are supportive of libertarian values.

Because the United States possessed these attitudes and because its social structure was pluralistic, de Tocqueville was ultimately optimistic about liberal democracy in the United States. Such was not the case in his analysis of democracy in France. That country did not possess a libertarian tradition, since it had been ruled by absolute monarchs up to the Revolution. Nor did it have a truly pluralistic society. The Revolution so thoroughly vitiated those associations that had traditionally checked the monarch's power, such as the church and the aristocracy, that once the old order was gone there was nothing left to check the centralizing tendencies of the new regime. Burke had foreseen all this and had warned of the inevitability of a Napoleonic leader. But once Napoleon had been defeated, the despotical tendencies continued. In *The Old Regime and The French Revolution* de Tocqueville showed that France was moving inevitably toward that bureaucratic centralism that he had warned his readers about in *Democracy in America*.

As we have said, de Tocqueville's analysis of liberal democracy had a great impact on subsequent liberal thought. Clearly, the strict utilitarianism of Bentham and James Mill would have to be revised. It would no longer be sufficient to speak of liberal reform simply in terms of expanding the franchise or creating the legal conditions for democratic rule. De Tocqueville's analysis had demonstrated that such reforms, in and of themselves, may actually contribute to majority tyranny and bureaucratic despotism.

Yet, the thinker responsible for beginning this process of revising liberal theory, John Stuart Mill (1806–1873), was himself a utilitarian. He was the son of James Mill and an important member of the circle of utilitarian reformers. Had John Stuart Mill not been the son of one of the leading utilitarians, he probably would have rejected utilitarianism outright. But so powerful was his father's influence upon him he could never bring himself to explicitly repudiate his upbringing, especially since that upbringing was aimed specifically at turning the younger Mill into a first rank intellectual defender of utilitarianism.

It is interesting that John Stuart Mill's turn away from narrow utilitarianism began with his reading of the Romantic poets, Wordsworth and Coleridge, who espoused in literature what Edmund Burke had espoused philosophically. They emphasized feeling and intuition rather than mere logic and rational categories of thought. And it was this emphasis upon the emotional level of human experience that attracted the younger Mill who, as a young man, was overly exposed to the scientific and coldly rationalistic doctrine of utilitarianism, and whose upbringing in that doctrine had cut him off from so much of what is genuinely human.[11]

But Mill also had read de Tocqueville. And just as the Romantic poets taught Mill that the utilitarian psychology was lacking in human terms, de Tocqueville pointed out to him its sociological inadequacies.[12] Both demonstrated the need for a certain conservative perspective on humanity and society. Taken together, they emphasized along with Burke the emotional aspects of human behavior and the need for human beings to be integrated into some sort of community. They made apparent to Mill the inadequacies of the strictly rational-individualistic perspective of classical liberalism.

What makes John Stuart Mill uniquely important in the development of liberal thought is his revision of the underlying assumptions of the classical doctrine. This de Tocqueville did not do; he was interested in critically analyzing a concrete example of liberal democracy, not in debating the validity of the liberal ideology as such. Mill, on the other hand, was precisely interested in the philosophical validity of liberalism. To his mind, the kinds of concrete reforms that de Tocqueville advocates in *Democracy in America* required a more fundamental reform of liberalism's basic philosophical assumptions.

His most important work in this regard is his tract *Utilitarianism*, published in 1859. He begins, as we would expect from the son of James Mill, by defending the principle of utility as a valid psychology of human behavior and as the basis of moral rules. But no sooner does he assert the validity of the principle than he quite literally modifies it out of existence. This is what he says:

> According to the Greatest Happiness Principle . . . the ultimate end, with reference to and for the sake of which all other things are desirable (whether we are considering our own good or that of other people), is an existence exempt as far as possible from pain, and as rich as possible in enjoyments, both in point of quantity and quality; the test of quality, and the rule for measuring it against quantity, being the preference felt by those who in their opportunities of experience, to which must be added their habits of self-consciousness and self-observation, are best furnished with the means of comparison.[13]

The Greatest Happiness Principle, of course, is Bentham's utilitarian ethics: What is pleasurable is good; what is painful, evil. But Mill's agreement with Bentham is actually a radical disagreement, for he qualifies the Greatest Happiness Principle in a way that actually refutes it. Note that while

Mill agrees that the good is identical to the pleasurable, he also insists that the pleasurable has a qualitative as well as a quantitative dimension. This means that some pleasures are qualitatively superior to others no matter how great a quantity of those others one experiences. It had been Bentham's whole point, however, that all pleasures are equivalent in that they can be quantitatively compared. The values Bentham employs in his felicific calculus such as duration, intensity, fecundity, and so forth, are all quantitative. Bentham assumes that given the choice between two or more pleasures, the best one can be determined by balancing these values against each other, the duration of one, for example, against the intensity of another. So long as pleasures are so conceived they can be quantified, and Bentham's legislator can create "scientifically" "the greatest happiness of the greatest number."

Once quality is introduced into the calculation, the felicific calculus no longer works, and the whole structure of utilitarianism collapses. And this is not only because it is extraordinarily difficult if not impossible to measure quality, but because quality can never be compared to quantity. For Mill, some pleasures are qualitatively superior to others no matter how quantitatively intense those others may be. To employ the felicific calculus to determine the best of such distinct pleasures would be equivalent to adding apples and oranges.

We can best illustrate Mill's distinction by employing a concrete example. Let us suppose we face a choice between spending our lives in the acquisition of wealth and property, or devoting ourselves to philosophical pursuits. Now if, as Mill would maintain, the life of the mind is qualitatively more pleasurable than a life spent in economic activity alone, no mere quantitative increase in our economic well-being can alter the distinction. No matter how wealthy we become, the intellectual life remains, qualitatively speaking, superior. The philosopher will always be happier than the capitalist no matter how successful the capitalist may be.

The question, of course, is how do we know that philosophy or any other pleasure we deem qualitatively superior is really so. Mill's answer is given in the previous quotation. "The test of quality, and the rule for measuring it against quantity," he argues, is the experience of those who in "their habits of self-consciousness and self-observation are best furnished with the means of comparison." Put simply, those who have had the intellectual and moral training necessary to discern quality are capable of determining which pleasures are indeed superior to others.

Now the objection will be raised to this line of argument that Mill has no basis for claiming that some have a judgment superior to that of others in matters of this kind. What right does he have, it will be asked, to claim his opinion is superior to mine? If I am satisfied spending my life making money, why should I take seriously his assertion that I would be happier doing something else? Mill's response has become one of the classic statements in Western political thought:

It is better to be a human being dissatisfied than a pig satisfied; better to be Socrates dissatisfied than a fool satisfied. And if the fool, or the pig, are of a different opinion, it is because they only know their own side of the question. The other party to the comparison knows both sides.[14]

The philosopher, in short, has experienced the lower pleasures as well as the higher. Thus, he or she has a basis for comparison that the average person does not possess. The problem, of course, is that precisely because their experience is limited, most people presume that their judgment is as valid as anyone else's. They do not have the experience to recognize their own ignorance and thus uncritically accept the Benthamite proposition that one pleasure is equivalent to another. In de Tocqueville's words, they imagine that their "petty and paltry pleasures" are every bit as good as the higher pleasures experienced by a Socrates. They make absolutely no distinction between quantity and quality. And to make matters worse, the emphasis upon equality that de Tocqueville had shown is the essence of democratic regimes confirms democratic people in their ignorance. To their mind, if all are equal, then the opinion of a Socrates cannot be in any sense superior to their own.

Two points need to be made here. First, it should now be evident that Mill's distinction between quantitative and qualitative pleasures is no mere academic exercise in moral philosophy. On the contrary, the distinction goes to the very heart of what de Tocqueville had shown is wrong with democratic society. Democratic people's erroneous belief that their opinions are as valid as anyone else's is precisely what lies behind the specter of majority tyranny. People who think differently, and particularly those like Mill who claim to have superior knowledge of how one ought to live, will be suppressed by the vast majority of the ignorant. And like de Tocqueville, Mill recognizes that this tyranny of the majority need not necessarily be political. The overwhelming power of public opinion may be itself sufficient to destroy intellectual liberty regardless of constitutional provisions protecting it.

Second, it is important to recognize that Mill's criticisms of democracy are much more radical than de Tocqueville's precisely because they are based upon a deeper critique of classical liberal philosophy. As we have noted, Mill's distinction between quantity and quality undermines the whole structure of utilitarian theory. Indeed, as many commentators on Mill's philosophy have pointed out, once it is admitted that pleasures are qualitatively distinct, there is little sense in employing the term *pleasure* at all. Clearly, the happiness of a Socrates is something that transcends what we normally mean by the word *pleasure*.

The problem, however, is in the political implications that would seem to follow from Mill's critique. These would seem at first glance to be antiliberal and antidemocratic. Indeed, Mill's argument in certain respects parallels Plato's. Plato had argued that philosophers ought to rule precisely because they have knowledge of what constitutes genuine happiness and well-being.

And, like Mill, Plato had recognized that the key problem with democratic people is their inability to understand that their idea of happiness is an illusion, a shadow in the cave world of opinion.

But Mill most assuredly is no antidemocratic and antiliberal Platonist. Like de Tocqueville, he wants to eliminate the defects of liberal democracy, not abolish it altogether as Plato would do. Mill's underlying epistemology does not admit of Platonic solutions in any case. Plato believed philosophers should rule because they alone grasp the true form of justice. But Mill does not accept the theory of form any more than he accepts the medieval notion of natural law. Despite his revision of utilitarianism, Mill remains an ethical naturalist. No less than Bentham, he rejects the idea of basing moral principles upon any transcendent or a priori ethical order.

Yet Mill agrees with Plato that justice is a crucially important political virtue. To know what justice is and to exercise it in one's life is precisely one of those qualitatively higher pleasures that Mill believes attracts the superior person. But if justice is not an a priori principle, how can it either be known or practiced? Unless this question can be answered, there clearly is no possibility of distinguishing between qualitative and quantitative pleasures, and the threat of majority tyranny remains.

Mill's answer, stripped to its essentials, is that all moral values, including justice, are rooted in utility. Broadly speaking, our concepts of good and evil reflect our self-interest. But not all matters of self-interest are identical. Some of our desires are much more basic than others. The desire for security, for example, is obviously more important than the other desires. Security, or the right to be safe in our person and property, is the basis of every other right we enjoy. As a consequence, Mill argues, the demand for security becomes transformed over time into a qualitatively higher demand for justice by gathering

> feelings around it so much more intense than those concerned in any of the more common cases of utility, that the difference in degree . . . becomes a real difference in kind. The claim assumes that character of absoluteness . . . which constitute[s] the distinction between the feeling of right and wrong and that of ordinary expediency and inexpediency.[15]

The desire for security, which begins as a simple utility or expediency rooted in a primitive self-interest in survival, becomes over time that moral value of a higher order we call justice. And what makes the desire for justice superior to other forms of ordinary expediency is the fact that our feelings and sentiments about it are so much deeper. What began merely as a quantitative difference in degree with other pleasures becomes a qualitative difference in kind. In this way the desire for security is transformed by the intensity of our sentiments into the higher moral value of justice.

The error that so many thinkers have made, Mill argues, has been to assume that because our moral values have the "character of absoluteness" they are rooted in some principle other than utility. Plato, of course, is the classic representative of this "erroneous" school of thought. Because justice had the character of absoluteness, Plato assumed that it is a transcendent form, something beyond the world of "becoming." But justice is neither a form nor a principle of natural law, Mill insists. Like all ethical values, justice is rooted in utility, but so intensely rooted that it becomes qualitatively superior to the "petty and paltry" pleasures associated with simple expediency.

Now, assuming Mill's ethical theory to be valid (and whether or not the intensity of sentiments establishes the objective reality of moral rules may well be debated), justice is indeed a moral value that can be known and practiced in one's life. And it is precisely this act of knowing and practicing the virtue of justice that constitutes the higher qualitative pleasure experienced by superior persons. They do not behave justly simply because they wish to ensure their security, but because they understand that justice is a value far more important than mere security. As such, they wish to embody justice in their lives, not for narrow utilitarian reasons, but for its own sake. Like Socrates, they find a higher form of happiness in the disinterested exercise of virtue.

Justice is not the only political virtue that Mill discusses in his revision of utilitarianism. He is, in fact, best known for his defense of liberty developed in his most famous work, *On Liberty*. Like de Tocqueville, Mill recognizes that liberty, particularly liberty of opinion, is crucial in a democratic society, for it is the one virtue that prevents the tyranny of the majority. And while he of course denies the theory of natural right since he rejects "the idea of abstract right as a thing independent of utility," liberty is nevertheless much more than a simple utility for Mill. It is, like justice, a moral value of a higher order because of its enormous importance to human well-being. Thus, Mill argues,

> I regard utility as the ultimate appeal on all ethical questions; but it must be utility in the largest sense, grounded on the permanent interests of a man as a progressive being. Those interests, I contend, authorize the subjection of individual spontaneity to external control, only in respect to those actions of each, which concern the interest of other people.[16]

Neither state nor society, in other words, has the right to interfere in a person's liberty unless the exercise of that liberty violates the legitimate interests of others. Mill recognizes that there are certain speech-actions that may rightfully be restrained. Shouting "fire" in a crowded theater is the classic case in point. But most actions are not of this nature, and liberty of opinion is almost never of this character, says Mill. As a consequence, he argues, freedom of thought and opinion must be kept free from external constraint in all but the most exceptional cases.

But bear in mind that this inviolability of liberty is based neither on abstract natural right nor on simple utility or self-interest. It is based upon "utility in the largest sense," that is, utility that is "grounded on the permanent interests of a man as a progressive being." What are these permanent interests? They are those that aid people in progressing morally. And moral progress, as we have just seen, is nothing other than the internalization of those complex social sentiments that surround our most cherished values. Liberty is itself one of those values, but it is in a sense the highest of all values according to Mill, for without it we would be unable to think critically about and debate those moral ideals by which we order our lives individually and collectively.

This may be said to be the key point of *On Liberty*. Liberty of opinion is the necessary precondition for human development, for without it we would have no way to determine the values that do constitute the higher qualitative pleasures of human experience. It is precisely in debating our values and ideals that we arrive at the truth of the matter, Mill insists. Thus, any attempt by the majority to prevent dissent actually prevents the truth from being expressed. What inevitably follows is the progressive debasement of humankind rather than its progressive development.

On Liberty has become the classic liberal statement in defense of freedom of expression. Every possible objection that might be raised against it is answered by Mill. Starting from the proposition that truth is the precondition for human development, Mill demonstrates that every opinion, if allowed to be freely expressed, brings us closer to the truth. If an opinion is false, says Mill, its free expression will elicit contrary opinions until the truth is found. If an opinion is a mixture of the true and the false, as is most often the case, freedom of expression and debate will aid in eliminating the false element of the opinion. And even if an opinion is true, says Mill, it should be subject to criticism lest it become meaningless to us, for truths that are not attacked and debated become hollow over time and thus lose their power to influence us for the good.

Apart from the question of liberty of thought and opinion, Mill concludes *On Liberty* with a general argument against governmental interference in the lives of individuals. On the whole, Mill argues, individuals are best left to themselves, both socially and economically (largely for pragmatic reasons, Mill is an advocate of laissez-faire in *On Liberty*, although he would later come to modify this position). And while the argument for limiting the functions of government is not, as Mill admits, strictly identical to the argument for limiting its power over the expression of ideas, the arguments are, in fact, quite similar. For aside from the fact that in most cases individuals are better able than government to do things for themselves, says Mill, individual responsibility encourages that same "progressive development" that freedom of opinion does. Hence, he argues, even when government could do a better job, it is best whenever possible to leave individuals to their own devices, "as a means to their own mental education."[17] And in any case, he concludes, the more functions government performs, the greater the danger that it will become that all-powerful and centralized bureaucracy that de Tocqueville so feared.

It should now be clear why Mill is a defender of liberal-democratic regimes despite his concern with their potential excesses. In theory, at least, they are most capable of creating the conditions for progressive moral development. In liberal democracies people are allowed to choose their leadership, express their opinions, and be responsible for their own lives. Nondemocratic and nonliberal regimes prevent the mass of people from ever experiencing these "qualitatively higher" pleasures and thus deprive them of that moral and intellectual improvement that Mill believes to be humankind's true end.

The problem, of course, is that liberal democracy contains within it contrary tendencies. In theory it encourages moral improvement; in practice it has the tendency to do the very opposite. Rather than encouraging freedom of opinion and individual responsibility, it creates the conditions for majority tyranny and bureaucratic despotism. What to do? Like de Tocqueville, Mill argues that certain safeguards must be built into democratic regimes to prevent these potential abuses. And to Mill's mind there are really only two possibilities: Either an intellectually and morally superior elite must be given special roles within government, or the intellectual and moral level of the mass of people must be raised. Mill advocates both.

The idea of guaranteeing intellectual elites a role within democratic government Mill develops most consistently in his *Considerations on Representative Government*. Among a number of suggested reforms, he proposes plural voting, which gives "intellectual elites" more than one vote as a means by which to check the overwhelming numbers of the majority. In addition, he advocates proportional representation (PR). A PR system (of which there are many different types) guarantees a seat in the legislature for those candidates who get a sufficient proportion of votes less than a majority. Mill believed that this type of electoral system would ensure representation for intellectual minorities, something impossible to accomplish in single-member district, winner-take-all systems in which only that candidate who secures a majority of the vote wins a seat in the legislature. The winner-take-all system was, to Mill's mind, a major contributing factor to the tyranny of the majority.

Plural voting never has been adopted by Western liberal democracies, and we now know that proportional representation does not really accomplish what Mill intended. But what is important for our purposes is the theory behind Mill's advocacy of these reforms, not their practical effect, which is that democratic decision making will lead to majority tyranny unless decisions are informed by something other than public opinion. In theory, Mill's reforms would create just such informed decisions by ensuring a legislative role for moral and intellectual elites. Thus, if riding the crest of popular opinion the legislature were to attempt to pass laws suppressing unpopular minorities—communists, for example—Mill's legislative elite would resist these illiberal tendencies. Understanding the importance of freedom of opinion, and grasping the qualitatively superior life that liberty brings, they would oppose any attempt on the part of the legislature to suppress unpopular ideas.

The idea of creating a legislative elite may seem, at first glance, to violate the premises of democratic decision making. But this is not necessarily the case; it was certainly not so for Mill. He was pursuing a line of reasoning that can be traced back to Aristotle and Cicero. These thinkers recognized, as Mill did later, that pure democracy inevitably becomes the unlawful "mobocracy" of the majority. They therefore proposed mixing "aristocratic" elements into democratic and republican constitutions to check the excesses of popular rule. Aristotle, recall, called this *polity,* Cicero the *composite state.* The purpose was to make democracy work as it ought to, not to eliminate it altogether. This is precisely Mill's objective—to ensure that liberal democracy functions in the manner of Aristotle's and Cicero's ideal rather than as an unlawful and illiberal tyranny of the majority.

Most important in preventing the tyranny of the majority is Mill's argument for raising the intellectual and moral level of the mass of people to an appreciation of liberty and, indeed, of all the "higher qualitative pleasures." This Mill believes can in part be accomplished by the state's providing mass public education for all. And while the idea of state-supported education seems hardly novel today, in Mill's time it was a radical proposal. This was still the age of classical liberalism, and any suggestion that the state involve itself in any but negative functions seemed heretical to many. This attitude was intensified by the fear that the state would destroy liberty of opinion by imposing its views upon students. But Mill makes a careful distinction between providing an education and determining what is to be taught. The state's function, Mill insists, is the former, not the latter.

But is mass education really the answer? It was part of Mill's genius to have recognized that it may actually contribute to the very problem it is supposed to resolve. Basing his argument upon de Tocqueville's analysis of democracy, Mill shows how European society is daily "advancing towards the . . . ideal of making all people alike."[18] Note, says Mill, that

Formerly, different ranks, different neighborhoods, different trades and professions, lived in what might be called different worlds; at present to a great degree in the same. Comparatively speaking, they now read the same things, listen to the same things, see the same things, go to the same places, have their hopes and fears directed to the same objects, have the same rights and liberties, and the same means of asserting them. Great as are the differences of position which remain, they are nothing to those which have ceased. And the assimilation is still proceeding. All the political changes of the age promote it, since they all tend to raise the low and to lower the high. Every extension of education promotes it, because education brings people under common influences, and gives them access to the general stock of facts and sentiments.[19]

In short, every extension of education, along with almost every other change in contemporary society, has the effect of generating a mass society and thus laying the foundation of majority tyranny. Rather than encouraging a variety of opinions, the extension of education has the tendency to produce a mass public opinion. And this, in turn, promotes a breakdown of what Mill terms a "variety of situations," by which he means a breakdown of associational life. Different groups espousing different ideals are destroyed by the very sameness of ideas that mass education promotes.

It is important to note that the problem of mass public education for Mill is not that the state will impose its opinion upon the students; this he believes to be a problem easily rectified. The problem is that mass education, as with any other mass endeavor, inevitably produces a common public opinion. It is not a problem, therefore, that can be overcome merely by changes in curriculum or other such modifications of the educational environment. Mill suggests that the very structure of mass education, and indeed of mass industrial society generally, tends to produce majority tyranny no matter what is done to prevent it. More than this, even what is done tends as often as not to promote it.

Despite these problems, modern liberals continued to make the expansion of mass education a central plank in their reform platform. There was really little else they could do. The egalitarian tendencies of democratic societies in fact precluded special roles for intellectual elites, at least in the legal sense Mill had in mind. Unless the intellectual and moral level of the masses could be raised, therefore, liberal democracy appeared doomed.

This certainly was the position of T.H. Green (1836–1882), an obscure Oxford don little known outside academia. His obscurity does not detract from his intellectual importance, however, for he and his followers, the Oxford Idealists, as they came to be known, laid the foundations of modern liberalism by making the final break from utilitarianism. (This Mill never did do, at least not explicitly, and he is therefore best seen as a transitional figure standing midway between the early classical doctrine and the later theory developed by Green.) As a consequence, Green and his students freed liberal thinkers from a psychological and ethical doctrine that was much too narrow for the kinds of reforms they were advocating.

Green made the break from utilitarianism, as well as from the earlier doctrine of natural rights, both of which were rooted in the British tradition of materialism and empiricism, by drawing upon the German, and particularly the Hegelian, tradition of idealism. (Idealism is the metaphysical opposite of materialism; it posits reality to be other than a material principle.) We shall have more to say about Hegel in the next chapter. For now it is sufficient to note that Hegel demonstrated to Green the existence of a spiritual reality beyond the purely material and the possibility of thinking about social and political matters from the perspective of spiritual ideals.

Following Hegel's lead, therefore, Green argues that a spiritual reality—God—constitutes the rational-moral ordering of the universe. Human beings participate in this ordering through their progressive ability to structure their lives around moral principles that they themselves comprehend and will.[20] They participate, in other words, through their teleological development toward moral autonomy. As a consequence, Green argues that the whole structure of liberal thought from Locke to the utilitarians needs to be revised; for given this larger reality, and humankind's participation in it, it was clear to Green that liberal ideals could no longer be justified in the name of strictly materialist principles, whether in the guise of Lockean natural rights or Benthamite utilities.

Yet, for all of this, Hegel's idealism simply pointed Green in a new direction and provided him with a nonutilitarian point of view. Beyond this, Hegel's influence is really not all that important. Indeed, it is perfectly possible to understand Green's revision of the liberal doctrine without referring to Hegel at all; for, in effect, Green founded the basic ideals of liberalism upon a classical basis. His psychology, sociology, and political theory are rooted in a tradition of thought that begins with Socrates and that in many ways is reminiscent of Edmund Burke.

Thus, Green's psychology or theory of human nature rejects the utilitarian view that the desire for pleasure and the wish to avoid pain is the defining characteristic of the human personality. This view, recall, followed Hobbes in presuming that the will is prior to reason, that we use our intellectual capacity only as a means to calculate how best to get that which our desires prompt us to want. For Green, it is quite the other way around. The utilitarians forget, he argues in his major political work *Lectures on the Principles of Political Obligation* that "in being determined by the strongest motive . . . the man . . . is determined by himself, by an object of his own making."[21] They forget, in other words, that human beings cannot will anything unless they first employ their reason to determine that which they really desire.

Now "the determination of will by reason . . . constitutes moral freedom or autonomy,"[22] Green argues, for it follows that if people themselves determine that which they will, they in effect determine themselves. They become that which they wish to become. This is a crucially important point, for it means, among other things, that it is possible for people to freely determine what kind of social and political order they wish to live in. They are not limited to creating a society that conforms only to the supposed unlimited and uncontrollable desires for property and power.

But what is it then that people ought to will? Green recognizes that human beings have evolved over time and that their ideas of what is morally valuable have changed. But in essence, he argues, this evolution has been increasingly toward recognition that it is reason itself that establishes the validity of moral rules. Whereas "primitive people" obeyed the law for reasons of social compulsion, at a later stage of development human beings obey because they themselves determine that they ought to obey. That is, the possibility of obedience to law as an act of moral freedom is open to them.

The moral person, that is, the one who understands the moral role inherent in their rational capacity, will do just this, Green insists. They will recognize that their completeness as human beings, their "realization of an idea of perfection," to use Green's words, lies in their ability to make their will conform to rational rules of ethical conduct. To do otherwise, to live the life of "pig satisfied," for example, would be to sacrifice one's moral autonomy, hence one's freedom. The moral person recognizes that freedom lies in the subordination of the will to rational rules or laws we ourselves have created.

It is clear that freedom, which Green identifies with rational moral conduct, is the highest human value attainable. In this he is at one with John Stuart Mill, and his idea that freedom involves the "realization of an idea of perfection" is essentially identical to Mill's claim that liberty cannot be conceived apart from "the progressive development of mankind as well." Both ideas of freedom involve the notion of moral development, and Green would certainly agree with Mill that those who argue differently simply lack the experience and the rational training to know otherwise.

But Green was more explicit and thorough than Mill in making this connection between liberty and moral purpose. Indeed, he was the first to employ the term *positive freedom* to describe the connection[23] and to counterpose it to the purely negative idea of liberty held by Hobbes and the utilitarians.[24] Like Rousseau and the ancient Greek thinkers, Green wanted to emphasize that unless there is a positive connection between our actions and some moral purpose, we cannot truly be said to be free.[25]

Green's revision of the classical liberal view of human nature and its corresponding theory of liberty carried with it a revision of the liberal conception of society as well; for if by nature humans are moral beings, it follows for Green, as it did for the Greeks, that they are by definition social beings as well. As such, Green views society not simply as a collection of self-interested individualists, as in the contractual and utilitarian theories of society, but as a structure of traditions, laws, and institutions that unite individuals into a larger ethical whole.

Now it is this larger structure of traditions, laws, and institutions, Green insists, that "constitutes the moral progress of mankind";[26] for if we recognize that human beings are moral (and social) creatures, it follows that their social and political institutions are reflections of their deepest moral impulses. And inasmuch as human beings progress morally over time, since they learn increasingly to live by inner moral reason rather than by outer physical compulsion, it also follows that the institutions they create over time progress morally as well. Liberal democracy, given this analysis, must then be in some sense morally superior to earlier forms of political organization.

But it also works the other way around. If human beings create institutions that embody moral ideas, they themselves internalize those ideas by acting within the institutional framework of their society. This means that in their social and political activities they move toward their goal of moral perfection, which Green has identified as the conformity of will to reason. In his *Lectures on the Principles of Political Obligation,* he puts his analysis in the following way:

> The value . . . of the institutions of civil life lies in their operation as giving reality to these capacities of will and reason, and enabling them to be really exercised. In their general effect, apart from particular aberrations, they render it possible for a man to be freely determined by the idea of a possible satisfaction of himself, instead of being driven this way and that by external forces, and thus they give reality to the capacity called will: and they enable him to realize his reason, that is, his idea of self-perfection, by acting as a member of a social organization in which each contributes to the better-being of all the rest.[27]

Green's analysis can be clarified by an example. Citizens of liberal democracies have a number of political institutions available to them that embody various moral ideals. The essential equality of human beings, the dignity of the individual, and the right of political participation are clearly some of the ideals implicit in the institutional structure of liberal democracy. It follows, then, that to the extent that citizens actively exercise their duties as citizens—vote, discuss issues, perhaps even run for public office—to that same extent they take in the ideals of society. They learn, for example, the importance of liberty of opinion, for they are compelled to recognize that without it they cannot make rational choices in the voting booth. But such recognition constitutes precisely what Green means by the conformity of will to reason. One's actions as a citizen lead to the internalization of the ideal of liberty of opinion such that one comes to actively will it, not simply to accept it as a legal requirement.

Green's political philosophy is simply the logical extension of these altered conceptions of humanity and society. Most importantly, he radically revises the earlier theory of rights. Since reason is not subordinate to the drives and desires, Green cannot accept the theory that rights are rooted in utility. Nor can he accept the even earlier doctrine of natural rights. Clearly, Green argues, if human beings are by nature social animals, "it is only . . . within society . . . that there can be such a thing as a right."[28] In Burke's words, rights are prescriptive.

This is not to mean that the rights of the individual are to be utterly subordinate to the dictates of society. Such a position could hardly be described as liberal. In fact, Green desires an expansion of individual liberty, particularly in regard to intellectual and political activities, for this is what makes moral reason rather than compulsion the basis of social order. Bear in mind that such a goal of "self-perfection" is the whole point behind Green's revision of the classical liberal doctrine.

It is to mean, however, that any claim to a right is a social claim. As such, it is one that must not only involve the recognition of the rights of other individuals, but must also contribute in some way to a larger social good. This holds for all rights including that most important of rights in the liberal tradition, the right to property. Property is a social right, granted by society, and justified only to the extent that it contributes to "the better-being of all," that is, to the moral progress of the whole citizenry. Indeed, like Aristotle, Green sees in the appropriation of property an essentially moral act through which individuals learn, in the act of appropriating, their responsibility toward others. Ideally they learn to control their acquisitiveness for a larger social good, and to use their property in ways that are conducive to the moral improvement of others as well as to themselves.

Herein, of course, lay a crucial problem, in fact the essential issue in the development of modern liberal thought. The conditions of late nineteenth-century industrial capitalism were not at all conducive to the moral use of property. Indeed, Green argues,

> the actual result of the development of rights of property in Europe, as part of its general political development, has so far been a state of things in which all indeed "may" have property, but great numbers in fact cannot have it in that sense in which alone it is of value, viz. as a permanent apparatus for carrying out a plan of life, for expressing ideas of what is beautiful, or giving effect to benevolent wishes. In the eye of the law they have rights of appropriation, but in fact they have not the chance of providing means for a free moral life, of developing and giving reality or expression to a good will, an interest in social well-being. A man who possesses nothing but his powers of labour and who has to sell these to a capitalist for bare daily maintenance, might as well, in respect of the ethical purposes which the possession of property should serve, be denied rights of property altogether.[29]

It cannot be stressed too strongly how serious this debasement of the industrial working class was to the internal coherence of the liberal ideology. Property had always been viewed by liberal thinkers as the very basis of individual freedom. But by the end of the nineteenth century it had become clear that the legal protection of the individual's property rights was in social fact destroying those rights for vast numbers of people. While the capitalist and industrial middle classes were getting richer, the workers were getting poorer. The result, as Green noted, was that for practical purposes the worker had no property rights at all and could not, therefore, be expected to acquire those social and ethical skills that the ownership of property ought to bestow.

Green's "solution" to this problem laid the foundation of the modern liberal theory of the state. According to Green, the state has a clear responsibility to ensure that the distribution of property is such that all citizens share in its benefits. It must take *positive* steps to see that the national wealth does not become concentrated in so few hands that others are deprived of its moral benefits. And Green applied this same logic to other areas of community concerns. He was a great advocate of state-supported public education, as he was of other public ventures that he believed would benefit the moral life of the community.

It was with this reasoning in mind that Green became an advocate of the *positive state* rather than of the strictly negative state favored by the classical liberals. Note here the logical connection between Green's new conception of the state and his theory of positive liberty, a connection discussed extensively in the chapter on Rousseau, for to define liberty positively, that is, in light of moral purposes, leads to the conclusion that the state has a positive responsibility to structure society in ways that allow those purposes to be realized.

Green, nevertheless, remains a liberal. His focal point is the individual, not the state. For this reason, he absolutely rejects the idea that the state should legislate morality, or that it should have the power, as Rousseau suggested, to force any of its members "to be free." The state is to play a positive role, Green argues, only insofar as removing those obstacles that prevent individuals from realizing their moral freedom, such as inequitable property relations, ignorance, lack of healthy living conditions, and so forth. If the state goes beyond this, says Green, if it goes beyond removing "obstacles to the realization of the capacity for beneficial exercise of rights, . . . [it defeats] . . . its own object by vitiating the spontaneous character of that capacity."[30] Put simply, the state cannot take from individuals their capacity for free moral choice without destroying the possibility of individual "self-perfection" that it was created to protect and encourage in the first place.

It is important to bear these points in mind, because they clearly establish Green and his followers as liberals and set them apart from those thinkers, such as Rousseau, who would carry the idea of the positive state to very illiberal conclusions. It is true that they reject the philosophy of utilitarianism and its emphasis upon negative liberty and the negative state, but they do not reject the ideal of the free individual, nor do they reject the corresponding idea that the powers of government must be limited. Liberal democracy remains the ideal political structure. And the sacredness of private property, a key element of the liberal philosophy from Locke on, is reaffirmed. Green wants to modify the principle of private property so as to secure real property rights for all, not to eliminate it altogether.

Such, in broad outline, is the philosophy of modern liberalism, a philosophy first articulated by Green and the Oxford Idealists. Modern liberals since then have not really gone beyond the framework established by these thinkers, although there has been a great deal of evolution within this basic intellectual structure. In Britain, L.T. Hobhouse was perhaps most responsible for carrying on the ideals of modern liberalism. In this country, the key figure was John Dewey who, while not sharing Green's idealist metaphysics, advocated essentially the same social and political ideals as his British counterpart.[31]

In this century, modern liberalism has become a profoundly influential ideology in the industrialized countries of western and northern Europe. Generally speaking, it now constitutes the theoretical basis of the modern welfare state. It took longer in this country for its influence to be felt. Not until Franklin D. Roosevelt and the New Deal were the basic ideas of modern liberalism put into political practice or, for that matter, even recognized as legitimate by most Americans. Until then, the radically individualistic, laissez-faire, and antistatist position of classical liberalism dominated American political consciousness.

A further comment about the liberal tradition in this country is in order here because that tradition is, not without cause, a source of great perplexity to many American students. For historical reasons rather unique to this country, those Americans who espouse the classical doctrine—those who advocate a free market economy, individual responsibility, and the negative state—typically call themselves conservatives. And while they may in fact hold to certain traditional values that are characteristic of Burkean conservatism, their basic perspective remains fundamentally liberal. Those, on the other hand, who call themselves liberal espouse the ideals of the modern doctrine as developed by Green and subsequent thinkers in that tradition.

The real political debate in this country, therefore, is best understood as a debate between an early and later variant of the same liberal ideology, rather than as one between liberalism and philosophical conservatism. Broadly speaking, this is a debate between those who favor an expansion of the welfare state and those who wish to reduce the role of government in society. The Democratic and Republican parties may be said respectively to represent these two positions, but only in a very rough sense, for one can find liberals of both types in either of the parties.

Taking now the modern liberal tradition as developed from John Stuart Mill through T.H. Green, what judgments can be made of it from the historical perspective of the last quarter of this century? On the positive side, most would agree that it possesses several theoretical advantages over the classical doctrine. Most notably, its underlying psychology provides a more real and comprehensive account of that which constitutes humanness than does Bentham's calculus of pleasure and pain. Whatever else may be said of classical liberalism, its utilitarian view of the species is hopelessly narrow, and modern liberals must be credited with recognizing this fact.

The same may be said of the modern liberal view of society: It gives us a much more realistic picture of social relationships. Surely the later liberals were correct in conceiving society as an organic structure of traditions, customs, and institutions that encompass and shape the individual. Every insight in contemporary social science indicates the validity of this point of view. Few serious political analysts today would agree with Bentham that society is nothing more than the sum of its individual parts.

Finally, in terms of political philosophy, modern liberalism's legitimatization of the positive state was the necessary precondition for serious thought about what role the state may appropriately play in social and economic affairs. We may or may not agree that the modern state should be involved in the economic and social life of the community to the extent that it is, or to the extent modern liberals say that it should be, but it is difficult any longer to avoid the issue altogether. Like it or not, the social problems generated by industrial society have impelled state intervention in a host of areas. At the very least, modern liberalism does make it possible to think seriously about the legitimate extent of state intervention.

On the negative side, there are clearly some serious problems inherent in the modern doctrine. As a theory of politics, it is unfortunately subject to various political interpretations. Green's emphasis upon the moral essence of historical institutions, including the state, has led some of his followers to a "conservative" emphasis upon the rights of the state and a corresponding deemphasis upon those of the individual.[32] Others have taken Green's theory of social rights to "socialist" conclusions, arguing for the extensive transformation of property relationships in the name of a higher social purpose (although few of them have been willing to jettison the principle of property altogether). In either case, working from the same philosophical perspective, Green's followers have derived contrary political conclusions.

That Green's political theory can be taken to such various conclusions indicates a basic ambiguity at its core. It may be that liberal ideals simply do not fit very well with the Socratic or "idealist" point of view, and that any attempt to bring the two together inevitably leads to theoretical confusion. Here, clearly, is the advantage of the classical doctrine. Whatever the validity of its underlying psychology and sociology, there is no question about what the respective roles of the individual and state should be.

Connected to these theoretical issues are various practical political problems that have continued to plague modern liberalism. Most seriously, it has not only been unable to avoid those conditions that give rise to majority tyranny, but in many instances has actually contributed to the problem. One cannot say today that public opinion is any less powerful than it was when de Tocqueville and the younger Mill first alerted us to its dangers. Nor can we say that the reforms advocated by modern liberals to aid people in their "progressive development" toward moral and intellectual autonomy always have had their desired effect. Indeed, as Mill in part anticipated, they often have had the very opposite effect. Many of the reforms initiated by the modern welfare state—mass education, social welfare, governmental regulation of the economy, and so forth—have actually contributed to the homogenization of our culture and to a commonality of opinion far beyond anything imagined by Mill.

Of course, the liberal welfare state cannot be blamed entirely for this state of affairs. There have emerged powerful private agents of homogenization that have had a profound impact upon the creation of a common public opinion. Television comes immediately to mind here, as does "Madison Avenue" and the whole technology of consumerism that surrounds it. (Mill had noted this dangerous potential of modern mass communications long before the invention of telecommunications or the development of modern advertising techniques.) But even here the modern state and the liberal philosophy upon which it is based cannot be held completely without fault, for they have been notably ineffective in regulating these agents of homogenization and of checking their sway over public opinion.

Another, related, problem plagues modern liberalism. Rather than removing the obstacles to self-development, many critics, liberals included, now argue that the welfare state itself poses a threat to individual autonomy. And the problem is not simply that people are becoming more dependent upon government and less upon their own initiative. The deeper problem is that as the state takes over more and more social and economic functions, that associational life that de Tocqueville had seen as the basis for individual autonomy and for a plurality of opinions is rapidly eroding. Private as well as local political associations inevitably decline as an increasingly centralized and bureaucratized state takes over functions these associations had traditionally performed. The ultimate consequences of this, the critics argue, may be what de Tocqueville most feared: the happy and willing enslavement of the multitude to a benevolent but all-powerful bureaucratic despotism that rules precisely in the name of equality and democracy.

This problem is intensified by an often elitist social policy on the part of liberals. In theory, the welfare state is to remove obstacles to self-development, not to take over functions best left to individuals themselves. But there has long existed among many liberals a kind of Benthamite belief in the efficacy of social engineering on the part of intellectually trained elites. The line between removing obstacles to self-development and the elitist manipulation of society for people's own good is thus sometimes blurred. The popular complaint about the "do-gooders" in government is, in effect, a complaint about this elitist and undemocratic strain in the liberal tradition.

At an even deeper level, some thinkers now suggest that liberal ideas themselves have become a central part of the problem. They claim that the arguments in *On Liberty* are no longer an alternative to mass public opinion, but have themselves become an integral part of it. And, they insist, it is not, as Mill might have hoped, that the majority employs its liberty to determine what really is socially and politically desirable, but, in the name of liberty of opinion ("everyone has a right to his or her opinion") the majority treats all opinions as equally valid and thus makes no effort at all to distinguish the true from the false.[33] The inevitable result, it is argued, and as Plato originally had foreseen in his account of democracy, is moral anarchy rather than the progressive moral development of the species.

All of these criticisms are ultimately rooted in the fact that the internal consistency of the modern liberal doctrine has begun to break down. The respective roles of the state and the individual have become blurred in modern liberal thought. This same blurring of what had once been clear and definite ideas can be noted in the other dimensions of liberal thought since Green, in the theory of rights for example. And, as we have seen, the doctrine as a whole can be taken to quite different political conclusions. It is no wonder, given this theoretical confusion, that modern liberalism has so often had in practice results contrary to its premises.

It is at least in part clear why theoretical confusion has occurred. The emergence of industrial capitalism, which compelled liberal thinkers to reconsider the classical doctrine in the first place, has created conditions that no longer fit terribly well with modern liberal assumptions. The ideal of ensuring a balance between individual autonomy and state intervention, for example, is very difficult to maintain given the problems inherent in industrial society. The enormity and complexity of those problems—economic, social, environmental, and so forth—seem inevitably to lead to the expansion of state power at the expense of the individual. And a theory that asserts the duty of the state to resolve these problems on the one hand, yet maintains the ideal of individual autonomy on the other, is sure to have problems with the internal consistency of its ideas.

Historically, when a tradition of political thought develops a lack of theoretical coherence, it is almost always a sign that it no longer conforms to social and political reality. It becomes incoherent because it is altered and stretched over time to accommodate changing conditions until, eventually, its initial premises neither correspond to existing reality nor logically fit with subsequent theoretical modifications. Assuming this to be the case with the liberal tradition, as many now do, there is a serious question whether liberalism can once again be revised to fit with the realities of the modern world better than it now does. Certainly the subject of the next chapter, Karl Marx, had no doubt that the liberal ideology had run its course. He not only rejected that tradition of political thought, but rejected it in a way that called into question the most fundamental assumptions about humanity and society that had characterized liberalism from Locke to T.H. Green.

But whatever criticisms we may make of liberalism, even the most radical, let us keep in mind how profoundly important that tradition of political thought has been to the Western world, and how much it expresses some of our deepest and noblest ideals. Beginning with Locke in the seventeenth century and culminating with T.H. Green in the nineteenth, these ideals have remained influential despite the underlying changes in philosophical perspective. Note the persistent affirmation of the worth of the individual, the essential equality of all human beings, the right of political participation, and the right to think, speak, and express oneself freely. Recall the unrelenting demand for limited government, and the invention of new constitutional techniques to accomplish this end. And let us not forget that these ideas and ideals were the basis for major changes in Western political institutions. Liberalism never has been a mere theory of politics; it has always been a major impetus for political reform.

Seen in this historical perspective, we can justifiably conclude that liberalism has in a crucial sense transcended its own theoretical limitations, for it is difficult to imagine any future political philosophy that does not incorporate in some manner those basic ideals that liberals have so long defended. In this sense, liberalism has become Aristotle's wisdom of the ages, for it has established certain principles of political life that most would now hold to be the sine qua non of any civilized state.

Notes

1. Alexis de Tocqueville, *Democracy in America*, 2 vol., rev. Francis Bowen, ed. Phillips Bradley, trans. Henry Reeve (New York: Alfred A. Knopf, Inc., 1945), I:7.

2. Ibid., p. 56.

3. Ibid., p. 274.

4. Ibid., II:336.

5. Alexis de Tocqueville, *The Old Regime and the French Revolution*, Stuart Gilbert, trans. (Garden City, N.Y.: Doubleday, 1955), p. xiii. De Tocqueville elaborates upon the connection between self-interested individualism, the decline of associational life, and despotism as follows: "in a community in which the ties of family, of caste, of class, and craft fraternities no longer exist people are far too much disposed to think exclusively of their own interests, to become self-seekers practicing a narrow individualism and caring nothing for the public good. Far from trying to counteract such tendencies despotism encourages them, depriving the governed of any sense of solidarity and interdependence; of good-neighborly feelings and a desire to further the welfare of the community at large."

6. De Tocqueville, *Democracy in America*, I:202.

7. Ibid., p. 282.

8. Ibid., p. 199.

9. Ibid., p. 198.

10. Although de Tocqueville is often considered to be the founder of modern political sociology, he was not in fact the first modern to grasp the intimate relationship of society to polity. Certainly Burke understood the connection, as did Montesquieu, and others even before them. What de Tocqueville contributed was a concrete understanding of the social conditions necessary for the existence of a viable liberal-democratic political structure. For a further discussion of these facts, and for a general analysis of

de Tocqueville's "sociology," see Jack Lively, *The Social and Political Thought of Alexis de Tocqueville* (Oxford: Clarendon Press, 1965), pp. 43–70.

11. See Robert Denoon Cumming, *Human Nature and History: A Study of the Development of Liberal Political Thought*, 2 vols. (Chicago: University of Chicago Press, 1969), I:378–88, for a discussion of the poetic influence of Wordsworth and Coleridge upon Mill. The influence was more important than simply putting Mill "in touch" with his feelings, for reading these poets caused Mill to seriously rethink the premises of utilitarian psychology.

12. Mill wrote glowing reviews of both volumes of the English translation of *Democracy in America*. These reviews, which demonstrate the profound influence of de Tocqueville's analysis of democracy upon Mill, can be found appended to the Schocken edition of *Democracy in America*. See Alexis de Tocqueville, *Democracy in America*, 2 vols. (New York: Schocken Books, 1961).

13. John Stuart Mill, "Utilitarianism," in *Utilitarianism, Liberty, and Representative Government* (London: J.M. Dent & Sons Ltd., 1910), p. 11.

14. Ibid., p. 9.

15. Ibid., pp. 50–51.

16. Ibid., "On Liberty," p. 74.

17. Ibid., p. 164.

18. Ibid., p. 130.

19. Ibid.

20. Thomas Hill Green, *Lectures on the Principles of Political Obligation* (London: Longman's, Green and Co. Ltd., 1941), pp. 20–21.

21. Ibid., pp. 12–13.

22. Ibid., p. 26.

23. Although Mill is often seen as a proponent of negative liberty, it is clear that his notion that liberty is an aspect of people's self-development puts him in the camp of the proponents of positive liberty. See H.J. McCloskey, *John Stuart Mill: A Critical Study* (London: Macmillan, 1971), pp. 127–28. The problem is that Mill is a transitional figure and thus is not always consistent, either in his theory of liberty or in other aspects of his social and political thought.

24. In his "Liberal Legislation and Freedom of Contract," in T*he Political Theory of T.H. Green* (New York: Meredith Corp., 1964), pp. 51–52, Green defines freedom as "a positive power or capacity of doing or enjoying something worth doing or enjoying." By "something worth doing" Green means something that contributes to our own and our fellows moral development.

25. See the now classic analysis of these two conceptions of liberty in Chapter 3 of Isaiah Berlin's *Four Essays on Liberty* (London: Oxford University Press, 1969).

26. Green, *Lectures on the Principles of Political Obligation*, p. 32.

27. Ibid., pp. 32–33.

28. Ibid., p. 216.

29. Ibid., p. 219.

30. Ibid., p. 210.

31. See L.T. Hobhouse, *Liberalism* (London: Oxford University Press, 1964); and John Dewey, *Liberalism and Social Action* (New York: Capricorn Books, 1963), for a representative example of their respective liberal philosophies. Both of these works provide short but good critiques of the classical doctrine, as well as defenses of modern liberal ideals.

32. Early in this century, a major debate ensued among Green's students about how his philosophy was to be interpreted in terms of the appropriate relationship between the individual and the state. Some argued that the state, as a "moral essence," is higher than the individual; others that the state exists only to aid individuals in developing their capacities as human beings. This latter view was developed most consistently by L.T. Hobhouse in *The Metaphysical Theory of the State* (London: George Allen & Unwin, Ltd., 1918), written as a critique of the ideas of Bernard Bosanquet, a follower of Green, who employed the Hegelian element in Green's philosophy to justify state supremacy. Hobhouse's book, written during World War I, pointed to "the direct connection between Bismarckian ethics and Hegelian teaching," (p. 24). Hobhouse, in short, grasped the illiberal possibilities inherent in Hegelian idealism, possibilities that he argues never led Green to advocate the subordination of the individual to the state, but that are nevertheless inherently dangerous to the integrity of the liberal philosophy.

33. See Herbert Marcuse, "Repressive Toleration," in Robert Paul Wolff, Barrington Moore, Jr., and Herbert Marcuse, *A Critique of Pure Tolerance* (Boston: Beacon Press, 1965), for an example of this kind of critique. See also Robert Paul Wolff, "Beyond Tolerance," in this same work.

═══ **14** ═══════════

Marxism

Communist ideas, in one form or another, have been around for a long time. Plato advocated a communist system for his philosophic rulers, and any number of thinkers since Plato have proposed reordering society along communal lines. But communism in its modern sense did not emerge until the nineteenth century. Like conservatism, it was an ideology created in opposition to liberal ideas. Unlike conservatism, it rejected any attempt to preserve the past. Communists and liberals were in agreement in this regard: The French Revolution had forever destroyed the ancien regime. No less than their liberal opponents, the communists understood that people would have to come to terms with modern industrial society.

In the nineteenth century, communism was simply one variant of a much broader ideological tendency called socialism, a vague term then used to classify a group of thinkers and activists of the most various intellectual and political persuasions. We are able to categorize them as a distinct group only because of their common opposition to the conditions of industrial society and to the liberal ideas upon which that society was based, not because their ideals necessarily had a great deal in common.

The key issue for the socialists, of course, was the deteriorating conditions of the new industrial working class. It is difficult for us in the late twentieth century to appreciate how extremely degrading these conditions were in the early stages of the industrial revolution. But the degradation was very real and, from the perspective of the mid-nineteenth century, it called into question the whole basis of modern society. For the terrible and paradoxical truth of that society seemed to be that every increase in technological progress was matched by an increase in human suffering.

Unfortunately, the early socialists—the most important of whom came to be called the utopian socialists—were neither equipped to explain the cause of this suffering, nor to offer realistic solutions to the problem. As we have noted, they were a group of thinkers of widely disparate tendencies. As such, they could neither agree on what would constitute a viable socialist society nor on how to arrive at it even when they could agree. It is true that the early socialists did as a general rule advocate some form of communal property and exchange, seeing Lockean private property not as the source of rights but, given the conditions of the working class, as quite the opposite. But beyond this there was little agreement. And there was just as much confusion over strategy as there was over theory. Some pre-Marxian socialists were mild-mannered reformers; others were militant revolutionaries. A thinker capable of grounding socialism upon a sound theoretical basis was needed. Only then could socialism be shown to be a real alternative to existing society, and only then could a viable political strategy be developed that would be capable of uniting socialists in a common cause.

Enter Karl Marx, a thinker who not only put socialist ideas upon a sound basis, but who called into question the whole tradition of Western social and political thought. Born in 1818 in Prussia to a middle-class family, he entered the university at the age of seventeen and went on to attain a doctorate in philosophy. Upon leaving the university, Marx moved in 1843 to Paris, which was then the center of the socialist movement. He became acquainted with a number of socialist thinkers and revolutionaries in Paris, and it was there that he met and began working with Friedrich Engels who was visiting the city at that time. The intellectual collaboration of Marx and Engels lasted until Marx's death in 1883.

In 1845 Marx was compelled to leave Paris because of his radical views. He moved to Brussels where he continued to develop his socialist ideas. In 1848, in collaboration with Engels, Marx produced the famous *Communist Manifesto,* a classic of polemic literature. In the same fateful year that the *Manifesto* was published, revolutionary upheavals shook Europe. Marx and Engels initially expected these upheavals to grow into a working-class revolt that would finally produce a socialist society. Their expectations, however, were quickly dashed. It was clear that the workers would have to await another opportunity to play their "revolutionary role," a fact that became of crucial importance to the integrity of the whole Marxian theoretical system, as we shall see at the close of this chapter.

In 1849, after several intermittent moves, Marx took his family to London where he remained until his death. During these years he helped organize the first International Workingmen's Association, an organization comprising some of the early "socialist" and labor groups worldwide. But Marx's most important contribution during the London years was theoretical rather than political. It was during this time that he began his mature work in economics. The result was the publication in 1867 of Volume I of *Capital*, his most important and, justifiably, most famous work. Volumes II and III of *Capital* were brought out subsequently by Engels after Marx's death.[1]

With the publication in 1894 of the final volume of *Capital* (Engels died the following year), Marx's ideas had become the dominant intellectual system within the revolutionary socialist movement. This is still true. Indeed, in this century Marxism has become not only the language of revolution, as much as was liberalism in the period following the French Revolution, but it has remained the source of a profoundly important critique of Western social and political thought.

It is this larger critique, as we shall see, that is important to political theorists, not the specifics of Marx's socialist doctrine, or his particular vision of communist society. Nonetheless, in order to comprehend this larger critique it is necessary to grasp the essential elements of his socialist theory. This is the case because the critique is contained within the theory, a theory that Marx claims to be scientific. Indeed, he termed his theory *scientific socialism* to distinguish it from the utopian variants. He was not content, as were the utopian thinkers, simply to paint pictures of ideal societies. He attempted to demonstrate the scientific validity of his doctrine. This required that he elaborate a much larger intellectual framework than had the early, and frankly primitive, socialists. Because of this larger framework, and because of the unquestioned brilliance with which it was articulated, it had and has continued to have a far larger intellectual impact than the socialist ideas of the pre-Marxian theorists.

Marx's scientific socialism is based upon what he terms the materialist conception of history. To assert the possibility of communism is by definition to assert a historical possibility. This requires, Marx argues, a scientific understanding of history, an understanding that he claims the materialist conception provides. This materialist view conflicts with the concepts of Hegelian philosophy, which in Marx's time, and particularly in Germany, influenced historical studies heavily. You will recall that Hegelian philosophy is based upon an idealist rather than a materialist metaphysics. In Hegel's view, therefore, history involved the working out of a spiritual principle and, as such, it was to be understood in that light. Marx insisted that such a perspective was only leading historians and social theorists further and further from the truth. Rather than studying human beings in history as they really are, as a part of the material world, German thinkers in the Hegelian tradition were caught up in abstractions that, in Marx's mind, simply stood in the way of a scientific comprehension of history.

For this reason, Marx developed his own materialist theory of history by way of a critique of idealism and the idealist interpretation of history. This critique, and the basic outline of his own materialist conception, was published in 1846 as *The German Ideology,* with Engels as co-author. The basic materialist proposition of this work is that "the first premise of all human existence, and therefore all of history . . . [is] that men must be in a position to live in order to be able to 'make history.'"[2] Before people can make history, much less philosophize about it, they must first exist, not abstractly as philosophical categories, but concretely as actual existing material entities. It thus follows for Marx that any valid historical analysis must begin with the ways in which human beings materially produce themselves, both as individuals and as a species. This involves the study of those basic productive or "historical acts," as Marx calls them, by which people provide for the necessities of survival: their modes of providing food and habitation, the technologies they employ in exercising these productive activities, and the social form of reproduction by which the species as a whole is perpetuated.

It is an obvious and indisputable fact, but one that Marx nevertheless insists upon making, that these historical acts of production have "existed simultaneously since the dawn of history and the first men, and still assert themselves in history today."[3] What does change, Marx argues, is not the fact that these acts must always be performed, but the ways in which they are performed. Over time human beings improve their technology and along with it their whole mode of production. Most important for Marx, they alter society as a whole, at the same time, for productive activity is inherently social. These historical acts of production conceived of in their social form Marx calls the *relations of production,* and it follows, given this analysis, that changes in technology must alter the production and along with it the entire society.

For Marx, these relations of production are constituted by the division of labor. In every society, he argues, we find a particular mode of cooperation, corresponding to a particular level of technological development, in which different productive tasks are relegated to different people. The most basic form of the division of labor, he argues, is that manifested in the sexual act. It takes two people each performing a unique role to produce a third. Almost as basic is what Marx calls the "spontaneous" division of labor found in very technologically primitive societies. Here different tasks are assigned on the basis of natural or biological attributes. The stronger will become the hunters, the weaker food gatherers, and so forth.

But there comes a point—the precise historical period is unimportant— at which the division of labor becomes for Marx not only a stable factor in social life, but the very basis of all subsequent social orders. This point, he argues, occurs when there first appears a division between material and mental labor. When a small intellectual class (a priesthood for example) separates out from the mass of manual workers and devotes itself solely to intellectual pursuits, the basic structure of society up to the present day is set.

That structure, Marx argues, is a structure of class exploitation, for while the division of labor is at one level simply a division of activities, at another it is a division of property, that is, of social class. Those who perform certain productive tasks are rewarded more than others, both in terms of the quantity and of the quality of the goods produced by society. For this reason, Marx asserts that "division of labor and private property are . . . identical expressions: In the one the same thing is affirmed with reference to activity as is affirmed in the other with reference to the product of the activity."[4]

In the liberal tradition, of course, differential rewards of property do not, in themselves, constitute exploitation. For Marx, however, since property is, in his words, "the power of disposing of the labour-power of others,"[5] it is inherently exploitive. For example, once the division between material and mental labor has emerged (and in Marx's analysis this is a division of property), the intellectual class is in a position to compel others to provide it with the leisure to engage in the "higher activities" of the mind. This division between mental and manual labor is, of course, a very primitive form of class structure, but it constitutes a model of all subsequent forms of class exploitation.

What is crucial in Marx's analysis is the fact that class exploitation must inevitably lead to class conflict. The exploited class will naturally resist its exploitation (although Marx is careful to point out that this resistance takes many forms and is not always recognized as resistance by the exploited class). Thus, the basic insight of Marx's materialist interpretation of history, summed up in the famous words of *The Communist Manifesto,* is that "the history of all hitherto existing society is the history of class struggles."[6] Capitalist society, in which the proletariat, or industrial working class, resists the exploitation of the capitalist, is simply the most recent example of this history.

Such then is the basic outline of Marx's materialist analysis of history. Beginning with the obvious proposition that "men must be in a position to live in order to make history," Marx logically and empirically derives a sociology of class conflict. This constitutes, as Marx intended, a radically different view of history than that propounded in the idealist philosophies of the Hegelian tradition. But in his rejection of this tradition Marx did more than offer an alternative to it; he attempted to demonstrate how idealist philosophies could themselves be explained in terms of his materialist analysis.

In order to understand Marx's critique of idealism, we shall need to elaborate in some detail the psychological implications of his materialist theory of history, implications summed up in his now famous statement that "life is not determined by consciousness, but consciousness by life."[7] What we think, believe, understand, the whole of our mental processes in short, is determined by our life, that is, by our real material life as it is expressed in the historical acts of production. This means that consciousness is determined by the structure of the division of labor, the resultant class system, and the corresponding modes of exploitation and conflict that are, as we have seen, the social consequences of human productivity.

Marx does not mean to suggest here that consciousness, "in being determined," is to be understood as something distinct from or independent of material life. Quite the contrary: Marx believes this to be the fundamental fallacy of idealism. Life determines consciousness, according to Marx, precisely because consciousness is a part of life. It is a particular manifestation of material life: an organization of the material mind that reflects a material reality. Nor, given this materialist view of consciousness, does Marx mean to argue that consciousness is mechanically determined. Clearly, if consciousness is an intimate aspect of material life, it must in some sense itself shape material reality, a matter we shall discuss in some detail subsequently. What Marx does mean to say, simply, is that consciousness must be understood within the context of a larger material (social) reality, and that this reality determines consciousness in the sense that it sets the basic parameters within which consciousness functions.

Now, bearing these qualifications in mind, Marx goes on to argue that a given class system will determine (that is, set the parameters of) a corresponding form of consciousness. He does not mean by this that everyone will have the same thoughts, or that every individual will think exactly the same way as every other individual. Indeed, different classes, precisely because of their different social positions and productive roles, will possess their own unique "class consciousness," according to Marx. He means simply that, in a general sense, every society possesses a common stock of values, beliefs, and attitudes that justify existing society and existing class relations.

It follows, therefore, that any change in the productive or class relations of society must lead to a corresponding change at the level of consciousness. For this reason, Marx asserts that "men, developing their material production and their material intercourse, alter along with this their real existence, their thinking and the products of their thinking."[8] In the act of producing, people change not only their real social existence—the division of labor and class structure—they change the very structure of their consciousness.

In his preface to *A Contribution to the Critique of Political Economy,* Marx elaborates upon this connection between social life and social consciousness. In every society, he argues, we find that the "relations of production . . . correspond to a definite stage of development of . . . [the] . . . material productive forces."[9] Broadly stated, a given class system (which, of course, implies a particular form of the division of labor, of property, and of economic life in general) always corresponds to a given level of technological development. And the sum total of these class relations or relations of production, Marx continues, "constitutes the economic structure of society, the real foundation on which rises a legal and political superstructure and to which correspond definite forms of social consciousness."[10]

This distinction between the economic structure or substructure of a society and its corresponding superstructure constitutes an important element of Marxian social analysis. Note that the economic substructure of society determines the superstructure of consciousness. This is simply another way of saying that life determines consciousness. But also note that this super-structure of consciousness corresponds to legal and political institutions that are also superstructural, that is, determined by the economic base of society. Thus, stated in its most general form, the economic (class) structure of society determines its political structure and determines as well corresponding social and political beliefs and values.

What does this have to do with the critique of idealism? The answer is contained in a final but crucial element of Marx's analysis. According to Marx, this superstructure of political consciousness, and indeed the whole cultural apparatus of ideas, beliefs, and values, constitutes misperceptions of social reality. Thus, while it is true that life determines consciousness, it does not determine it in ways that necessarily illustrate the true character of social life. Indeed, consciousness not only mistakes the nature of social reality, says Marx, it plays the role of justifying the very reality that gives rise to these misperceptions to begin with. Marx calls these forms of social misperception "false consciousness," his definition of ideology. (Bear in mind here that ideology has this special connotation for Marx and is not to be confused with the broader meaning we have discussed in the chapter on Burke and that we will continue to employ in the final chapter.) And this propensity to generate false consciousness or ideology Marx believes to be one of the chief characteristics of any social order divided by social classes.

There are a variety of ways in which consciousness may be characterized as ideological. We shall see subsequently why Marx believes most political ideas, and particularly liberal ideas, may be so characterized. For now, we want to understand the connection between Marx's theory of ideology and his critique of idealism. Obviously, Marx considers idealism to be an ideology, that is, a false perception of reality. What is important here, however, is its particular character as an ideology. It is, says Marx, essentially a religious ideology in the guise of a philosophy. And the key characteristic of any religious ideology, he argues, is that it assumes that God makes man. It is quite the other way around, says Marx: Man not only makes God, he makes the entire superstructure of consciousness in the process of his material development. Religious ideology thus promotes the greatest illusion of all, says Marx, for it posits consciousness, in the form of God or spirit, as something independent of, higher and more real than, the material world. This is precisely what idealism does. It is no wonder, Marx argues, that idealists who draw upon Hegel inevitably make the mistake of viewing history not as "a question of real, nor even of political interests, but of pure thoughts."[11] Rather than analyzing people's actual material life as it is manifested in real class conflict, they "move in the realm of the 'pure spirit' and make religious illusion the driving force of history."[12]

The problem with the ideology of idealism, however, is not just that it misperceives the real nature of social reality, although for the historian and social philosopher that is quite serious enough. The deeper problem is that, as with any ideology, idealism tends to perpetuate the very social conditions that give rise to it in the first place. At bottom, Marx argues, these are conditions created by the existence of social classes. Ideologies, idealism included, thus tend to perpetuate existing class relations. In the case of religious ideology, the problem for Marx is obvious. Religion acts as a mechanism of psychic escape for those—the worker for example—who, because of their class position, suffer real economic exploitation. By positing a God who will reward the worker with perfect justice in the next world for suffering gladly the injustices in this, religion, in Marx's analysis, prevents the worker who accepts its authority from ever changing those class relations that are the source of his or her misery. It is for this reason that Marx insists, in his now infamous statement, that religion is the *"opium* of the people."[13] Like opium, religion is a form of mental escape from real problems and real distress. And as a mechanism of escape, it prevents the sufferer from changing existing conditions as surely as does opium.

This same analysis, though less obvious, applies to idealism. As we have seen, in Marx's analysis idealism is simply a religious ideology in philosophical clothing. It could be described as the "opium of the intellectual" for, once accepted, it dulls the critical sense. In assuming the existence of some supposed spiritual reality that transcends such "mundane" matters as real human misery, the intellectual is prevented from ever grasping the class basis of that misery and thus from ever playing a truly critical role in social reform.

It is clear, then, that, as with other ideologies, idealism arises out of existing class relations and aids in their perpetuation. But precisely what is the mechanism by which this connection is created and maintained? Marx's answer constitutes the final and brilliant element of his critique of idealist philosophy. Clearly, Marx argues, if life determines consciousness, it follows that the idealist inversion of life and consciousness can only be explained by an actual "inversion" in social life itself. And, says Marx, this turns out to be precisely the case, for idealism emerges at that precise historical juncture at which the division between mental and material labor first appears. Once society has evolved to the point where it is possible for the mass of manual (material) workers to support a separate intellectual class, at that precise point idealism emerges, for now, says Marx,

> Consciousness *can* really flatter itself that it is something other than consciousness of existing practice, that it is *really* conceiving something without conceiving something *real;* from now on consciousness is in a position to emancipate itself from the world and to proceed to the formation of "pure" theory, theology, philosophy, ethics, etc.[14]

The conclusion to be drawn is clear. Idealism cannot exist without a separate intellectual class. This means, as a general theoretical proposition, that class exploitation is the source of idealist philosophies and, indeed, of all forms of false consciousness. And it is clear why this is so, says Marx. The division of labor has been shown to be a division of property as well as a division of functions. The intellectual class, therefore, does not merely perform a different activity than others; it is disproportionately rewarded for its activity. It becomes the first propertied class and, as such, is in real economic terms "superior to" or "higher than" others. This economic superiority constitutes the intellectuals' actual social condition and it is this that of necessity determines their consciousness. Since the intellectuals are in fact socially superior, they come to believe not only that their role within the division of labor is superior to that of others, but that the products of their activity, their ideas and philosophies, are superior as well. This superiority is affirmed by making ideas themselves "higher than" and "superior to" the real material world. This, says Marx, is why idealism conceives of reality as some purely intellectual category such as "God" or "spirit" that not only exists independently of the material world but that supposedly is the cause of its existence.

An obvious example of this relationship between social class and the ideology of idealism can be seen in Plato's theory of form. Form, according to Plato, is a transcendental reality that this world only imperfectly "participates in." In Plato's political theory, therefore, the object is to make justice in the state conform as nearly as possible to justice in its ideal transcendent reality. This, you will recall, is to be accomplished by making philosophers rulers.

This, of course, is precisely Marx's point: The idealist philosophy of form cannot be conceived apart from the notion of philosophic rulership. In Plato's time the division between mental and manual labor had reached that point where the philosophers were in a superior social position, believed their social superiority ought to be given political form, and legitimized their claim to power with an idealist theory of justice that they alone could understand.

It is now possible to grasp the truly radical character of Marx's critique of idealism. He in effect reduces the whole of the idealist tradition since Plato to the status of ideology. (As we shall see, Marx applies this same critique to earlier materialist philosophies as well, for he was convinced that, despite their materialist metaphysics, they failed really to go much beyond idealism.) Moreover, the critique of idealism was such that it seemingly confirmed Marx's own materialist interpretation of history. In showing the connection between social class and idealist philosophy, how the latter arose out of the former, Marx believed he had substantiated his basic premise that life determines consciousness and not, as idealism presumed, the other way around.

This rejection of idealism was the necessary first step in Marx's materialist analysis of history, but only the first step, for *"the task of history . . . once the other-world of truth has vanished, [is] to establish the truth of this world,"* [15] says Marx. It is the task of history, in other words, to analyze people's real material conditions and the social possibilities inherent in them once the illusory world of idealism and of ideology in general has been exposed.

What then is the truth of this world? The truth, Marx argues, is that the capitalist system is by its own inherent economic laws self-destructive. The disintegration of the capitalist mode of production, and thus of its whole political superstructure and accompanying forms of false consciousness, is historically inevitable. Most important, Marx insists, is the truth that communism must just as inevitably arise out of the ashes of the ruined capitalist order.

We can only briefly summarize Marx's actual analysis of the capitalist mode of production. (It is important to realize that what follows is the barest outline of a detailed economic analysis that took Marx an entire lifetime to complete.) The basic premise of that analysis, of course, is that capitalism, like every earlier economic system, is based upon class exploitation.[16] In the case of capitalism, this exploitation is inherent in capital itself, which, as with any form of property, Marx considers to be nothing more than expropriated labor. But it is a particular form of expropriated labor. What the capitalist makes as profit, says Marx, is the surplus value realized by the expropriation of the economic value created by workers. Workers are paid subsistence wages, that is, paid enough to maintain them sufficiently to ensure their continued capacity to labor; but they are required to produce much more value than they realize in wages. This surplus value, taken by the capitalist as profit, is called capital. (It is for this reason that Marx considers capital and wage labor to be equivalent terms.)

Inherent in this analysis is the labor theory of value, a theory often attributed to Marx but which in fact he took from the liberal economists themselves. The theory asserts that the market or exchange value of any commodity is the amount of labor embodied in it. (A commodity for Marx is any product produced for the purpose of market exchange.) It follows, therefore, that capitalist profit is the expropriation of the economic value created by workers, and the precise mechanism of this expropriation, according to Marx, is quite simple. The capitalist simply compels the workers to work longer than the time it requires to create sufficient value to pay them subsistence wages. He compels them, for example, to labor for sixteen hours rather than the eight or ten hours it requires to generate enough economic value to maintain them.

But why do workers accept such exploitive conditions? The answer, Marx argues, is that they have no other choice. The capitalist owns the means of production (factories, machines, the material instruments of production in general) and thus controls the only means of livelihood available to them. And, it must be added, the capitalist has no choice in this whole matter either. He must exploit the worker as surely as the worker must be exploited, for the capitalist operates within a competitive market system in which the failure to generate profit spells economic doom. In their own way capitalists are as much victims of the capitalist relations of production as are the workers.

Now it is clear, given this structure of economic relationships, that workers are transformed into little more than commodities, something to be purchased on the market at the lowest price possible. Their only value is the market value of their labor power, not their value as human beings. For these reasons, Marx insists that the exploitation, hence misery, of the proletariat is much more extreme than that endured by earlier productive classes. In his analysis of the feudal mode of production, for example, Marx notes that medieval workers were protected by institutions and long-standing traditions that ensured their livelihood and at least a modicum of economic equity. But capitalism, says Marx, "has put an end to all feudal . . . relations . . . and has left remaining no other nexus between man and man than naked self-interest, than callous 'cash payment.'"[17] Under these conditions, not only is the economic condition of the proletariat debased beyond human toleration, but the nexus between the worker and the capitalist ceases even to be a human relationship. Thus, unlike any previous productive class, the proletariat is not only made miserable in the narrow economic sense, it is quite literally dehumanized.

Marx employed the term *alienation* to describe this dehumanization, and he devoted much theoretical effort in his younger years to analyzing the nature of alienation in a capitalist system. His chief work on this subject is *The Economic and Philosophic Manuscripts of 1844*. In this work, Marx argues that alienation is the chief characteristic of the capitalist order, and by *alienation* Marx means the separation of our specific human qualities, our "species being," as he termed it, into structures of domination. The class divisions generated by the existence of capitalist private property, of course, constitute the chief example, and indeed the basic source, of such alienation. Given these class divisions, workers are separated from the capitalists and, once separated, dominated. Indeed, it is precisely in their separation, that is, in the alienation of their innate human capacity for community with their fellow creatures, that the domination of the worker becomes possible.

Given this basic form of separation-domination, the entire world of workers becomes an alienated reality, Marx argues. They are alienated from the fruit of their labor, which is expropriated by the capitalist as profit. What rightfully belongs to workers as a direct human expression of their productive life is separated from them and then, in the form of surplus value or capital, becomes the source of their domination and exploitation. More than this, the whole technological infrastructure of industry takes on an alienated character. Rather than the machine being an extension of their human powers, workers become an appendage of the machine, for inasmuch as they do not own the means of production, they are incapable of employing technology for their own direct human benefit but must use it as the capitalist dictates.

All of these various forms of alienation achieve their highest and most tragic character in self-alienation, according to Marx. Having alienated the power to act upon the world in a directly human way, the workers finally alienate the power even to comprehend that world. Given Marx's proposition that life determines consciousness, it must follow that where life has become alienated, so too must consciousness. It is clear from this analysis that alienated consciousness is nothing other than false consciousness, or ideology. The natural human ability to comprehend reality is quite literally separated from the workers by the conditions of their lives and replaced by false perceptions of reality. These perceptions, by blinding the workers to their real conditions and therefore preventing them from changing those conditions (as in the case of religious ideology), constitute structures of mental domination.[18]

Given such extreme misery and alienation, particularly the alienation of consciousness itself, one may well wonder how Marx could assert the inevitable demise of capitalism. He has described a seemingly perfect and unalterable system of exploitation. Workers have no choice but to submit to the expropriation of their labor, and in the very process of submission develop forms of consciousness that prevent them from even grasping the true reality of their condition, much less from changing it.

But there is a catch, a fatal flaw, an inherent contradiction that the capitalist system cannot resolve, Marx argues. No matter what the capitalist does, the inevitable tendency inherent in the capitalist system is for the rate of profit over all to decline until the system finally disintegrates in its entirety. Marx termed this tendency the "law of the falling rate of profit," a law that he believed to be every bit as inevitable and unchangeable as any law of physics.

Marx's reasoning may be briefly summarized as follows: Capitalists are subject to the exigencies of the market no less than workers, albeit from the other side of the situation. Whereas workers are in competition with each other to sell their labor, capitalists are in competition with other capitalists to purchase it. Given this demand for labor, the inevitable result is the tendency for the cost of labor to rise and, conversely, for the amount of profit or surplus value to decline. In order to maintain profits, the capitalist is compelled therefore to find some means to depress wages. This, Marx argues, is accomplished by the introduction of labor-saving machinery. As machines are introduced, unemployment increases, indeed increases to such an extent that there is created what Marx calls an "industrial reserve army" of unemployed workers. Given the inherent laws of the market, labor once again becomes cheap as desperate workers compete with each other for an ever declining number of jobs. Wages are thus depressed and profits increase.

But do they? Only in the short run, Marx insists. Since labor is the source of value, the less that labor is employed the less value overall will be created. (The machine cannot produce more value than it took to create it, but only increase surplus value by depressing wages.[19]) Moreover, the more that unemployment increases, the fewer the people capable of purchasing the products created by the capitalist. Hence, the very tactics used to increase profits must, in the long run, have precisely the opposite effect.

Let us emphasize that there is nothing the capitalist can do about these contradictions. The market, which is the essential precondition for commodity production and hence of capitalist accumulation, pits every capitalist against all others. Under such conditions of competition each capitalist is compelled to introduce new technologies lest he lose his competitive edge and is gobbled up by the successful capitalists. Indeed, the stakes in this game are extremely high, for the failed capitalist, Marx points out, will be forced into the ranks of the proletariat. In his own way, the capitalist is as desperate as the worker and is forced to behave in ways that are in the long run self-destructive.

Marx generalizes this analysis by noting that at a certain stage in every economic system, capitalism included, "the material productive forces of society come in conflict with the existing relations of production."[20] Put simply, the property or class relations come into conflict with the rational development of technology, and with the rational use of that technology. In the case of capitalism, for example, technological improvement only serves to increase the misery of the working class on the one hand (mass unemployment and extreme alienation) and further destabilize the capitalist class on the other (declining rates of profit). At that point at which it is no longer possible for the economic system to overcome the conflict, at the point says Marx where "all the productive forces for which there is room in it have developed,"[21] capitalism will disintegrate.

In the meantime, Marx paints a picture of capitalism driven to ever more desperate, and ultimately irrational and futile attempts to stave off the inevitable. The intensity of capitalist competition increases in precise proportion to the decline of the system as a whole. Technologies are introduced at a feverish pace with resulting overproduction of commodities on the one hand and increasing unemployment on the other. The consequences of this "anarchy of production," as Marx terms it, are periodic depressions in which all of the productive forces that had evolved up to that point are destroyed. Society, says Marx:

> suddenly finds itself put back into a state of momentary barbarism; it appears as if a famine, a universal war of devastation had cut off the supply of every means of subsistence; industry and commerce seem to be destroyed; and why? Because there is too much civilization, too much means of subsistence, too much industry, too much commerce.[22]

Any one economic collapse does not spell the end of capitalism, of course. Quite the contrary. The depression allows the whole process to begin anew, and the conquest of new markets temporarily forestalls the next crisis.

(Marxists view the age of colonialism in precisely this light.) But this does not prevent the law of the falling rate of profit from working its inexorable logic. It simply extends the range of the capitalist mode of production until the whole world has been transformed into a gigantic capitalist system. This, says Marx, paves the way for more serious and extensive economic collapses and diminishes each time the sphere of expansion in which capitalism can overcome its inherent contradictions.

Such, then, is the inevitable demise of capitalism according to Marx. But note that behind the "falling rate of profit" and the other economic abstractions Marx employs to describe this process is the actual fact of human misery and alienation. The more capitalism produces, exploits new markets, and advances technologically, the more miserable and alienated the proletariat becomes. And this, as it turns out, is the crucial fact, for the inevitable demise of capitalism described in abstract economic terms is the inevitability of the overthrow of that system by a revolutionary class that the system itself produces. As Marx notes, what the capitalist class "produces, above all, is its own gravediggers."[23] With the revolutionary rise of the proletariat, in the now famous words of *Capital,* "the knell of capitalist private property sounds. The expropriators are expropriated."[24]

How accurate is this analysis of the capitalist mode of production? We shall return to this issue shortly, for it played a crucial role in the later disintegration of the Marxist movement into various factions. But we must first add one more element to the analysis if it is to be complete. It is thoroughly dialectical. It is an analysis premised upon the dialectical model of social and historical change, which, paradoxically given his critique of idealism, Marx derived from Hegel. Hegel, in turn, had evolved the idea of the dialectic as a means of dealing with certain intellectual dilemmas arising out of modern philosophical thought. These dilemmas are not important for our purposes, nor were they for Marx. What was important to Marx was the form of social and historical analysis inherent in dialectical thinking, which he believed had certain advantages over other theoretical perspectives. In order to understand these apparent advantages, we must discuss briefly Hegel's dialectical philosophy and the modifications that Marx introduces into that intellectual system.

For Hegel, the dialectic was a method of analysis based upon the idea that truth is something that evolves out of contradictions. In dialectical analysis one cannot therefore grasp truth by normal logical means. Logic, as opposed to dialectics, is static and noncontradictory: Something *is* or *is not* and remains so eternally. In dialectical thinking, *is* and *is not* form a nonstatic and self-contradictory whole that transforms itself into higher truths. And while this form of reasoning might seem to roughly resemble the Socratic dialectic of philosophical disputation, there is this important difference: Hegel conceived the dialectic to be a cosmic principle inherent in nature, history, and thus the consciousness of humankind itself. This meant that the self-contradictory and self-transforming nature of dialectical logic (the transformation of the *is* and *is not* into higher truths) is also the logic of historical development. Hegel thus considers that each social stage in historical evolution must, over time, give rise to new and higher forms of society.

Hegel, of course, put his dialectical philosophy within an idealist framework. He believed that the dialectic was the working out in history (and in nature and consciousness as well) of an ultimate spiritual reality he called the Absolute Idea. When human consciousness finally recognizes this ultimate reality, the dialectic of history is complete. In the meantime, each socio-historical epoch represented for Hegel the highest stage of development so far achieved toward that end or completion, toward the "realization of spirit" as he would put it. For this reason, Hegel's dialectic became a conservative justification of the existing order, specifically of the Prussian state. In his words, "what is real is rational," that is, what exists is rationally or philosophically justified as the highest expression of the cosmic order of things then attainable.

While adopting the dialectic as a model of historical transformation and, hence, as a method of social analysis, Marx utterly rejected these other elements of Hegel's philosophy. In the first place, as we have seen, Marx viewed the whole notion of an ultimate spiritual reality as idealist nonsense, a religious ideology elevated to the rank of a philosophy. For Marx, the dialectic was an expression of the material reality of class conflict. Transformation to new and higher forms of society were to be explained by the periodic transformation of class relationships. In the second place, he rejected the conservative interpretation of the dialectic. In dialectical logic, the *is* and the *is not* are organically united into a self-transforming whole. Hence, while it is dialectically true that the "real is rational," its opposite—the "rational is real"—is (as Hegel himself recognized) also true. This means that it is perfectly consistent with dialectical analysis to actively strive for a more rational ideal of society than that which exists so long as it can be shown to be the next dialectically necessary stage in social development. Hence, as Engels puts it "in accordance with all the rules of the Hegelian method of thought, the proposition of the rationality of everything which is real resolves itself into the other proposition: All that exists deserves to perish."[25] In short, the revolutionary transformation of capitalism ("the real") into communism ("the rational") is legitimized by dialectical analysis.

It is by these inversions of the Hegelian system that Marx transforms the dialectic into a materialist and revolutionary doctrine. (In Engels's now famous statement, "the dialectic of Hegel was . . . turned off its head, on which it was standing, and placed upon its feet."[26]) What is ultimately important, however, is not so much the logic behind Marx's revision of Hegel, but the concrete ways in which he employs the dialectic as a method of social analysis once he has separated it from the idealist and conservative mold in which Hegel and his disciples had put it.[27] In Marx, the dialectic becomes the means by which to grasp the essential nature of the capitalist order, and to demonstrate its inevitable transformation into communism.

Yet, as Marx would be the first to insist, nothing is proven either about the nature of capitalism or the possibility of communism by the mere assertion of dialectical principles. What is required is a concrete, empirical analysis of the actual economic structure and tendencies of the capitalist mode of production. The whole point of Marx's critique of Hegel's idealism, after all, was to get to the empirical "truth of this world." But facts do not "speak for themselves"; the empirical world must be analyzed from some theoretical perspective. This is all the dialectic is for Marx: a perspective, a way of thinking that he believes best illuminates the nature of social reality.

We can now see in Marx's empirical examination of the capitalist mode of production the profoundly dialectical nature of his analysis. Note that the relationship between capitalist and proletariat is conceived of as an organic unity of positive and negative, as an *is* and *is not* relationship. In the drive to accumulate surplus value, the capitalist creates the proletariat, but it is just as true that in generating surplus value the proletariat creates the capitalist. It thus follows dialectically that the structure of mutual self-creation must become a structure of mutual self-destruction given the inherent suppression of one class by the other. This, of course, is precisely the conclusion of Marx's analysis. In degrading and alienating the proletariat to an extent unknown to earlier productive classes, the capitalist creates its own "gravediggers." But by the same token, the proletariat cannot destroy the capitalist as a class without destroying itself, for given Marx's analysis wage labor cannot exist apart from capital. (In the language of dialectics, this is known as the "negation of the negation.")

Finally, such a radical restructuring of class relationships, given Marx's economic analysis, must inevitably lead to the transformation of society as a whole, to a new synthesis or higher stage of social relationships. This is precisely the assumption upon which the dialectic, as a model of historical development, rests. And it is clear why this assumption holds in Marx's analysis, for he has already demonstrated that the radical alteration of class structure, in this case to the higher synthesis of classlessness, must lead to the wholesale transformation of the legal and political superstructure of society and, along with it, to the transformation of accompanying forms of consciousness.

How valid is this dialectical analysis? We have, of course, every right to question the appropriateness of the dialectical model, just as we do with any other theoretical perspective. And indeed, a great deal of criticism has been directed at the dialectic, particularly in terms of its underlying philosophical assumptions. But it is important, at the same time, to appreciate the potential advantages in any given perspective. In the case of the dialectic, Marxists argue that these advantages are clear, for the dialectic, they insist, constitutes a much more realistic conception of social relationships than that which we find in the liberal point of view. The dialectical model points not only to the "obviously" organic nature of society, but to the underlying reality of conflict that must pertain where there exists class exploitation. Moreover, they argue, this conflict view of society compels the theorist to conceptualize society as nonstatic and self-transforming, and therefore to look for those social tendencies that impel change to "new and higher forms" of social organization.

The classical liberal view with which Hegel and Marx were familiar, on the contrary, did not conceive of society as an organic whole. The early liberals were social atomists who, as we have seen, saw society as little more than a collection of individuals. They had therefore little appreciation of the existence of class conflict or, consequently, of the possibility of existing society ever being transformed into something radically different. It is for this reason that "the facts" of capitalist society did not mean for them at all what they meant for Marx. The question is, Which model of society (if either) best explains the facts? Here the reader must decide for him- or herself.

But here we confront two problems. First, even if we accept Marx's materialist and dialectical analysis of history, how does it follow that a proletarian revolution will of necessity produce a classless or communist society? We may, if only for the sake of argument, grant Marx his dialectical premise that the proletariat is the revolutionary negation of the capitalist system, but what is to prevent the proletariat from simply becoming a new exploiting class? This, after all, is what has happened in the case of every earlier revolutionary transformation, as Marx's own analysis bears out.

The answer is already contained in Marx's economic analysis of capitalism. Inherent in that analysis is the basic materialist premise that life determines consciousness. What this means, in terms of the revolutionary role of the proletariat, is that the worker's consciousness is an ideological misperception of the true nature of his condition only so long as capitalism remains viable. But at the point where that economic system can no longer function, a point at which the worker's misery has reached such an intolerable level that he has no choice but to revolt, he will, in Marx's words, be "compelled to face with sober senses his real conditions of life and his relations with his kind."[28] He will, in short, be compelled to recognize, by his unique social position within the productive apparatus of capitalism, that it is private property and the existence of social class that are the source of his dehumanization, and that only by their forcible overthrow can he realize his true humanity.

It is because of this capacity to grasp the true nature of private property, to understand its inherent exploitive character as such, that Marx accords such a unique status to the industrial working class. Unlike the utopian socialists who saw the proletariat as simply the "most suffering class," Marx saw it as a class with worldwide historical significance. Because of its real material life—its propertylessness and subsequent degradation—Marx believed the proletariat alone had the capacity to comprehend intellectually the source of alienation and dehumanization and, therefore, to eliminate it in its entirety. No earlier productive class could possess such a radical insight, nor therefore initiate such a radical revolution against existing conditions.

It is consistent with Marx's materialist view of history, then, that communism must inevitably arise out of the ashes of the capitalist order. (Whether it is true or not is another matter.) Yet, here we confront a second, related problem. Marx bases his assertion about the inevitability of communism upon the unique revolutionary role of the proletariat. In Marx's analysis, communism is inevitable in the final analysis only because a proletarian revolution is inevitable. Why, then, given its inevitability, does Marx constantly call for revolution? Why is it necessary to actively work to bring about that which must occur of necessity? Indeed, to work for it would seem to imply doubts about its inevitability and, by extension, about the whole underlying materialist conception of history.

The answer to these questions constitutes a final, and crucial, element in the Marxian philosophy. The issue, in its essence, is whether or not that philosophy is strictly deterministic. Are human beings utterly determined by historical-material conditions, or are they in some sense determining? Marx insists that they are both. To assert that the workers will revolt is, at the same time, to assert that they ought to revolt. Marx combines the *is* and the *ought*, the objective analysis of historical reality with a subjective call for revolutionary action. This combining is known as the unity of theory and practice, or *praxis,* and may be said to be the defining characteristic of Marxism. Theory constitutes objective analysis of historical conditions, practice, revolutionary action aimed at transforming those conditions. For Marx, the overthrow of capitalism must involve both.

Now the idea of praxis is most clearly developed in a short eleven paragraphs, or theses, that Marx had written to himself in 1845. These paragraphs, known as *The Theses on Feuerbach,* argue for the unity of theory and practice by way of a critique of another materialist social philosopher named Ludwig Feuerbach. What made Feuerbach important to Marx was that he was the first to transform Hegel's dialectic into a materialist doctrine, the purpose of which was to reground religious thought upon a more "real basis." Marx immediately recognized the importance of Feuerbach's revision of Hegel. But he also recognized that Feuerbach stopped short of carrying his materialism to its logical conclusion, to a justification of praxis. In this, Marx insists, Feuerbach had perpetuated the problem inherent in all earlier forms of materialism.

Thesis number one establishes the basic framework of the problem. According to Marx, "the chief defect of all hitherto existing materialism—that of Feuerbach included—is that . . . reality . . . is conceived only in the form of . . . *contemplation* . . . but not as *human sensuous activity, practice,* not subjectively."[29] The defect, in short, is that while earlier materialism recognizes that reality is material, it recognizes it only from a theoretical point of view, as something to be philosophized about, not as something that includes human action and can be altered by human action.

Put another way, earlier materialists failed to recognize that while material reality shapes human behavior and human consciousness, it is precisely that behavior and that consciousness that alters material reality. It is for this reason that Marx notes in thesis number three that "the materialist doctrine that men are products of circumstances and upbringing, and that, therefore, changed men are products of other circumstances and changed upbringing, forgets that it is men that change circumstances."[30] It forgets, in short, that human beings are both determined and determining. They are determined by material circumstances, but they determine the circumstances they are determined by. It works dialectically, both ways.

Here it will be objected that such a dialectical relationship violates the Marxian premise that life determines consciousness. But the objection fails to grasp the radical nature of what Marx meant by that premise. Recall that Marx believed consciousness to be itself a part of material life, not something independent of it. It was Feuerbach and earlier materialists who, in adopting the purely theoretical attitude, had made the mistake of divorcing mind from material reality. (For this reason, Marx argues, they in effect adopted the position of idealism despite their materialist metaphysics.) To assert that human understanding or theory can be carried over to changing existing social conditions is not only not contrary to materialist assumptions, says Marx, it is the necessary conclusion to be derived from them.

Any theory, of course, cannot be carried effectively into practice. The theory must accurately reflect actual social conditions or it will be incapable of changing anything. False consciousness will, of course, be ineffective. A correct understanding of actual social conditions, however, coupled with an attempt to change those conditions, must in the long run be successful, Marx argues. And herein lies precisely the crucial historical role of the proletariat. Their actual life conditions compel the workers to grasp the reality of their social order; those same conditions compel them to change it. Marxism is the theoretical comprehension of the capitalist order; the proletariat its practical revolutionary negation. The proletariat, in short, is the actual material embodiment of Marxian praxis.

But how do we in fact know that Marxism is a correct comprehension of the capitalist order, and that its prediction of the inevitability of communism is valid? The answer, Marx argues, is contained within the idea of praxis itself, for it is clear that praxis is the only way in which social theory, any social theory, can be verified. If the theory works in practice, then it is correct; if not, it must either be modified or rejected. This means, in the final analysis, that the ultimate truth of Marxist theory resides in the revolutionary capacity of the proletariat to overthrow the capitalist order and produce communism. We shall return to this role of the proletariat as the material validation of Marxist theory shortly, for it has obvious implications in any serious critique of that theory.

For now, it is sufficient to recognize that revolution is not simply a means to change the social order for Marx; it is a way of knowing. Revolution is an epistemology! This is an entirely novel idea in the Western tradition of political thought, and its implications extend well beyond the issue of communism or a working class revolution. For the idea that praxis is the only means of attaining valid social and political knowledge is a radical rejection of the entire Western epistemological tradition, whether in materialist or idealist form. Prior to Marx, to be objective meant to stand back, to separate oneself from that which was being studied. To intervene subjectively would be to alter the object being investigated and, thus, to invalidate one's theoretical analysis. Marx insists the opposite is the case. Unless one subjectively intervenes, the validity of theory can neither be proven nor can it evolve into higher understandings of social reality. Indeed, without this, theory is nothing more than ideology, Marx argues, for in never testing existing reality by attempting to change it, it takes that reality as a given and thus helps to perpetuate it.

This latter point is of particular importance because it illustrates Marx's ultimate critique of Western philosophy. We have already seen how, according to Marx, idealist philosophies obscure social reality. The same can now be seen to be the case with pre-Marxian materialist philosophies as well. In adopting the purely theoretical attitude, materialists such as Feuerbach simply perpetuated that division between intellectuals and others that constitutes in microcosm the division of society into social classes. They could not see, precisely because they remained aloof from society, that their theories were unwittingly a confirmation of a historically doomed social hierarchy.

For this reason, Marx believed that materialist philosophies from the seventeenth century on were simply defenses of liberal capitalist society. In thesis number nine, Marx argues that "the highest point attained by *contemplative* materialism, that is, materialism which does not understand . . . practical activity, is the contemplation of single individuals in 'civil society.' "[31] He means, simply, that in merely contemplating society, rather than attempting to change it, early materialists took for granted the radical individualism of existing society.[32] In the work of Hobbes and Locke, and throughout the tradition of classical liberal thought, this took the form of assuming that self-interest is the defining characteristic of human nature, and that human beings are innately individualistic property seekers. The early liberal's theory of human nature thus confirmed existing social reality; it did not occur to them that this reality is what gave rise to their theory.

In demonstrating the necessity of praxis, Marx believed he had overcome the ideological character of Western philosophy, earlier materialism included. Not only would revolutionary practice change social reality, it would expose in the process the misperception of that reality that had heretofore characterized Western social and political thought. Paradoxically, it would come to threaten the integrity of Marxist theory as well, as we shall soon see. But in order to understand this "paradox of praxis," a paradox crucial to any serious critique of Marx's philosophy, we need first to discuss the general outline of Marx's vision of communist society.

Most obviously, it will be a classless society since capitalist private property will no longer exist. (Personal property that cannot be used to acquire profit—one's clothing, house, and so on—will remain the only legitimate form of property.) But it follows that the elimination of private property in its concrete manifestation as capital cannot occur without its elimination as a division of productive activities as well. Recall that *property* and *the division of labor* are equivalent terms for Marx (social class being their highest expression). Hence, in a communist society people will no longer perform the same functions day after day but will perform a variety of activities. In Marx's words, communism "makes it possible for me to do one thing today and another tomorrow, to hunt in the morning, to fish in the afternoon, rear cattle in the evening, criticize after dinner, just as I have a mind, without ever becoming hunter, fisherman, shepherd, or critic."[33] Every human being will now be able to develop his or her own unique capacities and talents, and in a way that contributes to a larger social good rather than to increasing social exploitation. For this reason, Marx's own definition of a communist society is that it is one "in which the free development of each is the condition for the free development of all."[34]

Along with this transformation of the economic substructure of society must come a transformation of the whole legal and political superstructure. The state, and the entire legal and bureaucratic apparatus that surrounds it, must disappear. Since the state is nothing more than the political reflection of the economic structure of society (it is, according to Marx, the political arm of the ruling class), a classless society by definition must be a stateless society. In practical terms, this will mean that what had heretofore been political decisions made by the few will become social decisions made by the entire community.

But the greatest transformation effected in communist society will be that of humankind itself, and of its whole conscious conception of itself and the world around it. An alienated social structure of necessity produces alienated consciousness; the elimination of social alienation must have the opposite consequences. Hence, in a communist society people will not be driven by the desire for property and power since neither will any longer exist as sociological realities. They will be in this regard the very opposite of the bourgeoisie, who are incapable of thinking about life except in terms of the struggle for wealth and power. Having created a just and humanly satisfying society, moreover, they no longer need a God of eternal justice to rectify the wrongs of this life. Nor do they any longer need the consolation of "pure philosophy" as conceived by Hegel and the German philosophers. No longer is consciousness divorced from the reality of the material world, for that world is no longer an alienated reality. Consciousness can now aim at a scientific comprehension of material-social life for the purpose of bettering conditions for all.

How valid is this vision of communist society? The answer, of course, is that we cannot know until the attempt is made to actually create it. Past "communist" regimes have not done much to encourage optimism in this regard, a matter we shall discuss shortly. What we can say is that, in theory at least, there is nothing that would preclude the possibility of Marx's vision working in reality. With this in mind, let us for the moment defend him from the most commonly made criticisms of his communist ideal.

There are, to begin with, those who argue that the conditions of modern industrial society are much too complex to eliminate the division of labor. But Marx saw the other side of industrialization. He realized that the constant introduction of new machinery by the capitalist would ultimately create the possibility of freeing people from the necessity of performing the same drudging task day in and day out. And, long before most others, he noted the increasing automation of industrial capitalism and the simplification of productive tasks inherent in this process.[35] Under these kinds of technological conditions, the idea that one might, let us say, manage a factory in the morning and write poetry in the evening is not so farfetched as it might first seem. And even when the division of labor as a division of productive tasks could not entirely be eliminated, it need not exist as a division of property. The specialist need not acquire more than others simply because he or she performs a highly skilled function.

The usual objection to this argument is that people will refuse to perform socially necessary skilled tasks unless they are differentially rewarded. But this objection implicitly assumes a condition of scarcity in which well-being, even survival, depends upon the ceaseless struggle to acquire more. Such a condition will not exist in a communist society. The appropriation of the advanced technology of the capitalist order, coupled with the elimination of social class, will make scarcity a thing of the past. Under these conditions, fulfilling one's material requirements no longer need be based upon what one does for a living. More than enough is available for everyone regardless of what one does. Moreover, since the whole superstructure of capitalist consciousness will have been eliminated in the process of constructing communism, the desire for material incentives will no longer exist in any case.

Marx's claim that the state will be an unnecessary institution in a communist society has also drawn a number of criticisms. At bottom, these criticisms are based on the assumption that political power is essential in the maintenance of social order. But the assumption is by no means a demonstrated fact. Marx may well be correct in arguing that power is necessary only under certain kinds of social conditions, such as those in which exploitive class divisions pertain. Nor is it a demonstrated fact that making decisions, setting priorities, and regulating the social order require a bureaucratic structure separate from the larger society. Recall that a communist system is premised upon the simplification of economic life and the elimination of the division of labor. Under these conditions most decisions would not require vast amounts of expertise, and people would have available the leisure to participate meaningfully in public life.

It is important to understand here that Marx is not disputing the necessity of organization or leadership in a communist society. He is simply asserting that these tasks need not be performed by the state, and that power is not essential in their implementation. Clearly someone will have to see that the streets are maintained, trains arrive on schedule, and other such public matters are attended to, as much in a communist society as in any other.[36] But it does not follow from this that leaders must employ power. Remember that whoever leads does so at the behest of the whole community, not of a particular class, and we can therefore assume the leaders' relations with others will be cooperative rather than conflictual. Moreover, the role of leadership will be rotated, just like other social roles. Hence, there will be no opportunity for leaders to solidify their position into a new division of labor and a new structure of power. (And bear in mind that, given the transformation of social consciousness, they will have no desire to do so in any case.) They will lead without becoming leaders, just as they will fish without becoming fishermen, rear cattle without becoming shepherds, and perform their other social activities without becoming defined by them.

All of these criticisms are really technical or practical in nature. They assert that communism will not work because of the complexity of industrial society, the need for specialization, the necessity of bureaucratic regulation, and so on. But in fact they rest upon a much more fundamental critique of the Marxian vision, namely, that it is contrary to the facts of human nature. Almost invariably Marx's critics will conclude their criticism on this point, arguing that no matter how much society produces for the general economic well-being, the individual will always want more and will, as a consequence, always be in a competitive relationship with his or her fellows. It thus follows that the division of labor and social class cannot be eliminated, the state abolished, nor capitalist consciousness transcended.

Marx's response to this final criticism is, in effect, that it reverses the real relationship between sociology and psychology (that is, between material life and consciousness). It wrongly assumes that people's supposed innate desire for property and power determines the structure of society. It assumes, in short, the existence of an unalterable human nature to which society must conform. But, as we have seen, forms of consciousness and behavior are not psychologically innate for Marx; they vary depending upon the class structure of society, a fact that he believes obvious to anyone who studies history seriously. There is thus no such thing as a "human nature," only a social nature. Human beings, as Marx states in *Theses on Feuerbach,* are "the ensemble of the social relations."[37] In capitalist society, they are the ensemble of capitalist relations and think and behave as such. In communist society, they will think and behave as differently as the social relations that characterize that society.

In the final analysis, Marx's critics had simply espoused the liberal view of humanity and society, and herein, of course, lies Marx's ultimate criticism of their position. Liberalism is alienated theory; it is a social and political doctrine premised not upon people's species being, that is, upon people as they really are, but upon people as they exist under the alienated conditions of capitalist society. As we have seen in *Theses on Feuerbach,* Marx believes liberalism to be a form of false consciousness generated by the capitalist order. As such, it is by definition an ideology, that is, a false perception of reality that will disappear once the material conditions that give rise to it disappear. Thus, the ultimate rejoinder to his liberal critics, no less than to his religious and idealist critics, is the actual creation of a communist society.

Marx's critique of liberal theory may easily be expanded to a larger critique of the Western tradition of political thought as a whole, for, like liberalism, that tradition is essentially a manifestation of alienated theory for Marx. Let us briefly discuss that critique, for it constitutes a genuinely important contribution, albeit a negative or critical one, to the development of Western political thought. We may then conclude with a critical analysis of Marxism itself.

Let us begin by noting that Marx is not primarily a political theorist. Indeed we may term him an antipolitical theorist, for he rejects the ultimate reality of those very categories—justice, the state, law, and so on—by which political thinkers had heretofore organized their thinking. These categories, and indeed the whole mode of reasoning characteristic of Western political thought are for Marx nothing more than forms of alienated or ideological consciousness. It is for this reason that he does not give us anything like a coherent political theory. There is in Marx no consideration of the philosophical meaning of justice, no theory of the ideal state, and no analysis of the various forms of government. To his mind, these categories of political analysis are at best irrelevant, at worst ideological.

This same attitude applies to the recurrent issues of Western political thought. For Marx, most of these issues are themselves ideological; they constitute false perceptions of reality created by an alienated social structure. To take the most obvious example, "What is the just state?" is an important issue only assuming that the state is a necessary political structure. This Marx does not assume, or rather assumes to be the case only when society is divided by social class. And given his theory that the state is nothing more than the political arm of the ruling class, it is clearly impossible to create a just state in any case.

To take a more contemporary example, the issue of majority tyranny that so concerned later liberal thinkers cannot, in Marxian analysis, exist apart from the phenomenon of alienated consciousness and the whole liberal democratic and capitalist order that undergirds it. The majority cannot tyrannize the minority when it has no desire for economic or political advantage and, indeed, the distinction between majority and minority no longer exists, conditions that would supposedly pertain in a communist society. And any of the many other issues we have discussed in this book, from Socrates to the present day, can be subjected to this same kind of analysis.

In the history of Western political thought, then, the influence of Marx has been almost wholly negative. He is, as we have said, an antipolitical theorist rather than a political thinker in the traditional sense. But this is precisely what makes Marx so important. In adopting a radically negative stance toward Western political thought, he calls into question the very categories and issues of that tradition and thus compels us to rethink them in the most radical way. Indeed, he compels us to rethink that tradition of thought itself. Could it be that the whole of it is no more than an ideological misperception of social and political reality? Have we been on the wrong track since Socrates first raised the issue of justice in the streets of Athens? These are the questions that Marx raises, and they are raised so brilliantly and uncompromisingly that we cannot ignore them.

Yet, he raises them in a manner that calls into question the basic premise of his own theoretical system. Let us recall what that premise is: The truth of any theoretical system can only be confirmed in practice. The truth of Marxism, and hence its critique of all earlier political thought, rests then upon the ability of that theory to be put into practice. This, as we have seen, is dependent upon the ability of the world proletariat to produce communism through revolutionary praxis against the capitalist order. And herein lies the problem: The proletariat has either failed to perform its "historic task," or the social and political consequences of "successful communist revolutions" have been largely contrary to Marxian theory.

The most fundamental problem for Marxist theory, clearly, has been the general failure of the industrial proletariat to act as a revolutionary force. This failure may be attributed largely to improved economic conditions that have eliminated the extreme economic exploitation that existed in Marx's time, if not the more subtle forms of alienation. The working class has by now been thoroughly absorbed into society and, as such, generally supports the existing social and political order. Nationalism has largely replaced class identity and revolutionary ardor as the dominant form of working-class consciousness in the industrial West.

In Marxian analysis, there can only be one answer as to why this has happened. Clearly capitalism has been able to overcome those economic crises that Marx had argued are endemic to it. Recall that the conscious realization of the real nature of capitalism on the part of the proletariat cannot occur apart from the continued disintegration of that system. This is the only way in which consciousness and life, theory and practice, can come together to produce a revolutionary upheaval. The failure of the proletariat, then, may be interpreted as a failure of Marx's theoretical analysis of capitalism and, by extension, of the whole philosophy of historical materialism upon which it rests.

This interpretation was in fact made by a number of Marxists early on in this century, for it had become evident even then that the capitalist system was more stable than Marx had initially assumed. The founder of this new school of thought was Eduard Bernstein, an important leader of the pre–World War I German Social Democratic Party, at that time the largest mass-based Marxist party in Europe. Bernstein concluded that the growing stability of capitalism required a major revision of Marxist theory. (For this reason, Bernstein's brand of Marxism came to be known as *revisionism*.) This revision involved recognizing that the presumed dialectical necessity of capitalism's demise could no longer be accepted, and that socialism must therefore be viewed as a moral ideal to be striven for rather than an historical inevitability to be carried into revolutionary praxis.[38]

Needless to say, Bernstein's revision of Marx generated enormous opposition from "orthodox Marxists" who saw, quite correctly, that what was at stake was the scientific validity of the doctrine.[39] If socialism was to be a moral ideal rather than a scientifically demonstrated necessity, Marxism could hardly be said to have evolved much beyond utopian ideals. They argued, therefore, that Bernstein's interpretation of the situation was not the only one possible.

One of the most important of these arguments was made by V.I. Lenin. He attempted to demonstrate that capitalism was able to stabilize itself temporarily through the imperialist penetration of underdeveloped countries.[40] Such penetration, Lenin argued, allows for the expropriation of cheap labor and resources from these countries and, hence, for the realization of super-profits. These profits, in turn, are used to raise the wages of key elements of the industrial working class and thus to dampen their revolutionary ardor. But this simply confirms the essential correctness of Marx's analysis, Lenin insisted. Economic imperialism meant that capitalism was becoming a worldwide phenomenon as Marx had predicted. In the long run, as the "third world" itself became an industrialized and competitive component of the larger capitalist system, the disintegration of worldwide capitalism and the revolutionary triumph of the world proletariat inevitably must occur.

But even if we accept Lenin's analysis and its prediction of the final demise of capitalism, and they have not yet been borne out, there is another problem Marxists must now confront. In those countries where "Marxian socialist revolutions" had succeeded, the results were quite contrary to the Marxist vision of communism. In past ruling "communist regimes" the state did not disappear; indeed it typically grew to enormous proportions. And standing behind the state apparatus, both supporting and dominating it, was the communist party, an elite and nondemocratic structure that prevented any possibility of communal decision making on the part of the population as a whole. This structure of political domination reached totalitarian proportions in the Soviet Union during the Stalinist period; and while in that country and most other Marxist states the extreme conditions of totalitarianism were subsequently eliminated, one can hardly claim that the Marxist ideal of communism had in any sense been attained.

How this came to happen is a long and complex story, far too long and complex to discuss in any detail here. We can note, however, that the growth of the state was probably inevitable. This is what has occurred in every other industrialized country, although this is not what in Marxist theory was supposed to happen in a socialist society.[41] But the domination of the state, and indeed of society as a whole, by an elite and nondemocratic party is another matter. It deserves, therefore, some special comment.

The founder of the modern communist party was the Russian Marxist V.I. Lenin and not, as popular opinion tends to assume, Karl Marx. (Indeed, there is good evidence that Marx rejected the kind of political structure that characterized the Leninist party.[42]) Lenin was the leader of the Bolshevik party (the forerunner of what became the Communist Party of the former Soviet Union), which came to power in October 1917 at the culmination of the Russian Revolution. The Bolsheviks were initially only one faction of the Russian Social Democratic Party. Over time, they split entirely from the parent body. The split was based upon a dispute over how a Marxist revolutionary party ought to be structured. The majority of mainline Social Democrats argued that the party must be an open and democratic organization. Lenin and the Bolsheviks argued for a clandestine, tightly knit group of professional revolutionaries hierarchically organized into a command structure that would function almost as a military machine.[43]

There were a number of reasons behind Lenin's advocacy of this kind of party structure, but they can all be reduced to the fact that he believed a social democratic structure to be incompatible with the social and political conditions of prerevolutionary Russia. To begin with, the Tsarist autocracy prevented the existence of any kind of open antiregime activity. But the deeper problem was the fact that Russia was essentially an agrarian, peasant-based country. Modern industrial capitalism had yet to emerge in anything but outline form, and the Russian working class was, as a consequence, extremely small. Under these underdeveloped conditions, Lenin believed that only a small and tightly organized group of professional revolutionaries possessing a genuine socialist consciousness would be capable of leading the workers. In turn, Lenin argued, the workers would have to pull along large elements of the peasantry in any revolutionary transformation of Russian society.

Numerous objections to Lenin's reasoning were raised by his fellow Marxists, but they essentially revolved around the complaint that Lenin's idea of party structure contained an implicit admission that the necessary substructural conditions did not exist for a genuine socialist revolution. If they did, if, for example, society were composed of a majority of exploited class-conscious workers, the party would not be necessary. The workers, given their extreme exploitation and immiseration, would spontaneously revolt without the aid of professional revolutionaries.

The effect of these criticisms was to show that Lenin's party violated Marxist theory by attempting to "push history," to generate a socialist revolution before the conditions for it existed. In the language of the debate that ensued among Marxists at the time, it was argued that Lenin had replaced the classical Marxian notion of spontaneity with that of consciousness. His creation of the party was an implicit admission that spontaneity (that is, the spontaneous revolt of the proletariat) would not work, and that consciousness (that is, the conscious will of a vanguard party) was necessary for revolutionary success. For Lenin's critics this meant that his party involved a fundamental violation—a reversal—of the true relationship between material life and consciousness.

Lenin, needless to say, rejected these arguments. In the first place, he considered Russia to be an imperialist extension of the capitalist powers and thus believed that a revolution could legitimately begin on the periphery of capitalism's domain as well as in its center. Moreover, he assumed, as did all his fellow Bolsheviks, that a revolution in Russia would spark a worldwide revolution against capitalism.[44] Under these assumed conditions Russia would not find itself surrounded by hostile capitalist powers and would be able to build socialism quickly and peacefully with the technological aid of brother socialist states. Hence, the attempt to carry out a genuine socialist revolution in Russia by means of an elite party did not seem to Lenin to be a violation of Marxist theory.

But, again, in the Marxian system the test of any revolutionary theory is its outcome in practice. And just as the industrialized proletariat has so far failed to play out that revolutionary role predicted by theory, the Marxist movement in Russia, and in those other countries where it came to power organized along Leninist lines, produced consequences quite at variance with theory. Along with the growth of the state bureaucracy came a consolidation of the power of the Leninist party at the expense of the democratic and communitarian ideals of Marxism.

Indeed, Marxist theory was employed in these regimes to justify party dominance of state and society. The ultimate paradox of this was that the justification typically was made within the context of national ideals. This was the case as well with Marxist-Leninist revolutionary movements in the third world where Marxism was often a cover for nationalism. We shall discuss the enormous importance of these facts in the next chapter. For now it is sufficient to recognize the obvious contradiction inherent in the transformation of an internationalist doctrine into a nationalistic justification of rule by a party elite.

If we now take the whole of this analysis, we may well conclude that the unity of Marxist theory and practice has disintegrated. The history of the proletariat, as well as that of the revolutionary Marxist movement, has failed to confirm theory. Given Marx's own epistemological assumptions, we might then conclude that Marxism is wanting, for it is a theory that has failed in practice. Orthodox Marxists argue, of course, as they did when Bernstein first attempted to revise the theory, that the historical drama is not yet over. They claim that the apparent stability of capitalism is an illusion, that Stalinism was a temporary irrationality in a more general revolutionary movement, and that the ideal of communism will yet be realized.[45]

Non-Marxists would argue, of course, that it is difficult, and becomes increasingly so over time, to accept these predictions at face value. This would seem even more the case now that the Soviet communist regime and its East European empire has finally collapsed. For many, this appears to be positive confirmation of the failure of Marxism and, conversely, of the triumph of capitalism and classical liberal economics. To be sure, some communist states still exist, most notably the People's Republic of China, but they are few, marginal, or like China, developing increasingly free market economies.

But there is another side to this "end of communism" assumption. As we have noted, not all Marxists thought the Russian revolution a good thing, certainly not in its Leninist form, and many have continued to assert the classical view that capitalism must become a worldwide phenomenon before a genuine communist revolution can occur. Seen in this light, it could be argued that the spread of capitalism may actually be confirming Marx's analysis and, ultimately, creating the conditions for a genuine communist society as opposed to the perverted forms of the past. Moreover, the collapse of communism means an end to the cold war, and this may allow for a much less biased and ideological understanding of Marx than has heretofore been the case, particularly in this country. The end of communism may be what is required for a rebirth of Marxism; this at least is the view of more than a few Marxists.

But let us assume for the sake of argument that the theory of Marxism no longer conforms to historical reality. If so, a paradoxical fact emerges. Given Marx's own definition of the term, *Marxism* itself must be defined as an ideology, a false perception of reality. And in the case of those ruling regimes that had employed Marxism as a justification for party domination and as a cloak for nationalist ideals, it became an ideology in the fullest sense of that term.[46] For under those conditions it not only misrepresented reality, it acted much like a religious doctrine, sanctifying existing conditions and thus preventing people from changing them.

Nonetheless, from the broadest perspective, the value of Marxism is not diminished even if this analysis is accurate, at least not for the political theorist, for the Marxist critique of Western social and political thought may well be valid even if Marxism itself must now be included in that critique. While there is certainly no consensus among political thinkers that this is the case, it is cause for concern for those who do believe it to be so. For if Marx's indictment of Western political theory is valid, if the whole of that tradition is nothing more than ideology, then political thinkers no longer have an intellectual tradition that they can in good conscience draw upon, Marxism included. It is not without reason, then, that few political thinkers in the contemporary world have theorized about social and political matters without keeping this intellectual nemesis of Western thought always in mind.

Notes

1. A fourth volume of *Capital* was eventually edited and brought to publication by the German Socialist leader Karl Kautsky.
2. Karl Marx and Freidrich Engels, *The German Ideology*, R. Pascal, ed. (New York: International Publishers, 1947), p. 16.
3. Ibid., p. 18.
4. Ibid., p. 22.
5. Ibid. Marx took this definition of property from the liberal economists themselves.
6. Karl Marx and Freidrich Engels, "Manifesto of the Communist Party," in *Selected Works* (in one volume) (New York: International Publishers, 1968), p. 35.
7. Marx and Engels, *German Ideology*, p. 15.
8. Ibid., pp. 14–15.
9. Karl Marx, "Preface to a Contribution to the Critique of Political Economy," in *Selected Works*, p. 182.
10. Ibid.
11. Marx and Engels, *German Ideology*, p. 31.
12. Ibid., p. 30.
13. Robert C. Tucker, ed., "Contribution to the Critique of Hegel's Philosophy of Right: Introduction," in *The Marx-Engels Reader* (New York: W.W. Norton, 1972), p. 12.
14. Marx and Engels, *German Ideology*, p. 20. (Emphasis in original.)
15. Tucker, "Contribution to the Critique," p. 12. (Emphasis in original.)
16. Marx posits the existence of three earlier forms of productive life—the asiatic, ancient, and feudal modes of production.
17. Marx and Engels, "Manifesto of the Communist Party," pp. 37–38.
18. It is clear that the capitalist is alienated as well as the worker, although, unlike the worker, he is "content" in his alienation. Unfortunately, Marx did not analyze the capitalist's alienation in any detail. For a brief but excellent

discussion of what Marx did have to say about it, see Bertell Ollman, *Alienation: Marx's Conception of Man in Capitalist Society* (Cambridge: Cambridge University Press, 1971), pp. 154–57.

19. The idea that machines cannot produce more than the value of the labor it took to produce them is puzzling to most students. It must be kept in mind, however, that for Marx only human labor can create value; the machine, in and of itself, can therefore create nothing. There are several ways in which this can be "demonstrated," but the easiest is to imagine a situation in which all labor had been replaced by machines. If machines can produce more value than labor, it should follow that a completely automated society would be most capable of generating profits. Yet, it is clear that in such a situation economic value would not exist at all, for no one would be employed and thus no purchase of commodities could be made. This, according to the Marxist theorist Ernest Mandel, "proves the validity of the . . . [labor theory of value] . . . , for at the moment human labor disappears from production, value, too, disappears with it." See Ernest Mandel, *An Introduction to Marxist Economic Theory* (New York: Pathfinder Press, 1970), p. 28. In addition to Mandel's book, see Robert L. Heilbroner, *The Worldly Philosophers: The Lives, Times and Ideas of the Great Economic Thinkers* (New York: Simon & Schuster, 1953), chap. 6, for an easily comprehensible analysis of these issues.

20. Marx, "Preface to a Contribution to the Critique of Political Economy," p. 182.

21. Ibid., p. 183.

22. Marx and Engels, "Manifesto of the Communist Party," p. 40.

23. Ibid., p. 46.

24. Marx, *Capital: A Critique of Political Economy*, Friedrich Engels, ed. Samuel Moore and Edward Aveling, trans. (New York: The Modern Library, 1906), p. 837.

25. Engels, "Ludwig Feuerbach and the End of Classical German Philosophy," in Marx and Engels, *Selected Works*, p. 597.

26. Ibid., p. 619.

27. See Martin Nicolaus's forward to Karl Marx's *Grundrisse: Foundations of the Critique of Political Economy*, Martin Nicolaus, trans. (New York: Vintage Books, 1973), pp. 26–44, for an excellent discussion of Hegel's influence on Marx. According to Nicolaus, "the usefulness of Hegel lay in providing guidelines for what to do in order to grasp a moving, developing totality with the mind." (p. 33).

28. Marx and Engels, "Manifesto of the Communist Party," p. 38.

29. Marx, "Theses on Feuerbach," in *Selected Works*, p. 28. (Emphasis in original.)

30. Ibid.

31. Ibid., p. 30. (Emphasis in original.)

32. Whether or not thesis nine refers only to capitalist society is a matter of dispute. See Sidney Hook, *From Hegel to Marx: Studies in the Intellectual Development of Karl Marx* (Ann Arbor: University of Michigan Press, 1962), pp. 300–303, for a discussion of this issue. See also chapter eight of that work for an extended analysis of the entire *Theses on Feuerbach.*

33. Marx and Engels, *German Ideology,* p. 22.

34. Marx and Engels, "Manifesto of the Communist Party," p. 53.

35. See David McLellan's abridged translation of *The Grundrisse: Karl Marx* (New York: Harper & Row, 1971), pp. 141–52, for a brief discussion of Marx's views on the nature of work and production in a communist society. For those who wish to read this difficult but crucially important work in its entirety, see the Nicolaus edition of the *Grundrisse.*

36. See Friedrich Engels, "On Authority," in Tucker's *Marx-Engels Reader.* This short article was written in response to those "socialists" (actually anarchists) who advocated the elimination of authority as such. Engels insists that it is the authority of the modern state that must be destroyed, not authority in general. Says Engels, "wanting to abolish authority in large-scale industry is tantamount to wanting to abolish industry itself, to destroy the power loom in order to return to the spinning wheel" (p. 731).

37. Marx, "Theses on Feuerbach," p. 29.

38. Eduard Bernstein's major attempt at revision is his now classic work *Evolutionary Socialism: A Criticism and Affirmation* (New York: Schocken Books, 1961). This book marks a clear break from orthodox Marxism.

39. See Peter Gay, *The Dilemma of Democratic Socialism: Eduard Bernstein's Challenge to Marx* (New York: Collier Books, 1962), for an excellent analysis of the impact of Bernstein's revisionism on the theoretical integrity of the classical doctrine.

40. V.I. Lenin developed this thesis in his *Imperialism: The Highest Stage of Capitalism: A Popular Outline* (New York: International Publishers, 1939).

41. Marx conceded, in his "Critique of the Gotha Programme," that the state, under the control of the workers, would continue to exist for a time after the revolution, until full communism finally emerged. This form of the state he termed the revolutionary dictatorship of the proletariat (it was to be dictatorial vis-à-vis its relationship to the remnants of the bourgeoisie, democratic in its relationship to the proletariat). While Marx provides no time frame for the final withering of the workers' state, it is clear that the dictatorship of the proletariat is to be only a temporary stage in the development toward the statelessness of communist society. Yet, in "communist" countries the state, which never was a worker's democracy, which continued to grow in size and power, and which gave little indication of "withering," was officially justified as a legitimate form of the dictatorship of the proletariat. In

the former Soviet Union, where the state grew to truly enormous proportions, this official justification became less and less convincing. (It was perhaps for this reason that the 1977 Soviet Constitution asserted that the "state of the whole people"—a political form never mentioned by Marx—had been attained.)

42. Marx had rejected the organizational principles of a French revolutionary named Blanqui, principles that were close to those later advocated by Lenin. While there were, and still are among many revolutionary Marxists, disclaimers of any similarity between Lenin and Blanqui, there is good reason to believe that Marx's critique of Blanqui applies equally to Lenin. Rosa Luxemburg, a contemporary of Lenin and herself a radical Marxist, thought so, and criticized Lenin's theory of the party in a classic of Marxist literature entitled "Leninism or Marxism?" See Rosa Luxemburg, *The Russian Revolution and Leninism or Marxism?* (Ann Arbor: University of Michigan Press, 1961).

43. Lenin first expounded his theory of party organization in the pamphlet *What Is To Be Done?* (New York: International Publishers, 1929).

44. This idea was most consistently developed by Leon Trotsky (next to Lenin the most important Bolshevik leader during the 1917 revolution) in his theory of "permanent revolution."

45. See Isaac Deutscher, *The Unfinished Revolution: Russia 1917–1967* (Oxford: Oxford University Press, 1967) for an example of these kinds of arguments.

46. This paradox is brilliantly summed up in one sentence by Shlomo Avineri in *The Social and Political Thought of Karl Marx* (Cambridge: Cambridge University Press, 1968): "If Marx's point of departure was Hegelian, so was his blind spot: like Hegel himself he did not subject his own theory to a dialectical critique" (p. 258).

15

The Age
of Ideology

There can be no doubt that the age of ideology, that period of time that stretches from the French Revolution to the present day, has radically altered the intellectual map by which Western people orient themselves. Increasingly, however, thinkers have begun to question the appropriateness of ideologies, either as intellectual systems or as platforms for revolutionary change. Much of Edmund Burke's original critique of ideological thinking and practice is as relevant today as it was in his own time. Indeed, the rise of modern totalitarian movements, all of which have been based on ideological systems of thought, indicate that ideologies harbor potentialities dangerous beyond anything imagined by Burke.

In this century there have been a great variety of criticisms of ideological systems. Some have simply elaborated on Burke's original critique; others have gone considerably beyond Burke to question the whole basis of modern thought in light of the rise of ideological thinking, still others to a re-examination of the entire tradition of Western political philosophy. In this chapter, we will take this broad perspective and attempt to understand the logic behind ideologies from the point of view of the historical development of Western thought in general.

We have chosen in this book to think about that history in a particular way. We have argued that the defining characteristic of political thinking from Socrates to St. Thomas was the presumed unity of ethics and politics, and that the general thrust of modern political thought from Machiavelli to the age of ideology was to call into question that presumption. This was accomplished by denying humanity's essential ethical capacity, the natural character of society and polity, and the idea that the state exists as a "moral essence" whose purpose it is to direct human beings to some moral end. Indeed, the whole language of political theory is altered in early modern thought. In place of the classical language of moral reason we find the language of pleasure and pain, self-interest, and power, a language that many thinkers continue to employ.

Now let us apply this general view of modern thought to an analysis of modern ideologies. It immediately strikes the attention that ideologies seem to be characterized by their attempt to reaffirm the unity of ethics and politics, but in a radically new way. In the classical tradition, the unity of ethics and politics presumed the existence of the morally autonomous individual. This is why classical thinkers assumed that human beings possess by nature a social and ethical capacity. Ideologies, on the other hand, tend to replace the idea of personal moral autonomy with a "higher principle of moral progress" beyond the individual, a principle to which the individual is to subordinate him- or herself. Unlike the higher principles of the classical tradition, such as natural law, which include the individual as a moral agent, the higher principles characteristic of ideologies tend to subordinate the individual's moral agency rather than to actualize it.

Marxism is one of the clearest examples of this tendency. The Marxist revolutionary does not choose communism as a moral ideal, but as the dictate of the higher principle of historical necessity. To be sure, that necessity involves praxis, that is, the revolutionary action of the individual. Action, nevertheless, flows not from the impetus of ethical ideals but from a realization of a necessity transcending such ideals. This is crucial to the whole Marxian system and largely explains why Bernstein met with such hostility from fellow Marxists when he attempted to transform Marxism from a doctrine of historical necessity to one of ethical ideals.

Fascism is an even clearer and more extreme example of this tendency. In its less extreme forms, fascism posited the unique characteristics of a people, its "spirit" or "geist," as a higher principle to which the individual was to be subordinate. In its more extreme racist forms, as in the case of German National Socialism, the individual's moral judgment was subordinated to a supposed "biological law" that dictated the "decline" of certain races and the "triumph" of others.

What is true in these extreme examples is true also, albeit in a more subtle way, of the other ideologies we have discussed in this book. Tradition, which for Burke served simply to furnish guidelines for political thought and action, became for subsequent reactionary thinkers an almost sacred category, something above and beyond the individual. This was particularly the case when the conservative philosophy became connected to nationalist ideals.

Paradoxically, this tendency to subordinate the individual as moral agent to "higher principles" was true as well of liberalism, at least in part. Granted, the early liberal tradition, from Hobbes to the utilitarians, largely rejected the idea of any structure of purposes beyond the individual. Yet, in elements of its later development, liberalism was also characterized by the erection of "moral structures" transcending the individual. The market mechanism of Adam Smith, for example, constitutes an economic structure that is supposed to automatically produce a public good quite independent of individuals and their moral judgments. Indeed, it works precisely because they set aside moral judgments and rationally pursue their self-interest. (To argue in Benthamite fashion that self-interest is equivalent to the moral is only to say that the moral is identical to one's subordination to the "higher principle" of the market.) Spencer employs these ideas to posit an even higher structure of biological purposes to which individuals are to subordinate their moral sensibilities.

Most important, this erection of higher principles beyond that of the individual is characteristic as well of the most powerful and influential ideology of the modern world: nationalism. Nationalism posits the nation-state as the supreme value, and asserts that individuals ought to subordinate their moral judgment to the dictates of the nation. This is not to be confused with patriotism. Patriotism is the simple and uncomplicated love of one's country. Nationalism, as an ideology, justifies the subordination of the individual's moral agency to moral purposes supposedly embodied in the nation itself.

We have discussed the emergence of the modern nation-state extensively in this book and have noted the rise of nationalist sentiment that accompanied it. Beginning in inchoate form as far back as Machiavelli, nationalism had become the dominant form of political identification in Europe by the middle of the nineteenth century. It remains so to this day and is now sweeping the third world as new nations are being created and consolidated. But more than an emotional source of political identification, nationalism became a philosophically explicit ideology in the nineteenth century through the efforts of an Italian thinker named Giuseppe Mazzini. The results were not very impressive, but Mazzini did make explicit the logic of nationalism, particularly the idea that the individual was to be subordinate to the dictates of the nation.[1]

Nationalism is a uniquely important ideology, not only because of its political impact, but because it has profoundly subverted the theoretical integrity of the other major ideological systems of thought. This fact requires some elaboration, for, as we shall see, it plays a crucial role in the actual political subordination of individuals already inherent in their moral subordination to the higher principles of the ideological worldviews.

In this century, this nationalist perversion has been most dramatically evident in the case of Marxism. What had been an internationalist doctrine of revolutionary class conflict became a cover for nationalist ideals. Many of the revolutionary Marxist movements in the third world were in fact nationalist movements justified in the name of Marxist theory. This nationalization of Marxism is precisely what occurred in Russia once Stalin came to power. The same phenomenon occurred in China after 1949, as well as in other third world Marxist regimes. Particularly troublesome in the case of Marxist nationalism has been its propensity, most evident in the Soviet Union under Stalin, to justify totalitarian forms of political controls utterly at variance with the humanistic ideals of the classical doctrine.

In a different way, this same fate befell liberalism. It too was originally an internationalist doctrine. Bear in mind that the early revolutionary liberals, certainly those in France during the Revolution, considered themselves the advocates of the "rights of man," not just of the rights of a particular national grouping. But this internationalist and universalistic orientation was subverted once liberalism became the official ideology of the Western European nation-states. Initially, no problem was perceived in this link between liberalism and nationalism because liberals believed that the nation-state constituted that political structure in which the ideal of self-government could best be realized.[2] Their internationalist goals, in short, seemed most attainable within a national framework. But they could defend the idea of the nation-state only by recognizing, as they were logically compelled to do, the right of self-determination of all national groupings. In political fact this often meant defending national entities that systematically violated liberal ideals, and not just the ideal of self-government. This in turn suggested, if only implicitly, that the nation-state constituted an ideal higher than those universal values traditionally espoused by liberalism.

Moreover, even in those West European countries that were constitutionally structured along liberal lines, the conflict between liberal and national ideals remained. For the fact is that the nation-state, whether constitutionally liberal or not, constitutes a political structure not terribly compatible with the maintenance of liberal values. Most seriously, the emotional power of nationalism, coupled with the increasingly bureaucratic centralism of the modern state, inevitably diminishes the liberal ideal of individualism. Once again, this was not immediately recognized, for in the early tradition of liberal thought the nation-state was seen as the political form most conducive to the realization of that ideal. But the situation was quite different following the French Revolution. By then, the power of the state, including the liberal-democratic state, had taken on quite extraordinary dimensions. It was not simply power in the abstract that came to characterize the modern nation-state, but an ability to generate an almost universal acquiescence in the continued centralization and bureaucratization of that power at the expense of subordinate communities and associations. We have analyzed this fact extensively in our discussion of de Tocqueville, who clearly saw in this the tendency of liberal democracy to subordinate the individual to the bureaucratic state despite its defense of individualism and limited government.[3] And the attempt on the part of modern liberals to rectify the situation has, as we have seen, as much intensified the problem as resolved it.[4]

Conservatism was also subverted by its association with nationalism, an association forged in the struggle against the philosophy of the French Revolution. We have already discussed the fact that the Aristotelian and Ciceronian ideals of philosophical conservatism do not fit well within the political structure of the nation-state. But the problem is more serious than this. The creation of the nation-state required the destruction of those feudal entities that had been the bearers of the traditional values and traditional ways that constitute the core of the conservative philosophy. And this process of destruction has continued, for while the feudal world has long ago passed away, contemporary institutions and associations that might act as repositories of conservative ideals have been hard pressed to maintain their autonomy and viability within the bureaucratic confines of the modern state. Contemporary conservatism thus finds itself in the same paradoxical situation as liberalism. Its support of nationalist ideals renders it a doctrine at war with its own most basic principles.

We may, therefore, make the following general assertions: In becoming adjuncts to nationalism, the theoretical integrity of the major ideologies of the modern world has been subverted. In actual political fact, this subversion has had the effect of supporting the trend toward state centralization on the one hand and, correspondingly, of subverting the individual's moral autonomy on the other. This, of course, is most obvious—and most frightening—in the case of the totalitarian ideologies. But they are extreme examples of a more general process associated with the rise of ideologies.

Why did ideologies develop this way? The underlying sociological reasons are generally agreed upon. Most scholars concede that the industrial revolution and all that is associated with it (the emergence of modern science, the decline of religion, and the general secular thrust of the modern world) constitute the social basis of ideological thinking as well as its nationalistic perversions. That revolution destroyed the old agrarian "feudal" communities that had formerly encompassed the individual and provided him or her with a sense of ethical values and moral purposes. The individual was increasingly isolated from any meaningful communal structure that could provide a stable set of values. Ideologies, so to speak, entered this moral breach by providing a systematic value system that fit the conditions of industrial and secular society, just as the nation-state provided a new kind of community and nationalism a new form of communal identification. Inevitably, there arose a close connection between these various elements of industrial society. The new ideological value systems were thus almost inevitably incorporated into nationalistic justifications of state power. It is for this reason not at all surprising, paradoxical though it is in theoretical terms, that even the internationalist ideologies should be employed for nationalist purposes to the detriment of the individual's moral autonomy.

It is the philosophical or theoretical reason behind this development that is more difficult to determine. There is little in the way of scholarly agreement on this issue. We shall, nevertheless, make an attempt, basing our analysis upon the basic theme of this book.

Let us begin by noting that the problem began long before the nationalistic subversion of the key ideologies. That in becoming nationalized all ideologies have contributed to the subordination of the individual to the state is true. But this is merely the political manifestation of a more fundamental subordination of the individual to the "higher principles" of history, race, the economic marketplace, the forces of biological evolution, the spirit of a nation, or what have you. It was indeed this initial subordination that made ideologies so useful to the nation-state that could now legitimize itself by claiming to embody these higher principles.

This tendency of modern ideologies was recognized and opposed by those thinkers who attempted to reform these traditions of thought. The reason behind their opposition provides a crucial insight into the issue before us. For revisionists such as Green, and anti-ideologues such as Burke, no structure of authority can exist apart from individuals who demonstrate their moral capacity by self-willed obedience to law, and by free participation in the life of their political community. For these thinkers, authority means, by definition, a reciprocal arrangement between the individual as an autonomous moral being and the polity as a moral structure.[5] It means, in short, the unity of ethics and politics without which, as Burke in particular emphasized, there will exist little more than a political order incapable of integrating its citizens into a meaningful structure of authority, and a society of atomized individuals lost in an ethically meaningless world. Under these conditions, again as Burke noted, political force (and we would now add totalitarianism) becomes the only mechanism of control.[6]

Needless to say, the ideological subordination of the individual's moral autonomy to higher principles was not done with the intention of producing these consequences. Quite the contrary. As we have noted, ideologies arose precisely to establish a new basis of authority and meaning in a world in which the traditional value structures had been destroyed by industrialization and the triumph of the nation-state. But their methods had the contrary result; they stripped the individual of the very moral capacity that is the source of meaning and the basis of authority.

Why? This is, in fact, the real question before us, and while no definitive answer can be given at this historical juncture, it appears, at least in part, that the whole metaphysical and epistemological thrust of modern philosophy strongly encouraged thinkers to found the ethics of the state (or of whatever form of polity they envisioned) on some principle other than that of the morally autonomous individual. The classical idea of the morally free individual had been largely discredited in modern thought: in Machiavelli, in Hobbes, later in Bentham and the utilitarians. In an age of ethical naturalism, the concept of the individual as moral agent, at least in the teleological sense, was exceedingly difficult to maintain. But if the classical view of the individual could not be maintained, the same results could be had, or so it seemed, by subordinating the individual to higher principles that could be justified within the framework of ethical naturalism, in short, within the framework of modern science. Smith's market mechanism, Spencer's Social Darwinism, Marx's historical inevitability, and fascism's theory of race all were asserted to be not moral ideals, but scientific facts. This was a crucial claim, for a scientific doctrine is clearly "above reproach" in the framework of modern philosophy.

In our discussion of Hobbes, we stated that the defining issue in political thought since Machiavelli "has been to find some way of deriving a theory of authority from the metaphysical and epistemological assumptions of modern science." This statement now takes on particular relevance, for so many modern ideological systems of thought are characterized by precisely this attempt. Their proponents try to found a theory of authority upon what they presume to be scientific premises. That these premises may in fact not be scientific is irrelevant. (In the case of National Socialism they were patently absurd.) What matters is that they are believed by their adherents to be scientific, and that they are stated in the form of scientific certainties.

The paradox in all of this is clear. By claiming the authority of science, ideologies satisfied the requirements of modern naturalism and at the same time seemingly derived new theories of authority from within the very framework of assumptions that had to that point made such theories so difficult to articulate. The consequence, as we have seen, was quite the opposite of that intended. The whole basis of authority, namely the unity of ethics and politics, was in fact destroyed because the concept of the morally autonomous individual had been destroyed. And the ultimate paradox in all of this is that these new "sciences" became the rational legitimization of nationalism, the most irrational political force of the modern world and the factor most responsible for the political subordination of the individual to the growing power of the modern bureaucratic state.

It is all too clear what these paradoxes mean in real political terms. Worldwide, the nation-state system, the intensity of nationalism, and the division of the earth into competing worldviews, confront modern people with the very real possibility of a final holocaust. In this century the reality of this possibility has been made abundantly clear to all. And within the nation-state itself, the whole basis of authority rests upon very shaky foundations. Thus, the display of awesome power abroad by the major states may well be matched by an unforeseen weakness within. Beneath the apparent stability of the nation-state, and despite the emotional power of nationalism, the reality may be a Hobbesian society of atomized individuals, alienated and disconnected from any real source of authority and lacking any genuine sense of ethical meaning and purpose. Under these conditions the possibility of social and cultural disintegration may be greater than we care to admit.

CONTEMPORARY POLITICAL THEORY: THE FUTURE OF A TRADITION

Where do we go from here? From the perspective of this book, the answer is clear. We need to devise political philosophies that unify ethics and politics in a way that fits modern conditions. But how? We can only suggest here the basic elements of an answer, for there is little in contemporary political thought that indicates that a solution is at hand.

Let us begin by discussing those solutions that probably will not work. It seems, to begin with, increasingly unlikely that the major ideological systems of thought can be made compatible with this unification. They are a prime source of the problem; not a solution. And we are now painfully aware that past attempts at revision have largely failed in this objective; there is little reason in the present day to believe that further revision will change anything. We may well ask whether these systems of thought adequately comprehend the social and political conditions of the modern world in any case. We have suggested, in our analysis of each of the key ideologies, that there are clearly problems in this regard. Moreover, the nationalization of these ideologies has so much subverted their theoretical integrity that there now seems little hope of reconstituting them to their original vitality.

Further development of these intellectual systems has continued, nevertheless. Marxism has continued to evolve as a social science. So too has liberalism as a political doctrine, particularly in recent years.[7] These developments are by no means without value. Whatever criticisms we may make of modern ideologies, their further elaboration has produced new insights into the nature of political reality and raised new and important questions about political life. But these developments, as often as not, have only served to further the disintegration of the theoretical integrity of the original doctrines. They have not, in any case, really resolved the contemporary disjunction between ethics and politics; at least there is no consensus that this has occurred.

Reviving the classical tradition of political thought in its entirety does not seem a terribly fruitful way to resolve the problem either. Granted, this tradition does unite ethics and politics; indeed this is its defining characteristic. But, for better or worse, modern philosophy since the Renaissance, including political philosophy, has long since altered our intellectual map of the world. It would not be easy to discard that map for one that, taken in its entirety, presents what is to most an alien terrain. Simply returning to the past is no solution, although there have been some notable attempts to do so.

Yet, the classical tradition does suggest at least an approach to the problem, for while we cannot draw upon the whole of classical thought, we can at least isolate those elements in it that characterize the ideal of the unity of ethics and politics and determine what in modern and contemporary political thought is compatible with the ideal. This is possible because, in the broadest sense, that ideal has never really disappeared. It has been attacked, but constantly returned to. It has been perverted by the rise of ideologies, but, paradoxically, for the purpose of recreating it. And it is an ideal shared by a large number of contemporary thinkers, including a number of those "ethical naturalists" who reject the metaphysical and epistemological assumptions of classical thought.

What, then, does constitute that ideal? The reader should now be well acquainted with its key elements. They are those, first of all, that affirm the idea of the individual as an autonomous, self-developing, and self-fulfilling entity. So powerful and pervasive has this conception of the individual been in Western thought that it is characteristic of thinkers of the most various philosophical persuasions. Aristotle, St. Thomas, Rousseau, Burke, Green, and many others not discussed in this book, all view the individual in this light. Granted that the specific character of that view varies, and certainly there is little agreement among these thinkers in terms of underlying philosophical assumptions, but all share in common this basic perspective on the individual.

It is, moreover, an ideal that conceives of the individual within the context of community. In the broadest sense, it is an ideal premised upon the Aristotelian notion that human beings are political animals, that is, creatures who by nature need and desire to fulfill themselves through common endeavors with their fellows. So influential has this idea been that even for many of those thinkers whose theoretical contributions are most hostile to classical theory, such as Marx for example, the emphasis upon community and, correspondingly, upon the self-directing and self-fulfilling individual has remained.

These facts, of course, do not a theory make. Political theory, certainly great political theory, is the product of a unique mind confronting a social and political order that no longer makes sense. We await the conjoining of these conditions. In the meantime, it is sufficient to recognize the recurrent ideal that runs like a thread through the Western tradition of political thought. For in the present age the problem is not simply how to conceptualize that ideal within the framework of modern philosophy, but how to keep before us its importance as a humanizing and civilizing factor. This is the ultimate danger before us: The present subordination of the individual to the forces of nationalism and to the bureaucratic centralism of the nation-state threatens even the memory of the ideal.

With these thoughts in mind it is only appropriate that we end this treatise where we began, for if there is, as we maintain, an underlying continuity to Western thought in terms of its ideals, if not in its philosophical methods, then the end of our speculations should in some sense be contained in its beginnings. When Socrates first confronted the Sophists of his time, he faced the very issues that stand before us today, albeit in less serious and less terrifying dimensions. Is there or is there not an order and purpose to things, and if there is, how do individuals and their polities fit into it?

Socrates' answer, contained in his admonition to Callicles, "that this universe is . . . called cosmos or order, not disorder or misrule" was unambiguous. The cosmos is an order of justice, and it comprehends the state as well as the individual. This was the theoretical principle upon which Western political thought was first founded and which we have identified as the unity of ethics and politics. Whether or not we can reconstitute that principle on a modern basis only the future will tell. It remains, nevertheless, a recurrent ideal in Western political thought; it should be the task of those of us who have studied that tradition to think through the ideal once again.

Notes

1. See Gaetano Salvemini, *Mazzini,* I.M. Rawson, trans. (New York: Collier Books, 1962), for a short, classic study of the basic elements of Mazzini's political philosophy.

2. See Guido de Ruggiero, *The History of European Liberalism,* R.G. Collingwood, trans. (Boston: Beacon Press, 1959), p. 410.

3. Frederick Watkins, in *The Political Tradition of the West: A Study in the Development of Modern Liberalism* (Cambridge: Harvard University Press, 1967), p. 295, frames the problem broadly as follows: "liberalism called for a pluralist organization of society, while the tendency of nationalism lay in the direction of uncompromising monism. The resulting conflict did much to reduce the effectiveness of modern liberalism."

4. Ibid. See chapters 10 and 11 for an extended discussion of the negative impact of nationalism upon liberal internationalism and liberal ideals in general. Watkins notes this same subversive influence of nationalism upon the conservative doctrine (which he shows was itself initially internationalist in outlook) as well as upon the socialist worldview.

5. T.H. Green, as we have seen, was particularly insistent upon this point. In his major philosophical and epistemological work, *Prolegomena to Ethics,* A.C. Bradley, ed. (New York: Thomas Y. Crowell, 1969), p. 356, he makes his position even more emphatically clear. What he terms "external authority," that is, political obedience based simply upon obedience to external rules, is not genuinely authority at all.

6. See Hannah Arendt, *The Origins of Totalitarianism* (Cleveland: World Publishing Company, 1958), for an analysis of the role of ideology in modern totalitarian regimes. Arendt defines totalitarian ideology (in particular,

Stalinist Marxism and German National Socialism) as "the logic of an idea." The "idea" constitutes supposed biological or historical "laws" from which is derived a logic of action against specified groups (for example, the Nazi's "law" of race, which asserted the inevitable demise of "non-Aryan races" provided, by logical deduction, a justification for genocide). Thus, in Arendt's analysis of totalitarian regimes, the higher principles of the ideology are transmuted into insane modes of "political action."

7. What is commonly called Marxist Humanism, a term that comprehends a variety of schools of thought, has become increasingly influential. In clear opposition to the totalitarian perversion of the Marxian system, this brand of Marxism attempts to revitalize the humanist ideals, and the radical social perspective, of the classical doctrine. In liberal thought, the most important recent development may be found in the work of John Rawls, particularly in his *A Theory of Justice* (Cambridge: Belknap Press, 1971). What is important about Rawls's political thought is his attempt, via a critique of the utilitarian position, to rethink the philosophical underpinnings of liberal ideals.

Glossary

A priori: a philosophical term referring to knowledge that is *prior* to any sense experience; knowledge that is derived from reason alone or that is inherent in the rational structure of the mind.

Authority: as distinct from power, the condition in which obedience to the laws and customs of the political community is self-willed. (See **Power.**)

Being/Becoming: in early Greek philosophy, a basic distinction constituting two different conceptions of reality. The philosophers of becoming claimed that all things are in a state of ceaseless change or *becoming*. The philosophers of being, on the other hand, asserted that beneath the changeable world of sensation exists a perfect and unchangeable reality of *being* as such. While these distinctions were originally employed by the pre-Socratics in their investigation of physical nature, they were carried over into social and political philosophy. Plato's theory of form, for example (and, indeed, any theory of form or teleological perspective), assumes the reality of being, that is, of the existence of a cosmic order of unchanging rational principles, ethical as well as physical. (See **Form; Teleology.**)

Civitas: the ancient Roman term for state, which comes closer to its modern meaning as a constitutional entity distinct from the political community than does the Greek term polis. (See **Polis, Polity.**)

Classical: the ancient Greek and/or Roman periods. (See **Renaissance.**)

Consent: in modern political theory, the idea that the state and government exist by the consent or agreement of the citizenry. (See **Divine Right; Social Contract.**)

Dialectic: in ancient Greek philosophy, a method of disputation (also known as the Socratic method) beginning with opinion and leading to ultimate conceptual knowledge. In the modern philosophies of Hegel and Marx the dialectic is conceived not only as a mode of understanding, but as a principle inherent in nature and history as well.

Divine Right: the idea, derived from medieval thought but actually early modern in content, that the monarch's right to rule is of divine origin. Modern contract-consent theories arose in opposition to the theory of divine right. (See **Consent; Social Contract.**)

Empiricism: an epistemology that claims that sensation is a valid source of knowledge. (See **Epistemology.**)

Enlightenment: roughly the period from Locke to the beginning of the nineteenth century. The enlightenment was characterized by an emphasis upon the new scientific method and rational modes of inquiry.

Epistemology: a theory of knowledge. An epistemology establishes what can be known and the methods by which knowledge can be attained. (See **Empiricism.**)

Ethical Naturalism: any ethical system in which values are derived from empirical facts rather than from a transcendent or teleological principle. Naturalistic ethics typically reduce ethical principles to the empirical "facts" of human psychology. In the naturalistic system of utilitarianism, for example, the empirical fact that people desire pleasure is erected into the ethical principle that they ought to desire it. (See **Ethics; Normative; Teleology.**)

Ethics: moral philosophy; the study of normative issues. (See **Normative.**)

Form: in ancient Greek philosophy, the rational principle that gives order and meaning to both the empirical and ethical domains. In the theory of form, a human being is human because he or she manifests the form (intelligible principle) of "humanness," just as a just action is just because it manifests the form of "justiceness." In Plato, form is transcendent or "separated" from empirical reality. In Aristotle, it is immanent or inherent within matter. (See **Being/Becoming; Teleology.**

Hellenic: Derived from Hellenes, as the Greeks termed themselves, Hellenic refers to the period before Alexander the Great's conquests ended Greek autonomy and intermixed Greek and Oriental cultures until his death in 323 B.C. (See **Hellenistic.**)

Hellenistic: That period after Alexander the Great's death in 323 B.C. to the middle of the second century B.C., and for some well into the era of the Roman Empire. The Hellenistic period was one in which Greek thought and ideals spread throughout much of the civilized world including, most importantly, Rome. (See **Hellenic.**)

Idealism: a metaphysics asserting that ultimate reality is something (God, spirit, or mind, for example) beyond the material world; the opposite of materialism. (See **Materialism; Metaphysics.**)

Ideology: originally a term used to describe the philosophy of a group of French thinkers of the period surrounding the French revolution. Since then, the term has taken on a number of different meanings. Sometimes it is used loosely to mean nothing more than political belief. In Marxist theory, it means a false perception of social and political reality. In contemporary social and political theory, it refers to those systems of thought since the French revolution that are marked by their worldview character (that is, their claim to universal validity) and their theoretical justification of mass revolutionary action. Liberalism, Marxism, nationalism, and fascism constitute some of these major ideological systems of thought.

Liberal Democracy: a form of government based upon an extensive franchise and the protection of basic rights and liberties.

Materialism: a metaphysics asserting that reality is material and that matter alone is real; the opposite of idealism. (See **Idealism; Metaphysics.**)

Metaphysics: the study of the nature of reality as such; our basic assumptions about what constitutes ultimate reality. (See **Idealism; Materialism.**)

Nationalism: the most influential ideology of the modern world, nationalism posits the nation-state, as the political organization of the nation (whether conceived in ethnic, religious, or linguistic terms), as the supreme political value. In its extreme form, nationalism requires the total allegiance of individuals to national ideals and their subordination to the dictates of the state. (See **Nation-state.**)

Nation-state: a territorial and autonomous sovereign political entity administered by a government possessing ultimate power to enforce law and typically legitimizing its authority as the representative of a particular national grouping, real or imagined. The nation-state constitutes the most common form of polity in the modern world. (See **Nationalism; Polity; Sovereignty.**)

Natural Law: universal moral rules of obligation known by reason alone. As such, natural law principles are higher than positive law and thus operative whether reflected in positive law or not. In natural law theory, for example, reason establishes the universal wrongness of murder and the obligation not to hurt our fellows, whether or not these principles are established by civil law. (See **Natural Right; Positive Law.**)

Natural Right: universal moral rules, known by reason alone, that establish those basic rights or liberties that all human beings by nature possess. Whereas natural law establishes obligations or duties, natural right establishes liberties or freedoms. (See **Natural Law.**)

Nature/Convention: a fundamental distinction in Western political thought. The state, and even society, may be conceived as either natural (institutions that, by nature, human beings require) or conventional (artificial institutions created for pragmatic reasons). In classical thought, the state and society were generally viewed as natural; in modern thought—in contract-consent theories, for example—as conventional. (See **Consent; Social Contract.**)

Negative Liberty: liberty conceived as freedom from restraint. In the negative conception, where no positive law exists to restrain action, the individual may be said to have liberty. In contrast to the theory of positive liberty, freedom is not defined in terms of moral purposes. (See **Positive Liberty.**)

Negative State: a state that involves itself in performing only those basic functions necessary for the maintenance of order, such as police and defense functions. The idea of the negative state was particularly important in classical liberal theory and corresponded to the liberal ideal of a *laissez-faire*, free market economic system. (See **Positive State.**)

Nominalism: a theory asserting that truth is a function of language, that is, nothing more than the logical consistency of language. It denies that abstract terms represent an objective reality (for example, that the word beauty refers to an actual existing reality of beauty as such). For the nominalist, such terms are no more than symbols used to classify objects and ideas, and truth is no more than the logical manipulation of those symbols.

Normative: that which has to do with values, with matters of good and evil, right and wrong, as opposed to the empirical domain of facts. The field of ethics deals with normative issues. (See **Ethics.**)

Pluralism: a social condition characterized by the existence of many diverse groups and associations; the opposite of mass society where there exists little or no social differentiation.

Polis: the small city-state of ancient Greece, at that time the common form of polity in the Hellenic (Greek) world. (See **Hellenic; Hellenistic; Polity.**)

Polity: the generic term for any form of political community. (See, **Civitas; Nation-state; Polis.**)

Positive Law: law made by human beings; legislative or civil law. (See **Natural Law.**)

Positive Liberty: liberty conceived not simply as freedom from restraint, as in the case of negative liberty, but as a positive freedom to perform those actions that are socially and morally beneficial. In the positive conception, liberty cannot be conceived apart from some larger moral end. (See **Negative Liberty.**)

Positive State: a state intimately involved in the affairs of the community. In classical thought, the state was believed to have the positive function of inculcating moral virtue in its citizenry. In modern liberal thought, the state is asserted to have the positive function of removing those obstacles, such as poverty and poor working conditions, that stand in the way of the full (social and moral) development of the individual. The "welfare state" is the modern form of the positive state. (See **Negative State.**)

Power: the ability to compel obedience. (See **Authority.**)

Realpolitik: a theory asserting that politics is nothing more than the struggle for power.

Reformation: the religious movement, beginning in the sixteenth century, that led to the establishment of Protestantism and was crucial in the development of the modern nation-state.

Renaissance: that time, roughly from the late fourteenth into the seventeenth centuries, which marks the beginning of modernity. Empiricism, realism, and humanism characterize this historical period. The humanistic (human-centered) view of reality involved a return to classical (and particularly Roman) literary sources. (See **Classical.**)

Republic: A term of Roman origin referring to a form of government based upon some level of popular rule and the existence of a degree of personal liberty and freedom. The term passed into general usage to refer broadly to constitutional and democratic states as opposed to monarchical or absolutist ones. Thus, the United States was termed a republic by the founders.

Social Contract: in the early modern period, a theory of politics that asserted that the state is created by the mutual consent (contract) of its members. Such consent was typically viewed as either express (an actual formal agreement or contract) or tacit (an implicit agreement based upon obedience to the laws of the state, or the use and enjoyment of the benefits of citizenship). For the most part, contract theorists did not believe express consent, that is, an actual act of contracting, had ever occurred in historical fact. Rather, they employed the idea of contract as a hypothetical construct to determine what political principles rational human beings would consent to assuming they could in fact contract, and whether or not existing political institutions corresponded to those principles. (See **Consent; Nature/Convention; State of Nature.**)

Sophistry: the early Greek philosophy that emphasized the conventional (that is, relative) nature of social and political knowledge, and that encouraged individuals to realize their desires by triumphing over society's rules. In political theory, this led to a glorification of power and to a focus on the means by which to attain it. Socratic theory arose in opposition to these principles.

Sovereignty: the ultimate locus of power. In modern political thought the state has traditionally been conceived as sovereign, that is, as the ultimate center of political power, independent of all other external political authorities, and supreme over all domestic groups and associations. (See **Nation-state.**)

State of Nature: in contract theories the prepolitical, sometimes presocial, condition existing prior to the act of contracting into political society. For most contract theorists, the state of nature, like the contract itself, is a purely imaginary construct. (See **Consent; Social Contract.**)

Teleology: the study of phenomena from the perspective of goals or purposes. A teleological perspective presupposes that things develop to some end (*telos*) which, in its completeness, manifests an underlying order or principle. In Aristotle, for example, matter has the potential to actualize itself, that is, to manifest in the process of development the principle of form inherent in it. (See **Form.**)

Bibliography

GENERAL READINGS

BERKI, R.N. *The History of Political Thought: A Short Introduction.* Totowa, N.J.: Rowman and Littlefield, 1977.

PLAMENATZ, JOHN. *Man and Society,* Vols. I and II. New York: McGraw-Hill, 1963.

SABINE, GEORGE H. *A History of Political Theory,* 4th ed., rev. Thomas Landon Thorsen. Hinsdale, Ill.: Dryden Press, 1973.

STRAUSS, LEO, AND JOSEPH CROPSEY. *History of Political Philosophy,* 2nd ed. Chicago: Rand McNally, 1972.

WOLIN, SHELDON. *Politics and Vision, Continuity and Innovation in Western Political Thought.* Boston: Little, Brown, 1960.

I. SOCRATES

CORNFORD, FRANCIS MACDONALD. *Before and After Socrates.* Cambridge: Cambridge University Press, *1968.*

GULLEY, NORMAN. *Plato's Theory of Knowledge.* London: Methuen & Co., Ltd., 1962.

GUTHRIE, W.K.C. *Socrates.* Cambridge: Cambridge University Press, 1971.

TAYLOR, ALFRED E. *Socrates: The Man and His Thought.* Garden City, N.Y.: Doubleday, 1953.

VERSENYI, LASZLO. *Socratic Humanism.* New Haven: Yale University Press, 1963.

II.   PLATO

BARKER, SIR ERNEST. *Greek Political Theory: Plato and His Predecessors.* London: Methuen & Co., Ltd., 1918.

BARKER, SIR ERNEST. *The Political Thought of Plato and Aristotle.* New York: Dover Publications, 1959.

GRENE, DAVID. *Greek Political Theory: The Image of Man in Thucydides and Plato.* Chicago: University of Chicago Press, 1950.

GRUBE, G.M.A.. *Plato's Thought.* London: Methuen & Co., Ltd., 1935.

NETTLESHIP, R.L. *Lectures on the Republic of Plato.* London: Macmillan, 1901.

TAYLOR, ALFRED E. *Plato.* New York: Books for Libraries Press, 1911.

III.   ARISTOTLE

ARENDT, HANNAH. *The Human Condition.* Chicago: The University of Chicago Press, 1958.

ARMSTRONG, A.H. *An Introduction to Ancient Philosophy.* Boston: Beacon Press, 1965.

BARKER, SIR ERNEST. *The Political Thought of Plato and Aristotle.* New York: Dover Publications, 1959.

GRENE, MARJORIE. *A Portrait of Aristotle.* Chicago: University of Chicago Press, 1963.

JAEGER, WERNER. *Aristotle: Fundamentals of the History of His Development.* Oxford: Clarendon Press, 1934.

VEATCH, HENRY B. *Aristotle: A Contemporary Appreciation*. Bloomington: Indiana University Press, 1974.

IV. CICERO

COPLESTON, FREDERICK, S.J. *A History of Philosophy: Greece and Rome*. Vol. I. Garden City, N.Y.: Doubleday, 1962.

HAMMOND, MASON. *City-State and World State in Greek and Roman Political Theory Until Augustus*. Cambridge: Harvard University Press, 1951.

HICKS, ROBERT. *Stoic and Epicurean*. New York: Russell and Russell, 1962.

LONG, A.A. *Hellenistic Philosophy: Stoics. Epicureans. Sceptics*. Berkeley: University of California Press, 1986.

MITSIS, PHILLIP. *Epicurus' Ethical Theory: The Pleasures of Invulnerability*. Ithaca: Cornell University Press, 1988.

REAL, GIOVANNI. *The Systems of the Hellenistic Age*. 3rd ed., ed./trans. John R. Catan. Albany: State University of New York Press, 1985.

STOCTON, DAVID. *Cicero: A Political Biography*. London: Oxford University Press, 1971.

WENLEY, ROBERT. *Stoicism and Its Influence*. New York: Cooper Square Publishers, 1963.

ZELLER, EDWARD. *Outlines of the History of Greek Philosophy*, 13th ed., rev., ed. Dr. Wilhelm Nestle, trans. L.P. Palmer. New York: Dover Publications, 1980.

V. ST. AUGUSTINE

DEANE, HERBERT A. *The Political and Social Ideas of St. Augustine*. New York: Columbia University Press, 1963.

FIGGIS, JOHN NEVILLE. *The Political Aspects of St. Augustine's "City of God."* Gloucester: Peter Smith, 1963.

HEARNSHAW, F.J.C., ed. *The Social and Political Ideas of Some Great Mediaeval Thinkers*. New York: Barnes & Noble, 1967.

MARKUS, R.A. *Saeculum: History and Society in the Theology of St. Augustine*. Cambridge: Cambridge University Press, 1970.

OTTLEY, R.L. *Studies in the Confessions of St. Augustine.* London: Robert Scott, 1919.

VI.   ST. THOMAS AQUINAS

COPLESTON, F.C. *Aquinas.* Harmondsworth: Penguin Books, Ltd., 1955.

D'ENTREVES, ALEXANDER PASSERIN. *The Medieval Contribution to Political Thought: Thomas Aquinas, Marsilius of Padua, Richard Hooker.* New York: Humanities Press, 1959.

GILBY, THOMAS B., *The Political Thought of Thomas Aquinas. Chicago:* University of Chicago Press, 1958.

GILSON, ETIENNE. *The Philosophy of St. Thomas Aquinas.* ed. Rev. G.A. Elrington and trans. Edward Bullough. Freeport: Books for Libraries Press, 1937.

HEARNSHAW, F.J.C., ed. *The Social and Political Ideas of Some Great Mediaeval Thinkers.* New York: Barnes & Noble, 1967.

VII.   MACHIAVELLI

ANGLO, SYDNEY. *Machiavelli: A Dissection.* New York: Harcourt, Brace & World, 1969.

CASSIRER, ERNST. *The Myth of the State.* London: Yale University Press, 1946.

CHABOD, FEDERICO. *Machiavelli and the Renaissance,* trans. David Moore. New York: Harper & Row, 1958.

POCOCK, J.G.A. *The Machiavellian Moment: Florentine Political Thought and the Atlantic Republican Tradition.* Princeton: Princeton University Press, 1975

PREZZOLINI, GIUSEPPE. *Machiavelli.* New York: The Noonday Press, 1967.

STRAUSS, LEO. *Thoughts on Machiavelli.* Glencoe, Ill.: The Free Press, 1958.

VIII.   HOBBES

GOLDSMITH, M.M. *Hobbes' Science of Politics.* New York: Columbia University Press, 1966.

JACOBSON, NORMAN. *Pride and Solace: The Functions and Limits of Political Theory.* Berkeley: University of California Press, 1978.

MINTZ, SAMUEL I. *The Hunting of Leviathan.* London: Cambridge University Press, 1969.

OAKESHOTT, MICHAEL. *Hobbes on Civil Association.* Berkeley: University of California Press, 1975.

STRAUSS, LEO. *The Political Philosophy of Hobbes: Its Basis and Its Genesis.* Chicago: University of Chicago Press, 1963.

WARRENDER, HOWARD. *The Political Philosophy of Hobbes: His Theory of Obligation.* Oxford: Clarendon Press, 1957.

IX. LOCKE

DUNN, JOHN. *The Political Thought of John Locke.* Cambridge: Cambridge University Press, 1969.

FRANKLIN, JULIAN H. *John Locke and the Theory of Sovereignty.* Cambridge: Cambridge University Press, 1978.

MACPHERSON, C.B. *The Political Theory of Possessive Individualism: Hobbes to Locke.* Oxford: Oxford University Press, 1962.

PATEMAN, CAROLE. *The Sexual Contract.* Stanford: Stanford University Press, 1988.

STRAUSS, LEO. *Natural Right and History.* Chicago: University of Chicago Press, 1953.

TULLY, JAMES. *A Discourse on Property: John Locke and His Adversaries.* Cambridge: Cambridge University Press, 1980.

YOLTON, JOHN W. *Locke and the Compass of Human Understanding.* Cambridge: Cambridge University Press, 1970.

X. ROUSSEAU

CASSIRER, ERNST. *The Question of Jean-Jacques Rousseau,* ed. and trans. Peter Gay. Bloomington: Indiana University Press, 1963.

CHAPMAN, JOHN W. *Rousseau—Totalitarian or Liberal?* New York: AMS Press, 1968.

CHARVET, JOHN. *The Social Problem in the Philosophy of Rousseau.* Cambridge: Cambridge University Press, 1974.

COBBAN, ALFRED. *Rousseau and the Modern State.* London: George Allen & Unwin, Ltd., 1964.

ELLENBURG, STEPHEN. *Rousseau's Political Philosophy: An Interpretation From Within.* London: Cornell University Press, 1976.

MASTERS, ROGER D. *The Political Philosophy of Rousseau.* Princeton: Princeton University Press, 1968.

SHKLAR, JUDITH, N. *Men and Citizens: A Study of Rousseau s Social Theory.* Cambridge: Cambridge University Press, 1969.

XI. CONSERVATISM

CANAVAN, FRANCIS P., S.J. *The Political Reason of Edmund Burke.* Durham, N.C.: Duke University Press, 1960.

COBBAN, ALFRED. *Edmund Burke and the Revolt Against the Eighteenth Century.* London: George Allen & Unwin, Ltd., 1960.

KIRK, RUSSELL. *The Conservative Mind: From Burke to Eliot.* Chicago: Henry Regnery Company, 1960.

O'GORMAN, FRANK. *Edmund Burke: His Political Philosophy.* Bloomington: Indiana University Press, 1973.

OAKESHOTT, MICHAEL. *Rationalism in Politics.* New York: Basic Books, 1962.

WILKINS, BURLEIGH TAYLOR. *The Problem of Burke's Political Philosophy.* Oxford: Clarendon Press, 1967.

XII. CLASSICAL LIBERALISM

CUMMING, ROBERT DENOON. *Human Nature and History: A Study of the Development of Liberal Political Thought,* Vols. I and II. Chicago: University of Chicago Press, 1969.

DE RUGGIERO, GUIDO. *The History of European Liberalism,* trans. R.G. Collingwood. Boston: Beacon Press, 1959.

LONG, DOUGLAS G. *Bentham on Liberty: Jeremy Bentham's Idea of Liberty in Relation to His Utilitarianism.* Toronto: University of Toronto Press, 1977.

MACPHERSON, C.B. *The Life and Times of Liberal Democracy.* Oxford: Oxford University Press, 1977.

MANNING, D.J. *Liberalism*. New York: St. Martin's Press, 1976.

PLAMENATZ, JOHN. *The English Utilitarians*. Oxford: Basil Blackwell & Mott, Ltd., 1958.

XIII.   MODERN LIBERALISM

ANSCHUTZ, R.P. *The Philosophy of J.S. Mill*. Oxford: Clarendon Press, 1963.

BERLIN, ISAIAH. *Four Essays on Liberty*. London: Oxford University Press, 1969.

CUMMING, ROBERT DENOON. *Human Nature and History: A Study of the Development of Liberal Political Thought,* Vols. I and II. Chicago: University of Chicago Press, 1969.

DEWEY, JOHN. *Liberalism and Social Action*. New York: Capricorn Books, 1963.

HOBHOUSE, L.T. *Liberalism*. London: Oxford University Press, 1964.

MACPHERSON, C.B. *The Life and Times of Liberal Democracy*. Oxford: Oxford University Press, 1977.

MANNING, D.J. *Liberalism*. New York: St. Martin's Press, 1976.

MCCLOSKEY, H.J. *John Stuart Mill: A Critical Study*. London: Macmillan, 1971.

WATKINS, FREDERICK. *The Political Tradition of the West: A Study in the Development of Modern Liberalism*. Cambridge: Harvard University Press, 1967.

WOLFF, ROBERT PAUL. *The Poverty of Liberalism*. Boston: Beacon Press, 1968.

XIV.   MARXISM

AVINERI, SHLOMO. *The Social and Political Thought of Karl Marx*. Cambridge: Cambridge University Press, 1968.

GAY, PETER. *The Dilemma of Democratic Socialism: Eduard Bernstein's Challenge to Marx*. New York: Collier Books, 1962.

HOOK, SIDNEY. *From Hegel to Marx: Studies in the Intellectual Development of Karl Marx*. Ann Arbor: University of Michigan Press, 1962.

MEYER, ALFRED G. *Leninism.* New York: Praeger Publishers, 1962.

MEYER, ALFRED G. *Marxism: The Unity of Theory and Practice.* Ann Arbor: University of Michigan Press, 1954.

OLLMAN, BERTELL. *Alienation: Marx's Conception of Man in Capitalist Society.* Cambridge: Cambridge University Press, 1971.

TUCKER, ROBERT. *Philosophy and Myth in Karl Marx.* Cambridge: Cambridge University Press, 1969.

XV.   THE AGE OF IDEOLOGY

ARENDT, HANNAH. *Totalitarianism.* New York: Harcourt, Brace, & World, 1968.

GERMINO, DANTE. *Beyond Ideology: The Revival of Political Theory.* New York: Harper & Row, 1967.

LICHTHEIM, GEORGE F. *The Concept of Ideology and Other Essays.* New York: Vintage Books, 1967.

PLAMENATZ, JOHN. *Ideology.* New York: Praeger Publishers, 1970.

WATKINS, FREDERICK. *The Political Tradition of the West: A Study in the Development of Modern Liberalism.* Cambridge: Harvard University Press, 1967.

Index